To
Katherine -
with appreciation
for your journey
John

Finding My Way

Healing and Transformation
Through Loss and Grief

Finding My Way

Healing and Transformation
Through Loss and Grief

John M. Schneider, PhD

Seasons Press

Colfax, Wisconsin

Editor:
David Johnson

Design and layout:
David Johnson

Proofreading:
Sienna S'Zell

Cover painting:
"The Roads of Life"
by Jim Leff
170 Duboce #8,
San Francisco, CA 94103.

Library of Congress Number: 93-087812

ISBN (hardback): 0-9638984-1-8
ISBN (paperback): 0-9638984-2-6

Seasons Press, Route 2, Box 75, Colfax, WI 54730.

To my parents,

Maryanne Keaveny and Edward Charles Schneider

Acknowledgments

This book on grief could not have been written without many lives touching mine. Now in my mid-fifties, I am grateful and privileged to have witnessed the processes of living, dying, loss, change and growth of many people: family, friends, clients, students and colleagues. The richness of this book lies in their stories and what I have learned from them.

I could not write about grief without including my own losses. My father, Ed Schneider, died suddenly of a heart attack when I was 18. It transformed me, my mother and my sister Liz in different ways. At times we grew together. At other times, our grief separated us. I am thankful that I had the time to mature, forgive and be forgiven before the death of my mother, Mary Keaveny Schneider. I am grateful for the ongoing love and support of my sister Liz and her family—Kent, Christopher and Sarah.

Many contributors will remain anonymous because they were clients of mine. It has been a privilege to know these people with the intimacy that therapy permits. It remains a source of both inspiration and caution to witness the therapeutic process and the importance of validation in all our lives.

Some of my friends, clients and family have died. In dying they have taught me lessons I could not have known otherwise: Mom, Dad, Jim, Kathy, Mark, Matt, Lis and Bob. Some live in desperate or lonely circumstances, demonstrating the courage to remain alive spiritually while little else exists: Carol and Betsy.

A profound and career-changing loss for me was the suicide of Bob, one of my psychotherapy clients twenty years ago. The inability of my colleagues to help me with my grief issues raised my awareness of just how little professional training does to prepare us for life's existential issues. Bob's gift has been to free me of many of my fears. That freedom has allowed me to help others explore the depths of their awareness without my getting in their way quite so often.

Jean Newman was a friend and writing colleague at the time of Bob's suicide. She gave me permission to write long before I knew how to do it— or knew what I knew! Many ideas had their origins in the discussions we shared. Donna O'Toole had two children live and eventually die with cystic fibrosis. I have gained an enormous amount from her ability to transform tragedy into opportunities to grow. Cheri Saylor's self-awareness and will to live, in spite of sometimes overwhelming obstacles, has long inspired me. Her capacity to celebrate her new health has awed me. She has been an important fellow traveler and co-facilitator of grief and imagery groups for many years.

I knew Jan Romond long before she, Ed and John lost Mark in a traffic accident. Over the years we have grown closer while working together and grieving the quite different loss of yet a second child while celebrating the birth and wonder of Katy and the growth of John. She has inspired me as I've witnessed her courage and growth, creativity and humor.

Lee Battey has been a friend and source of inspiration through thick and thin. We met long after the transformations resulting from the losses of several children and after her evolution from a farmer's wife into one of the most successful hospice directors in the country. Lee's sensitivity and grace, forgiveness and spirituality have blessed me many times—along with her sharp editorial sense. Jean, Donna, Cheri, Jan and Lee have shown me the power of creative expression, ongoing friendship and a keen sense of humor.

Susan Zimmerman began the widow groups in Lansing many years ago after the death of her husband. We were two ships passing in the night for many years—until the common vision of INTEGRA, the Association for Integrative and Transformative Grief was born. We've seen ourselves as siblings who share the best of transgenerational grief—her organizational and leadership skills have made communicating the importance of loss and grief work to many others possible.

Sally Mead Schneider was my wife for eighteen years and remains co-parent of our three wonderful children. She was a key supporter in my early professional years. The resiliency and love of my now adult children Betsy, Anne, and Rachel, through their parent's divorce and their own life changes, continue to challenge me and give me hope for the future. It is their generation and beyond that I hope will profit most from what we learn now about grief.

I've found male colleagues who have been sensitive to their own process in ways which validated my own journey. Some have come by way of typical male bonding activities, the "warrior" activities. My tennis partner and friend, George Leroi, has shared much of his life with me, as well as exchanging lessons about winning and losing, as had John Boler and Tom Parmeter before him and Dave Reisinger since. Tennis provided us all with the safety to explore our vulnerabilities, feel our competencies, savor aces and nurture each other.

I have witnessed other male friends find the value of a religious commitment or a therapeutic community as a forum to experience grief and forge their spirituality. Ron Abraham has a sense of devotion to a simple life of nurturance and love. His openness to his own grief and his support of Donna, Steve and Matt while Matt was dying demonstrated to ix

me that a good heart can be worth so much more than intellectual understanding. Tom McGovern has shared his grief over the many changes in his life, a journey through spiritual change, addiction and loss of homeland to enter marriage, parenthood and a new career. His Irish humor and spirit, along with his sensitivity to grief, have been invaluable to me. My spiritual brother Jake Foglio has also given me a deep appreciation for making commitments with passion, even when those commitments involve celibacy and remaining a loyal dissident in a religious system conflicted about change. Reed Schroer has a wonderful knack of facing life's contradictions with humor, patience and an earthy wisdom uncommon among clergy. He has inspired me with his openness to suffering without getting consumed by it. Dave Voorhees has shared his interest in grief and training pastoral counselors. His enthusiasm for story telling as a way to give permission for grief and growth represents a shared interest which I use throughout this book. Jim Haase tapped his creative process to rediscover the power of music and playing to reach into both hope and despair, to make peace with his own dying.

Diane Deutsch came from her ministry background to challenge me to sharpen my thinking in many ways. Her enthusiasm and willingness to participate in the development of the Response To Loss Inventory (RTL) adds an exciting dimension to this work. Ellen Leroi has combined an ongoing friendship with a willingness to work together therapeutically and apply models of grief to the problems of family and children across generations. Ellen, her husband George, and their sons John and Benjamin, generously share their home with me on a regular basis, providing opportunities for many discussions. Lois Frears was a counselor to my children in middle school when we first met. As a result of her taking my year-long grief course, we jointly developed a model to compare existing theorists on the grief process.

I am grateful to Jim Heavenrich and Ole Almstrup for their feedback on the effects of loss and separation on development and childhood. Jim has also been my sharp and loving "devil's advocate" for my approaches to therapy and to life in general. Jim, Shelley, Karyn and now Benjamin keep me in touch with the awe and joy of growing families. Ole and Inga showed the remarkable capacity to maintain a loving friendship with the entire Schneider family throughout the time of the divorce. They, along with Sine, Jakob, Jonas, Dorte, Oskar and Lukas, are our Danish family.

Gordon Deckert has been a mentor and colleague, and it was he who first introduced me to the importance of grief as a phenomenon separate from depression. His permission to enjoy myself in my professional identity has been invaluable. Oz Parsons shaped my writing skills and validated my talents through his support and enthusiasm in graduate school. Norm Kagan was a mentor and colleague during my early professional years who helped me sharpen my thinking and put it into researchable terms.

There have also been a number of physician friends who have alerted me to the particular grief issues they face. Greg Lyon-Loftus was one of the first, a psychology graduate student and then a medical student who loved to challenge my thinking. Our occasional visits are still as lively and stimulating as ever. Dave Stoller is one of the more recent, as he shared the power of letting go of what was already lost, the Iris Principle which he introduced to me. Jim O'Brien has co-taught with me for many years, largely from his willingness to share his vulnerabilities in working with death and dying. Karen Blackman has been a fellow traveler throughout her professional career which spans family medicine and psychiatry. Her exuberant sense of humor and sharing of existential approaches to therapy has been refreshing. Susan Cunningham and Karen Johnson, residency rebels bent on revolutionizing medical education, shared much of their journey and grief through medical education and beyond. Scott Monteith and Anne Batdorf-Barnes were enthusiastic members of a loss and grief course who went on to research physician self-care and put it into practice, accepting the losses that come with respecting their personal limits and having a personal life.

I've learned much about the nursing perspective on grief, starting with my mother, who, long before I was born, was the rural public health nurse at the time of the Bath (MI) school disaster on the day Lindbergh flew the Atlantic. I learned a great deal about dignity amid loss when "rounding" with her in rural New York State in the 1960's. I learned about grief and dying from the Danish nurse's perspective from Lene Andersen, a good friend and soulmate, and my wife Sharon.

A number of people have help me expand the cultural, sexual and ethnic context of how I view grief. Peter Elsass is a warm, witty, personal version of Hans Christian Andersen for me. He has a wonderful way of telling stories with a message for examining loss from a cross-cultural perspective that is not quite so European and middle class. His work with the Indian tribes of South America and his penetrating style of inquiry have added exciting dimensions. So has the enthusiasm and commitment of Karen de Correa and Doris deRamilla and their devoted volunteers at FORJAR in Bogota, Colombia, who adopt abandoned terminally-ill children. Teresa LaFramboise has personally sensitized me to the many grief issues faced by the Native American population. From a distance, I have appreciated the efforts of Kathleen Ritter and Craig O'Neil to apply this model of grief to the gay and lesbian community and their unmistakable and profound losses.

Many professional colleagues in Michigan, Texas, California and Denmark shared their efforts at grief counseling. Some examples in this book come from their personal and professional experiences. In 1972, Ray Riskey invited me to lecture to his death and dying class and help him facilitate a group of terminally ill individuals. Little did he know what a monster would be created! Jean Gilreath created a wonderful retreat—The Maples—for us to meet at for many years. Hospice of Lubbock, Texas, has provided me a home away from home, giving me enormous support on many levels from the financial to the spiritual.

My professional colleagues collaborated with me in research interests, psychotherapy supervision and training programs: David Price, Phyllis Landick, Pam Montgomery, Joe Guilani, Charles Dahlstrom, Tom Helma, Bill Hinds, Marilyn Schneider, Don Melcer, Chris Minning, John Casbergue, Jerre Corey, Denise Tracy, Lori Eyres, Kai Bjørn and Lis Jensen, Dave Peradotte, Dave Picone, Virginia Brown, Linda Hayward, Angie Hoogterp, Linda Prong, Ruth Rosenthal, Ed Gibeau, Kris Freeark, Marc Levine, Inger de Fine Licht, Peter Mortensen, Paul Gandil, Jim O'Brien, Jim Scott, Steve Shelton, Gert Rasmussen, Anne Viskinge Jensen, Bodil Talamona, Hans Martin Svarre, Amy Zamkoff, Anne Thompson, Max Thome, Gloria Tuma, Joanne Zimmerman, Peter Bruhn and Cy and Marsha Worby. These and many others who have contributed greatly to my work.

Psych 590—The Psychology of Loss and Grief—was a course I taught for over fifteen years at Michigan State University. Tom McGovern formed a similar group at Texas Tech that gave me feedback on the manuscript and enriched the writing process. Those who passed through that course—students, professionals, fellow travelers through grief—have profoundly affected what is said in this book. Pam Washam and Sandy, LeJeune Witt, Lee Battey, Elsa Sadoth and others in "the group" in Lubbock critiqued the thinking, shared their experiences and edited the writing of a "prof," which was essential in the first edition and in the transformation that this edition represents.

Carol Green, Debby Kloosterman, Elaine Kaufman, and Sr. Juanita Gonzales also took part in a long-term grief leader group training program. Their grief was an integral part of learning to minister to others. As my friend Jeanne Achterberg says, it is *wounded* healers who minister to others, not just the *healed* ones. They, along with Dave, Jim, Sue, Ellen and

Julie, have given much back to me and have put up with a lot in their training.

Kim Sangster, Steve Schmidt, Jack Lewis, Shawn Fulton, Kelly Rhoades, Tim Chiang, Cindy Morgan, Virginia Brown, Julie Turner, Robert Geiger, Kathy Seitz, Lynn Darling, Barbara Coulton, John Bellingham, Kathy Klco, Lynn Breer, Joanne Karpinen, Sue Kollmeyer, Martha Bristor, Pat Potter, Vi Halpern, Marilyn Viera, Anne Lauer, Carol Miller, Pam Hahn, Winnie Rome, Mary Christine (MC) Seeley, Marty Wong, Matt Zarontenella and Carla Parent shared their grief as friends and from their professional sensitivity and expertise. They allowed me to witness their growth in ways I could not have otherwise.

Susan Bruce, INTEGRA and Hospice of Lubbock, Texas, have generously given financially to make this volume a reality. Many have given me explicit feedback on how this model of grief applies to their own lives. Betsy Johnston, Dorothy Mirkil, Diana Donovan, and Sienna S'Zell all went through the manuscript with a fine-tooth comb, attending to details I overlooked.

Near the end of the process, Marianne Davidsen Nielsen stopped by and offered many constructive suggestions and validations, using her Danish cultural base to remind me of my American biases. Jeanne Achterberg, Frank Lawlis, Sister Monica Mai and Peg McCuistion reviewed the final manuscript and put in print their impressions.

The enormous job of editing and producing this book was done by David Johnson, a former student of mine who is now a colleague and managing editor of the *Noetic Sciences Review*. He also serves on the INTEGRA Advisory Board. Dave was one of those young mavericks who broke the developmental mold. Due to several significant losses of family members and a personal health crisis, Dave became interested in loss, grief and transformation at an age when his cohorts were seeking immortality and fast career advancement. Our friendship has blossomed over the years and he is now one of my key supporters. He has challenged me to sharpen my thinking about transformation, and encouraged the important changes in my writing style. The "last word" on *Finding My Way* is Dave's.

It is hard to cite all the people whose own grief process has been instrumental in my awareness and perspective on grief. In noting some, I am aware that I have forgotten others just as influential. I apologize for that unintended oversight. Memories and appreciation of such contributions are in my heart even if they are not in this acknowledgment.

Sharon Olson took me up on my wish for "future contacts" at the time I signed her copy of the first version of this book. She is now my wife and my best friend. She, too, has wandered through the maze of this book many times and has helped me "lighten up" when I have taken myself too seriously. Together we have found ways to make validation and celebration of life experiences healing and energizing in our personal and professional lives.

Preface

As Howard Brody, a physician, philosopher and colleague, says, when we seek help from professional caregivers, we may be indirectly saying, "My story is broken. Can it be fixed?". We seek others help or advice when we can't keep our life story running smoothly. Sometimes out of fear or pain and sometimes out of frustration, we ask, "Is my story broken? Is it still worth living?"

When we experience a trauma, a significant change in our relationships and in our everyday lives, we may believe that our life story is broken or meaningless. Our attachments, beliefs, our anchors to our past aren't stable any more. We feel lost, the path before us no longer clear or predictable. Life as we have known it may be over. Our current reality fills with lonely, helpless, empty and loveless times. We fear we've lost a significant part of ourselves—our best self—along with everything else. Our lives feel broken, transformed into a living nightmare.

Paradoxically, we can also feel such breaks when we are successful. Our accomplishments, love or luck dazes us. It seems too good to be true—and it is too good to last forever. Still, mastery, loving attachments and fortune can create discontinuity with our past. We may have fame, possessions, pleasure, wealth and security we never dreamed possible. We *hope* we've lost contact with our old selves—the parts of us that were ordinary, sometimes selfish, often helpless and incompetent. Our lives feel changed beyond recognition.

Our responses to trauma and to success are examples of what transformation is all about. The word "transformation" means a significant alteration in the form of something has taken place—a moving across or beyond the old form to something unknown or unknowable before the change began. In its healthiest sense, transformation is opening to a larger reality than the one our personal ego could admit previously. During the process of transformation, we experience being broken or of breaking with the past. We sense discontinuity in our lives as we go through any major transitions. That sensing of discontinuity, the healing that begins with acknowledging change, is an important part of the transformative journey we often call grief.

We need to trust ourselves. In spite of the broken or liberating appearance, we aren't changing what is meaningful to us. We are altering its form and its appearance. The essence of who and what we are remains. The gossamer thread that weaves its way through our story remains unbroken.

Finding My Way is planned as a two-volume series about the types of transformations that come when we recognize loss and permit ourselves to grieve. Grief is a process of mending the breaks in our stories, moving beyond our successes and peak experiences to integrating the broken parts—the good and the bad—forgiving our human weaknesses and enjoying the experience of just being ourselves, capable of loving and relating in ways more encompassing than we were before.

Major life changes can be stressful, especially if we fail to recognize that any life change contains an element of loss. We can't start something new without relinquishing something old. Unless we grieve such losses, our shattered dreams and broken stories cannot heal. We cannot move forward without acknowledging both our gains and our losses.

Transformation and change include many possibilities. From the moment we experience change, life is transformed into something it was not before. It may take time, perhaps a lifetime for the full extent of that transformation to be realized. We are living *in process* along the way.

My Own Transformations

Professionally, I've gone through periods when many ways of responding to trauma, broken attachments and other changes have commanded my personal and my professional attention. My training as a clinical psychologist taught me to look first for pathology and health risks. Depression, co-dependency, addiction, panic disorders and post-traumatic stress are commonly diagnosed as responses to loss in medical or mental health settings for people traumatized by suicide, accidents, war, divorce, incest, the death of a child, etc.

My professional training coincided with those remarkable years in the United States that erupted with the assassination of John Kennedy and quieted with the resignation of Richard Nixon. In between were civil rights battles, the Vietnam war and protests, more assassinations, men on the moon, sexual freedom, televised riots, massacres and murders. We were too much in shock to know it at the time, but we had experienced another collective loss within our country like the Great Depression and the Civil War a hundred years before. It is left to future generations to understand the collective grief we experienced and how it transformed this country. It has obviously affected me and my cohort generation.

We may not recognize vulnerabilities until we meet situations that trigger them. I didn't know, for example, how little I had dealt with my own issues about dying until, in my early thirties, I was working professionally with a group of terminally ill individuals. In the course of one week, three of them died, a separate client attempted suicide and a young woman was killed by a train outside my office window just as I happened to look out. I was in over my head.

When I tried to "treat" that group of terminally ill people for their "depression," I found myself feeling helpless and out of place. I finally realized they weren't depressed. They knew—in great detail—why they felt the way they did. They were dying. Their illness had isolated them. They were lonely. They were afraid—of dying, of untreatable pain (and of poor treatment generally), of abandonment by family and health care providers alike. I added to their loneliness and fears by disappearing when the first members of the group died. I did not validate the stresses in their lives or their way of coping. I was unprepared to deal with dying.

I then behaved as if my professional training was all wrong. I reverted to the other extreme. Everything must be due to the stress of normal grieving. Then Bob, a chronically-depressed client of mine, committed suicide. My support, nurturance and attempts to validate how hopeless he felt hadn't helped. My own ensuing grief caused me to ask the question: Was there more I could have done? I had offered several alternatives, including additional psychotherapy, medication, even shock treatment. Bob refused them all. Still, I doubted—had I been persuasive enough, insistent enough? Could I have prevented or delayed his suicide? How responsible was I?

My colleagues, all about my same age, were unprepared to recognize my grief or to help me with my guilt. One told me he was glad it wasn't his client, but that I should accept it as an "occupational hazard." In his attempt to explain the hazard we shared, I felt like a helpless victim, with more suicides lurking in my future. Another colleague insisted that I could have prevented the suicide if I had hospitalized my client, gotten electro-convulsive therapy and taken him off drugs. This, too, heightened my guilt and sense of incompetence. I had considered those, but I hadn't forced Bob to do them (which would have been impossible—he was a therapist himself, bright and not so depressed he couldn't fake a good front). Characteristic of being in our thirties, my colleagues and I believed we would succeed if we could get rid of one or two nagging shortcomings, become more assertive and more objective. We would make it—if our patients never committed suicide.

It's taken years for me to grasp both the extent and the limits of my responsibility for that suicide. The result is that I'm more sensitive to times when I can truly help others with professional intervention, and when that intervention will confirm my personal feelings of helplessness and validate my clients' existential dilemmas. For example, in working with people with chronic and life-threatening conditions, I've discovered that even if disease is treated effectively, irreversible loss results. Life is never the same after we've had a brush with death or endured a suicidal depression when death seemed preferable.

As a helper, I've learned that I can't change anything for others encountering stressful changes. Whether they are in a survival mode or their response is a pathological one, I have diagnostic and therapeutic tools. And I still respect their process. Then, too, I admire willingness to explore losses or to keep going at whatever the price. And sometimes my validation provides support to take the next step.

By my late thirties, my own stressful life-style led to two near-death experiences. My own death became an indisputable possibility. In due time I accepted that my own grief had to be my priority. I discovered ways to grow and to live a less stress-filled life. I found the means to feel empowered in the human potential movement and by the spiritual openness of transpersonal psychology.

In the newness and excitement of my personal discoveries, I pre-sumed that any change could lead to growth. It's taken the years of my forties to grasp how miraculous it really is when change is evolutionary and positively transformative. Such an optimistic viewpoint can be sug-gested much too soon to be acceptable. Some people have interpreted my message of hope as discounting the power and devastation of what they had lost or their particular limits or handicaps. The same criticism has applied to well-known professionals like Elisabeth Kübler-Ross and Bernie Siegal, who have found growth potential in facing death and life-threaten-ing illness. In our enthusiasm, our greatest challenge is to understand that some will feel diminished by a suggestion of hope for growth out of their particular loss or change.

Depressed or dying people may lack the resources to find hope. Relationships end without opportunity for expression of grief. Inexcus-able betrayals occur. Change can be disruptive and destructive. The physical pain of a chronic illness can be so incessant that death seems preferable. Not everyone has the time, energy and inner resources to make sense of the changes, betrayals and misfortunes of their lives. To say that *every* loss has significance can communicate to those who do not detect it that they have "chosen" not to, or that they are responsible for that "deficiency". It becomes a way to blame the victim.

Sharing the Journey through Grief

That which validates our own process of growth and transformation becomes a part of us. We don't need to distinguish between the ideas, feelings and process of someone else if our own corresponds to it—unless of course, we need to give them proper credit for stimulating our process.

Readers will find that I use the personal pronouns "we" and "us." It has helped me to identify with the process while I was writing. Occasionally my editor Dave Johnson and I have found my writing switching from "we" to "they". I have found myself wondering what it is that I am having trouble accepting about my own grief. It has often led to new discoveries.

The reader may find the use of words such as "ourself" and "our life" awkward at first, because this is not strictly correct usage. However, I chose to use this style because I realized that I am most likely speaking to an individual who is reading this book to help in his or her own grieving process. The style used, I believe, will speak more directly and personally to the reader, rather than making these concepts seem as though they are part of a college textbook. As an aid to understanding the concepts in this book I have included a glossary of terms in the appendices.

I've also used bits and pieces of people's "stories" rather than "case studies" for similar reasons. It's easier to identify with stories that are similar to our own. Some stories are my own. Many are disguised to protect privacy.

Yet it's not so easy to mend our stories, much less have someone hear our fears about twists and breaks. There are times, for example, when we just aren't very good champions of others who are grieving. This usually happens when someone's story comes too close to the rawness of our own unexamined losses or is a fulfillment of our worst nightmare. Anxious, we are more likely to distract people from their grief by our concerns about what can go wrong. What can go wrong, of course, is that we'll have to deal with something we'd rather not. We'll have to mind and to mend our own stories.

To be helpful, we, too, need to feel safe enough to "let go," have our own losses "validated," have the time and support for reflection, learn new ways to find meaning and eventually learn how to be playful again. Then we'll better know when to accept the natural course of grief, and when professional intervention is needed.

This book is intended for anyone who wishes to understand the transformative potential of grief. Some may appreciate an approach that supports the holistic nature of the grieving process which elucidates just how extensive the range of normal responses to significant losses can be. *Finding My Way* is comprehensive in scope, intended to be inclusive of reactions to all types of losses and changes, from birth to death, ranging from everyday losses to major life changes, including those we inherit from our ancestors.

Years ago, as I began my exploration of my own losses, I read one of Clark Moustakas' books on loneliness. Hours would pass. Suddenly I'd realize I had only read a few paragraphs. I had spent the rest of the time with the thoughts and feelings his words had triggered. It can be frustrating for the reader who expects this book to be a "page turner," only to discover it's hard to get past a notable chapter or a story that hits home. You, the reader, need to acknowledge where you are on your own path. Some chapters may not reflect your current process, or what you expect to happen. After all, we must consider and *validate* our own process of grieving and where that leads us. Only then can we give regard and validation to others.

I met a woman named Eileen several years after I published *Stress, Loss and Grief,* the early version of this book. She said that someone had given her the book just a day after her son had died. Over the next year she had read it. "I've recommended it to many friends . . . but I don't remember anything from it" she mused.

"Don't be offended," Eileen smiled, noting my crestfallen face. "I mean that positively. At that time I was looking for anything that validated what I was going through. Anything that did not I found jarring. What I remember from that first year was people's insensitivity, evidence that others didn't know what I was going though. It must be that what you had to say back then was right for me. It didn't distract me from where I needed to be."

Comments such as Eileen's validate me as a writer on the grieving process. I do not wish to objectify or distract people from their grief, only to validate its fullness and its permutations. Perhaps you, too, will remember nothing from this book—except those ideas which affirm your process and your story.

Contents

Section I

The Essential Ingredients for Transforming Loss; Our Dilemma with Change

For everything there is a season;
a time to be born, a time to die,
a time to weep and a time to laugh,
a time to mourn and a time to dance,
a time to get and a time to lose,
a time to keep and a time to cast away,
a time to love and a time to hate,
a time of war and a time of peace.

—Ecclesiastics 3: 1-8

Life has its own seasons and changes. As we grow naturally, our lives change in distinct patterns and cadences, like seasons. These transformations can be so profound that we are as different from ourselves as we grow older as are the seasons of the year from each other.

Seasons are annual cycles, witnessed many times in the course of a lifetime. Change in nature is at one moment destruction, at another, renewal. Human changes involve loss and gain, aging and birth, pulls toward togetherness and towards individualism *and* a process called grief. Grief is the healing mechanism we have in order to deal with change: it restores laughter, releases tears, admits both delight and regret. From the experiences and repetitions of our personal cycles and expanding narrative, we learn what to keep or to cast away. Together, our personal seasons and changes weave a delicate fabric that tell our unique and collective life stories.

This first section of *Finding My Way* introduces themes that appear throughout the book. It provides a context to examine loss and the choices that go into healing and positive transformation. Knowledge of how we attach emotionally, how we change and the ways we have of responding to trauma and loss can enhance our appreciation and respect for the process of grieving.

Change, Adjustment and Transformation

Change characterizes today's world. We are a planet in flux: New nations, the downfall of governments, the explosion of information technology, the AIDS epidemic, uncertain employment, the high cost of health care, regional and civil wars, drug addiction, natural disasters make the news daily, to mention just a few. The way we form emotional bonds, engage in or abstain from sex, and what is considered healthy are concepts that are being redefined. Very little of life is untouched by change in modern times.

Some thrive on change. Art, often seen as a precursor of change, invites us to experience the world in new ways, challenging basic ways of experiencing life which had remained the same for generations. Chaos theory insists on a state of flux. Science, technology and modern modes of travel have opened a world unimaginable a century ago. In the process, basic ways of living that had endured for centuries have been destroyed and often forgotten.

Ilya Prigogine is one of many who suggests that it is disintegration that enables structures to re-form at higher levels. Change is an essential ingredient in challenging no longer functional beliefs, in the simultaneous evolution of ideas and invention (e.g., Rupert Sheldrake's (1980) morpho-genetic fields), in personal and transpersonal paradigm shifts, biological mutations and spiritual awakenings.

Change involves relinquishing the old and embracing the new. Letting go of what is no longer functional or essential involves accepting loss and the need to grieve it. Many resist such acknowledgment. Some say that all we need to do is hold on until we can resume old ways, get back on our feet or past the crisis, since we'll never be free of our basic attachments, no matter how hard we try. Some say we just need to adapt, to change to whatever is needed by our circumstances. Let go, they say— it doesn't really matter anyway.

When we hold on, we resist change, waiting to get back to the old ways. When we let go, we give up anything and anybody that doesn't help us achieve our goals. Either extreme implies that we need not acknowledge that the core of who we are might be violated.

Sometimes neither *holding on* nor *letting go* is sufficient. The complexity and overwhelming nature of today's changes can demand transformation—a wholesale abandonment of old ways in order to develop larger, more inclusive realities. *Change that is transformative is more than coping; it is akin to dying in the magnitude of redefining who we are and what we are about.* Out of an awareness of the uniqueness of what we lose emerges a greater whole. The universal experience of grief liberates the old self and changes us in deeper ways than we imagined possible.

Losses diminish what we have. Loss also transforms us if it liberates us from a too narrow view of ourselves and what we are about. Without experiencing the common bonds of loneliness, suffering and grief that precede liberation, we can only adjust or cope, and in so doing distract ourselves, ignoring or dreading both the gradual and sudden erosions of life that accompany major changes.

Any major modifications frighten us. We even feel helpless with seemingly minor shifts in routine, hopeless to change the things that matter most. We hold on to the predictable, the familiar old ways that may no longer work. We worry what else can go wrong—and sometimes it does.

Still, we carry on. Our capacity to respond to life's variety can be our greatest strength—or our greatest weakness. It is a peculiarly late-twentieth-century American belief that suffering is an *optional* life experience, one that we have the capacity to avoid altogether through more effective ways of coping and adapting. It is a great American myth that we can overcome anything and, in an age of extremes, a perplexing American dilemma, because when change becomes unavoidable we are particularly predisposed as a culture to minimize or avoid it.

Cultural Roots of Our Dilemma with Change

It is a myth of modern society that success in relationships, individual accomplishments, technology, fame, wealth or knowledge can eliminate the necessity of grieving. We occasionally discard that myth—for example, in the process of surviving wars and natural disasters. People put aside their personal agendas to fight, shelter, shovel and sandbag for collective survival.

Individuals, communities and nations who go through such profound catastrophes are rarely the same afterwards. Old bonds are disrupted by war or drugs: when brother betrays brother, our attachments to family and childhood can be lost. Common adversity creates bedfellows of strangers: when outsiders help us, old suspicions are discarded and new bonds result. When our earthly possessions are destroyed, we have to look beyond the material to find a reason to go on living. Whether it is a private or shared tragedy that cracks our fragile eggshell of individuality, we open to new, more inclusive definitions of what makes life worth living. A critical window of opportunity for transformation opens. *That window is grief.*

When that crucial window is closed, missed or unsafe to explore, grief is denied. We may lack safety to admit something has become real, verify its full extent and find the motivation and hope for transforming it. We may lack encouragement to trust our individual and communal best selves when facing the worst nightmares and cataclysmic realities of our lives. We may lack the courage to make the internal changes necessary to identify what is enough, let go of what is already gone, share available resources and reformulate our life-styles accordingly.

Once crises pass, we often revert to our learned responses about change, loss, attachments and dying. We may reinterpret defeat and loss as temporary setbacks. We distract ourselves with work and play, avoid time to reflect on what has not returned. We may even deny the experience, as Ernest Becker pointed out years ago (1974), to the point of distorting reality.

Unlike the rest of the world in the past hundred years, where losses due to war, famine, disease and poverty were a palpable part of life, we in the United States haven't endured such realities on a massive scale. Our "American Dream" has protected us: Bad things don't happen to good people, or else they occur somewhere else. The two World Wars did not destroy *our* homes. The Holocaust was way over in Europe. Famine may bring people to our shores, but it rarely occurs here. Since the time of the Great Depression, poverty and disease just haven't existed in suburban America. Nor do people die at home; we take them to hospitals.

Even though our attempts at coping occasionally crumble, we still want to believe that loneliness, suffering, death and poverty are optional experiences, as long as we we shore up our ego strength, keep busy or have sufficient loyalty, will power, condoms, education, money or credentials. Winning the lottery or a major lawsuit are new ways to reach the Great American Dreams of wealth, fame and power, of doing better than our parents did, or of living forever young. We'll rebuild on the hundred-year flood plain because the flood of the century has already happened. Cancer, AIDS, heart disease, and depression will be cured in our lifetimes, leaving us with fewer ways and reasons to die. Average life expectancies, now nearing eighty, will continue to increase. If we can just stay young, immortality is within our grasp.

Many Eastern religions have long held that suffering and mortality are necessary parts of life. Suffering, they say, results from material attachments to people, life-styles and beliefs. They see current American culture as creating enormous suffering for itself by our belief in myths about youth and success, in our unquestioned attachments to the sensory and the material. Enlightenment in their view comes from revising such beliefs and challenging the nature of our attachments in order to discover deeper meaning and connection. Letting go of what is already gone, called the Iris Principle in Greek mythology, is an essential step in transformations that lead to enlightened existence.

It's easy to see why such philosophies evolve elsewhere, where poverty, early death and suffering are more visible and commonplace. The United States, still a relatively young country in love with adventure, change and pushing back frontiers with great technological and medical accomplishments, can flirt with the notions that suffering is an option, that possessions always enrich lives and that fame guarantees immortality.

Yet pursuit of the American Dream is why we've struggled so much with the Vietnam War, why poverty and homelessness seem intractable and why we've denied a need to change our sexual behavior as a response to AIDS.

We resist the radical changes in life-style that saving the environment or reducing the national debt demands. We adhere to religious rituals even when they are devoid of spiritual nourishment. Our models for health promise immortality, based on warnings or avoidance, and a preoccupation with winning battles over disease and romanticizing the extension of life. Acceptance of loss and death is at best "un-American," at worst defeatism.

Understandably, those who resist the transformative potential inherent in grieving a loss are those who have the most to lose. They already have credentials, intelligence, education, careers, money, health, talent and fame. They insist that there are alternatives to grief through logic, rewarding work, understanding, entitlement, luck, mastery or cure. Some may intellectually appreciate new paradigms of transformation while failing to integrate them into ways of living. They are the greatest beneficiaries of the American Myth. Naturally, they object to losing those benefits.

I recently moved to a new community and was having my hair cut by Carol, a woman in her forties. Carol did not know much about me and my work. Spontaneously, she commented that she had seen a television program recently about people who lived the longest. She said that a lot of factors were considered in studying these people who were well over a hundred years of age. The overriding reason for every one of them was their ability to deal with grief. "I've learned that, too," Carol commented. "A few years ago I had a whole mess of losses. It was the most painful time in my life. Today I am the richer for it. I have grown in ways that would never have been possible otherwise." Life experience has made Carol wiser than many of my colleagues—indeed wiser than I often feel as I search for answers in theory, research and my own material comfort.

We struggle when we fail to note the dimensions of what needs to be relinquished or when we place too much emphasis on accomplishments. In our optimism about abilities and our special qualities, in emphasizing youth and traditional religious beliefs, and in romanticizing our pioneer spirit, we risk underestimating the magnitude of the change we face and the importance of knowing what will always endure.

What Is Essential for Transformation?

There are so many ways to respond to change. We know little in advance that can tell us how we'll undergo a transformation or if we'll employ preplanned tactics in answer to a particular change event. We can learn different approaches. Just when we think we've got the answer, we find there is another level, another way to understand change. The wisdom to know what is needed comes from our own life experiences.

Grief is both a process and a state of being, analogous to an electron in physics, which has matter and position as well as velocity. Heisenberg's principle of uncertainty, originally applied to atomic theory, observed the impossibility of simultaneously measuring and knowing both the position and velocity of an electron. It is similar with grief. Attempting to define its state belies its process. Attending only to the process does not permit us to know just where we are at a given moment. Transformation includes both process and state, impossible to appreciate at the same moment.

Socrates is quoted as admitting he never made a mistake by saying yes. When he had a choice, "yes" was clearly a natural consequence from which he learned and grew. As described above, *the American dilemma is the perception that we have the opportunity to say no to suffering as a part of life.* As long as this myth persists, we'll mistakenly seek alternatives to grief. As Elizabeth Harper Neeld has noted in her book *Seven Choices* (1990), saying yes to facing the loss and the resulting suffering is essential to growth through grief.

At the other extreme, we may perceive that saying yes is not possible. When we say no to life experiences, it may also be because we do *not* having a choice, that it is *too soon* or that the seemingly positive options are premature, too frightening and dangerous to our immediate emotional and physical safety. Additional factors from our past, individual and aggregate, genetic and transgenerational, accompanied by an absence of safety in the present can limit our immediate options.

Add to the dilemma the common professional view that all responses to loss are inadequate, signs of pathology or poor reality testing. To say that *all* losses lead to illness, stress and calamity is to disparage the human capacity for understanding, healing and forgiveness. Losing a parent is undeniably a significant loss. But as Eisenstadt and his colleagues (1989) have found, some find it a profound creative challenge while others find it a profound limitation.

I have met people who have transformed major losses in their lives and are the richer for them. I've seen, read, and heard about individuals who have survived concentration camps, combat, torture, the death of their children and the suicide of a spouse, but nevertheless have found ways to give their life a new sense of meaning and abundance. Some sexually and physically abused children have been able as adults to uncover the reality of their abuse, confront and express their rage, forgive themselves and their abusers and alter their lives in positive ways. Some traumatized war veterans have found their way back to a life of self-respect and health.

Such reintegration does not come easily or quickly. It requires the courage to accept arduous challenges, apparently bottomless grief, immeasurable anger and the wellsprings of despair. But it doesn't take place until we discover that we're not experiencing a loss in isolation—some power, force, friend or higher being is necessary for us to recover and go on. We need to concede that support may not always be where it *should* be—in our families of origin, friends during the good times or in people with impressive credentials. We may find support as we develop relationships with others who are able to witness our changes, give us comfort and safety, absolve and receive forgiveness, as well as provoke and hold us to standards—often new people we meet in our grieving process.

We need to risk losing the comfort and security of our support groups; we need to abandon the protective identity of being forever bereaved so that we can grow and move on. We must choose to stay open to every effect of living and dying. Then we can experience the full spectrum of what transformation is about. We can find connections that extend beyond our egos and this lifetime.

Transformation:

The process of revolutionary, sometimes evolutionary change.

The discovery of choice through experiencing its absence.

The journey through life, with all its detours and surprises.

We experience love and loneliness.

We find times to keep and times to let go,

Times to begin and times to end.

Transformation of loss is about finding our way.

Sharing the Human Experience

In this book, I've included examples of loss and separation based on my own odyssey as well as those of family, friends, clients and students. Their life stories, their questions, confessions and struggles are vital to my understanding of grief as a transformative process. So is their fortitude, growth, forgiveness, humor and love. I am grateful for their sharing and for the hope, wisdom and questioning that their lives exemplify.

I have slightly altered the stories to protect their identities and their privacy. Sharing their stories affirms the importance of examining our own life experiences and discovering our own process throughout life, whatever form that may take. Hopefully you, the reader, will feel revitalized to be in touch with your *own* life story. People can be inspired when they know others struggle equally hard to find their way.

John MacDonald, a novelist, had his fictional character Travis McGee note that "Sometimes *not* finding treasure is as valuable as finding it." (*The Turquoise Lament*, 1973) Some people I've met did not find growth or meaning. Some did not survive. Perhaps I have discovered the most from them. I've wondered if their tragedies were intended only to help us accept that some losses are not worth recovering from. Perhaps their choice not to seek new definition was an opportunity for me to learn that choice involves a wider range of possibilities, not just what I wanted them to choose. Perhaps their loss of meaning is intended to enhance our appreciation when we have it.

My loss of such people has been a strong motivation to comprehend the grieving process across the life cycle. I am thankful for the opportunities they provided me to detect and to embrace my own shadow and my own destructiveness, my occasional inability to witness suffering or validate despair or to provide the safety and support they desperately needed. Sometimes I respected their choices and stayed present as they died or resigned themselves to a life empty of passion and meaning. Sometimes I have *held their hope* while they experienced the full extent of what they'd lost. Sometimes they challenged me to be more realistic and appreciative in appraising growth potential.

Limitations

I've endeavored to break my professional straightjacket by looking for both support for *and* disagreement with my ideas about change, stress, loss and grief. My observations and illustrations come from people I have met and from those I've read about, learned about through research, movies, literature and conversations with friends, family and colleagues. John Bowlby (1969, 1979) wisely warned professionals *not* to assume that people with losses who come to us in our offices, hospitals and clinics reflect the entire spectrum of grief experiences.

Still, we often arrive at a point where we see what we expect to see, not necessarily what's there. What is written here also reflects where I am at a moment in time. Remembering Heisenberg's Uncertainty Principle, what is lost by writing is the ongoing process of discovery that extends beyond the time of this book.

Chapter One
The Transformative Power of Grief:[1]
A Discovery Process

> *You and I were created for joy,*
> *and if we miss it, we miss the reason for our existence . . .*
> *if our joy is honest joy,*
> *it must somehow be congruous with human tragedy.*
> *This is the test of joy's integrity.*

> **—Louis Smedes in Tim Hansel's**
> **You Gotta Keep Dancin'**

In times of rapid change, it's easy to lose sight of ourselves and our potential. We struggle to adapt to new information, and to keep up with the latest technology. We see conventional wisdom shifting rapidly enough to make each generation out of date before its prime. At the same time, we're excited by life's multiple opportunities. We work to build careers, raise children, find love and to express ourselves. More often than not, however, we put aside personal priorities in the face of society's demands.

In today's world, there are numerous external forces causing widespread changes in our basic behaviors. Added to the social, political and ecological forces are the natural changes, losses and deaths that are inherent in the growth and aging of individuals and families.

Our lives are continually transformed. Sometimes we have a choice; at other times, we are radically changed by life events that challenge, even threaten our very lives. It is my experience that we continually discover opportunities for growth, by choice or not, and that one of the most universal opportunities comes through loss and grief. How grief can create opportunities for growth, rather than a tragedy of life, comes from understanding:

---

1. An earlier version of this chapter first appeared as an article in the *Noetic Sciences Review*, Autumn 1989.

- *The role of loss throughout life*
- *The transformative potential of grief, pain and suffering*
- *The nature of the grieving process*

The Role of Loss

Loss disrupts meaningful parts of our lives as well as changes the ways we experience, anticipate and express ourselves. There are two types of losses: *natural* and *developmentally disruptive*.

Natural Losses

Change is a natural process of our growing up, maturation, aging and dying. These changes include the everyday "necessary losses" (Viorst, 1986). For example, we lose the comforts of the womb and the closeness we had with mother as a baby. We stop being picked up and carried after we learn to walk. As children, we lose favorite teachers, pets, or friends who move away. In time, we lose our parents and siblings as a central focus of our lives even though we carry with us a legacy of the experiences we had with them during these formative years.

In our early adult years, we cope more effectively with loss by believing we are the exception to the rules, especially ones about limits and death. We challenge, revise or discard the assumptions and beliefs of our childhood, creating loss experiences for ourselves. We're convinced we'll be better off without the hindrance of family, culture or conventional wisdom.

Eventually, we come to acknowledge that our parents weren't always wrong, cultural tradition has a place in our lives, we're no longer as young as we used to be, we have limits, our dreams have been reached, or they never will be. We lose our innocence—many times over. Sometimes we may feel we are dying under the weight of our commitments and responsibilities. We grow weary of meeting unanticipated complications and limits.

Natural losses continue throughout life. Eventually we will lose family, friends, work and sometimes our health as a part of living long enough. At the end is our own death—our final, natural loss. Before and during that event is the loss of everyone and everything we have loved and cherished.

Developmentally Disruptive Losses

Natural losses are a normal part of growing and aging. There are many losses that aren't natural or universal. What is natural at one age is disruptive at another because it happens too soon—such as losing our parents as a child—or too late, such as leaving home for the first time at age forty. Such losses disrupt our ability to do what "comes naturally," to grow and separate from our parents, secure in the belief that they will always be there for us.

Disruptive losses also include traumatic, often sudden occurrences that exceed our capacity to continue life as usual. These include such wrenching events as life-threatening illness, death of a child, divorce, rape or murder. They demand that we change and adjust as they challenge us to find any remaining threads of normalcy. They can demand all our energies to cope and adjust for a long time afterwards .

Both natural and developmentally disruptive losses can profoundly challenge what gives our life meaning and pleasure. We may challenge our illusions about security, immortality, fame, success and material wealth, and acknowledge our losses, limits, and our own dark side. We may do things we are ashamed of, things that can have disastrous consequences for our marriages, careers or self-respect. *We focus on what no longer exists, what is missing now, or what will never be*. It can be painful to find out how alone we are, the price we are paying for our achievements, our secret passions, our betrayals or our procrastination. We may even come to the realization that we are dying and will be dead for a very long time.

For transformation to have a base in our life experiences, we need to be sensitive to loss. Transformation, after all, means starting with one thing and ending up with something quite different (a loss itself!). We must know our origins, talents and legacies if we are to appreciate the magnitude and awesomeness of the transformations that later occur. We need to understand how our attachments, dreams, beliefs and myths have created either a solid foundation or a motivation for growth. We need to affirm what our lifestyles, routines, and habits have allowed us to accomplish or how our shortcomings have pushed us to overcome them. In short, we need to validate the talents, limits, opportunities and betrayals we begin with and experience along the way. Only then can we appreciate how we "played the hand we were dealt"—one measure of our transformations.

The Transformative Potential of Grief

Personal transformation can be the result of *and* the cause of joy and grief. *Transformative potential is created when we can reassess what we have lost and discover an internal richness never appreciated before.* Transformation involves making use of our internal resources. It involves not being fettered by roles and rules, but finding ways to be empowered by them. We transform by finding strength in acknowledging our weaknesses instead of denying them, discovering new realms of consciousness and rediscovering innocence through renewal and forgiveness.

Transformation doesn't seem possible during times of emptiness and loneliness. My client Tim was far from seeing his transformative potential during the year he went through a divorce, bankruptcy, the death of a friend, and a move. "Just when I thought things couldn't get any worse, sure enough, they got worse," he sighed.

The life cycle itself is a process of such fundamental change that even a few years from now we may not recognize ourselves. Physically, these transformations are often obvious, yet our life experiences can similarly age our emotions, imagination, curiosity, thinking and our willingness to live fully. To appreciate the full range of human experiences associated with growing up, aging and death, we must also have the time to grieve, heal, understand and challenge ourselves again.

How does it happen that people find the strength and courage to go through their grief, to eventually transform loss into creative life experiences? Living fully means we accept every consequence of living and dying: that we will indeed experience loss, joy, change, laughter, success, failure, love, anger, guilt, betrayal, good health as well as periods of pain and illness. Birth, change and death are universals of our existence. All of these need *validation*, which simply means we use all the resources of our mind, body and spirit working together to strengthen our being.

On the occasion of each loss, whether natural or disruptive, we can *choose* to grieve. Grieving provides opportunities for "midcourse corrections," to make sometimes radical shifts in where we are going based on what we know about our past, present and future. Not grieving involves distortion of or dissociation from reality—a decision made at the time because we find we lack sufficient resources or safety to fully experience the reality of the loss. Not grieving is a hazardous, stressful alternative that can lead us down an irreversible path—at least one we cannot reverse without a great deal of help (see also Chapter Ten).

In the wake of one significant loss, we often realize that we can't afford to leave our assumptions, illusions and myths unchallenged. They may increase our vulnerability and helplessness or they may contribute to our passivity and rigidity in times that demand change. How we make these adjustments in the grief process is critical in determining how we will adapt to life thereafter—whether we drift aimlessly, or whether we find our way. *Finding my way* means we are eventually able to recount the fullness of our story, not just its high points or its endings. It can mean we are able to continue to experience a life with times of fulfillment and meaning.

In essence, we carry within us the love we have received long after the source of that love has departed from our lives. Gandhi once noted that grief over the loss of a loved one was perhaps our greatest delusion, for we retain within us the essential character of that relationship. That it is only form, not substance, that we lose, however, is something most of us can only appreciate after experiencing the full cycle of grief. This level of transformation is usually achieved only by experiencing the *paradoxes* of authentic feelings—too many of us want to jump to this final phase to avoid the hard emotions.

Transformation is not without its obstacles. Our loved ones don't like to see us in pain. They may interpret our grief as a sign of their failure as a friend, lover or helper, or they may fear that if they get too close the pain and grief may become their own. *Our grief often stimulates grief issues in others.*

Grieving as a Discovery Process

Transformation through grief occurs when we decide that what remains is sufficient to go on living, and when we *discover* what is possible with the resources we have. This process includes several phases:

- *What is lost?*
- *What is left?*
- *What is possible?*

Phase One: Discovering What is Lost

The task of this first phase is to discover how extensive the loss is. How does it affect us? We discover what we have lost, what isn't there now or what's no longer possible. With time, these painful and often isolating discoveries give us a picture of how extensive this loss is. Melissa, a former client of mine, wrote in a journal:

> *It is impossible to think—I shall never sit with you again or hear your laugh. Every day for the rest of my life you won't be here. No one to talk to about my pleasures. No one to call me for walks, to go to the mall. I write an empty book. I cry for an empty room. And there never will be comfort again.*

Grief as a process of discovery often begins with *shock,* followed by attempts to overcome or escape from the loss interspersed with admissions of its reality. Common questions during this phase include:

- *Has it really happened? (When Grieving Begins)*

- *I can beat this! (Fight—Holding on)*

- *Why face it? (Flight—Letting go)*

- *How bad is it? (Awareness)*

This phase involves the need to acknowledge that something is missing and to find ways to cope while gradually discovering the extent of the loss.

Losses usually cannot be absorbed fully at one time. We need time away from them, to discover if we have to deal with them or not. Our methods of coping help us limit our vulnerability to our losses. However, they require enormous amounts of energy. "I can't admit to myself that he/she is gone" is a typical statement during this phase. Our coping style helps us conserve our remaining resources by allowing us to detach and distance ourselves from the loss. This way we can pace the amount of awareness we let in so that we can begin to adjust. Many models of grief emphasize the pathological aspects of denial and distraction.

During the initial phases of grief, coping involves adaptive ways that *limit awareness.* Coping that *expends* energy involves *fighting,* or what can be called *holding on.* We try harder. We're optimistic. We try to understand why it happened and then find a cure for it. We keep active, perhaps throw ourselves into our work, creating a distraction from the awareness of our loss. We take care of others so we don't have to focus inward. We believe that what we are doing will make the loss and grief disappear, at least temporarily.

Methods of coping that conserve energy involve flight or escape, or what I call *letting go.* We escape through our dreams and fantasies, as if in a trance or stupor. We limit our vulnerability by becoming passive or separated from everyday life. We engage in pastimes, collude with friends to give ourselves a break. We might acknowledge that the loss did happen, except we'll also say it "isn't all that bad" or we "don't care."

For example, Peter found temporary escape with his friend John during the last days of his mother's life:

> *During my mother's last six weeks, I played tennis with John every other day. It was my only time away from the tensions, details and demands of her care. I knew that if I wanted to, John would willingly listen to me talk about what was happening. We had known each other for years, and it seemed there wasn't anything we couldn't discuss, including his own reactions when his parents died.*
>
> *I needed to escape during those tennis matches. We played evenly, as we usually did. We enjoyed each other's company. We laughed, told jokes, complimented each other on our play.*
>
> *John validated me by letting me be where I needed to be, knowing it could be different if I needed that, too. Later, I did talk. Again, I felt his real presence, his strength permitting me to go as far as I needed.*
>
> *After Mom died, John's first comment after giving me a hug was "Well, Peter, now we're both orphans." His comment challenged me to look at this life change in a way I might not have, at least for a while. That challenge soon led us to laugh about our common fate as orphans. In playing together, and in being challenged, I felt strengthened.*

Such coping allows awareness to be a gradual or episodic process. It is important to recognize this as a valid part of grieving. *Escape is vital in grief and gives respite from the ruthless emptiness of awareness.*

Still, reality of the loss catches us when we are most vulnerable—when we go to sleep, make love, are touched, hear a particular song. "I was walking along, enjoying the sights of the city, when I realized that the last time I was here was with Ellen," Tracy, a recently divorced man, reported: "It was as if I got hit in the stomach."

Awareness can be a turning point, a time when we either find some strength to go on or we give up. One of the mysteries of the grieving process is how some people go on living in spite of devastating losses, while others give up in spite of relatively minor setbacks. It's as if at some

Figure 1-1:
Discovering What Is Lost

level we make a choice whether to go on to the second phase of this grieving process or not. Perhaps it's a matter of whether our motivation toward living exceeds our pull toward death or stagnation.

Leon Uris identified the nature of this turning point in his novel *Trinity* (1977):

. . . all [people] in that instant of ultimate agony make a decision to live or die. It's not a conscious decision, but one your spirit makes. Apparently I made the decision to go on living . . . in one form or another.

When the choice is not to go on with living, physical death may not be the immediate outcome. Many people have given up on life long before they die. They simply exist, cope and abide by their unchallenged beliefs and myths.

Phase Two: Discovering What is Left

When we've found out the extent of our loss and can still go on, healing begins. We find the sources of support and nurturance that helped us make it through the darkest and most vulnerable times. We'll remember what we've lost and restore what we can.

The tasks of this second phase allow the meaningful aspects of what remains in our lives to be recognized and remembered. We find ways to contain the loss, rather than only limit our awareness of it. It can be a time-consuming and exhausting process.

It takes time and energy to find the resources necessary for such exploration and restoration. Healing often involves the rediscovery of the simple and the sensory, of negotiating a truce between our mind, body and spirit. Taking time for a massage, a walk in the woods, or a day at the beach are examples of helpful self-nurturance.

For perspective to emerge, we need to have objectivity *and* openness, vulnerability *and* strength. Integrating loss involves remembering the way it was and finding ways to rebuild.

Does enough remain? Is enough recoverable? We may choose to discover ways to grow from our losses or for accepting and adjusting to them. Choice involves risk, knowing that life is fragile and success has no guarantee. It can also mean accepting that *all* we have, we have *now*.

Grief transforms us when we risk growing. We ask if enough remains of ourselves and our resources to risk living fully again. Is it worth the hurt and fear to date again after a partner's death? Can we make plans, knowing that disaster has struck in the past? Can we tolerate feeling disloyal if we turn our energies to new possibilities, new challenges, and away from our loss?

When we make such choices, we are often motivated by a sense of incompleteness. "There has to be more to life than this," commented Alayne two years after her husband died:

> *I can't accept that I'm supposed to sit back and live off his pension. My life has to have meaning once again. Yes, I can be hurt. That's a price I'm willing to pay.*

Sometimes, the process of healing from a loss can be rushed too quickly, just as the healing of a broken leg can be tested prematurely by running on it too soon.

Figure 1-2:
Discovering What Is Left

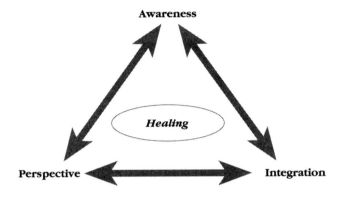

A second alternative is to live within the bounds of what's left. Such a choice may not seem like a decision at all. It's hard to know if we've decided not to grow or whether we're still healing and waiting for a better time.

How often have we heard statements like: "She never recovered from her husband's death." Was a *choice* made not to discover one's transformative capacities resulting from a significant loss? When we choose not to risk transformation, our lives will remain fixed around the loss. When we continue to mourn for what once was and cling only to what is left, we may live lives further diminished by each new loss. The greater the accumulation of losses that have gone unprocessed, the greater the risk we take when finally choosing to grow.

Phase Three: Discovering What is Possible

The worst has happened. With time, we accept the reality of the loss. Then we find out what we have left. We discover life's potential. Living fully after a significant loss means we bring together the resources of mind, body and spirit, and act accordingly. We act "in sync" with ourselves and our values. We alter our long-standing beliefs and myths, or reaffirm them. We reform and re-explore; we risk, giving up the comfortable and familiar.

Figure 1-3:
Discovering What Is Possible

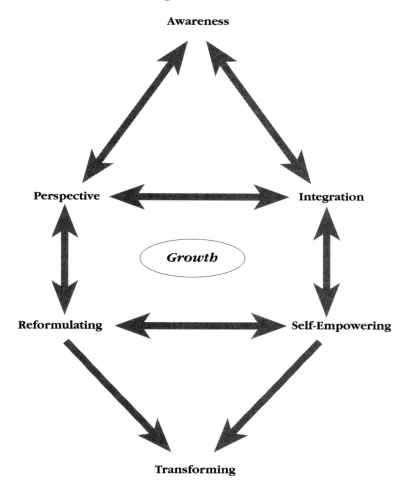

Having accepted the reality of the loss and the limits of what we have left, we take on tasks that include the discovery of life's potentials. Some people, with little or no opportunity to improve the quality of their life, choose to die or, at least, not to prolong life. This can be a valid choice for some. Clark, a young client with AIDS, demonstrated this choice when he said, "I've changed my motif from dying with AIDS to living as fully as I can with it."

Those motivated to grow from their losses don't have it easy by any stretch of the imagination. As my client Sheila noted many years after her divorce:

> *The most painful part of my grief was becoming aware of every-thing I lost as a result of the divorce. By far, the hardest part was choosing to move on, to give up the comfort and support of my grief and the soothing familiarity of my anger at my ex-husband.*

It is at this time in the grief process that people often undergo some type of *rite of passage* (saying good-bye, finishing business, etc.) as a test of their commitment to growth. In doing so, it is not uncommon to find people doing things with others who can bear witness to their process (e.g., having a personalized memorial service or a special graduation).

It is also not uncommon for people to "move on," which has other consequences and possibly more losses. We might lose friends and loved ones who are willing to be present during hard times, but are frightened or mystified by our desire for growth and challenge. Two of my clients, Arlene and Jack, experienced this when they left their support group for bereaved parents ten years after the death of their son:

> *When we left, no one from that group ever came to see us again. We weren't supposed to ever get over Tony's dying. It was as if they thought Jack and I had betrayed him—and them too.*

We may be ready to move on while others around us are not, even others who were important to us earlier in our grieving.

Often transformation requires altering the ways we look at the world. This process of reformulating and re-exploring means that we choose to risk loss and give up comfortable resolutions because we know that it is necessary for our own empowerment. Karen, whose mother had died when she was fourteen, related this dream:

> *I dreamt my mother was alive and living in Chicago as a very successful lawyer. When I met her I said, "I thought you were dead." She laughed. She told me it had all been a hoax she had carefully planned. "The life of a wife and mother wasn't for me' she told me in my dream.*
>
> *"How could you do that to us?' I demanded angrily. "That was a pretty cruel thing to do. You could have at least seen us once in a while."*

"I never could have left otherwise," she responded. "Besides, I like being a lawyer."

What a wonderful gift from my mother.

Here I am struggling with a career and raising two children, and she pops up with a great but impossible solution! There sure are times when I'd love to do just what she did in my dream. Letting myself dream about her this way gives me a freedom to be more imaginative. It's as if Mom gave me back the playfulness I'd lost when she died.

Grief can help us shift from seeing ourselves as the center of the universe, to seeing the universe as the center of who and where we are. It's similar to Flaubert's reflection that "One does not chose one's subject matter. One submits to it." A client, Ron, reflected, "After I got my personal ego deflated, I realized I was a part of something much bigger than my physical self." This statement came many years after losing his livelihood and reputation as a scholar and psychotherapist. Years of soul-searching had led him to realize that he had exceeded his limits prior to his losses, and this realization allowed him to choose a much simpler and happier life as a teacher.

Transformation that results from grieving can be characterized by a shift from limits to opportunities. Whether we believe in an afterlife or not, we can appreciate what contemplating it does for us. Transforming loss allows us to discover new ways to relate, understand, create and commit ourselves to an ongoing process of renewal and discovery. We come to know that loss, grief and the potential for transformation are parts of the cycle and the celebration of life. That knowledge permits us to grieve with less resistance and fear as we encounter new losses.

Chapter Two
Recognizing And Validating Losses

*Let us endeavor to see things as they are and then inquire
whether we ought to complain. Whether to see life as it is
will give us much consolation, I do not know, but that
which is drawn from the truth, if any there be, is solid and
durable; that which may be derived from error must be like
its original, fallacious and fugitive.*

—Samuel Johnson

Art, 38, came to a medical clinic with back pain, fatigue, headaches, and sleeplessness:

*For months I've felt as if there was something wrong with me. I've
not been myself. It scared me. It started after I finished building the
house. I reached my dream—with many compromises along the
way. So why was I feeling so down? It should have been a time to
celebrate. I couldn't. All I could think about was how tired I was.
I wondered if it was worth it.*

*Sometimes I have this thought—like things would be better if I
could build another house. Am I crazy?*

*After hearing Art's story, his doctor asked, "Art, did you lose
something?"*

*Art looked stunned. Then he replied, "I guess I did. I lost my dream.
The new house I just built isn't the same as I'd hoped. A lot of
changes start to finish. We couldn't afford the big fireplace I
wanted. It's fine, though it's not what I dreamed it would be at the
start.*

*I don't know what to do with myself these days. All my spare time
for two years went into that house. It's like I've lost a sense of
purpose, a goal, an everyday routine that made it worth getting up
in the morning.*

*It's crazy, I know, but I keep thinking about building another. My
wife would kill me!*

Doc, does this mean I'm just grieving? Is that all this is?

Years ago the term *success depression* was coined by Martin Seligman (1968) to explain the phenomenon of grief after succeeding at a sought-after goal. At a time to celebrate, such as completing a house, graduating, getting married, or having a child, we are sometimes unable to do so. We have not recognized that we have lost things in the process of reaching a goal, a dream, or new status in life. When we cannot *validate* its reality, we may diminish or exaggerate its significance.

For many people there is tremendous relief in authenticating their losses. Grieving is a familiar process once we understand that we have experienced a loss. Yet we often fail to recognize significant losses in our lives, even those shared with others. And even if we do, we may feel we have no right to grieve and move on from it. We are supposed to *adjust* to change, not succumb to it.

The failure to verify a loss makes it difficult to understand the subsequent process of mourning. As Art discovered, sometimes all that is necessary is help in recognizing the losses encountered in change, even positive change. Our behavior, "not being myself," makes sense as grief. Art understood that. In completing his house, he reached *and* lost a dream. His daily routine was altered. He lost a purpose for each day. But he finally recognized his loss: "I'm just grieving—that's all it is."

What makes it so difficult to recognize, much less validate loss? "It's not the American way," said my client Tom. "It's a sign of weakness, lack of optimism, incompetence" was another's reply. Another: "It's the male macho stuff," smirked Carol, "Guys can't admit anything that makes them look bad!" Caroline observed: "Our family never shows grief. It's a weakness we can't indulge in. It's our aristocratic heritage." Our attitudes reflect our culture's belief that loss can be overcome by image, competence, desire, being "macho" or by virtue of our entitlement.

Prior to 1930, over 80% of people in the US died somewhere other than a hospital. Now, 80% die in hospital settings. Avoid hospitals and we avoid death or its reminders. The rise of the mass media has both brought death into our living rooms and separated us from the real experience. As a result we think that dealing with loss and death is an option, similar to switching channels. This attitude suggests that grieving is a morbid indulgence, a sign of character failure, a source of shame, evidence of incompetence. It is characteristic of a youth-oriented society that has not been forced, unlike other parts of the world, to face the reality of death, limits and loss in times of rapid and profound change.

Samuel Johnson long ago noted that there is no solace in discovering the presence and fullness of loss. Without *validating* loss, however, there is also no hope to transform dysfunctional societies or individuals hell-bent on self-destruction. With validation of what is lost, there is that possibility.

In this chapter we will define some key terms that are used throughout this book, such as *validation* (Olson and Schneider, 1988, 1990). This chapter will also identify the situations leading to significant losses: life experiences, alterations in life-style, self image, families and the world. What is involved in recognizing when a loss has taken place? What are the different types of losses we may experience? In this chapter *disenfranchised losses* that Ken Doka speaks of, which lack support for grief will be identified, along with *communal* and *transgenerational* losses that we share with many others, living and deceased.

Validation in Recognizing Loss

Validation becomes "therapeutic" when it intentionally affirms the fullness and the reality of our struggles, crises and grief. Therapeutic validation has the potential to occur in many circumstances:

- *Times of decision-making*

- *Crises, love affairs, friendships, anger, or creativity*

- *To strengthen our capacity to undergo and share any life experience*

- *With those whose work involves high levels of stress*

Therapeutic validation includes the following:

- *Genuine communication—within the self and with others. It is usually without intention to change, manipulate or control.*

- *It has an existential focus. It acknowledges the reality of universal human conditions, such as love, joy, loneliness, pain, birth, genuine humor, success, grief and the search for meaning and happiness.*

- *It can be used to acknowledge potential for both the enhancement and renewal of the self as well as the potential for stagnation and death.*

- *It contains an acknowledgment that we are doing the best we can under the circumstances.*

- *It admits and accepts the existence of our shortcomings, weakness, shadow or dark side in ways which permit understanding, forgiveness, healing, integration and wholeness.*

- *Therapeutic validation does not distinguish between an honest response and what may be the more enduring truth. We often contradict ourselves, feeling intensely one moment and seeing it differently when feelings have cooled. A validating response does not point out apparent contradictions. It affirms the moment and the process, the honest response and the seeking of truth. This is the emotional paradox we must go through to get to integration.*

- *Finally, therapeutic validation endorses the human condition, whatever that might be. It affirms strength and encourages self-care. It can challenge us to renew and to forgive.*

Therapeutic validation results when it

- *Provides safety, nurturance and hope for health and for the well-being of relationships.*

- *Neither exaggerates nor diminishes the reality of life's existential conditions.*

The formulations of many late-twentieth-century European (Miller, 1983,1984; Frankl, 1974; Bowlby, 1979) and American (Gendlin, 1964, 1977; Moustakas, 1972; Kopp, 1977, 1979; May, 1977) existential approaches support the genuine acceptance of human conditions. Such acceptance includes the belief that our attempts at coping represent our best efforts at the present time. It allows us to make sense of what we are experiencing and to explore creative alternatives.

Loss and Therapeutic Validation

Loss requires affirmation in the face of real external and internal stress and change. To pursue our process of natural grief, we need validation that:

- **What we are experiencing right now is real.**

It's frequently the case that people in helping roles feel the need to "protect" others from reality or else go to the opposite extreme of confronting them with it. Protection, when it distorts or denies reality, does not provide the safety needed to discover our own strengths. Confrontation, at the other extreme, can attack our method of coping, weaken our self-concept and self-esteem and destroy the safety network we have established. Therapeutic validation of a loss finds its place somewhere between protection that distorts and confrontation that injures.

• *Our reactions and methods of coping "fit" the stresses currently being experienced.*

One of the essentials of working with people with loss is to provide an environment that can acknowledge their shortcomings and offer creative mechanisms to enhance their self-care.

"Am I going crazy?" is a commonly voiced concern after a significant loss. "Craziness" is the common explanation in modern culture for behavior which deviates from the norm, regardless of the circumstances precipitating it. *In therapeutic validation, until it is proven otherwise, we assume that the reactions are appropriate to the circumstances and the stress.* I have found that people are their own best judges of "not being themselves." If someone can state their fear of going crazy (in the absence of a history of mental illness), they are likely to be validating the uneven and often unpredictable course that normal grief produces. These fears can be lessened when people can discover the nature of those circumstances and gain a better understanding of their influence.

Validation involves "resonating" with another human being, or with oneself, to enhance awareness and growth. Such resonating includes a sense of connection which transcends different life experiences.

There are psychological schools that believe that early life experiences are always more important than current ones. But they may dismiss, diminish or overlook the significance of the present loss or stressful situations, preferring to explore its historical origins. Such a focus on the dominating influence of the past may not be helpful at the time of a significant loss. There can be a loss of trust in the therapist and in oneself when the emotional impct of the current loss is not acknowledged. The rigidity of the helper in focusing primarily on the past can detract from opportunities for the whole family to grieve and experience fully what is happening in the present.

Human beings in helping roles cannot be "trained" to be more humane in their response to dying or to other existential issues. Usually training does the opposite: It protects them from feeling the need to respond as a fellow human being who knows what loneliness, joy or grief is like. Their responses to their own personal losses may be so profoundly "trained" that they are insensitive to the struggles and tasks required for others to face their losses. Unfortunately, such insensitivity can and does occur among the most highly trained therapists, especially when they have little or no support or validation for their own losses and stresses.

• **We are doing the best we can under the circumstances.**

Validating the process of coping involves suspending the notion that we are not really trying to deal with the situation at hand, or that we are consciously and willfully avoiding our issues. Therapeutic validation has as a basic tenet that a person will allow full awareness of a loss when the strength, safety, and energy to do so are available.

Circumstances can be overwhelming. We aren't usually open to more issues than we can handle. Validation involves accepting limits and acknowledging the need for time, patience and gentleness with oneself. It also respects the person's vulnerability rather than using it as a sign of weakness. Validation is therapeutic when it acknowledges that we are doing the best we can, and when no attempt is made to alter or take advantage of our current emotional state.

From a therapeutic perspective, validation provides possibilities, not guarantees. It enables us to acknowledge our vulnerabilities and to understand and appreciate our strengths and weaknesses. Whether we consider validation in terms of everyday experiences or in times of stress and loss, it remains a powerful tool for communication within ourselves and with others. Any of our life experiences can be validated. This can give us, our families, friends, colleagues and clients the necessary strength to meet our losses and our challenges. We can know that our story is worth listening to. With validation, suffering can gain meaningful expression, joy can find ways to be shared, and love can create and fulfill its potential to empower and enrich.

What is a Significant Loss?

The Chinese symbol for "crisis" is the combination of two symbols: one for "danger," the other for "opportunity." A significant loss produces feelings of chaos, the loss of connections to other people, meaning, or our way of life. During such chaotic times, we are more sensitive and vulnerable. Our potential for transformation reaches its peak.

It's common to think that a significant loss involves death. In recent generations, we've accepted that divorce is a significant loss as well—

especially when we don't choose to divorce. In this book, we have broadened the definition of loss to include any life change, from birth onward, chosen or unchosen. The healing of any significant loss involves grief.

Change has the potential for both gain and loss. That does not mean we'll always experience a sense of loss every time something changes— or the opposite, that we'll always be able to find a silver lining. What constitutes a significant loss varies tremendously from one person to the next. The same event can affect two people quite differently, even when they share it. For example, the death of a parent can be a relief for one child and a catastrophe for another, depending on the relationships they had prior to the death.

People can feel mistrustful when someone says "I know just how you feel." The reader is encouraged to consider the potential for loss in this chapter in the light of the impossibility of knowing just what constitutes a significant loss for another—or the opposite, when change might be the source of relief and even joy.

Steps in Recognizing Our Losses

How do we recognize when a significant loss has occurred? There are several common elements:

• *Loss of external and internal predictability*

We can lose our sense of security and trust when a loss reminds us of how fragile our control over life events is. There is a risk in loving, moving, graduating, marrying or having a child. When we've experienced a loss, we're acutely aware that the future is unknowable, and the present is all we have.

The loss of *external* predictability and trust in our relationships and in our surroundings can signify permanent changes in behavior and life-style. Some people may find it difficult to love again. People living in flood- or tornado-prone areas come to understand the peril hidden in stormy weather. We may become more sensitive and vigilant in monitoring our environment. *We modify our behavior in order to decrease the chances of having a significant loss happen again.*

Here is an example from Denise, whose niece was killed in an auto accident:

> *My husband Butch says it's silly, and it may be. I won't let my three kids go on the same plane, train or even car together without me.*

I keep thinking about what happened to Sara and I think that I couldn't stand it if I were to lose one of my children. I know I wouldn't be able to go on living if I lost all three of them. I can't take that chance—unless of course I'm with them.

The loss of *internal* predictability (of some aspect of our self) can be even more threatening. It frequently deprives us of our capacity to orient ourselves, maintain access to our inner resources or rely on experience to carry us through. We see the world through new eyes, and we may feel alienated from our old way of doing things. After experiencing a loss, we meet the same old external environment with our new internal self, but we experience again a new sense of loss. The "old shoe" is there but it no longer fits. When the change is a positive one, we assume we'll "get over it"—and often we do, though we may miss the "old" self. But when the loss is negative, we may find it harder to believe we'll ever recover, worrying that the old self we've lost took the best of us with it.

We also can be unpredictably moody, easily distracted, forgetful and frightened when we grieve important losses. *We become unpredictable to ourselves.* We question the basic truths that have always guided us. Without those truths, we have lost the rudder that guides us, the anchors that gives us safe harbors. Grief over a significant loss is a precarious ride through a tempestuous storm.

Sometimes the unpredictability is in the loss itself, not our reaction to it. As we see in the example of Jeremiah, struggling with the early signs of Alzheimer's:

It's helpful to know that what is happening has a name now— Alzheimer's. As terrible as this is, it still gives me a way to make sense and make what is happening more predictable. Before I had the diagnosis, I thought I was losing my mind—emotionally, I mean. I'd call somebody on the telephone and hear their voice. I recognized the voice and I knew I knew them, only I couldn't recall their name or why I had called them. I'd get lost, even though everything around me was familiar. At night sometimes I forget where I am—especially if we're staying away from home. As frightening as losing my memory is, it's better now to know what it is.

For those of us not facing such an illness as Alzheimer's, it's hard to know which would be worse—to be mentally ill or to have this mentally degenerative disease. Loss of predictability can devastate us if we have no way to anticipate or control our responses. Jeremiah eventually retired from his job, and his wife Meg was able to help him compensate for his slowly progressing condition. He found many things he could still do where memory wasn't so crucial. Jeremiah's recognition and acceptance of what he couldn't do any more gave him the energy and the desire to explore new ways of experiencing life, still knowing that his time was limited. He was better able to *limit the scope of what he lost*—for the present.

• *Loss shifts our relationships*

Many losses challenge our friends and loved ones to know how to respond to our grief. Some are so profoundly affected by their own experience of the loss that they are not available to us emotionally to support our grieving. We grow closer to those who know what our loss is like. Few relationships are left untouched.

• *Loss changes our self-image and self-confidence*

Loss also affects the way we look at and experience ourselves. While we are grieving, it's hard at times to find our "best self," the parts of us that can usually rise to the occasion, be empathetic and tolerant. We wonder if these good, passionate, loving, positive parts of us have been lost or damaged. We become all too aware of our shortcomings and have a tough time finding self-esteem and inner strength.

• *Loss is multidimensional*

Losses are multi-layered. They are comprised of many smaller losses. If we recognized every aspect of a loss at one time, we'd feel overwhelmed and confused. We may be disappointed because we thought we had gotten over our loss, only to find we're dealing with still another aspect of it. With recognition comes validation and grief—one piece at a time. We can eventually appreciate, understand, and even accept the importance of each bit and piece, finding new ways to respond. Here is a good example of this:

> *While walking through a wood on a university campus, Mary Ellen was attacked and raped at knife point. Over time, she painfully discovered that she had experienced a number of losses connected to the rape. One was a loss of her sense of control and ownership of her body. Another loss was in her ability to enjoy solitude and the beauty of nature without having to be concerned for her own safety. In addition, Mary Ellen experienced the loss of a number of illusions—that people are trustworthy; and that if you*

try hard enough, you can cause—or prevent—anything. The failure of law enforcement officers to indict her assailant deprived her of her belief in fairness and justice. She lost her relationship with her boyfriend, who was unable to be supportive and understanding of her "unusual" behavior and feelings in the weeks following the incident.

It took over a year before the awareness of each of these losses emerged in her post-rape counseling sessions. Yet as she discovered each one, Mary Ellen felt herself regaining ownership of herself. But each time that she found a new aspect, she initially became discouraged and wondered if she would ever get over the rape:

Time and effort to adapt to this loss have brought many changes to Mary Ellen's life. She was able to find solitude in new ways, often going places with a companion. She also learned a martial art for self-defense. The friendships that withstood her initial fears and pushing away became even deeper than before. "I'm a stronger person for what happened," she commented three years later. "I've regained my playfulness and my enjoyment of sex. But I don't think that I'll ever lose that sense of needing to be aware of what's going on around me when I'm alone. I'll never have that sense of innocence and freedom when out walking by myself I once had."

• Losses have different significance at different times

Not all losses have the same importance to us, nor does the same loss remain fixed in its significance. However, when we are in the midst of acute awareness of the fullness of our loss, it's inconceivable that anything could be worse than what we're going through—even if it is "only" getting a traffic ticket. We learn its *relative significance* later. Profound losses have greater continuing consequences. Sometimes our reappraisal of the meaning of the loss comes and goes for many years—perhaps the rest of our lives.

No one else can know the true significance of our loss because no one else has lived our life. Our unique experiences and personality, the nature of our relationships and our beliefs, hopes and dreams define how we experience change. A traffic ticket can be overwhelming if it means losing our license or opportunities to earn a living.

Many times, the process of grief brings with it surprises concerning how significant—or insignificant—someone or something was to us. For example, losing a partner or spouse of many years can produce unexpected feelings of relief. The awareness of this can produce guilt over not "loving" the partner, which may force us to examine a new aspect of our personality never explored before.

The significance of a loss depends on:

• *The intensity of the attachment, dream or feeling*

When we invest ourselves in someone or something, we form attachments. We form bonds with people, objects, ideas, dreams, expectations and places, to mention a few. When we lose any of these, we feel diminished. If we win an Olympic gold medal in world record time, we lose the feelings associated with striving for the dream. The *anticlimax* defines that feeling which athletes sometimes report after the big win. They experience an emptiness or a sense of loss because they no longer need to strive after the big dream—the goal has been removed. As Emily Dickinson observed, the greatest tragedies in life involve not getting what we dream; the second greatest come from achieving them. Successful athhletes lose one role and its expectations and take on a new one—from contender to champion, from anonymous to famous.

As children or adolescents, sometimes we are ambivalent about our personal attachments. We love and depend on our parents, yet we resent the limits they place on us. In leaving home for college, a job or a marriage, we feel a loss, but we also feel relief. What we may have failed to recognize is that our ambivalence has complicated our grief. Before we can fully understand what we have lost, we must acknowledge the complexities of our attachments.

We get connected to intangibles as well. We have ideals and they get shattered. We grow up with assumptions about the way the world is, the way our parents, partner and heroes are, the way *we* are—only to have something come along and destroy these images. We feel betrayed. We grieve the loss of the way things were or seemed to be.

• *The number of related losses*

It's rare when losses come one at a time—a single loss can encompass several losses. For example, divorce is more than separation from a spouse. Initially, one or both partners may feel relief from constant conflict and emotional tension. But then the related changes begin to occur— relationships with children, friends, family; financial changes; loss of home—these always compound the loss. We may have the illusion that divorce should be quick and clean, only to find years of alimony, co-parenting, awkward and sometimes painful reminders at the children's graduations and weddings and at holidays. One loss, such as divorce, radiates many other losses.

There are no guarantees that one loss will insulate us from others. "Just when I thought it couldn't get worse, sure enough, it got worse" is frequently heard from people experiencing multiple losses:

> *"Give me a break!' pleaded Mike when he found out that he was losing his job. Only a month earlier Tommy, his six-year-old, had been diagnosed with leukemia and a year ago his wife had died in a car accident. "I think I could survive one of these, but, my God—all three!'*

A new loss can unexpectedly bring up old ones—sometimes we didn't even know they were losses. Years after having had two abortions, Michele had a miscarriage when she wanted to have a child:

> *I wasn't prepared for the tears. I was crying for three, not one. It wasn't all right to grieve the abortions when they happened. After all, they had been my choice—and I still believe they were right. It took the miscarriage to realize I'd carried these two little ghosts around.*

• ***The extent to which our daily routine or life habits are disrupted***

We are sometimes surprised and feel guilty that a loss didn't seem to affect us as much as we thought it should:

> *"I can go days without thinking about Mom dying," admitted Jane only a few weeks after her mother died. "Didn't I love her? I thought I did."*

For the thirty years since she'd left home, Jane lived thousands of miles from her mother. Except at holidays, they'd rarely see each other. Jane's daily routine was not altered by her mother's death. There were few reminders of her mother in what she did each day.

On the other hand, we are sometimes surprised and disturbed at how much a seemingly minor loss bothers us:

> *When I gave up smoking I had an awful time. You would have thought I'd lost my best friend. I was moody and irritable, restless. I couldn't figure out what to do with my hands or with coffee breaks. I'd always smoked after making love, at times to reflect on*

the pleasures of life. I don't do that any more. In fact, I even avoid sex and coffee breaks because they tempt me to smoke.

Even when we want to change habits such as smoking, knowing their injurious effects on our health, we may realize more of a loss than we imagined because of the number of activities that were affected by it. Perhaps smoking was always associated with times of pleasure or reflection. Initially, in our grief, we may have difficulty separating what we are losing (smoking) from what can be kept (improved health).

Recognizing When a Loss Has Occurred

A loss is a loss, isn't it? Unfortunately nowadays, in a culture that prides itself on overcoming obstacles to happiness and material wealth, it can be hard to validate our own losses, much less gain support from others. It's not that we need to be morbid or preoccupied with loss in everything. It may be a matter of a few moments in an otherwise positive experience to savor or mourn what is gone.

It's easy to recognize some of the losses we experience, especially those related to death, devastation, accidents and illness. Others aren't so easily recognized. We know something has changed, perhaps, but we can't put our finger on it. In change, there is generally something new introduced and something old lost. In some changes, we can clearly see the old that is lost and only with time will the new become apparent. In others, the positive is so clear we can't see the loss or we consider it trivial in comparison.

Failure to Recognize a Loss

When we experience growth, we experience joy. Failure to recognize a loss can leave us puzzled by the absence of joy, burdened by the recurrence of sadness and anger, and ashamed of our lack of the gratitude and happiness that accompany usually positive changes. We feel that we should experience happiness for such events and, as a result, discount the significance of our experiences instead of looking for what losses may be part of a mainly positive event. Judy sought the help of a trusted friend as she wrestled with "things going too well":

Judy was embarrassed to talk about this. She felt as if she was being ungrateful or morbid. Yet, she needed to discuss her reactions with someone. No one else seemed receptive.

In the past few months, everything in her life had gone beautifully. She had finished her doctoral dissertation, which her advisor said was one of the best he had ever chaired. She had lined up a publisher for a book she was writing. During very difficult times for getting jobs, she landed a job at an Ivy League university.

Now she felt strange. Everything seemed unreal. She felt she was a phony. She didn't deserve all this. To be so successful didn't fit her self-image. Sometimes, she wondered if she was going to wake up and all of this would go away.

In describing how she felt, Judy identified what was changing in her life as a result of all these positive events. One was that she was soon going to be moving to a new community, where she would lose her support and the respect she had developed in the community. Her self-image as an "average, nice person" had been over-whelmed by her successes. She was frightened by her own compe-tencies and her new self-image. The old one was familiar, comfort-able and predictable. The new one was exciting, though unpredict-able.

Judy's relationship with her husband was changing, too. For the first time, they were moving for her job. He would have to find something there. They hadn't talked much about it. The change meant giving up an old way of relating.

Judy felt excited as she left the session. Now she looked forward to what was happening. Validating losses freed her to experience and share the joys of the positive events fully.

Validation of a loss is often only a first step. For Judy it turned out to be enough. She had the support and resources to do the rest.

External, Internal and Shared Aspects of Loss

Significant losses can contain internal, external, shared and transgenerational aspects.

External Losses

External losses have to do with our attachments to people or pets (relationships), places (environment) and things (objects). As a result, the disruptions of these kinds of connections constitute significant *external* losses. Table 2-1 shows examples of these types of losses:

Table 2-1: External Losses

	Loss of Relationship	*External Losses*	*Environmental Losses*
Obvious Losses	Death of a loved one Separation Abuse Incest	Theft Destruction of propoerty Desecration	Natural disaster Loss of shelter, food or safety
Loss as Part of Change	Divorce Role reversals Temporary separation	Moving Buying/selling valued objects Now job	Perceptible changes: Seasons Noise levels Space Pace of life
Unnoticed Losses: Growth-related	Being in love Marriage Birth of a child Ending therapy	Wealth Winning a prize	Imperceptible changes: Seasons Noise levels Space Pace of life

Relationships

There are two types of loss of relationship: 1) the loss of a relationship through death or divorce and 2) losses as a part of an ongoing relationship. The death or disappearance of a loved one is an obvious loss. More difficult to recognize are those losses embedded in continuing relationships, such as having children together, committing to marriage, or staying in a partnership over time. Because no growing relationship stays the same, loss and its recognition become an important part of its vitality. Anne Morrow Lindbergh reflected on the changing nature of relationships in *Gift from the Sea* (1975):

One learns to accept the fact that no permanent return is possible to an old form of relationship and more deeply still, that there is no holding of a relationship in a single form. This is not tragedy but part of the ever recurrent miracle of life and growth. All living relationships are in the process of change, of expansion, and must be perpetually building themselves new forms. *But there is no single fixed form to express such a changing relationship.*

Because there is no single, fixed form to express a changing relationship, the old is constantly being altered. When old, no longer functional ways of relating are released, there is room and energy for the new, for revitalization. Sometimes our failure to recognize these changes leads to alienation, misunderstandings, and, in some instances, a dissolution of the relationship. For example, "You don't treat me the way you used to when we were first together" can be an invitation to explore how the relationship has changed, what is missing now, and, if possible, what can take place to revitalize. Unfortunately, such statements are often only complaints—or else the invitation for discussion is misunderstood. In this example, a couple provides a familiar response to the gradual eroding of their relationship:

> *George and Pat had been married for twenty years. During that time, they had three children, all healthy and growing. During the early years of the relationship, they had to struggle a great deal. George lost several jobs and Pat was a very important source of support to him during those times. More recently, George became quite successful in his business, receiving much recognition and financial reward. Pat, who saw her role in life as principally one of support for others, became increasingly depressed and jealous as both husband and children needed her less. George became increasingly confident and outgoing and shared less and less at home. Neither recognized the changes in this relationship until George announced the marriage was over.*
>
> *Pat felt deserted, unappreciated for the role she had taken in life. She failed to recognize that her role was no longer a functional one in a family that grew less dependent on her. George, on the other hand, failed to recognize the need to mutually grieve the loss of what they had shared early in their relationship, so that his joy and success could be shared and a new relationship emerge. Pat couldn't realize the role she had played had been appreciated, but was no longer necessary.*

People don't ordinarily view as a loss something we choose to do or that may on the surface seem positive. A sense of loss can result from a job promotion or the birth of a wanted child. But because people might think we're crazy, self-indulgent, or morbid in our reactions, these can be as difficult to grieve as the death of a loved one. Without support and understanding, grieving is difficult:

> *Mike was a popular faculty member at a midwestern medical school. He was an overwhelming choice of the search committee and the faculty to become dean of the medical school. A month after assuming office, Mike returned from a meeting very upset and depressed. He related to a colleague that he had just gone to visit the lab that he had helped establish years before. Most of the people in the lab, including the faculty, had been recruited and hired by him—and were people he had considered friends. This was his first visit since he became dean. After a few minutes, someone had asked him to leave—they were uncomfortable with his being there. After all, he was the dean now.*
>
> *This experience was not quickly resolved. Some noticed his bitterness—he left after two years in the post, a short tenure.*

Mike had not anticipated the losses involved in his promotion. Yet similar reactions are experienced by many who are promoted above their peers. Friendships change and are sometimes lost. The basis of trust, forged over time, does not always transfer when roles change.

External Objects

We think we don't need many things until the time comes when we have to do without them. Then we have the opportunity to examine how important—or unimportant—something is. As we have discussed, the most significant losses concern our basic needs—for shelter, comfort and predictability. But less obvious are things that have memories or achievements associated with them. We often miss most those things that we rely on for self-expression and as ways to enhance our sense of self-worth. A musical instrument, a boat, our native country or the language and customs we learned while growing up are often such agents of self-expression. This is profoundly felt in people who have emigrated from their native country:

> *Birgit met Peter during his sabbatical year in the Netherlands. At the end of the year, they decided to marry, and she emigrated to the*

United States with him. It wasn't until several years later, during a course on couple's communication, that Birgit began to discover some of what she had given up in coming to this country. She had felt vague resentments, guilt, and loneliness for several years. It had never been enough to bring up, for she was very much in love with Peter and had put her effort into solidifying their relationship.

She discovered that she missed her family, particularly on the holidays. She also felt cut off from old friends, and that making new ones in the US was very difficult. New friends were likely to be Americans who did not share her cultural heritage. Part of her vague discomfort also came from speaking a non-native language, English, which often did not permit her to communicate exactly what she felt. Since her husband and her friends didn't understand Dutch, there was no way to let them know.

The most difficult time came when her mother died. She was not able to be with her mother at the end, or attend the funeral. It was then that she felt how much she had given up to move to the United States.

Our relationships with objects are highly personal. Most of us have "treasures" that are of little monetary value or consequence to anyone else, items that represent ties to our past, our friends and ancestors (e.g., photographs and trophies)—all of which are sources of comfort, prestige, and pleasure or ways of expressing self. Losing these can be a source of tremendous grief, as happens during natural disasters:

In June of 1972, hurricane Agnes left a trail of devastation in the Eastern United States. Many people were killed, homes destroyed, and communities disrupted. Crisis teams helped people beyond their initial shock and got them functioning again. Homes were rebuilt and new community spirit developed. Yet months and even years later, many individuals discovered losses from this devastation that they had overlooked in the struggle to survive. There was more divorce and child abuse, both measures of the strain of losing so much. A frequent awareness was the loss of irreplaceable photos of parents, grandparents and children, and of mementos that were precious in preserving memories.

Environmental Loss

As the previous example illustrates, part of the human story is the desire to live in a predictable, supportive environment. Because of the fundamental importance of this, disruptions and losses at this level can be devastating—no longer can we take the world for granted. Our sense of security in our home environment isn't usually conscious. Yet when a disaster strikes, it's difficult to confront our unconscious needs:

> *The natives always laughed at the foolishness of these housing developers, only to find out afterwards that the place wasn't secure from floods. Now we have the Great Flood of the Millennium. There isn't a place for miles left untouched. They'll probably try to rebuild, convinced it can't happen again. It proved that it can happen, not that you can ignore its possibility.*

This was a common observation after the worst flood in recorded history had, in the summer of 1993, destroyed entire housing developments in the central United States built on what was referred to as the "one-hundred-year flood plain"—safe because no flood had reached that level in the previous one hundred years. This one did.

It's less obvious when we lose something predictable about our environment to "progress." For example, when an interstate highway is built two blocks away, or the local airport changes its traffic pattern so landings and takeoffs are directly overhead, we might not even notice the change after the first few days. Yet we may be spending energy blocking out the noise in ways we don't recognize until we get some place quiet. If we've lived in an environment filled with activity and traffic noise our whole lives, we can be disrupted by the "boring" stillness of a farm or a lake. What we've lost is the rhythm, pace and stimulation we've grown used to. "I couldn't sleep a wink last night," complained Willie while visiting her sister in the country. "It was so quiet I could only hear my own high pitched whine in my ears and it kept me awake." To be sure, major disruptions in our environment are serious threats to our sense of trust and predictability.

Internal Losses

Losses have a way of changing something inside us. Grief itself is an unsettling process that causes us to wonder if we're going crazy, if we've lost a part of ourselves that can never be restored. It's a rare loss that doesn't cause us to stop and question the basic premises we have about life—fairness, immortality, the ability to love. We may not always want to know why we do what we do, but when significant losses occur, they shake loose some of our internal anchors.

Table 2-2 show examples of internal aspects of losses:

Table 2-2: Internal Aspects of Loss

	Identity, Roles, Habits	*Developmentally Based*
Obvious Losses	Fired from job Widowed Divorced Chronic illness Rape	Birth Death
Change-Related	Leaving home Change of job Change in life-style Retirement Master new skill Form new relationship	Weaning Start school Changes at puberty Aging
Growth or Success	Graduate or finish school Job promotion Become popular or celebrity Creativity	Maturation Learn to walk and talk Gain insight or judgement

• *Our assumptions, stereotypes and myths: spiritual*

There are aspects of our life that we define as essential to being alive. These include what gives our life meaning—our values, our beliefs, our way of being. Losses can challenge this essence. We may lose a sense of connection to anything and anyone. The resulting feeling of loneliness challenges our spirituality, our willingness to reach out, to believe in our "best self," and to place hope in powers stronger than the forces beating us down. If a loss is severe enough, we may even decide that life is not worth living.

It's obvious that our spiritual well-being can be disrupted when our belief system is challenged. Validating spiritual losses is important if we are to grieve them. Without grief, we have no capacity to discover a more mature and robust spirituality that fits our present circumstances and helps us understand the new—and old—meaning of our lives.

There are challenges that everyday life makes on our values and our will to live. Our will to live is a compilation of all the forces within us—our mind, body and spirit—that determines what it takes for us to survive. With every significant loss, a spiritual question asks: is there enough left to keep going? We may think we know the answer only to discover that life has something else in mind for us.

Sometimes we go on when it makes no sense to do so—living in pain, fear, humiliation, poverty, illness. Years later we may find our suffering has given us a depth, a credibility, and a message of hope for others and ourselves. But some lose their spirit while continuing to exist physically. One definition of depression is the loss of a spiritual self.

The loss of assumptions is, in a way, a loss of innocence. To function in life, we take many things for granted, including assumptions, prejudices and routine ways of behaving. A loss may force us to examine and discard these old ways. We lose our innocence. Table 2-3 suggests some of these "losses of innocence":

Table 2-3: Significant Assumptions Challenged by Loss

I am responsible
I am not responsible

I can only live moment to moment
I will live on indefinitely

I can control anything important to me
No matter how hard I try, I am helpless

I will always find something meaningful in life
There's no real future for me

I can count on things staying the same
I can't count on anything or anybody

Justice and fairness will ultimately win out
Justice and fairness do not exist

Everything has a purpose and a meaning
Life ultimately has no purpose and meaning

This is the best of times
This is the worst of times

I am different from everyone else in the world
I'm just like everybody else

Someone will take care of me
No one cares about me

Losses threaten assumptions. In some instances, such as a "mid-life crisis," every presumption or belief we have seems invalid and disrupts the way we view our world. They change the way we behave, adding another set of losses:

> *Seamus was devastated when his wife divorced him. He could not believe she would do it. He assumed that if he carried out his end of the bargain (he would provide financial security, she would do household chores), the marriage would go on indefinitely. He was angry. Her decision was unfair; his hard work had not been rewarded.*

> *Seamus knew that things were not going so well. He'd assumed everything would always work out for the best. After all, his mom and dad had their problems, but they hung together.*

> *Seamus had assumed he would never be alone. He had never learned how to take care of his basic needs, such as cooking or managing the money he earned. At one point he asserted: "I guess I can learn to cope with all these changes. I don't know if I'll ever be able to trust anyone again, even myself, in the same way as I used to. My faith is shattered. What can I count on?"*

Seamus had a number of his assumptions and beliefs challenged—including fairness, the way things have always been, his parents as role models, that effort pays off, what men and women are supposed to do. Seamus' questions were disruptive and life-altering. In grief, we question our judgment when something goes wrong, even when we have done nothing. "If only I had kept him home that morning!" sobbed a mother after her son was killed on the way to school.

Loss of Identity

Doubts about our self-worth—who we are and how competent we are—can result from change. We can lose a sense of worth as a result of either a firing or promotion. We can lose our goals and dreams as a result of both success and failure. Our habitual ways of doing things don't always work when we move, stop smoking or start a love affair. Our attractiveness, health, prowess, self-concept, identity, ego strength, body image, or our sexual drive can be altered if we gain or lose weight, fall in love, exercise regularly—or become disabled, chronically or terminally ill. *In every instance, our identity changes.* We may even find ourselves saying things like "this isn't me"; "This is the new me"; "I can't believe I'm thin.

In my mind, I'm always fat" or "I've never thought about myself as attractive." Such statements reflect our struggles with defining—and sometimes losing—who we are.

Retirement can also deprive us of an important role as well as our work, something to do every day. Our identity is central to our sense of worth. Unplanned retirement or being fired can take from us an image of who we are and have been for years, as well as our chief purpose for living and a comfortable, familiar, predictable way to relate.

Internal losses are often not observable from the outside. They can come about at times of apparent positive growth and change:

> *Maureen felt joy and relief after her final back surgery. However, she also felt uneasy. She had lost a habitual way of responding to herself and her environment, as well as a familiar role, predictable relationships and freedom from responsibility.*
>
> *Maureen had been operated on twelve times for lower back pain over a fourteen-year period. None of the previous operations had any lasting effect. As a result, she lived in pain. Her family life was frequently disrupted by acute episodes. She was unable to work regularly or carry out routine household tasks.*
>
> *By attending a pain clinic for several months following the surgery, Maureen discovered that the pain had disappeared. But after an initial euphoria, she felt depressed and sought counseling. She felt like a stranger to herself, did not know what to do with herself. Besides, her family was often angry with her.*
>
> *At one point Maureen realized that she wanted her pain to return. "At least I had a focus in my life then." In time, she realized that with the absence of pain, she was now expected to assume responsibilities she had not had for fourteen years. It was the loss of freedom from those responsibilities and the loss of a familiar, predictable way of behaving (i.e., focusing on her own pain) that created feelings of grief.*

Developmental Loss[1]

Occasionally, we stop and reflect on what's happened to that little girl or boy we used to be—or as we get much older, how did we get to be this age when we still "feel so young." How could our children be the age

---

1. Developmental losses will be explored in greater detail in an upcoming book.

they are when we still think of ourselves as being so young? With such times of reflection, we often realize how much we've changed—and what we've lost in the process of getting older. Yes, we're wiser; but that wisdom has come at the price of our innocence, childhood spirituality, myths and assumptions that no longer fit. We have lots of experience— and a limited amount of time left.

Shared Loss

Whether we admit it or not, none of us is an island, complete unto ourselves. This is certainly true where loss is concerned. Inherent in grieving is identifying and remembering what connects our "island" to the rest of the world, our family, community, religion and culture—all major sources of validating shared loss.

Events of change do not only affect single individuals. The death of a spouse, for example, is also the death of a parent, child, sibling, friend, or co-worker. There are unique aspects to the loss for each person. The death of that one person, however, is a shared loss.

Shared losses are sometimes easier to validate. People willingly share the impact of an assassination of a public figure like John Kennedy, Martin Luther King or John Lennon. We tell stories of where we were at the time, or what others said about it. As in the saying "misery loves company," loss can create or strengthen bonds between people. That certainly applies to grief. It can also be critical that those in positions of power give permission for loss and grief to be acknowledged.

Many self-help groups are based on the desire to validate shared losses. Family and friends may not understand what it's like to lose a child, parent or sibling, face an addiction, go through a divorce, or become a widow. We may want to protect the ones we love from seeing how angry, sad or disgusted we are with what's happened, or how ashamed we are of what we've contributed to the loss. We need to feel validated by others whose loss experiences are like our own.

Shared losses can also be times of loneliness when others are unable to be open about their grief. We may also experience the same loss in such different ways that it lacks a sense of commonality. Such differences certainly characterized the divisiveness of the Vietnam war, when some saw the enormous loss of national face and integrity, while others struggled to keep up the image. Supporters of "my country right or wrong" fought with those who saw "the whole world watching our shameful war." It has taken well over a decade to begin seeing how common our loss was, and how divisive our way of responding to the loss had been.

Positive life experiences can also be a mixture of shared joy and loss. At a wedding, the couple focuses on the joy of the commitment they make to each other. Parents and siblings may be genuinely happy for their joy, but also feel a sense of loss of the special relationship they had with one member of the couple. We can be happy for a friend at work who gets promoted while personally saddened that it means they'll no longer have the same work relationship with us.

In many instances of shared loss, we don't recognize the loss at the same time. It may be many years later that we can look back and see how graduation was the last time we saw our classmates, or the birth of a child changed our relationships with childless couples. As soldiers, we were so relieved that the war was over, we didn't acknowledge to each other how much a loss it was not to have the life-essential companionship of a buddy or the thrill of living-on-the-edge that never happened again. It's often at reunions, holidays or chance meetings years later that the shared value of what we lost can finally be recognized.

Table 2-4 shows some examples of shared losses:

Table 2-4: Examples of Shared Losses

Communal
Death of a public figure
Loss of a national/state/community/religious image
Catastrophe/natural disaster
War
Recession/economic depression
Connection to a community/cause/collective goal

Familial
Loss/death of a parent/sibling/child
Birth of an exceptional child/sibling
Chronic illness/disability of family member
Adoption
Abortion
Divorce/separation/abuse/incest
Leaving home/staying at home
Retirement

Transgenerational
Incest
Abuse
Alcoholism
Family secrets
Early death
Homeland
Connection to land/ship/farm

Communal Loss

Communal losses are major changes which affect both the image and the life-style of a community, nation or religious group. In Biblical times, Moses held the Jewish nation in the desert for forty years after leading them from slavery in Egypt. A generation who experiences the shared loss of slavery had to lose their influence before those born later were able to become the leaders of the Promised Land. The fall of communism, as positive as it seemed, meant a tremendous loss of a predictable way of living for millions of people, with life getting much worse for some. It may take several generations of freedom to overcome the shared losses of those nations.

Natural disasters, war, and economic recessions affect whole communities and nations with common losses of home, jobs, food, family, and lives, to mention a few shared aspects. The crash of an airliner deprived my home town of its favorite book store owners—a loss mourned by family as well as community. "I never knew John," people would say, "but he did so much for our community. Good people like that shouldn't die!" They were expressing their communal grief.

Here in the early 1990's, publicly documented cases of sexual abuse by Catholic priests and other ministers of faith are frequently in the news. Such practices are hidden, a source of shame for the church. Many Catholics experience a loss of trust in church authority, a sense of outrage at the offending priests, shared losses by the many victims who were now adults. Many also struggle in their grief to identify what had been lost.

Familial Loss

Marianne was forty-four and Eric fifty-three when they gave birth to their sixth child, Tom, a Downs Syndrome baby. Everyone in the family grieved and celebrated the birth, and participated in the raising of the child. Ten years later, the older children began to realize that as their parents age, Tom will eventually be their responsibility.

A loss to one member of a family is rarely isolated. Incest, for example, may occur between only two members of a family, yet its effects alter every relationship within the family. For some the effects may not be felt for many years, yet its potential is still there.

Divorce is obviously a shared loss in one sense but it is not in another. When the decision to divorce is not shared by both partners, the experience of the loss is quite different. When child custody becomes a struggle, a legal battle, or is left entirely up to one person, there is usually more that is divisive about the divorce than is shared. The ways of coping with the loss or defending against it can be so diverse and painful that one cannot support the other, much less acknowledge the loss of the love and dreams they once shared.

Adoption and abortion are losses that often are not recognized as such, much less as shared losses. The circumstances leading to either way of resolving an unmanageable or undesired pregnancy may be composed of numerous losses. The very decision to give birth or not may also be a shared loss. Denise struggled with her decision many years later when the son she gave up for adoption indicated he wished to contact her:

> *He had been conceived during the New York City power blackout in 1966. I was only sixteen at the time, trapped on a elevator at school with my boy friend at the time. We broke up shortly after I found out I was pregnant. I never told him. I didn't think he deserved to know. I left school, gave birth at this horrendous hospital, saw my baby once. Only my best friend knew.*
>
> *I've since married and have three daughters. My husband never knew. I've told them about this new situation, that I was being contacted by the child I'd given up. Manny started crying, "I've always wanted a brother, especially an older one." Sandy wondered if that was why I wanted them to be such tomboys when they were growing up. I honestly don't know.*
>
> *It's changed my relationship with my husband. In some ways we're closer. Ken let me express my grief over what happened. We had some long discussions about his not knowing, wondering how that had affected our relationship over the years. We grieved the impact of having such a secret between us.*

Denise and her family found both gains and losses in the new discovery. Denise had the opportunity to openly grieve. Not so fortunate was another woman, who had an abortion:

> *We already had five children. I hadn't been pregnant in ten years. I was finally in a position to make something of my own life. We used protection. It didn't work.*
>
> *Here I was, at forty-three, pregnant again! I wasn't sure I could handle it. When the amnio test came back suggesting Down's*

Syndrome, I felt something snap. I couldn't do it. I had to have an abortion.

My husband's Catholic—at least that's how he was raised. He went along with my decision, although he argued a bit at first.

Things have never been quite right between us since that time. I remember crying many times about the child I lost even though I knew it was the right decision. My husband never said anything after that day when we had the abortion. "We have to live with what we've done' he said, staring straight ahead as we drove home.

We don't make love anymore.

Transgenerational Loss

Transgenerational loss is the effect of a particular loss on succeeding generations. In many instances the loss began in a traumatic event that may have never been discussed because it was so painful. So we know nothing of, for example, what happened in the concentration camp our parents survived, or where they lived before moving to our hometown. We know dad was in the war, but nothing about what he was like before then, except for that one picture where he was smiling—something he's rarely done during our lifetime.

In transgenerational loss, the focus is often on the person shunned or excommunicated—the adopted child or the victim of incest. Transgenerational loss can manifest as alcoholism and abuse, or wars between clans, communities and religious groups that span decades, even generations. What's difficult to recognize in transgenerational loss is that each generation is responding to the loss in similar ways until it is too late to rectify the pattern.

Difficulties in Validating Loss

Some losses are difficult to recognize and support because they are what Ken Doka (1989) calls "disenfranchised": They involve unpopular or antisocial behaviors, or the breaking of social taboos. For example, families often discredit the losses of a member who admits incest and thereby violates the family secrecy rule.

Some losses aren't legitimized because of intense feelings about them, as in torture, rape or incest. We can't imagine ourselves in those situations without feeling rage or disgust, so we avoid people who have such losses, victims and perpetrators alike. Sometimes we fail to give support because their loss is frightening, our own worst nightmare. Table 2-5 shows examples:

Table 2-5: Losses Difficult to Validate

Complicated	_Long-lasting_
Divorce	*Chronic illness*
Birth of a child	*Life-style change*
Child custody	*Death of a child*

Controversial	_Chosen_
Murder	_(when choice is available)_
Insanity	*Abortion*
Abuse	*Marriage*
Torture	*Promotion*
Taboo	*Job resignation*
Incest	*Moving*
Rape	*Divorce*
Life-threatening illness	
Losses due to sexual orientation	

There is very little, if any, grief support for the spouse who murders, the incestuous or abusive parent who loses children. Who wants to endorse the losses experienced by parents who voluntarily give up children, have an abortion, attempt suicide or fall in love with the "wrong kind," get AIDS from "promiscuous" sex or dirty needles, give up home, family, and community for "no-good" reason? We generally respond to such individuals with an attitude of "you're getting what you deserve—you asked for it":

> *I was desperate—married at fifteen, a baby every year for seven years. My husband got ill and couldn't work. Out of desperation I became a hooker. I couldn't live with myself, so I started drinking. When I drank, I went crazy. I beat the kids so bad. When I got sober enough to realize what I had done, I couldn't stand it, so I'd try to drown myself again in liquor. I tried to kill myself—unsuccessfully.*

> *Eventually, the courts took my kids away, and a couple of years later my husband died. I have survived—but God, what a price. There has been no one, no one, who was ever willing to support me at the time.*

Ned came along later. He saved my life—kept me from committing suicide. We married. Eventually I discovered God. My faith has been my only solace. I loved my children, but I know now the best thing that ever happened to them, and perhaps even to me, was having them taken away.

It's not surprising that Angie hadn't found much support over the years. What is amazing is that she found one person, Ned, who believed in her. Over time, Angie saw that what happened was the best she could do under the circumstances. She forgave herself because she discovered love and a belief in God. Angie realized she couldn't do it by herself. Life circumstances had been so overwhelming she had been unable to cope effectively on her own. Then she could grieve the disenfranchised losses of her children.

Whenever choice seems to be involved in a loss, we rarely feel sympathy for those making the choice. The small business owner who is forced to lay off workers rarely gets public sympathy in making such decisions, though this is a valid loss. Neither does the military commander who sends troops to battle, some of whom are killed. "I'm everybody's friend when the money is flowing," stated the head of a university department. "But it's a lonely spot when the budget is so tight cuts have to be made."

Perhaps it is too much to expect from the people in our everyday lives to empathize with these types of losses. Even professional therapists struggle with accepting their legitimacy. But with these situations, the need for validation from at least one source becomes essential if grieving is to take place.

The Life Change Inventory: Assessing Your Own Losses

You, the reader, may wish to identify your losses and their current impact. Appendix I at the end of this book contains the Life Change Inventory. You may wish to fill this out to give yourself a clearer idea of how extensively loss is affecting your life. It can also help define areas where the loss/change may not have affected you, or how that impact has changed with the passage of time and your grieving.

Summary

Loss can pervade any life experience. Recognition and support of the reality of a loss are essential for grief—the mechanism we have for renewal—to take place. Losses can be disenfranchised by families and society: We often fail to recognize significant losses because we lack safety and validation—from our family, friends or our culture. We can learn to recognize external and internal losses—losses that are obvious, a part of change or even losses embedded in primarily positive experiences that unexpectedly dim our joy. We learn to recognize when our beliefs are based on faulty or no longer valid premises. We learn that many losses are shared even if our grief processes differ.

From validating the extent and the limits of our losses, we gain an appreciation of what we have lost and what we have left. From expressing our grief, we gain motivation to live fully, the zest for celebrating life's moments of success, pleasure and transformation. We can affirm life's worth and our appreciation for the opportunities we still have.

Section II

The Nature of the Grieving Process: Themes and Discoveries

The meaning of life is arrived at . . .
by dark gropings,
by feelings not wholly understood,
by catching hints and fumbling for explanations.

—*Alfred Adler*

Alfred Adler's quote captures the essence of the process of grief—our attempts to give meaning to the ways we respond to loss. It is a risky, uncertain, frustrating and overwhelming process. There are times when my own grief process has greatly aided me in understanding another's. And sometimes it prevents me from doing so. Understanding helps if we can relate it to our life experiences. Models may only reflect where we are at a moment in time. Although their purpose is always limited, they can be helpful in capturing some essential elements. A model can also represent a life philosophy—a perspective that is continually validated, challenged and revised.

Knowing something about grief does not hasten the process nor lessen its pain. At times, this knowledge makes it even harder to *limit awareness* of the loss—a necessary aspect during grief. Knowledge can reassures us that we're not crazy and not alone in our journey, even if the path through loss is clearly our own.

In this section of the book, I will give the reader an overview of my model of the grieving process.

Definition: Grieving is a process of discovering the extent of *and* the limits of what is lost, what is left and what is possible as a result.

"Discovery" may seem a strange term to apply to grief, for finding out the full measure of our losses is rarely a pleasant task nor is it one we look forward to experiencing. The "harm-avoidant" part of ourselves, in fact, will argue persuasively that we've already wasted too much time with our loss. Yet discovery is exactly what we experience, when we have appropriate support and validation for the process. The health-seeking part of us wants to know what it is we have lost and what remains afterward, so we can know what we can do with it. It is, in this model, also a creative process. Not surprisingly, creative activities often intensify during grief because pain, suffering and chaos open us to our deeper self.

Models of Loss and Grief: How to Understand Them

Grief and normal bereavement have taken a more prominent place in the literature of the helping professions in recent times. The interest in personal experiences of loss has also grown. Story-telling and fictionalized accounts of survival and grief have been a popular theme in literature, music and the creative arts for thousands of years. Existential philosophers have addressed the central themes of grief for well over a century.

It seems to me at least four separate movements have developed that address issues of grief. I present them here in brief overview:

The Medical Model of Stress, Loss and Grief

Since the time of Eric Lindemann's (1944) pioneering work with the Coconut Grove disaster and studies of the aftermath of the Second World War, we have become more aware of how devastating losses can be on our lives. The medical profession has discovered that psychic trauma can cause physical as well as mental ills, shorten life expectancy and increase the risk of suicide and depression. The impact has been so profound that debates have been held whether grief is actually a disease process or a healing one (Engel, 1968).

The media exposure given to Elisabeth Kübler-Ross (1969) in the Vietnam War era helped Americans acknowledge the importance of dying and of grief. Until the 1970's, the pervasive philosophy of many health professionals about grief was that it was not a legitimate focus for research or treatment. Grief and the process of mourning were viewed as a natural, but very private process and therefore not amenable to traditional psychotherapeutic intervention (Averill, 1969; Freud, 1917). It was something best left to the clergy (Grollman, 1975; Westberg, 1962), or to family and friends. When it did appear in the professional literature, we debated its "stressfulness," whether or not it was a disease and what could go *wrong* in our lives if we had a death in the family.

The Death and Dying Movement Model

Schools of thanatology that focus on death and dying have been in existence for quite a while, long before the 1970's. Columbia University in New York, King's College in London, Ontario, and the University of Minnesota have some of the more prominent centers. Elisabeth Kübler-Ross, Stanislov Grof, Helen Bonny and many others gave considerable impetus to the clinical applications of thanatology. There are now extensive college and medical school courses, the hospice movement for care of the dying, and the controversial self-controlled death programs as promoted by Derek Humphries (1991) and the Hemlock Society in *Final Exit*. Stephen Levine (1982, 1984) and Anya Foos-Graber (1989) are leading advocates for conscious dying and "deathing" as a part of this renewed emphasis on quality in the dying process, while David Feinstein and Peg Elliot Mayo (1993) have inspired people to see how working with rituals for impending loss and grief can lessen our fears of dying.

The Self-Help Movement Model

In the late seventies, the self-help movement discovered the importance of loss and grief in life transitions and in programs such as Alcoholics Anonymous, divorce and widow self-help groups, cancer support and many other chronic illness groups. Self-help groups for many other types of loss and life transitions have emerged since that time, many emphasizing the importance of *coping* and *normalizing* the grieving process. These groups have often come into existence in reaction to the tendency by health professionals to pathologize grief by calling it depression, and through resistance to paying for expensive psychotherapy when what is needed is validation and support.

The Holistic Health Movement

A fourth emphasis has also emerged that has begun to combine its efforts with the self-help groups. Grief as a natural response to a wide variety of losses has gained legitimacy in the eyes of many in health professional roles, including nursing, pastoral care, psychology, social work and medicine. Likewise, it has extended to alternative health care practitioners—massage and music therapy, occupational and respiratory therapy—and to the non-professional helpers—hospice volunteers, parents, lovers and friends. This change in view is a part of the new emphasis on holistic health, taking into account the *whole person* in considering their health needs. As facilitating health and growth is becoming a legitimate function for health professionals along with intervention in pathology and disease, so is loss and grief.

The Need for a Comprehensive Model

In addition, those of us in helping roles are increasingly aware that people can have difficulty with the process of mourning, as previously described. Holistic practitioners are less likely to ascribe this difficulty to personal deficiencies in coping than are our medical model colleagues. Rather, difficulties are thought to be due to the absence of safe, supportive relationships or effective rituals that facilitate the process. Cultural changes that have brought about increased mobility and less reliance on organized religion, family and ethnicity are more likely to be seen as contributing to these absences.

At the end of the millennium, we are more sensitized to issues of loss than we have been for many years. Articles appear that describe the "end of the American Dream" or pessimism about continued prosperity as our salvation. We are coming to realize the fragility of our environment and our economy. Careers aren't nearly as stable as they once were. With the onset of diseases such as AIDS and increasing violent crime, we've lost the protective myth that death doesn't happen until you're older. We're increasingly in need of ways to make sense of the many losses and changes in our lives. We need more than ever to understand and respect our ways of responding to loss.

We can learn about coping with a particular kind of loss, but it is difficult sometimes to comprehensively view the nature of grief or to appreciate its transformative potential. Is the process different depending on the type of loss (e.g. death, divorce, murder, leaving home), the suddenness or violence of the loss, our age, available resources or the degree of choice we have over the loss?

Although there are a number of observers who write sensitively about grief, many questions about grief remain unanswered. Many approaches focus on a single loss, such as murder, suicide or the death of a child, and cover its issues in great depth. It is still relatively rare to distinguish between grief, a natural self-correcting healing process, and depression, which often requires professional intervention. An exception is the excellent and readable book by Klein and Wender (1993) which specifically discusses the differences, and emphasizes the importance of medically treating biologically-based depression. Post-traumatic stress is less frequently missed when it is a part of post-catastrophic treatment programs. Providers like Jeff Mitchell and Grady Bray (1990), Ben Colodzin (1993) and Alan Wolfelt (1988) have extensive programs to address treatment of emergency service personnel, war veterans, and family members. PTSD (Post Traumatic Stress Disorders) is still frequently missed among health care providers in non-acute settings.

Support for a comprehensive understanding of grief is still quite limited. Most research, treatment and training funds still emphasize treatment approaches that deal with pathological outcomes, not healthy ones. For example, the diagnosis of normal bereavement isn't reimbursable by most insurance companies. While bereavement support and follow-up is mandated by federal law in accredited hospice programs, no reimbursement requirement is provided for such services.

Other Models of Grieving

Reviews of the models of grief and bereavement have appeared over the years (Averill, 1969; Schneider, 1984; O'Toole, 1987; Gilliland and James, 1988). Such reviews have found that some models have arisen out of the study of a single event (the Coconut Grove fire by Lindemann, 1944), a particular trauma (Peter Sifneos' [1972] work with post-traumatic stress and alexythymia; Henry Krystal's [1968] study of Holocaust survivors), a particular age group (John Bowlby's [1969, 1973, 1980] work with infants and young primates) or with a particular type of loss (Elisabeth Kübler Ross' [1969] work with the terminally ill; Teresa Rando's [1986] work with bereaved parents). Some approaches have emphasized universal themes common in grief (e.g. Clark Moustakas' [1962; 1972] studies of loneliness; Irvin Yalom's [1989] clinical cases on existential crises; Ausburger's [1981] views on forgiveness). Others have emphasized the growth potential that any life experience can provide us (the existential-humanistic-experiential approaches of Eugene Gendlin [1971, 1974, 1978], Rollo May [1968, 1978, 1983], Fritz Perls [1969], Carl Rogers [1961], Norm Kagan [1980; 1984, 1987], Alvin Mahrer [1986] and Moustakas). Men's grief has received a boost from the popular work of Robert Bly (1989) and Lon Elmer (1990).

Time Since the Loss

Time since the loss is an important consideration in the helpfulness of various approaches. Some focus on the immediate response and the times of *acute risk*—the funeral, post-traumatic response, the time of shock. Others are concerned with *coping and adjusting* to the reality of the loss, with particular emphasis on the first year. Still others look at *long-term outcomes* of grief.

Acute Risk

Many approaches to grief have focused on acute risk and crisis—the first days after a loss. How we conduct ourselves at funerals, the necessity of debriefing a trauma victim, and assessing the risk of heart attacks after shock are among the types of responses studied. Such approaches are critical to survival and to people's openness to their grief.

Coping and Adjusting

Perhaps most research has been published on helping people *cope* with a loss—especially in the few months or first year after a loss. The danger of maladaption is high, as is the risk for developing stressful patterns of avoidance and denial. We are most afraid of being *judged* in these initial months, and most in need of people who understand what we've gone through. As a result, people with particular losses are much more likely to seek support from those who share their experience. There is much written from this perspective, both in ways to be helpful and personal accounts of a loss (e.g. Elizabeth Harper Neeld, 1990; Lynne Caine, 1974; James Agee, 1957; C. S. Lewis, 1953). Support groups have developed for many types of loss, from pets to widowhood to divorce, addiction, prison and even success.

Such group and community approaches are helpful, even essential, to validate and legitimize a loss. We need to know our response is normal—in spite of our fears that our grief isn't as justifiable as someone else's, that swings in mood and thoughts are not signs that we're going crazy, nor that meaning has totally and irrevocably gone out of life.

It is not helpful to be caught up in comparing the significance of our loss with that of someone whose loss differs greatly from ours. Many professionals who have attempted to combine different support groups find difficulties that couldn't be anticipated. For example, I was involved in bringing together parents who had lost a child from leukemia with parents of children ill with leukemia, and found the parents of the ill children very uncomfortable and resistant to talking with the bereaved parents. They weren't ready to accept that the death of their child was a very real possibility.

Combining groups with different losses—or who are at different stages of loss—too early can also result in some people inappropriately becoming helpers because they see their loss as trivial in comparison to that of others in the group. There need to be groups for people dealing with pet loss, moving or holiday stress for example, that don't compete for validation with people who are dealing with incest, divorce, murder or a terminal illness. It doesn't help to invalidate our own losses because others seem to have it worse than we do.

Long-Term Approaches to Loss and Grief

At some point, we all need to feel a part of the greater human condition once again, despite our losses. We need to know that while others may not have experienced the particular kind of loss we did, they know what it is like to suffer, to be lonely, and to struggle to keep going. There is a large community out there who can appreciate what it is like, for example, to have known times when death seemed preferable to life, yet who have savored life's gifts, and who have learned not to take for granted what we have or how long we might have it.

Models of grief are needed that look for the universals—the common bonds, challenges, decisions and risks of responding to a wide array of losses. It would help to see the process of grieving that goes beyond the acute phases, when we put one foot in front of the other. We desire models hopeful that life can eventually have meaning restored or newly developed; that we can find a place for loss in the context of our lives; that transformation to new levels is possible.

The model that is suggested here attempts to include our responses to all types of loss and the time spectrum of grief. It is based on a series of assumptions and the belief that losses can positively transform life.

Assumptions about the Grieving Process

• *The natural outcome of experiencing a significant loss is a process of grieving.*

It is my belief that grieving is the *natural* consequence of losing something or someone we value. It is our way of making sense of change. Peter Marris (1974) has developed a definition of significant changes in attachment and/or habitual ways of behaving and perceiving, by looking at both the intensity of the attachment to what was lost and how extensively day-in/day-out routines or habits were disrupted by the loss or change.

When we experience a loss, we may not be at all sure we can make it through. Before we can grieve, we must know we can survive. Abraham Maslow, in formulating his hierarchy of needs, noted that *survival* is a basic need, which must be met before higher needs can be fulfilled.

There can also be a period of time when grief stops before it is completed or even begun. It is characterized by a time when we are victims of a severe trauma, attempting to survive or to avoid the loss. There are a number of environmental pressures that can distract us from grief or distort our perception of the loss. These interfere with the natural process of grieving until they can be rectified. (See Chapter Ten)

Learning to survive can take everything we've got. Without safety and validation of our losses and resources, we may wait for decades for the opportunity to grieve a loss. As a result, while grieving may be the natural response to loss, it may not always occur.

• *Grief is a natural healing process.*

Grief is a universal human reaction that allows us to recover from and even grow as a result of a loss. Healing can occur if external factors (validation, resources and support) and internal factors (safety, ego strength, flexibility in coping styles) are available.

• *The ways we have dealt with previous crises in our lives will affect our reactions to current and future losses.*

Patterns of dealing with loss are handed down through family traditions, cultural legacies, and religious rituals. If we've feared or experienced abandonment earlier in our lives, losses escalate our separation anxieties. It's very hard to alter our responses, especially in the middle of a crisis—like trying to teach someone to swim while they are drowning. Yet it is possible to change our responses and to break with the limits placed on us by others or by our past experiences.

• *The loss of any significant attachment is a threat to all significant attachments, including our own life.*

We'd like to believe that a particular loss doesn't raise the possibility of other losses, but it does. Awareness means we'll look at every way this loss could affect us. If we are to reorder the priorities in our life, as often happens after a loss, we need to examine what those priorities are—including our commitment to life itself.

• *We can't take it (a loss) all in at one time.*

We don't take in the whole of our loss and its significance in a single moment, unless of course the loss is relatively minor. We're likely to make successive approximations to the true impact of the loss or to only take in a piece at a time. Life needs to go on in between the moments we spend in awareness.

• *We don't "get over" a significant loss, but we can move on.*

Grieving involves "abstracting what was fundamentally important about the loss and rehabilitating it" (Marris, 1974, p.34). Instead of getting over what we lost, we incorporate its meaning and its memory into the fabric of the rest of our lives. Such integration and reformulation allows us to see growth potential in tragedy, learning in suffering, new direction in chaos and continuity in change. It takes some time to reach this theme in grief, often long after the time of painful awareness.

• *Facing our greatest fears can be liberating.*

We can place our smaller fears in a larger context when we've faced our greatest fears—dying, loneliness, helplessness, loss of meaning and purpose—that can result from facing a significant loss. If we fear abandonment, for example, and someone important to us dies or leaves us, we are faced with a fulfillment of that fear. When we choose to face our greatest fears, they can no longer imprison us.

• *Grief is a holistic process.*

We are affected physically, emotionally, cognitively and spiritually by a significant loss. Grief pervades our thoughts, perceptions, and behaviors. We may not always be aware of it nor will our grief always be apparent to others, yet it can affect every aspect of our lives.

• *Men and women are likely to have different strengths and vulnerabilities in the process of grieving.*

Men and women often misunderstand each other's grieving processes. Men are more likely to want to put the loss behind them quickly, cope by being productive, and fear shaming. Women tend to be more open, helpless and inclusive in viewing their loss. Because of the relative emphasis we place on our masculine and feminine characteristics, we may tend to see men as not grieving at all, and women as grieving too much and too long when in reality both are grieving, but emphasizing different aspects of the process.

Sequences and Themes in the Grief Process

It's tempting to think of grief as going through stages or phases. It's also tempting to think that once we've arrived at a transformative phase, we're finished with grief—only to discover the whole process can recycle once again with a new loss or with another aspect of the same loss.

The term "stage" suggests that a particular behavior occurs for a length of time and then disappears or is somehow resolved. It can imply one stage is developmentally more advanced than another. The term "phase" has some distinctions from stages. Phase implies a transient quality, that may endure for a few moments or for a much longer period.

In my experience, people in grief do not go through a linear progression of grief stages—a common misperception. Grieving is a process that has its ebbs and flows, ups and downs, exhilarating insights and plunges to the bottom of the pits. People in grief often cycle back and forth through various phases and emotions, but in the larger picture there is a progression toward integration and growth.

The notion of cycles of grief has its appeal and also its limits. We go through the grief process many times, often cycling through the same loss several times as we get new information or a new perspective. The goal of grieving to many people is to get back our best self—who we were at the start—wiser, and sadder perhaps, but still of the same substance.

William Worden (1983) invites us to consider the "tasks" of grief— essential issues that must be worked through. There is a certain heaviness to the term "task" which certainly fits some of the time in grief. At other times it seems to add to the burden of grieving to think of what we are doing as just another "task."

As stated in Chapter One, my model of the grieving process is based on a *sequence* involving a discovery process for each aspect of a loss:

- ***Discover the extent of what was lost.***

- ***Discover the limits of what was lost (what is left).***

- ***Discover what is possible as a result.***

Each time we allow a particular loss or aspect of a larger loss into our awareness, we cycle through the discovery process. Except for simple losses, we don't go through this discovery process once—we do it many times.

I consider grief to be composed of themes, or phases, which occur in the context of the three-step discovery sequence described above.

Figure II-1: The Process of Grieving

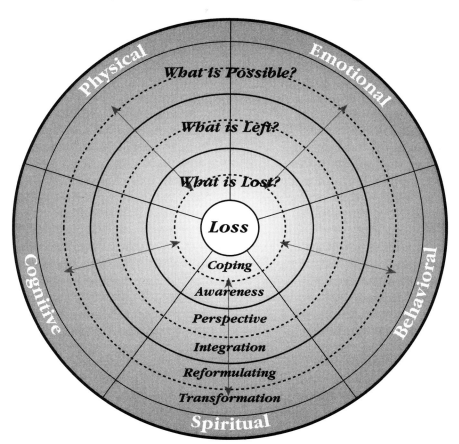

There are themes within and across these successions which at times ascend in importance and at other times are less important. These themes can overlap and complement each other, or at times even contradict each other.

Dimensions of the Grieving Process

There are multiple dimensions to the ways we experience our world. There are the ways we act (behavioral), how we think (cognitive), the feelings we have (emotional), the responses of our body (physical), and the meaning and values we have (spiritual). Significant losses involve all aspects of ourselves in ways that challenge the integration we've made of mind, body and spirit. Section II is a description of responses to loss based on these dimensions.

Figure II-1 suggests my concept of the different dimensions of the grieving process. Imagine this figure as if the loss were a pebble dropped into the middle of a still pool. The waves radiate out from the loss, with less intensity further away from the place or time of the loss. And, like the waves from a pebble dropped, the discovery process cycles and recycles, back and forth, with a gradual slowing back to stillness at the center. If we watch closely, we'll note that it's not a single wave that goes back and forth but a whole series—many grief processes moving back and forth.

Phases of discovery are discussed in order of occurrence for losses in general. Individuals differ considerably in what themes are prominent in their grief. Especially diverse are the ways we have of limiting awareness or coping. Any specific loss may vary both the order, intensity, and length of any of these themes within the grieving process.

Discovering What is Lost: The Beginning of Grief

The most painful and difficult aspect of grief is to know just what it is we have lost. It is necessarily the first phase of active grieving. In order to become more fully aware, we must at some point decide to face the fullness of our loss. The *beginning of grief* can be filled with shock and disbelief (see Chapter Three). Consequently, we need to *limit that awareness*, for to continue to submerge ourselves in the fullness of our loss could paralyze us. We use our ways of coping—fight or flight—to give us times of respite and delay, to "come up for air" and keep what aspects of our life routine we can. The themes this aspect of grief involve the going back and forth between *awareness of a loss* and *limiting that awareness* through holding on (fight) and letting go (flight) strategies. (See Chapters Four and Five.)

The beginning of grief has the following theme:

• *To permit the loss to be a reality.*

Awareness usually marks the beginning of grief itself. It is the time when the reality of the loss reaches our awareness. It is a *shock* because a new reality intrudes, often unanticipated. This first glimpse at awareness can come at the time of the event, or it can be delayed from days to many years, depending on our survival needs and the irrefutability of the loss.

Coping: Attempts To Limit Awareness (Chapter Four)

Sometimes it takes a long time before we become aware of what it is we have lost—or will soon lose. We continue to cope after we begin to know what it is we're losing. We need a respite from the initial shock, so we delay our response.

An additional function of coping is to search for some alternative to grieving. As Peter Marris (1974) noted, it represents an attempt :

> . . . to hold onto all that is meaningful or to rapidly move forward to a time and place where the loss is forgotten or no longer a part of the person's life. (p.32)

When we consciously cope (i.e., we know we're doing it), we're more likely to actively grieve as circumstances permit. When we're not conscious of our coping, we avoid or distort our grief. This can keep us from completing it.

There are two radically different ways we cope that account for what we call the "ups and downs" of grief. One theme involves fighting the loss—to *hold on*. The complementary and sometimes opposite theme is to try to escape from it—to *let go*.

Fighting/Holding On as a Coping Style

Our intent here is to find some way to prevent, overcome, or reverse a loss. During such times, we believe that if we try hard enough, we can overcome anything, including the threat or the reality of loss. *Holding on* ways of coping with loss have the following themes:

- *To overcome the loss.*

- *To prevent change from happening.*

- *To solve problems.*

- *To hold us to our responsibilities and our past.*

- *To enhance and maintain attachments.*

Escape/Letting Go as a Coping Style

The complementary response to fighting is letting go. We convince ourself that we didn't lose anything—at least nothing of importance. We withdraw, hide, distract ourselves from facing what we've lost. *Letting go* ways of coping with loss allow us to rest. We pull back from involvements and commitments and diminish our fear that everything meaningful has been taken. Letting go reinforces the belief that we are helpless in the hands of fate, God, or powerful others. These strategies reflect our helplessness or represent attempts to escape from or even destroy reminders of the loss. These escape/letting go ways of coping have the following themes:

- *To free us from the loss and its consequences.*

- *To conserve our energy.*

- *To find ways to enjoy life at the present time.*

- *To limit dependence.*

- *To get rid of attachments, roles or beliefs.*

- *To free us from guilt and obligations.*

Awareness of Loss (Chapter Five)

The major theme in awareness involves:

- *To know the implications and extent of our loss.*

- *To experience the full extent of our loss.*

Awareness is the central part of the grieving process. It is what we have to experience in order to know our loss. It emerges when our defenses and ways of coping give way: We are caught by surprise, have nothing else to do, or someone or something reminds us of the loss. We face the reality that what is lost is gone, it cannot be recovered. In awareness we feel helpless, deprived, hopeless, and fragile.

Awareness can be a challenge to our will to live, physical stamina, emotional depth, search for meaning, and our capacity to limit helplessness. It is the phase that is most frequently identified as "grieving," and is sometimes confused with "depression" (Kübler-Ross, 1969; Schneider, 1981; Deutsch, 1982; Klein and Wender, 1993).

Awareness is a turning point in grief. In finding out how much is lost, we may discover that it is too much to live with. On the other hand, we may decide to go on with life.

Discovering What is Left: The Limits of the Loss

We cannot know what is left or what needs to be restored until after we have discovered what is gone. It is necessarily the second phase in active grieving, the result of having gone as far as is necessary with the first phase. That may mean only a sliver of the entire loss has been fully explored, and that discovering what is left is only of that small portion. It involves a choice that at least for the moment, in light of this particular aspect of the loss, it is worth going on. It activates the themes of healing and restoration—of *perspective* and eventually *integrating* the results of our discovery with the rest of our lives. (Chapters Six and Seven)

Perspective (Chapter Six)

I have observed that grieving people take one of three directions at this time: 1) they return to coping to further limit awareness; 2) they move into a time of healing, passivity and resignation; or 3) they proceed to a more active discovery of what is left or can be restored.

Awareness may only be partially completed—a result of dealing with some aspects of our loss but not with others. As a result, we return to our ways of limiting its intrusiveness through coping until another time of awareness emerges. For a period of time, we may not want to look at our grief or its implications.

To return to coping usually means that awareness is incomplete or we somehow lack what it takes to face what is left. We haven't yet defined the full extent of our loss. Because our awareness is partial, we may lack perspective—we may assume we've lost *more* than we have or, the opposite, assume we have lost *less.* Perhaps we have yet to look closely enough at how responsible we were for the loss and, as a result, continue to exaggerate or minimize our guilt.

If we don't have the energy to go on, as can happen in terminal illness, we may relinquish coping. We feel resigned, accepting, detached, at peace. We live the moments we have. In terminal illness, this is often seen shortly before death. It can represent a perspective on factors outside of our control that we must simply accept.

If life is still worth living, our energy may now shift. We're less concerned about our honest, immediate responses and more interested in finding enduring truths. The themes in perspective include:

- *To discover what we have left and what can be restored.*

- *To consider forgiveness.*

- *To find the positives and the negatives.*

- *To consider the longer term implications.*

- *To remember as much as possible about the loss.*

- *To rediscover the little things that keep us going and bring pleasure.*

Integrating Loss (Chapter Seven)

At some point, effective grieving involves an active, shared act of self-forgiveness or restitution. This action functions as a personal rite of passage, a necessary part of integrating the loss into the rest of life. When we integrate our losses we are able to find motivation for change and growth. In accepting the fragile nature of life itself, we have the motivation to change. We build on the extent *and* the limits of responsibility for our loss. We reinvest our energies elsewhere.

Integrating loss allows us to *move on*. Sometimes that moving on is toward death. We say our good-byes. We let go of life. Sometimes moving on means relinquishing roles that tie us to our grief, identifying ourselves as survivors or victims.

Integrating loss involves the following themes:

- *To end active focus on the past.*

- *To say good-bye; finish business.*

- *To forgive; release feelings.*

- *To commit to the future.*

Discovering What is Possible: Moving Toward Transformation

When all the pieces of loss have been discovered and the full extent has reached awareness, we know what is left or can be restored. Then we can move on and use the loss as a motivation for new life. We can choose to do something with what we've got, whatever that might be. It may involve a radical and challenging process of *reformulating* the loss. *Discovering what is possible is an empowering process that leads us to the fullness of the transformation of the loss* (see Chapters Eight and Nine).

Reformulating and Self-Empowering (Chapter Eight)

Reformulating tests how far we've gone with integrating a loss. It challenges our strengths and determination to move on. There is often comfort when we first experience perspective. That's not necessarily true when we're reformulating the loss. There is a change in how we see things; we're more likely to focus on potential than on limits and shift from acceptance to challenge and passive to active. Reformulation extends perspective and expands the meaning of our lives. We find new patterns and themes in our lives, and in our families, relationships and culture. We reframe others' goals and expectations as less central to our own life.

Reformulation is also empowering, a test of our self-trust and self-awareness. Without the incentive that integrating loss provides, such self-awareness would not lead to the necessary follow-through to make significant life changes durable.

Self-empowerment initially involves being self-centered. Paradoxically, reformulating a loss can involve picking apart an over inflated ego— questioning our place in or near the center of the universe. We learn humility. Our sense of self can change—to be more *inclusive*. Empowerment comes from being a part of something that transcends our material being. Reformulating loss involves the following themes:

- *To focus on potential.*

- *To challenge limits and reformulate beliefs.*

- *To expand definition of self to be more inclusive.*

- *To find new patterns and life themes.*

Transforming Loss (Chapter Nine)

Transforming loss involves placing the loss in a context of growth, life cycles and unifying experiences. Loss is a change in form: Grieving is the means for transformation.

Transforming loss permits us to be less bound by the physical or by societal imperatives while appreciating even more our transgenerational connections and symbols. It extends the process of reformulation beyond the focus on our loss or our individuality to ways we are connected to all things by means of love and rituals of continuity with past, present, and future. We can extend our consciousness to include others, living and dead. By this definition, transforming loss is also a transpersonal process. Transforming loss involves the following themes:

- *To place the loss in the context of growth.*

- *To expand our notion of consciousness.*

- *To understand transgenerational continuity.*

Progression Through Grief: A One-Way Street?

It's tempting to believe that we automatically arrive at some higher plane once we complete a cycle of grieving. In those moments when we feel the fullness of our transformation, we'd like to believe we'll stay there forever. Unless we are dying, other losses and other connections will bring us back to the realities of living in a material world and in a sensory-rich body. Life has other losses, including the episodic loss of feeling of being at one with the universe. What we gain from the grief cycle is wisdom and the recognition of our choices in that process.

The Response to Loss Inventory

The chapters of Section II will expand the themes of grief. In the succeeding chapters, there are statements in the text, written in small type, that represent a way of viewing the loss. These statements are taken from the *Response to Loss Inventory* developed from this model (Appendix II). It is being used clinically and as a research tool to better understand how different aspects of this model apply to the grief of people with various losses. If the reader wishes to study the full spectrum of the grieving process, the RTL provides a useful tool.

Chapter Three

When Grieving Begins: Apocalypse or Clarion Call

The story of any person's real experience finds its startling parallel in that of every one of us.

—James Russell Lowell

Everything looked hopeless when Cliff died. I knew I could just let go and join him in death. All I had to do was lie down and accept the inevitable. But I couldn't give up. I had to keep going. I don't know where I got the strength. God and Cliff must have been with me then.

—Jane, 35, after being lost in a blizzard when her husband died.

I keep going over it again and again. I can't get it out of my mind. I keep seeing that scene—it's branded in my brain. The hand—the little girl's hand—lying there, holding those broken flowers—cut off from everything else. I wake up in the night, seeing that hand.

—Mike, 22, ambulance driver after a two-year-old girl was killed.

I keep reliving that wonderful time when I fell in love with Jonas. The setting was beautiful—an old mansion by a lake near a deep and lovely woods. He was sensitive and attractive. He drew me like a magnet. He helped me to open up in ways I had never known before. I felt so vulnerable and yet so safe with him. Our lovemaking was almost poetical, like a beautiful dance moving to a rhythm deep inside of us.

I never wanted it to end. It did. Now every once in a while when I close my eyes I can see and feel it all again. My life has changed since then, often in very painful ways. It has never been so beautiful, so poetic.

—Rose, 29, after a brief affair.

Stories like these commonly follow events that insist we remember them, incidents that transform our lives. They become our personal Apocalypse—they awaken us to realities and capacities we never dreamed existed. The impact of such occurrences is shockingly powerful, often imprinting itself in our memory so vividly that months, even years later, they can still feel painfully or poignantly fresh. Our lives are transformed from that moment forward.

Both positive and negative events and losses profoundly affect us in ways that can destroy our innocence or radically alter our way of life. Our life story seems broken—or filled with new meaning. We feel disconnected from our past, or more deeply a part of our universe. We see no hope, or we sense a transformation beginning. We may feel shattered into little pieces—broken elements of our stories and our lives. Or we may feel liberated from a past we're eager to forget. Significant changes can produce either response. We're more likely to react in extremes—our life is "completely over" *or* we have "been saved"; life is sheer agony *or* sheer joy. It's clearly not both at the same time.

Either our consciousness is heightened to the point that we are acutely aware of everything or we may be totally in a fog. Our biology is in alarm status: we are roused to either fight or flee. Heroes and cowards are defined in such times. So are fools and prudent responders.

At this time, there is often a blending of consciousness and coping. We are both vividly aware of our loss and struggling mightily to limit its impact. We are at the extremes of Holding On and Letting Go, while also acutely aware of what it is we want to fight or flee.

The beginning of grief involves first impressions. Sometimes these impressions accurately portray what's ahead or what has changed. Sometimes they represent our worst fears or our greatest hopes. It's only with time and perspective that we'll know the degree of correctness of these first impressions.

It's not only traumatic experiences that lead to these feelings of disruption. They can also be a part of success or peak experiences. We keep reliving that moment of triumph when we won the state track meet, fell in love, got the promotion. We yearn for the wonderful, intense living-on-the-edge feelings that characterized being in-love, the good-old-days, the comradeship of sports, the sense of mission and teamwork helping victims after a flood. These events change lives. We never feel quite the same.

When change is gradual or anticipated, the shock or disruption may not be obvious. Still, there may be a moment in time when the reality of the loss becomes clear: we know things will never be the same. It can be the realization that we are an alcoholic, or a celebrity, or that we have to leave an impossible or life-threatening situation. That awareness stays with us. We can't go back to the protection of our denial.

How does the beginning of awareness of loss differ from times when awareness will dominate? This beginning of grief is an attempt to take in what has changed, *but it is too much at this time.* Only with time and exploration do we make successive approximations to how bad *and* how good we have it. Time permits us to find less extreme ways to cope and to be less overwhelmed by awareness. We haven't completely changed— the resources we have to go beyond the loss, agony *and* joy are still available. Our feelings of abandonment or love are less total.

We have the tendency to treat times of heightened awareness as special—or as unreal. When it is special and positive, we want to keep it, preserve it, relive it time and again. When it was life-threatening or a source of shame, we want to believe it never happened—it was a bad dream, a nightmare. We struggle to give it a place in our life that allows for ordinary experiences. It may be a long time before we can remember anything about a loved one except the way they died or abandoned us.

In this heightened, beginning state of awareness, our coping can reach extraordinary levels. Our *best self* takes over and we do things we would never be able to do otherwise to delay or prevent the loss. We lift cars off trapped children. Soldiers charge an enemy bunker without regard for their safety. Physicians and nurses work ceaselessly to save lives at the site of a catastrophe.

We love the way we are at those moments—something gave us courage to rise above our usual self to actually prevent a loss from happening. Even if a loss was not eliminated, we can at least look back and feel that we did everything we could. Guilt, as a part of our grief, is removed.

Alternatively, what we sometimes do in this heightened state is the opposite. We become paralyzed. We'll do anything we can to eliminate the pain or the reminders of what's happened. We're so scared we can't even move, or we swiftly run away. We compound our loss by the destructive way we respond to it. We've let go of our usual self. And we feel ashamed or guilty for the way we responded to our loss. Not only did we not prevent the loss, we now have the additional loss of self-trust and best self to mourn.

Dimensions of the Beginning of Grief Awareness

If the loss itself doesn't change us, our way of grieving it will. The imprinting of details and the intensity of feelings occur with many losses. They are characteristic of this beginning of grief. Figure 3-1 outlines the dimensions of the beginning of grief. The earliest moments after a loss, when all aspects of our nature—physical, emotional, cognitive, behavioral, and spiritual—are in shock:

Figure 3-1: Dimensions of the Beginning of Grief

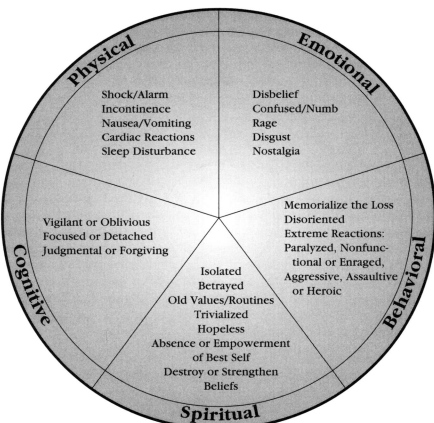

Physical
Shock/Alarm
Incontinence
Nausea/Vomiting
Cardiac Reactions
Sleep Disturbance

Emotional
Disbelief
Confused/Numb
Rage
Disgust
Nostalgia

Cognitive
Vigilant or Oblivious
Focused or Detached
Judgmental or Forgiving

Behavioral
Memorialize the Loss
Disoriented
Extreme Reactions:
Paralyzed, Nonfunc-
tional or Enraged,
Aggressive, Assaultive
or Heroic

Spiritual
Isolated
Betrayed
Old Values/Routines
Trivialized
Hopeless
Absence or Empowerment
of Best Self
Destroy or Strengthen
Beliefs

Behavioral Aspects

Memorialize the past and accept anyone who helps us relive it.
We may constantly search for people who will listen appreciatively to our reliving of the experiences we had. In finding a receptive audience, we can pretend the past is still alive and current. When our audience tires of our story, we leave them and find someone fresh and eager to listen:

> *I can remember exactly what I was doing before, during, and after I heard that Kennedy had been shot. I couldn't believe it. I was stunned, speechless, filled with horror. For years, I used to talk to others, often at parties, about what was happening to me then. So did everybody else. I never got tired of telling about it, although others did , particularly those too young to remember it.*

We may want the moment to be as full and expressive as we can. Disbelieving the shock of the loss, we seek a moment of closeness, intimacy and pleasure—to postpone the impact of what's changed, even at the price of violating conventional barriers:

> *Father Ira was Joe's best friend. He was our pastor. He told me of Joe's death in Vietnam. We hugged as he spoke, cried, wiped away each other's tears, kissed and then found ourselves making passionate love—both pretending that we were keeping Joe alive a little while longer, I guess. I don't know for sure. I don't feel guilty about what happened. I wanted to feel as close to another human being as I could—and Ira was safe. I wanted that moment of lovemaking to last forever, for it was Joe in my arms one last time.*

Disorientation
It's almost impossible to get our bearings at the time of a loss. Our actions often reflect how disoriented we feel. How did we get to the hospital, or home afterwards? We have no memory of driving or getting there:

> *I don't know what happened those first few days. I have vague memories of the funeral, being at the emergency room, our kids being home. I felt as if I was numb from head to foot. I didn't know what I was feeling—stunned, unsure, confused. There were times I almost felt glad and then I felt guilty about that. I got so confused I didn't know what I felt. I cried.*

Some of my crying wasn't for Rosie. I don't know—I'm still sorting out all the different things I was feeling.

Extreme reactions

After shocking or life-transforming news, our range of responses tends to become extreme. Our strength is superhuman—or totally absent. We are enraged or totally calm. We cry hysterically, weep softly, or not at all. We become totally organized—or dysfunctional.

Become paralyzed, nonfunctional or accepting of our helplessness

During natural disasters, it is common for some people to become totally immobilized or dazed by the event. They become disoriented and have difficulty functioning normally. Simple tasks such as eating or sleeping, finding shelter, family or friends are also difficult in this state of shock. People may wander aimlessly, even into harm's way, and may need help from others to get from one place to another. Peter had such an experience when his lover ended their relationship in a letter:

> *I remember vividly the feelings. It had been a long time since I'd received a letter from her. My hands trembled. I opened and scanned the first few sentences. I saw what she was writing—our relationship was over.*
>
> *I was stunned. I couldn't believe it, even though I knew something would happen. I wasn't prepared. My whole world ended. Tears flowed out in gasps and sobs. Everything felt so futile. Nothing could bring her back. I felt split in half.*
>
> *I don't know what I would have done if I hadn't been with Jim at the time. He pulled me back to the curb once when I tried to cross the street with traffic coming. He insisted we get something to eat and in taking me home. He kept asking me what I was going to do next, forced me to think of myself. Gradually I emerged from the plastic wrap that shrouded my consciousness and my behavior. I'm not sure I could have done it on my own.*

If we have to get away from impending danger, others may have to resort to shocking us to get us to respond. Under emergency situations, as happens during battle or when danger is imminent, faces get slapped, shoulders are shaken and yelling is necessary to break the trance.

Without having the opportunity to work through the many aspects of a trauma, someone cannot be expected to function or respond normally, which can invite further loss. Just as a baseball player unconsciously "bails out" on inside pitches after being beaned, so do pilots, oil rig operators, soldiers and train drivers reflexively flinch or hesitate after a trauma in the line of duty that has not been debriefed.

We may find that the loss allows us to let go of certain activities or responsibilities and accept "what is." We stop CPR, give permission for a loved one who is suffering to die, and accept the inevitability of change or defeat. We trust our intuition, which tells us: "Enough!"

Become enraged, aggressive or heroic

We can become bent on revenge or on eliminating the source of our loss. The bearer of unwelcome tidings needs to be aware that they may be the object of such rage, much as the Spartan messenger in ancient Greece who was killed when he brought bad news from battle. That's because we don't want to hear news that our life has changed forever in ways we do not want them to.

With the same intensity, we might throw ourselves into taking care of others, and thereby totally let go of our own needs. We can push ourselves past exhaustion to avoid or diminish the loss. Later, we're as amazed as everyone else about our superhuman efforts.

Cognitive Aspects

Experience disbelief, confusion or clarity

Our beliefs tell us that things should remain the way they are if the rules are followed. When something unexpectedly traumatic happens, that belief is challenged. Tim felt disbelief when his pet dog was hit by a car:

> *I couldn't believe it. How could he be dead? He never hurt anyone. He never went out in the street. He was just standing here beside me. I just was petting him! It couldn't be him!*

Tim was struggling with the belief that if his dog didn't hurt anyone, he would not be hurt in return. In the awakening of active grief, it is our additional loss of beliefs or the illusions of the stability and predictability of the rules we live by that shocks us.

When our usual rules are disrupted, we don't know how to think. Irene's response was strikingly similar to Tim's in her description of unexpectedly winning an award:

> *I couldn't believe it! I felt totally numb. I didn't know what to do—how to get to the stage. I was glad, except I felt like a phony. I was angry—I couldn't hide anymore. I felt ungrateful, though I really was. It was so . . . unexpected. Here it was—me, just an ordinary person—getting this award. How could it be me? People like me just don't win things like this.*

> *I couldn't speak—there were no words. I was confused, in a daze. It wasn't until days later that it began to sink in what had happened. I was shocked beyond words.*

At the opposite extreme, we could believe that things had never been clearer, that what has happened is more real than anything we have known before. The event makes sense of our life in ways it has never done before. It is a clarion call to a new direction in our life.

Vigilant *or* oblivious

When we know something unusual is happening, we may become unusually observant. We note details we'd otherwise miss. We experience sensations and feelings with greater clarity—for example, the victim of a car crash who can remember the license plate number of the oncoming car. Time perception slows down. It's as if we know we'll want to remember as much as we can of this moment for later—as a part of sharing our story about this event, or as a way to try to make sense of it.

Alternatively, our feelings can be so overwhelming that we're oblivious to anything going on around us. We may not have much memory of what happened. Pupils dilated to blackness, we may believe we are somewhere else in the universe.

Focused *or* detached

In addition to being oblivious of others, there may be an intense focus on the loss. We may be unaware of what others are experiencing, or be unable to communicate with them during this time. For example, funeral arrangements or the presence of so many friends and relatives at the time of a death can overwhelm us. Yet we note who is there—and who is not.

We may also feel detached from what was happening, as an observer rather than a participant. We may even feel separate from ourselves, watching from a distance our own behavior as well as that of others. We're separate from our feelings as a way to protect ourselves.

Judgmental or *forgiving*

We're quick to draw conclusions during this time, as a way to recover self-esteem and control. When people don't come to the funeral, for example, we conclude they didn't care. When someone prematurely tries to reassure us that things will get better, we're certain they don't understand us. We're just as quick to forgive someone who clearly shows remorse, even defend them against others. We often make snap judgments that we're unwilling to challenge for a long time.

Emotional Aspects

Emotions can be painfully strong and arousing. We find them difficult to control or, at the other extreme, to express. So many feelings become awakened simultaneously in the beginning of grief that many people report feeling confused, disoriented, or numbed. Agony and ecstasy are remarkably complex feelings with many similarities. We are not sure what we feel, or we feel several different things at the same time. It engages all our senses. We feel them vividly, clearly.

Numbness

The emotional equivalent of confusion is numbness. We may feel numbness of the shock, with so many feelings competing for our attention simultaneously.

Anger and Rage

We may become enraged as a way to protect our self-esteem and defend against the loss, because of an overwhelming sense of responsibility for what's happened, or as a way to elude our feelings of shame or guilt. Our initial reaction to the news of a loss can be directed outward, wanting to destroy the messenger and the message. Moira felt such intensity at discovering her husband's infidelity:

> *If he had been there when I found out about his sickening affair, I would have killed him. How could he do that to me? That son-of-a-bitch!*

Revulsion

The emotion that coincides with being judgmental is disgust. Extreme disgust—revulsion—involves rejection and distancing, a pushing away from something we feel is dangerous or alien to us. We may reject or feel revulsion for people who aren't as affected by this loss as we are, or who seem insensitive to our plight.

Shame

Shame may result from an inability to maintain an image of perfection in a role or the failure to accomplish a mission. It can result from being defeated in competition and from not realizing our potential. Whenever our goals or dreams are known by others and we fail to achieve them, we may feel a sense of loss while being shamed or ridiculed.

Reacting to the feeling of shame can itself produce further losses. It is a threat to our sense of self. It can destroy our sense of innocence and our curiosity. It invites us to judge ourselves, to discount the significance of our process (i.e., we did the best we could) or forget that our intentions were not entirely evil. If we accept shame and do not grieve the losses involved, our will to live can erode.

Helplessness

Helplessness is a common initial feeling at the time we first experience a loss. There is nothing we can do to change what's happened. This feeling of helplessness can be a combination of anxiety and lack of control.

It is often a combination of shame and helplessness that initially dominates our emotional reactions. Showing helplessness in an environment that is hostile or competitive can be destructive, if not physically, at least to our self-esteem by subjecting us to ridicule. As a result, loss, especially for men, is often associated with failure, disability, impotence, helplessness—and shame.

Nostalgia

A very different response to change is an attempt to keep the past intact, as we remember it to be. We look at the photos, tell the stories of how good it used to be as if they were current and real in the present, cherishing them this one last time.

Physical Aspects

Physically, we respond in extremes as well. We are either in a state of shock or a state of alarm.

Shock

Physically, a state of shock paralyzes us. It is characterized by immobility, trance, a lack of awareness or responsiveness to anyone or anything. After natural disasters, for example, it's not uncommon to find people sitting in a daze hours or even days later. During that time, they may have not eaten, moved or responded to anyone.

Alarm

Hans Selye (1976), in his pioneering work on stress, vividly describes how we respond physically to sudden change. He calls it the *alarm reaction*. Our bodies mobilize for change as if under attack. We believe that we could be killed if we don't respond correctly. We prepare ourselves to either fight or flee—in these moments, we prepare for both. Damon describes this experience after learning he had been fired from his job:

> *It felt as if someone had hit me in the stomach. I had trouble breathing. I felt dizzy and nauseous. I wanted to run away from my body. I felt paralyzed, rooted to the ground.*

> *Later I realized I had been clenching my teeth because my jaws ached. My arms were so tight. I wanted to lash out, to make the news go away. But I didn't, thank God.*

Incontinence/nausea/vomiting

In extreme instances, when death appears imminent, we may even lose control of our physical functions. Mike recalled one of his harrowing experiences in Vietnam:

> *We'd been under fire for over an hour when we realized we were running out of ammo. We each kept a couple of rounds to use on ourselves. Our guns fell silent. We watched as the Viet Cong began running towards us through the underbrush. It wasn't until afterwards—we got ammo at virtually the last second—that we could smell and see what had happened to all of us—we'd shit and pissed in our pants! Death had never been so real to me as it was in those moments.*

We can feel nauseous and even vomit at the news of the loss, a natural, physical, protective action. We try to protect ourselves from its overwhelming nature by "getting it out of our system." Nausea and vomiting are attempts to rid ourselves of this horrible information we don't want to believe or accept.

Cardiac vulnerability

It's no accident that the heart is associated with love and the connections with have with others—it is a vulnerable organ when we experience a loss of those bonds. For example, George Engel (1971, 1977) was one of many observers who noted that in some circumstances the response to unexpected news can be a heart attack, sometimes fatal. He saw these sudden deaths as one powerful piece of evidence that the body experiences stress at such times.

Sleep alterations

So intense and all-encompassing is our focus on the event that we may be unable to sleep for days, even weeks. Each time we close our eyes we see what happened over and over again, like a videotape stuck on replay. If we are able to sleep, our dreams contain fragments of our experience.

Sometimes these dreams can be restorative. Angelina took care of her dying mother during the last year of her life. She'd grieved her loss gradually over that time. Still, her death, while not a surprise, was a shock in its finality and irreversibility:

> *My mother had cancer for two years. I went home frequently to see her. Each time, I was shocked at how much weight she had lost, how much pain she was in. That wonderful sense of humor wasn't there very much anymore. She used to love to dance, to be out in the fresh air. Gradually she couldn't do that anymore.*

> *The day she died, I felt a real sense of relief. We had said our good-byes, and I was glad she wasn't suffering anymore. The next night I saw her in a dream. Only she was as she was two years ago— dancing, beautiful to look at, full of smiles and love. My tears when I awoke were for the mother I had lost—two years ago.*

Out of the body

There is often a physical component to feeling detached or oblivious: We may feel separated from our physical being. A state often described in near-death experiences and as the result of profound relaxation and trance, the experience of being out of the body can reflect a state of shock as well.

Spiritual Aspects

The spiritual theme in the beginning of awareness involves a willingness to *face reality*. Any major change can challenge our spiritual selves. Sometimes we are capable of meeting the challenge, sometimes we aren't.

Our spirituality either comes unglued or rises to the occasion, as our beliefs are either strengthened or diminished by the event.

Isolation or *deeper connection*

There are few times in life when we feel as isolated and alone as when we first experience the full impact of a significant loss. Lacking words to describe our experience, still in shock from the explosion of awareness, we cannot imagine ever being connected to the human race again.

At the other extreme can be the experience of feeling more deeply connected to what we lost, at least for a brief period of time. As we go to sleep at night, we hear the voice and sense the presence of our lost loved one, feel their guidance at times we need it, feel closer to others who have the same loss in common. This happened for Todd, a therapist after Ed, his client, committed suicide:

> *For several nights after his suicide, just as I was falling to sleep, I could have sworn Ed was standing there beside my bed. I could see tears in his eyes. He kept saying "forgive me, forgive me." I felt a great deal of torment. After I expressed my anger at him, that image went away.*

Such connections can happen as we are going to sleep, awakening, or during dreams. They can also occur at times when our contact with the missing person was most likely, such as when a deceased spouse would be coming home from work.

Although such spiritual contacts can reflect emerging awareness of the loss, Colin Murray Parkes (1981) has noted their presence for many years in the cases of women suddenly bereaved. Imaginary conversations with the lost person are particularly frequent. Sometimes they are ways of talking to ourselves. Sometimes they are more. Sometimes contacts occur right at the time of death, in ways not explainable by rational phenomena. Maria had such an experience when her twin sister died:

> *I woke with a start at two o'clock in the morning, sitting bolt upright in bed. I saw my sister Mary sitting there by my bed, saying "Help me, help me." I knew she wasn't there. I felt something very ominous was happening. I called her at home, five hundred miles away. I knew she was terminally ill. My mother answered the phone. Mary had died five minutes before.*

Feeling betrayed or affirmed

Everyone and everything we ever trusted has failed to prevent this loss. We don't know who or what is responsible, but we feel betrayed—by our belief that bad things don't happen to good people, that friends and loved ones will always be there in a pinch, or by our faith in a kind and merciful God.

In contrast, we can feel affirmed in our beliefs during this time of initial awareness. Our beliefs do help us understand why this is happening—how this loss is a part of a bigger picture. We can feel buoyed by the love that pours into our lives at such times, by the genuine tears of others who also mourn, by the memories that are shared and the stories that are told.

Old values or routines seem trivial or essential

We see others going about their everyday tasks as if nothing has happened while we find such routines totally meaningless in light of our loss. Things we never stopped to question, we look at now through different eyes, and see how little they mean in comparison to our loss.

These same values and routine can also seem essential at such times. We must prepare the meals—our deceased spouse or child "would have wanted it that way." We go out and plow the fields—it is the only thing that is meaningful and growth-producing in the midst of such a catastrophe. We must make the casket for our lost infant—every stroke that planes the surface, that carves the image, expresses the grief that has no words.

Hopeless or life-giving

Life feels meaningless and empty. Our old values seem trivial or naive. All hope seems gone. The unforgivable, the unthinkable has happened. Barry experienced such devastation at the time his son died:

> *As I went through those first few days, it was as if nothing was important anymore. I couldn't understand why people bothered to go to work, to eat, to sleep. Every conversation seemed so meaningless, so superficial. A part of me wanted to go up and shake these people and say, "Why are you wasting your life in such trivia? Don't you know that none of that will make any difference in the long run? Don't you know that nothing like that matters?" Another part of me said, "Why bother?" Life seemed so empty.*

"She died so others may live more fully" is a statement that reflects inspiration gained from a loss. The heroism and courage of someone we lost can affirm a greater purpose to life than we knew before their death or absence. In many indigenous cultures an entire family, clan or village will cease normal activities in support of the bereaved. In those initial moments after a loss, we may be most aware of the gift their life meant to us before we experience the personal agony of their absence.

Absence or *empowerment of best self*

Our initial response to a loss often reflects the nature of the loss and our usual ways of coping with life in general. Some losses cannot be overcome, the appropriate response is to let go. Attempting to reverse it, such as sustaining life support when all vital signs are absent, is a futile and inappropriate use of resources. Some losses can be reversed with super-human or highly creative efforts. Parents who insist on new treatments for their dying child may actually produce miracles in spite of all the odds against it. Some losses could have been prevented if action was taken at the appropriate time instead of too easily accepting that nothing could be done.

It's also true that how we *usually* cope plays a role in how we react to a loss. If we generally let things happen, roll with the punches, we're likely to take this approach when a loss occurs. If we're a fighter, always challenging the status quo, we're more likely to respond this way.

It is the interaction between the circumstance and our usual mode of coping that determines whether or not we've engaged our best self at a time of first becoming aware of a loss. Being laid back can be the best way to respond when it's important to let go. Fighting or not giving up is a sign of the best self when the loss could be avoided or limited.

The Shock of Awareness: How Long Does It Last?

Beginning awareness of a significant change is profoundly affected by the extent of our shock. Sometimes we can be in a daze for days, weeks, months, even years afterwards if we don't have the support or the confrontation to get going again.

Still, we come back and revisit the experience of our loss for as long as it takes to accept the full reality of what has happened. At first, we can't know the true extent of the change. That is a task that lies ahead. What we need is validation:

- *that the change happened*

- *that it cannot be reversed*

- *that others know it has happened*

When Does Grief Begin?

Grieving begins when we have experienced a loss. *Validating our awareness of the loss allows us to begin the steps of discovery.* As compelling as the evidence might be, we don't always respond quickly at the time of the loss or trauma. Sometimes we have premonitions or a sense that something has happened without any direct evidence. In those instances the awareness comes before we have confirmation of the loss. Sometimes in the midst of the most painful events, we must stay functional, often caring for others. Reality doesn't sink in until later—sometimes much later.

It's possible—if we are very young or mentally impaired—that we don't grasp what's happened. We may recognize that something has upset our family. We're not sure what, exactly. Somebody may have died. If we've yet to develop an understanding of death as irreversible, it's not necessarily so bad. Later, perhaps years later, it hits us that our loved one isn't coming back. We've lost them.

It's also true that we will resist accepting a loss until we have evidence that we can't rationalize away. An open casket and a dead body may be the proof we need to believe that someone close hasdied.

It can be difficult to accept reality when we remain hopeful that something will undo the loss. For example, it was ten years for Terry before his divorce became real and his grieving began:

> *When Stephanie left me with the kids, I was sure she would come back. In fact, we did get back together—twice. She needed her independence, I knew. I also knew she loved me. She knew I was a good dad. We never had any problems about sharing custody— for three years we moved in and out of the same house so the kids wouldn't have to be the ones to move. We've even made love on occasions. It was more satisfying than when we were married.*
>
> *So I needed to wait and let her sort things out. She'd come around.*
>
> *It came as a shock to me when she told me she was getting married to Toby. I even had to go to the ceremony, as painful as that was for me, to be convinced that it was over for us. When she kissed him, it registered: "This is it. I've lost her." For the first time I cried— almost ten years after the divorce.*

Similar stories surface when loss becomes valid. Marilyn had an intermittent relationship that needed time for her to accept its ending:

I went on for many months holding on to the belief that things would be the same between us when he came back. My everyday life wasn't any different, because he only came every six months or so. So I was fine—until the time came for him to return. He never came to see me—or even called. Then I knew it was over. I had lost him.

Mike realized his loss, not at the time of his promotion, but when he had to change offices:

It didn't hit me until I had to change offices. Then I realized I was leaving friends behind, and the place where I grew up professionally. I wouldn't be the same.

Jim didn't accept his illness as a loss until the pain came:

When the doctor told me I had cancer and only a few months to live, I couldn't believe it. I felt fine. I was active. He would not have detected it had I not come in for a routine physical.

I guess for quite a while I went on believing I was OK—that maybe he had made a mistake, or the things I was doing were curing me.

Then the pain came—in the middle of the night. It came in waves. I threw up—but not from the chemo I'd had. I felt weak. I was in a sweat. Then it hit me—I was going to die.

Mary was with her husband a few minutes before and a few minutes after he died of a heart attack. Even seeing his body didn't make it real. It took seeing his shoes:

I was doing okay until I got home. Even then, it wasn't until I saw his shoes where he had placed them by the bed. He would never wear them again. Then I broke down.

Sometimes we can see the loss coming. We *know* our partner has AIDS, that she is going to die eventually. We *know* we're retiring in a year. We can *anticipate* the effects that advancing Alzheimer's will have on us. We *know* the kids will graduate and leave home in a year or two. In some instances, being able to anticipate means the realization hits us sooner, or that it comes and goes. Sometimes we won't let it in until the very last minute—not even then if we can help it. The reality that lies ahead can be so compelling that suicide becomes an option we consider long before the symptoms of the disease debilitate us.

From the moment that we realize a potential loss is in the offing, we have already lost something. We have lost certainty, predictability, the illusion of permanence and immortality. What strikes us first may be how vulnerable the human condition is; how alone we are; how helpless we feel; how trivial life can seem when our priorities aren't straight. We may not accept the inevitability of death, our children leaving us, or our own dementia until we have to. However, we may accept many accompanying losses along the way. Kate had two children with muscular dystrophy. One died very young and the other not until his twenties. There were many real losses along the way—and many reversals of previous losses:

> *There were some things I kept learning over and over again. With one hospitalization, I prepared for death. Then it would hit—Jess wasn't going to die. I'd have to accept that I couldn't live ready for him to die. There was no certainty for me. Oh, there'd be periods of time when I'd get a routine going and it seemed like it could last. Then Jess'd get sick again. Nothing was for sure.*

> *Along the way, I accepted that I'd never see him grow up—and then he did! Jess even moved out and was living on his own for five years. I'd grieve one thing and then have to undo it! Each piece along the way had its own fullness. It was also living in the moment. It was not a prediction of the future—not of course, until Jess died at the age of twenty-five.*

Mario had the shock of reversal when he discovered his parents were alive in his Cuban homeland:

> *I was one of the few soldiers at the Bay of Pigs to escape on a tiny boat to the mainland. I left behind my family who couldn't get out. A year later, I received word that my parents were murdered because I had been involved in the counter-revolution.*

> *I was beside myself. I struggled with my guilt for surviving. I had support and my faith that carried me through. It took five years. I finally got on with my life—an education, a good job.*

> *It was eight years after I'd escaped that I got a phone call from a man and a woman in Miami. They claimed to be my parents. I refused to believe them. My parents were dead. It wasn't until they called me by my nickname and told me something only they would know that it hit me. They were alive! I was in shock. For days, I struggled with accepting that they were alive. It wasn't until I actually saw them that I could begin to put them back into my life.*

Many of us have jobs where we'll see more than our fair share of life's traumas. Many emergency service workers, for example, are in daily contact with car accidents, heart attacks, victims of murder and abuse. Psychotherapists may have suicides among the people they see. Doctors and nurses, indeed almost anyone who work on the wards of hospitals, often witness death. Train engineers may run into cars stuck on the tracks. If each event immediately became real to us, we'd run the risk of becoming paralyzed at a time when our help could be crucial for the survivors. As much as we'd like to believe we grow immune to such occurrences—after we've lost our sense of innocence—they take their toll. Sometimes they unexpectedly become real—as happened for Mike the ambulance driver in the example at the start of the chapter, when he saw the severed hand of the little girl.

Our First Reaction to a Loss

The constant companions to our grief over a loss are our ways of limiting our grief. When loss threatens our very existence, we defend against it. When it frightens us, we postpone active grieving as long as we can. Disenfranchised losses lack validation: grief is absent. "Anticipatory grief" occurs before the actual loss is final (as in a terminal illness, an expected retirement, birth, etc.), and is often characterized by coping to delay awareness. In sudden, catastrophic losses, coping can't hold back the reality until later, when we can have time for respite and relief. As a result, sudden losses are impossible to avoid: we are immediately aware of their reality. Anything more than first impressions, however, can be delayed due to shock, the apocalyptic or clarion call of that experience.

When Grief Begins, What Helps?

Chapter Ten will discuss what is necessary to overcome the blocks to grieving. When grieving begins, the most basic issues involve safety and trust. Safety can be both a matter of protection while in a state of shock and an awareness of the likelihood of extreme reactions. Trust is a matter of having someone who can stay with the bereaved as they experience the extremes of their emotions, or fall into total paralysis. It involves someone whose ways of testing reality are compatible with our own. When loss has begun to emerge as a reality we need to:

- *Make the loss a tangible reality.*

- *Get permission to express shame, if present.*

- *Validate that something profound has changed.*

- *Get permission to see that there is more to life than losing, or having, everything.*

- *Admit that we can't grieve alone.*

- *Recognize when professional help is needed.*

Make the loss a tangible reality

Without safety and support, our story will remain fragmented or frozen. Who we are today will not bear a resemblance to our old selves. The stressfulness of our lives will remain high. Our grief *and* our gains will remain unexplored—incomplete. Whatever it takes to make the loss real is necessary.

Get permission to express   shame, if present

We fear shunning and shame: When shame is involved in our grief, we need safety and non-judgment in order to come to grips with the loss, the shame, and to move on in the grieving process.

For example, in the light of great public protest over the Vietnam war, many returning soldiers were not allowed to tell their stories. For many a wall of shame surrounded the realities of their war experiences, which produced recurrent nightmares, flashbacks, drug addictions, suicide, abuse and other destructive behaviors. There was not an aura of safety in which to grieve their losses and witnessed horrors. Unlike previous wars, a judging public saw their deeds as a source of shame.

A pediatrician came to talk to me after hearing a presentation I made on self-care. I had mentioned my own struggles with the suicide of a client and the shaming I had experienced from two of my colleagues. Tom shared with me that he had misdiagnosed two children with Reye's Syndrome and that they had both died. "One I can accept," he almost sobbed through his tears. "But two—that's unforgivable." He had been unable to share this with his fellow doctors: "They would think me incompetent and force me to leave my practice." Sharing with his wife would also not help, he said: "She would tell me she loved me and that she knew I hadn't meant to do it."

Tom then proceeded to tell me what happened. I pushed him for details of what happened, what he had done, what he had considered, what had influenced his decisions. Fatigue had played a major role in his mistakes. So had his lack of experience with death and dying among children. "I went into pediatrics to save lives, not to be part of losing them," he cried during our session. He talked about wanting to leave medicine, his fears of being sued for malpractice, and of being shunned by his colleagues.

We only met once. I talked to him on the phone six months later. He had a vitality in his voice I hadn't heard before. "I'm still in peds," he chuckled. "I'm enjoying it more than I have in years. I've learned to take better care of myself—and to forgive myself."

What had helped Tom? He needed to confess what he had done to someone who *would not judge him*. He needed to explore in detail what had happened without being reassured too quickly and easily that he was OK, as his wife would have done. It needed to be with someone with whom he felt safe—myself, in large part because I had admitted to having gone through a similar shameful experience. Both of us knew that what he had admitted to me could be considered malpractice. My own mistakes and vulnerabilities, however, made me aware that saying that would distract him from admitting his shame and discovering his grief. Tom needed someone to witness his confession and *validate* the intensity of his feelings. He needed to consider leaving medicine and of facing the shunning that might occur—perhaps as his punishment or as an escape from his shame and his fears of repeating it.

When shame is involved in our grief, we can profit from confiding in someone we respect, who can *validate, witness,* and *legitimize* what we've experienced. We need validation of the fullness and the extent of our loss and our shame. We need a witness to our confession and later to what we've done with it. We need a chance to examine our values in light of what's happened. To continue doing something that contains risk, we need to learn what it was that led to our mistakes and failures—was it something within our control?

Validate that something profound has changed

Many of us have individually and collectively found ways to make our losses real—even ones as traumatic as war. Many remember the bombing of Pearl Harbor, the dropping of the atomic bomb on Hiroshima, Kennedy's assassination, or disasters such as the Challenger explosion, hurricanes, floods or devastating fires. We can recall in great detail what we were doing when the Gulf War started, when the US beat Russia in Olympic hockey, or when our favorite team won the World Series. We remember not only the moment, but also the time before the event and hours, sometimes even days afterward. By telling our stories and hearing those of others who shared this common event, we *validate* what we experienced. We experience the joy and the sadness, the disbelief and the reality, the loss and the gain.

More personal events, such as divorce or death, evoke similar reactions and emblazoned memories. There aren't nearly as many people around who share or appreciate the significance of the event. When the trauma was more than a single event, as often happens in incest, war, torture and abuse, there may be no one who will willingly confirm the reality of what happened. Our loss may remain unvalidated until some legitimate support exists.

When we validate the reality of our loss, we need to find people whose experiences are so close to our own we don't fear their judgment, nor discount their empathy. Sometimes we can find support from others with similar losses. In recent years, a variety of self-support groups have emerged for numerous life experiences, from life-threatening illness to divorce, from the loss of a pet to the death of a child, from alcoholism to weight loss.

As painful and a frightening as it might have been the first time, *re-experiencing the loss is necessary.* One of the ways we get trapped in this phase of grief is with the frozen images we have of what happened. As long as it remains "as clear as it if happened yesterday," our grief cannot progress. That moment is still real—today is not. Usually that means we've not had the opportunity to authenticate it by sharing it fully with someone. We may have tried several times, yet experience no sense of relief from the sharing. When our feelings are separated from what we're saying, we aren't reliving the event.

For example, I've mentioned before that three people from a support group I was working with died within a span of a week. Next, a client of mine attempted suicide. To top it off, a student was killed by a train right outside my office window while I watched. When I tell others about this incredible week, they inevitably feel terrible, imagining what it must have been like for me. Describing the facts of this week in this way, however, did little for me other than make me realize I could make others feel terrible about what I went through, but *I wasn't feeling anything.* Reciting the list of events doesn't produce strong feelings in me. At the time, what I needed was someone to say something like: "My God, John, that sounds awful! What was it like for you?" I needed *permission*, which I got almost two years later from a friend and colleague, to feel the experiences of that week, to recall in detail what happened, to validate the fullness of those traumatic events that changed my life. Simply reciting the facts wasn't enough.

Usually, when an event is very positive, the images are so wonderful we're reluctant to give up the specialness of the memory or to acknowledge the negative or ordinary aspects. We grow fond of telling and retelling exciting stories or recalling great athletic accomplishments. We often do so in a way that makes us a hero rather than convey other feelings we also had about what happened. People love great stories, though they may not permit the less positive, often shame-filled aspects of the experience to be admitted:

Jackson was a retired pilot, a war veteran of Korea, whose principal way to play was to tell stories about his accomplishments during the war. He shared with a friend about his feeling that he'd lost his playfulness during his war years.

His friend asked him how that had happened. Tears came to Jackson's eyes. For the first time, he talked about the event where he had been injured and his best friend had been killed. It led to his discharge on disability, something he had never discussed with anyone. His reluctance stemmed in part from feelings of shame. He was ashamed of the mistake he'd made. He felt guilty that it had cost his friend's life:

For years I've told as many war stories as anybody else. I have always looked on that time of my life as very special. I was alive then. It was one of the few times in my life when I could let myself play.

I've never told anyone what I told you today. I was so ashamed. It wasn't until today that I could admit that it happened. For the first time, I can feel my grief over losing my best friend while flying his wing. For the first time, I realize—that time of my life is over. I can't live on the memories of achievements or avoiding the painful ones. I want to feel how much I miss Ted. I must find ways to forgive myself, to play again, to live fully now.

Jason's family had such an experience five years after a tragic boat accident took the lives of his brother Art and his uncle Burt:

During the intervening five years, they'd never spoken of the two missing family members—for fear of causing too much pain for each other. Theirs was a growing family with new babies being born, growing children who were curious about the people in the photo albums. Jason was one of the curious ones—four years old, born a year after his brother's death. He'd ask his parents about the child in the photos but they'd fumble to avoid responding. "Oh, he's just a little boy we used to know," they'd say, feeling guilty in the process. How could they ever explain to Jason what had happened when they could barely stand going on from day to day themselves?

One day his parents realized they could no longer avoid the issue. Jason had been standing in front of the mirror in his room, making faces and changing hats. "Now I'm Jason," he grimaced and frowned. "Now I'm Art," he smiled and laughed.

Jason's dad had been watching unnoticed from the doorway. He was stunned by Jason's performance. Jason knew. Not only that, the performance told him that life wasn't very happy for Jason— in contrast to the pictures he'd seen of Art who had lived during a happier and more innocent time in the family.

With the help of two people who helped others with grief, the family met. Jason's parents had already let him know that the boy in the pictures was his brother who had died. Now it was time, Jason's mom asserted, for everyone to bring the memories of Art and Burt back into the family.

The family—the brothers and the sisters, the parents, grandparents and the children—spent the better part of the day sharing, crying, answering questions, telling each other what it had been like at the time of the accident and since. The children had many technical questions, like where it happened and how it happened—testing the waters of how much these adults, who had been so secretive, would be willing to share. Many expressed surprise at how close they felt to each other, how healing it felt to share the tears, how many misconceptions they'd had about what had happened.

It was a beginning. It was OK now to talk. Jason had questions that came up periodically over the years. "I'm glad everybody can smile like you did in those pictures with Art," he noted a few weeks later.

To smile again. The gift of revealing secrets and releasing frozen images can give permission to grieve and to live fully—laughter and tears, joy and sadness. Jason's family was alive once again—changed, now able to grow.

It's often the case that we are in such a fog at the time of a tragedy that we're not sure what happened. In the case of incest, torture or abuse, foggy memory may be a defense against knowing what happened. We split our minds from our bodily experiences to protect ourselves from the pain, helplessness and humiliation. Afraid we may be guilty for the trauma, we want to destroy the evidence linking us to it—even when that "evidence" is someone we love.

Feel safe enough, long enough, to discover what has changed

We may have been too young to safely explore our loss. Families often keep the truth away to protect us. Or else our own shock caused us to stop noticing anything except what was going on inside. To make loss real, we may go back to the scene with someone safe—to validate the event:

Diane's husband died in an air accident that she witnessed from the air terminal. The demands on her life, including small children and a medical residency, were such that she had returned to work immediately after the funeral. She felt she had done some of her grief work. Still, on significant anniversaries, particularly on the anniversary of his death, she would get extremely depressed and anxious, often withdrawing abruptly from relationships.

Diane had described the event to several people, but said she had never "felt" it. Finally, she decided to return to the scene of the air crash. She asked me to help her.

Diane's first step was to write out what she remembered of the accident. It helped her get in touch with her feelings in a safe way. She discovered what she wanted to look for in the visit. By luck, the Air Force colonel who had witnessed the accident with her five years before was still stationed nearby. He joined us.

Diane was moved by his recollection of the crash. The impact of reviewing the scene together again heightened both the memories and the sense of validation. Diane remembered the feelings of shock and disbelief. In discussing the crash with the colonel, he indicated it had been "pilot error" rather than weather that had been a major factor in the crash. Diane had not known this previously. She suddenly felt relieved of a layer of guilt she had not ever realized she had been carrying. She had assumed some responsibility for her husband's death because he was coming to see her and his pilot had tried to land in an unsafe place, despite the weather.

Now she knew that the weather wasn't the cause of his death, nor was she. As she went to the scene of the crash, Diane felt for the first time a depth of reality she had not known before—a release, a permission to move into her grief she had not had previously.

Diane was completing an incomplete story, adding pieces to a puzzle that wasn't clear. Important parts of it were missing—facts, a safe atmosphere to express her feelings, and people who could validate feelings and perceptions. It is the incompleteness of our stories that traps us in the past.

There is also a physical reality to the safety we need. Because the *alarm reaction* and the related experience of shock pose significant dangers to our physical well-being, someone may need medical care or observation. Engel (1971) has found that during or just after a stress event where a personal loss was experienced, some individuals suffer heart attacks. Many had existing physical problems, particularly cardiovascular ones. Others were taking medications that affect the heart.

Compared with all those who experience losses, the proportion of people who experience a loss and have a sudden heart attack is very small. Still, when something stressful happens, our health can be at risk. In order to minimize danger, it is advisable to be told of a significant loss when and where we have someone supportive with us and have access to medical help.

Get support to see that there is more to life than losing, or having, everything

During this time of emerging awareness the only thing that does not seem trivial or meaningless is what we've lost. We need validation that what we lost clearly had meaning for us. We may need to know that others made it through tough times too, times like our own.

Admit that we can't grieve alone

So many feelings surface at the time we become fully aware of a powerful life-changing experience. We often struggle to find words that can adequately express what we feel even in normal activities. But during a loss, we may only have gestures, tears, hugs, silence and the need to talk privately to ourselves.

We may believe we may have to manage our grief by ourself, but we cannot—we need others at times. Helping us begin our grieving is one such time. We find solace in the presence of others who don't ask for anything, including conversation, in return.

Melissa found that touch helped her release her feelings after she'd been diagnosed with AIDS:

I was doing so well until somebody put their arm around me. Then I broke down and cried and cried until I couldn't cry anymore.

Tony's mother was an ally in his grief when his wife died:

Knowing she was there, taking care of the kids and cooking the meals, was all I needed. I let my hair down and felt everything I'd been holding back—the rage, the loneliness.

Sometimes it's the one we're losing who gives us solace and permission to feel. Jeraldine received a tape in the mail from the man with whom she'd ended an affair:

He sent me a tape, acknowledging and accepting that we had to end the relationship. Hearing his voice got to me. He played music that had been so meaningful to us both. It deeply moved me and pulled me into my tears and my sadness. I realized then how much I was giving up—how much I would miss him.

Permission to feel can be received even when we struggle to resist showing our feelings. Matt's friend Denise stayed with him after a phone call telling him of his son's arrest for drug dealing:

She held my gaze and wouldn't look away. It was as if she could see inside, see my feelings, and wouldn't let me run away from them. I said "Damn your eyes." Then the tears came.

Recognize when professional help is needed

Sometimes we need help as our grief begins, some way to provide for safety and nurturance to explore the extent of the loss and to go on coping. We need to balance being distracted by people insensitive to our loss with others' encouragement to explore our feelings.

Such help is often not something we want from friends and loved ones—nor is it something that they can easily provide without distancing themselves or being overwhelmed.

We may not want a friend or loved one to be the one to tell us of the bad news. We don't want them to bear the brunt of the anger that wells up in us—the desire to destroy the message *and* the messenger.

We rarely want further contact with bearers of bad news. They've done their job. That's why "critical incident stress debriefing" (Mitchell and Bray, 1990) is composed of a group of outsiders that come in to the scene of a catastrophe for a few days and then leave. It's why hospital chaplains are often asked to tell families that a loved one has died and wonder why they have no further contact.

Professional caregivers must sometimes destroy the illusion that the loss hasn't happened. We accept the role of being the bearer of bad tidings—even when that news is finally heard years after the loss. Therapists and friends can be puzzled and dismayed by the abrupt termination of seemingly helpful contacts by a bereaved client or friend. When the loss becomes real, often by confrontation or returning to the scene, the bereaved may not want to continue treatment. The role of caregiver is temporary—to help the bereaved become unfrozen and get on with grieving and the awakening of awareness.

Grief is essentially a private process. "I'm tired of being a patient" was the comment of Irvin Yalom's client (in his book, *Love's Executioner*) who, after many years, had broken through an illusion of love. Her grief was her own, something she wanted to experience in private, away from anyone else's presence, especially professionals.

Family members will react in diverse, sometimes opposite ways, which can create misunderstandings and compound grief. Professional intervention can play a critical role in helping families proceed with grief more smoothly. For example, the Tennyson family lost their parents and one of their children in an airplane accident, leaving five siblings and their spouses to grieve. They asked two therapists to help:

> *Seven years have passed since the accident where three members of our family died in a small plane crash. Tanya and Ken were the most devastated—they had lost a child as well as the parents we'd all lost. We've all talked to our partners about it over the years. We've also been able to share a lot with each other—with the exception of Tanya and Ken.*

> *The other day we finally decided to talk. We were all taking a family vacation together, with all the kids—many who had been born since this happened. We found that some of us had moved a long way emotionally from the accident—to our surprise, especially Tanya and Ken!*

> *We had all been very supportive of them, in some cases to the exclusion of our own grief. What was most surprising to me was that neither Tanya nor Ken had much memory of the days after the accident. They remember next to nothing of the funeral.*

Surprisingly to us, it was our spouses who felt stuck back at the event. They remembered everything as if it had happened yesterday. My husband Greg burst into tears, saying, "I can see it so vividly, over and over, how you looked when you heard Jimmy (Tanya and Ken's son) and your parents were dead. I held back. My grief wasn't as important as yours. Now I want to feel sad—to be part of the family again."

Greg spoke for the other partners who also needed to share their stories from the time of the event. They had stood aside, helpless, not knowing what to do, not feeling included in the grief of the siblings. They observed, waiting. They knew exactly what happened. Now that Tanya and Ken wanted to know, they had something to contribute to the family's grief—and healing. They grieved their own losses: a nephew, their in-laws, their spouse during this long siege.

Sometimes differences in a family's grief leads to mistaken assumptions and distortions about what happened. What we forget is that emotional involvement with the loss means we're likely to remember events as we think they were, not necessarily as they actually were. Andy discovered how his own distortions had affected his family relations:

For years after my father's death, I felt a distance from my sister Joyce because I thought she had gotten there before he died and had a chance to say good-bye. I resented that she had the opportunity and I didn't. I resented my mother having those last moments with him.

It wasn't until twenty years later, when my mother made a tape recording for me of those painful days, that I found out. Joyce hadn't been there, and neither had my mother. They hadn't been withholding from me. Since then, we have talked a great deal about what happened, and it has brought us all closer. I regret the loss of closeness all those years—by my mistaken assumptions.

When a long time has passed and we are still reacting from shock or alarm, we may need professional help. Facilitating the start of long-delayed awareness can require overcoming or bypassing the defenses that block awareness. Sometimes unusual or alternative techniques are especially helpful, such as the use of sweat lodges and group ceremonies in the treatment of Vietnam veterans who are Agent Orange victims (Colodzin,

1993). These are approaches that are best handled by professionallt trained individuals (see also Chapter Ten).

Summary

Our lives take unexpected turns—with the experience of a traumatic loss, what we counted on is gone, never to return. We're not the person we used to be. Our relationships, our world will never be the same. These are turning points. Appreciating their significance and consequences are more than we can handle at first. We are shocked by the unexpected suddenness and our loss of control.

The beginning of grief is a time of great vulnerability. We begin to grieve when the loss and our feelings and reactions to it are *validated*. We may eventually discover that there's more to life than what is missing. We may also discover that there is not. With support, we find the courage to grieve, to grow and to affirm life's transformations. "A journey of a thousand miles begins with a single step" is an ancient Confucian saying. The beginning of grief is that first step on the pathway to our healing and transformation.

Chapter Four
Coping with Awareness:
Holding On or Letting Go?

If you haven't the strength to impose your own terms upon life, you must accept the terms it offers you.

—*T.S. Eliot,* **The Confidential Clerk**

Any time we face change, a part of us resists. We want to preserve our lives as they are. We want to hold on to the threads of love, our dreams, whatever connects us to our world and to ourself. We want to feel secure and predictable as long as we can. Yet change, both internal and external, is inevitable. When it happens, we need to adapt quickly and move on, rid ourselves of behaviors and ties to the past that are no longer functional. Our dilemma is to discover when to hold on and when to let go.

We are often ambivalent about whether to hold on or to let go. This ambivalence is a natural consequence of the two basic dimensions of being human: we are both social and solitary creatures.

The social part of us needs others, fears abandonment and prolonged separations, yearns for ways to stay attached and to make new attachments. That part of us wants to hold on.

The solitary part of us needs recognition that if we are to find our identity and be creative, we must rid ourself of encumbrances, tolerate aloneness and accept our uniqueness. Letting go of that which is no longer functional is a prime need of our solitary selves.

Both sides are a part of our nature. People differ considerably in the balance between the two, just as grief reflects that balance as we cope by holding on and letting go. The process of grieving itself often transforms that balance, especially if over reliance on one side or the other contributed to the loss itself.

This dilemma, to hold on or to let go, is a combination of resisting change and quickly adapting to it, representing the two sides of a profound ambivalence about facing the reality of loss. Both sides serve the same end—to *limit awareness of the full extent of what is changing.*

Peter Marris (1974) described this as the *conservation impulse*— our basic reaction to loss and change. This impulse serves a function on each side of the ambivalence that characterizes the early phases of grief. With these tools we believe we can:

- *Overcome the loss* or *avoid its consequences*

- *Prevent change from happening* or *limit its impact*

- *Solve problems and find meaning* or *enjoy what we can of life*

- *Enhance and maintain attachments and continuity* or *detach in order to maintain our sense of identity and uniqueness.*

When our loss is traumatic or represents a violation of our belief system, it can be an assault on our basic sense of being. Attempts to limit awareness are necessary buffers, protecting us from the full impact of the trauma until we can process it more gradually. Two ways we limit our awareness of trauma are by *coping* and *defending.* Coping strategies are analogous to a dam on a river after a heavy rainstorm that allows the flood waters to gradually go through to the valley below. A defensive strategy, by contrast, would be a dam that lets no water through—and eventually may break from the force behind it, washing away everything in its path.

The difference between *coping* and *defending* is that in coping we want a break, a respite from awareness of the loss. We'll not easily give up our problem-solving abilities, our meanings and attachments in order to prevent change. When we are defending against a loss, we are desperate to avoid the loss altogether.

Because they are often confused by professionals and the public, it is important to understand that coping is seen as a normal and adaptive response to a loss. However, a person may engage defending strategies against a loss, which I consider a way to stop grieving (see Chapter Ten).

Basic Mechanisms for Coping: Fight or Flight

We share with other mammals a biological mechanism for responding to a threat. When faced with a threat, we instinctively react in one of two ways—to fight or to flee. We may not even know until the last second which direction we'll go. We may feel paralyzed by the pull to fight and the desire to flee. At any cost, it seems, we want to avoid this threat—this loss.

Fight

If we choose to fight, we believe we will destroy or overcome our loss or the threat of one. We won't give in to it. We'll conquer or master it. With a little more effort we can beat it. If we don't give up, we'll make it. We're determined not to relinquish what's meaningful. Our will to live won't quit despite the beating we're taking.

There are times when our capacity to fight prevents losses from happening. There are also times when we limit the extent of the loss by our capacity to resist and our desire to rescue. *This urge to resist destruction is essential in our capacity to transform losses, for it allows us to search for and hopefully retain the essence of what is changing.*

Fighting or holding on as a way of coping is also a belief in our strengths, in the power of our connections. We ask "why?," expecting an answer that makes sense according to our lifelong beliefs. We believe that love can conquer all, that our relationships can meet the test, that everything we do has meaning and purpose. We will never walk alone. We will climb every mountain. We are truly free. We *shall* overcome.

Flight

The opposite extreme of coping is considerably more cynical and insists on its version of realism. Yes, the loss has happened. The way to deal with it is to find ways to escape or avoid its impact. We retreat in order to fight another day. We need a break to restore our energies. We give up. We quit. We laugh in the face of death, humiliation or tragedy. We avoid or destroy whatever reminds us of the loss. We relinquish our feelings of connection because the connection now feels poisoned, limiting, not valid. We may even reject or be revolted by what once may have been positive but now poses a threat to our existence. At the extreme, we'd rather die than face this loss.

Letting go, or escape, as a way of coping with loss can also be an admission of weaknesses, alienation and abandonment. We realize we were born alone and will die alone and are likely to be abandoned at critical times in between. Nothing really helps. No one cares. God is dead. Life is hell if you care too much.

Letting go is also a way to avoid or minimize the underlying loneliness and feelings of abandonment that are raised by each new loss. If we can convince ourself that we don't care or limit the overwhelming sense of deprivation or isolation that results, we can somehow keep going.

Sometimes letting go or fleeing adds to our loss. We didn't hang in there when to do so might have changed the outcome. By fleeing, we add new losses—the loss of self-respect, and guilt for surviving.

Flight or letting go is also essential for transformation. *We need to have ways to detach from the details, let go of what is no longer there and disconnect from the form of our losses so we can see a bigger picture and a new tomorrow.*

We can't escape from losses without a price. We can't completely avoid them, for significant losses are inevitable. All we can do is give ourself a break, a respite from the pain, a delay until a better time for grieving. Eventually, bits and pieces of what we've lost catch us when we're least expecting it—while we sleep or dream, when we let down our guard, when we feel joy, love, hope, appreciation, when we pause to reflect. Jokes give way to tears when they unexpectedly sidestep our ways to limit awareness of our losses.

We can't permanently continue to escape without deadening our senses and our other attachments, without minimizing the extent to which we care and love—for ourself as well as others.

Discovering What is Lost: A Balancing Act

As we begin to comprehend our loss, we may not be so afraid of it. We haven't been destroyed. We can decide how much to let in at one time, or how long we want to stay with it. We can distract ourself. We can stand it—at least so far. Bit by bit, we discover the extent of our loss.

It's a natural part of childhood and early adulthood to learn a variety of ways to fight and to flee. Sometimes we find one way that works so well it becomes habitual, and we don't learn other ways. To lose such a powerful way of coping can be very frightening, for we may have nothing to fall back on.

Grieving proceeds when we are able to use both holding on and letting go strategies adaptively. When we learn a variety of ways to cope, we can be flexible. Some ways of coping can keep us from awareness.

Others, like humor, help to distract us when we're overwhelmed. Together they give us confidence that we can survive. In our ways of coping, we can find hope, rest and needed strength.

In the next two sections, we will explore ways we fight and flee from loss. The wider the range of coping strategies we use, the more effective we'll be when we face a loss.

The separation into holding on and letting go is an artificial one in many ways. There certainly are times when our dominant strategy for coping is one or the other. We may hold on one way, for example, physically, while letting go another, perhaps emotionally. In couples and in families, however, it's possible that one member might specialize in holding on, while another seems only to let go. More often, we do varying degrees of both at different times—sometimes within a few minutes of each other.

Holding On: Fight

> *We shall overcome*
> *we shall overcome*
> *we shall overcome someday*
> *for deep in my heart*
> *I do believe*
> *We shall overcome someday.*
> *—African-American spiritual*

In the US in the 1960's, civil rights and anti-war demonstrators were fond of singing this spiritual. Its message of hope at a time of despair— assassinations, war, disillusionment—helped people believe in something. It captured the essence of holding on, the desire or belief that we could overcome a loss and keep going.

Holding on is a way to remain hopeful. We try hard to believe the loss did not happen, that it can be reversed, that it won't always be. We believe we can learn from it in ways that will prevent future losses. Elissa was holding on after her husband abandoned her with two small children:

There were days in those first weeks when I thought I couldn't stand it anymore. I knew there was no real escape—he would still be gone no matter what I did. Doing the housework, feeding the children, going to work helped me. I don't know what I would have done if I wasn't able to keep busy.

For Elissa, the reality of her new circumstances as a single parent meant delaying her grief for months, even years. She had to cope by holding on to her roles as housekeeper and mother, and by adding a new one, as breadwinner.

It requires a lot of energy to hold on during a major loss. Things aren't the same and we know it. If we stop to grieve, the fear is that we will lose even more—those things rewarding in our lives which have not changed. We see no alternatives, for now. We have to wait for a time when we can figure out what has happened—perhaps until next summer vacation or until the kids are old enough for us to leave them for a day or two. That may take years—years of simply coping as best we can.

We amaze people by how much we can do when we've experienced a loss. What they witness is the result of our fighting off the full impact of the loss. We're finally able to lose those excess pounds. We've found the incentive to write that book, finish the college degree, start an aerobics program. People wonder how we manage, knowing what's happened. But we're happy not to explain why we have so much energy right now. We just keep going.

There are many aspects to holding on. Our behavior changes. So do our thoughts and feelings. Our physical and spiritual selves shift. Figure 4-1 suggests some ways that holding on can take form:

Figure 4-1: Dimensions of Holding On/ Fight

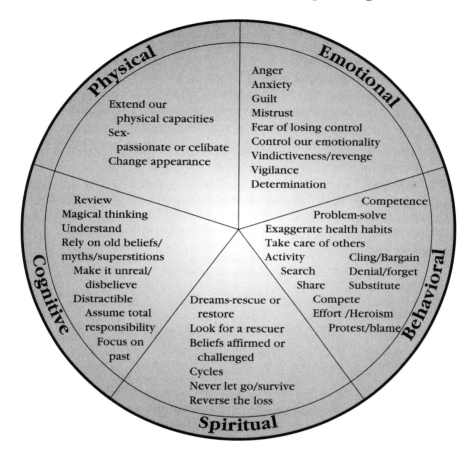

Behavioral Aspects of Holding On

As the words fight and holding on imply, this style of coping is an active one. It mobilizes our resources in ways we rarely employ except in times of crisis. There are numerous ways we act to fight off the effects of a loss.

Over competence

Keeping active and busy helps me feel less anxious about this loss.

During times of holding on, many people divert much energy into their jobs, social responsibility and such. When we do this, we become more effective in our work. We may actually become more competent, but it is at the expense of personal growth, health and flexibility.

We become suddenly motivated, able to overcome long-standing ambivalence. We break with our dependencies and show a remarkable capacity to make it on our own. Marlo discovered this about herself at the age of forty-four when her husband died:

> *When John died suddenly, my whole world collapsed. I had depended on him for everything outside the home. He had wanted to take care of me and I let him. I did know how, even though I was a bit rusty. I can get the car fixed, manage a budget, and plan trips. I'm going to school now, and I hope to get a job in a year or two. For years I'd put off my career. I felt comforted staying home, even though the kids no longer needed me there. Now there is no choice. I have to get going.*

Problem-solving/being responsible

I've been the one to make the necessary decisions.

The threat of loss can mobilize our ability to make decisions and solve problems. In fact, we may feel obliged to take on responsibility. Martin did, when one of his children was born with Muscular Dystrophy (MD):

> *When I first found out that Mark had Muscular Dystrophy, I didn't even know what the term meant. Since then, I've studied every-thing I could get my hands on about the disease. Being a scientist to begin with, I guess it was my way of getting control again. I've decided to make MD a major focus of my research. It's strange now—I know more about MD than our pediatrician does. It doesn't change that he is ill, though I feel less helpless.*

We become the one in our family who manages to take care of details while the rest fall apart at the funeral. After all, *somebody* has to do it!

Exaggerated health habits

I am smoking more.

I exercise more.

It is not atypical to experience a wide swing in health habits during times of holding on—either positive or negative swings. That means we may smoke or eat more—or, by contrast, exercise and diet more. We'll do what we need to do to *limit our sense of helplessness*.

Increased activity

> I keep active to avoid thinking about what happened.

It doesn't matter what we do as long as we do something that helps us limit the feelings triggered by a loss. If we are not busy, we fear we will have to take time to reflect on the loss.

Devoting ourself to the care of others

> Taking care of others distracts me from thinking about my loss.

We can also lose ourself in taking care of others. Parents and professional caregivers find someone who needs help—or create that need. It's a distraction from what's going on inside. We may feel guilty if we "indulge" in our own grief, knowing that someone else is hurting. Sensitized to the word "selfish," we feel we don't deserve the freedom to mourn.

It's only our turn when everyone else's needs are taken care of—if that ever happens. Doris, a forty-five-year-old therapist, had to wait several days before it was her turn to grieve the suicide of a client:

> *I went to the intensive care unit as soon as I heard of Tom's suicide. I was shocked, yet not surprised. As his therapist, I saw it coming for months, and I felt helpless to do anything about it. Thank God, his family was there. I could devote myself to their needs, then to his friends, and delay having to deal with my own pain. It worked, reasonably, for a couple of days. Then there wasn't anybody to take care of—except me.*

Doris was fortunate that it was only a matter of days before she got to her own grief. She waited until everyone else was well past their grief before she began—only to discover very little support within the family or community for her own grief. "But you are such a strong person" is a common response to professional caregivers who seek support during grief.

Search

> Until it is proven to be beyond a doubt that this loss is real, I will keep looking for it/him/her.

Individuals search as a reaction to loss. Search is often necessary to confirm the reality of a loss. Confirmation may release us from hoping that there had been some mistake or from hanging on to a miraculous escape:

A newspaper article describes Herb's forty-day, exhausting search for the body of his son, missing and presumed dead when his river raft overturned. He finally said, "I couldn't stop until I was sure."

Eleanor, adopted as a child, insists on finding her biological parents and hires a detective to aid in her search.

Twenty years have passed since Tom was reported as missing in action in Vietnam. His family looked for evidence to either confirm his death or that he is still alive. That finally arrived in the form of a ring that he always wore. "We knew he was dead then," sobbed his mother. "He never would have parted with that ring."

Amy, jilted by her boyfriend, keeps going over to his house, peering in his window, calling him on the phone despite repeated rejections. When he had her arrested for stalking, she finally came to her senses.

Sometimes this reality only comes in bits and pieces. Margo found this to be the case after her son Abe died in a fire that had burned his body beyond recognition. His dental charts confirmed his identity. Nevertheless, Margo never saw the body. Her husband did, though that still did not totally convince her:

It took me a year before I accepted that Abe was dead. On some level I knew, of course. The evidence was clear from the start. I never saw him—never saw his body. It took him missing every holiday, every birthday, every family celebration for that year. Each time, I'd say to myself, "Well, if Abe's alive, he wouldn't miss this." He didn't come. On those days, every time the door opened or the phone rang, my heart would leap—maybe it's him. It was when he wasn't there for his own birthday, almost a year later, that it hit me. Abe was dead.

Search behaviors are powerful, compelling ways to overcome loss as well as ways to delay grief.

Sharing

I want/need to tell others what happened.

Disclosing the experience of a loss makes it real. While holding on, we may share more than usual. We need to know that others struggle to cope as well—that they have it as rough as we do. This is usually the time when people join support groups—as awareness of the loss increases, the need to hold on and for validation also increases. Denise found this to be true in joining a support group for people with AIDS:

I was amazed the first time I went to the group how powerful it was for me to share the experience of my diagnosis and treatment when I first became symptomatic. I was with these wonderful people who knew exactly what it was like. They had already been there. I cried more deeply than I ever had before. I could look at dying. I could feel the sadness for what would never be. I could be angry about the injustice of it all.

It wasn't the same in the times after that. It was comforting to share my story, especially when someone new came to the group. Most of the time, it felt like I was someplace safe, and that my story of having AIDS was an admission ticket to this wonderful source of support. The time may come when it won't be so comfortable any more—especially when someone in the group dies. Right now, it's what keeps me going.

Competition and effort

Winning at something helps distract me from the loss.

If I try hard enough, I can bring back what I lost.

Competition requires concentration and gives us the opportunity to concentrate on something other than our loss. It allows us to play or express our frustration in the form of a game. On the other hand, competition confronts the threat of loss head-on. We beat the odds when defeat seems to be staring us in the face. Sherman was diagnosed with an inoperable cancer at the age of forty-two:

The doctor told me two years ago I had almost no chance of being alive a year later. I was determined to prove him wrong—and I have. Here I am, two years later—and still going strong! I know I can't ignore that I've had cancer, though I won't give in to this. I'm going to beat it, even if it's the last thing I do!

There are many instances when a loss is not clear-cut or inevitable. Effort does make a difference. Why else do we search through rubble after an earthquake and continue to look for cures for cancer or AIDS? Now, with a loss staring us in the face, we'll give it all we can to try to overcome it.

Effort and competition go hand in hand as ways to fight potential losses. We talk of the "battle" against cancer, the "war" on poverty and drugs, the need to defeat enemies who would destroy our way of life. We are holding on to whatever we can of a meaningful life.

Heroism

I've been able to do things I ordinarily could not.

In the face of disaster, we can perform feats well beyond our usual capacities. The soldier in battle, the firefighter in a raging fire, or the paramedic with the cardiac patient may respond in ways that are exceptional. Heroism, however, can come too late or in ways that do not help. For example, people risk their lives to bring life back to the body of someone they already know is dead, or to rescue someone who is drowning and lose their own life instead.

Protest and blame

I'm looking for who made this loss happen.

Significant losses frustrate us. We look for someone to blame for our frustration. We rage against the loss. We look for someone who looks or acts guilty hoping, by blaming them, to alleviate our frustration and limit our pain.

Our protest can focus on the lost person. How could they die? Didn't they know what it would do to us?

Our blame and protest can blind us when we believe others are responsible for a loss. This is not to say that blame is undesirable at this time. Expressing this, in a safe way, can help to relieve the pent-up emotions and allow us to gain a little perspective. It can also serve to protect our threatened self-esteem until we get further along in the grief process.

Sometimes there is evidence that someone did not do their job, did not care enough, gave up, or was out to create our loss. When people *feel* guilty and we have yet to sort out our role in a loss, we may want to believe they *are* guilty. It can be a relief to have someone to blame, to punish. On the receiving side, we may childishly believe that being punished will restore what we've lost.

Anger and blame continue to serve us when a loss was intentionally caused by others, as in theft, murder or kidnapping. To see someone punished can keep us going and eventually be a relief.

On the other side, we may need others to be angry with us to free us from our guilt. We may need our partner, as we initiate a divorce, to feel hurt. We absorb some of the fury that we know we deserve for leaving *them:*

> *We had both been so reasonable about the divorce, even though I was the one who was leaving. I knew June was hurting a lot, but she'd always put up a brave front, trying to be understanding. Then one day, standing in the kitchen, she let loose, began pounding me on the chest, crying, swearing at me. Then we both burst into tears, held each other, knew for the first time the pain we shared in this separating.*

Blame becomes a frozen, fixed form of protest if no one validates its coping function. Unfortunately, the present nature of litigation in the United States tends to overemphasize this way of coping. The rate of malpractice suits and bitterly contested divorces are evidence of an exaggerated blaming process. It can prevent reconciliation. In many cases, it delays grief until after the suit is finally settled. That may be many years, and the outcome is usually unsatisfactory because it does not bring back what we've lost, nor can it ever adequately compensate us for our loss. In some instances, winning the suit is supposed to fully compensate for the loss, eliminating altogether our need or permission to grieve.

Clinging

I keep reminders of my loss around me (e.g., pictures, mementos).

I remain involved with friends and family to stay connected to my loss.

I avoid being alone.

I haven't given up the rituals and habits that connect me to my loss.

As babies will grasp desperately to their mothers during a separation, we, too, can cling to a slim hope that a loss will be reversed. We keep reminders around us, wishing to bring back the past. We distance ourself from people who distract us from missing the one who is no longer there. For example, after my Uncle Tim was killed in a train accident, his fiancé became a member of our family. She was in my parents' wedding and took frequent trips with us. She never dated or married, dying at the age of 83.

In another example, Jane clung to hope in spite of the letter that her son had been killed in battle:

Every day I went to the mailbox, hoping another letter would come, saying it had all been a mistake. I kept hoping, even though I knew.

Bargaining or superstitious behavior

I would do almost anything to get back what I've lost.

We're often not aware that we are bargaining. We don't know how vulnerable we are until someone comes along with the promise of a cure, a way to eliminate our loss—and we grasp at it without critically evaluating its validity. When we bargain, we tolerate very small odds. How else can we explain our willingness to have surgery when chances are heavily against our survival?

Many assumptions give us a basis for bargaining. Rewards will come if we do our fair share, for example. We won't have to experience loss if we work hard enough. When the threat of loss exists, we'll bargain with higher powers, or very low characters. We become docile and accommodating to the doctor who suspects we have a life-threatening condition, for if we're a good patient, a cure will result. We'll go to faith healers, listen to charlatans intent on making money on our misfortune by promising the impossible. We pray a lot. We make sacrifices. We make promises. We'll try anything, do anything that might reverse our loss.

We are quite vulnerable when we are bargaining. Others can take advantage of us financially and emotionally in our desperation to believe that what we've lost isn't gone. For example, they may offer us ways to connect with our loss through channeling and other ways of mediating connections with a deceased loved one. Some people may suggest their favorite superstitious behavior: if you do this, your loss will be restored. If it holds even the faintest glimmer of hope for connection or restoration, we'll try it.

Bargaining involves assumptions we haven't challenged. Clarence, at the age of fifty-nine, had a life-long assumption challenged when the truck factory he had worked at for thirty years went bankrupt:

All my life I've believed that if you work hard enough, things will work out. Until now that's worked out okay for me. Then the plant closed and they declared bankruptcy. I lost my thirty years of retirement benefits.

I realized how wrong I was. All that hard work, and for what? It's too late for me to start over. It just isn't fair!

As with Clarence, when bargains fail we also kick ourselves for being so naive as to believe in them. We are furious at others who "duped" us into thinking we could beat the odds—furious at ourself.

Bargaining can also become a defense to eliminate grief when we'll do *anything* to avoid it. There needs to be a limit on what we'll do or sacrifice, especially when it comes to our sense of integrity.

Denial and forgetting

I look as good as I always did.

I find myself talking or acting as if nothing has changed.

A common way to cope is to deny it happened or to forget it for periods of time. That takes many forms.

One way we deny that anything is different is to try to create the illusion of everything still being the same. We can get ourself to look good—a way to delude ourself that we are doing OK. In a society where appearances matter, we can succeed for periods of time in convincing others.

We use denial to help us pretend that nothing has changed. We're waiting until our loved one returns. So we go ahead and fix up their room, prepare for their birthday or the holidays as we usually do. But then reality crashes in. Norma experienced this in the months after her husband left her:

It's strange! I find myself when it's 5:15 looking at the door, wondering when he will come in. Then I remember. He won't be coming anymore.

We may go about our business as usual after being diagnosed with a life-threatening condition that hasn't any symptoms—yet. When the first symptoms appear, or when we can't do the things we usually do, our denial no longer works.

Forgetting, more likely to be seen in holding on, can be distinct from denial, which is more often associated with letting go. In holding on, we may forget what has changed and operate as if it was still a part of our lives. We may not yet have acknowledged the implications of the loss that necessitate changes in our life-style.

The paradox of denial is that in order to deny, we must first admit that a loss has occurred. We aren't grieving. We know we're not being ourself. There is a tension between our denial and what we know exists—the loss. That tension remains until we grieve the loss. If denial remains for an extended length of time, it becomes a defensive strategy, which stops grieving.

Substitution

I've found someone or something to replace what/who I've lost.

Substitution is an attempt to replace the lost object, person, or beliefs by new ones. Substitution gives us the opportunity to discover if what we lost was unique, irreplaceable. *If it can be replaced, then we don't need to grieve it.*

Substitution is a form of denial. We put someone or something in the place of who or what is lost. In some cases, the substitute may closely resemble the lost person or object. In other instances, we attempt to meet the needs that are no longer being met. For example, someone may become promiscuous after a divorce, find a new partner too quickly, or have a baby as soon as possible after another one dies.

Sometimes, using substitution as a way of finding out if the loss can be replaced will work, depending on the severity and nature of the loss. Usually it does not. There are instances where we don't realize it hasn't worked until years later when we realize something is still missing in our lives, or when the substitute partner or child becomes dissatisfied with being only a replacement.

Recapturing the moment

Every time we think of the first moment we knew of our loss, we may want to share it as it was. When the event is positive, the fullness of the experience stands in contrast to the relative emptiness prior to it and today. We can't maintain the highs of yesteryear. The stress of today is in the attempt to recapture those moments by always romanticizing those times in our life when we were "living on the edge." Minerva, once a star athlete, candidly admitted she was addicted to finding ways to recapture the glorious moments of her past:

> *I'd do just about anything to get back that feeling I had back then. It was truly a peak experience. Since then I've turned to drugs, drinking, and sex as I tried to get back that sense of being so fully alive as I had then. I thought for a while that I'd rather not live than miss out on the excitement of times like that.*

> *I finally realized I can't live in the past. It was hard to admit that to myself. Now it's just a memory.*

Cognitive Aspects of Holding On

What we think, see and remember can be attempts to prove that the loss did not occur, or that it is reversible. At first, we can't accept its reality. We go over and over the events surrounding the loss, convinced that if we could find something everyone else has overlooked, we can change what's happened. We look for ways to prove it hasn't happened. We need to find a way to solve the problem of the loss—to overcome it or reverse it. We struggle to understand why it happened. We look to our assumptions and beliefs that have worked in the past to help us avoid or soften the crisis. When that doesn't work, we look for who's responsible for the loss.

Sometimes we've already come to an acceptance of the reality of the loss. We spend our time looking backwards—to the time before the loss happened—clinging to the memories and remnants of the past.

Making it unreal

This whole thing seems unreal.

I don't believe that this loss happened.

I hope I am dreaming and wake up to find it never happened.

The circumstances under which a loss occurs can be vivid and clear, or can be a shock. If it is the latter, we may later question whether it really happened. If everyone acts as if nothing has happened, that can confirm our desire to believe that the loss didn't happen in the first place.

There is a difference between a loss seeming to be unreal and true denial. When validation of the loss is provided, its reality is admitted, however grudgingly. In denial, even validation does not make a difference.

When we lack confirmation of the reality of a loss, we want to believe it didn't happen. Memories of many childhood traumas are later dreamlike because no one upheld what happened; to accept what happened would have dire consequences. To survive those consequences, we may have to dissociate mind from body.

When feelings of unreality are maintained for longer than a few months, one is likely to require professional help. There may be too many obstacles to the needed safety and validation to admit that what happened was real.

Magical thinking

I keep thinking something could be done to bring back what I lost.

I think that if I am good or perfect enough, what I lost will return.

Childhood is a time when we develop superstitions. We hold our breath so we won't end up in the cemetery. We avoid stepping on a crack in the sidewalk so we won't break our mother's back. We don't walk under ladders, so bad things won't happen to us. When faced with the threat or reality of a loss, we may fall back on such magical thinking. "If I had only known what was going to happen" is an example of magical thinking—if only we were so powerful that we could see things before they actually happened, we could prevent what we didn't want to happen.

We grasp at straws. If we pray hard enough, think only positive thoughts, or punish ourselves, perhaps we can beat this. Magical thinking undergirds the holding on style of coping, especially when we try to reverse the inevitable.

Review and understanding

> I go over the loss in my mind, trying to figure out how it could have been different.
>
> Something could have prevented this loss.
>
> I try to figure out why this loss happened to me.
>
> If I could find the reason this loss happened, I wouldn't feel so bad.

Martha, recently fired as an elementary school teacher during budget cutbacks, repeatedly reviews all the incidents leading to being fired. She looks for how she might have been able to prevent it. In attempting to solve a problem with no solution, when the loss has already occurred, there is a tendency toward repeated review of the events that occurred before and after the loss. These ruminating search behaviors often involve comparisons to other situations, people, and events similar to the loss and the repeated review and analysis of all the information available to the bereaved about the loss.

Herb's thinking fueled his search for his son's body:

I kept going over it repeatedly in my mind. Sometimes, I'd try to convince myself it hadn't happened. After all, they never found his body. Then at other times, I'd try to convince myself that I could have prevented all this, if I had insisted he not go on the trip. There are even times when I see couples I dislike and wonder how come they are so lucky. It seems so unfair.

Review is an adaptive approach when something can be done about a loss—that's why we try it. In other circumstances, however, reality and the irreversibility of the loss persuade us to let it go.

There is an impression many of us share that making sense of something lessens its impact. We're thinking that being able to understand or explain something takes the mystery out of it—and that it is the mystery that creates our misery. To some extent this is true. Fear results when we don't understand why something happens. When one bad thing happens, what's to keep other bad things from happening too? Understanding permits us to limit our sense of vulnerability to other losses. It doesn't prevent us from feeling the sense of loss.

As someone whose career in the past twenty years has revolved around understanding loss and grief, I can attest to being a "world-class expert" at this way of defending against my own losses. It's both a blessing and a curse. On the one hand, I recognize grief easily and know how it will be for me. I know that coping is only going to delay the inevitable, which helps me validate my own grief process. On the other hand, I've discovered that being an expert on grief doesn't lessen the pain, the loneliness, the empty feeling or the wondering if this time might be the time I don't make it. As Shakespeare wisely observed, "Well, everyone can master grief 'cept he that has it"—so it is with coping by understanding.

Rely on old beliefs and myths

"If I could only understand" is one of our more sophisticated myths about how to cope. We also develop ways *not to think*. We rely on our beliefs and assumptions throughout life as a way to make our daily living easier, a way to explain what is happening to us. When a loss occurs, as Table 4-1 shows (page 124), we'll search through the familiar beliefs to see if any of them fits to explain or soften the blow of this loss. Sometimes they fail us by activating maladaptive coping styles.

Table 4-1: Holding On Beliefs and Myths

If I don't concentrate on remembering what has happened, I'll forget it.

If I work hard enough, nothing bad will ever happen to me.

If I'm good enough, nobody I love will ever die.

Cheer up—things could be worse.

It will all work out in the long run.

If I can understand why it happened, everything will be all right.

Every cloud has a silver lining.

It's God's will. He has something better in mind.

People get the respect they deserve in this world.

Don't question it. Just accept it. You have to go on.

The show must go on.

I must learn to accept it.

Idle hands are the devil's workbench.

There must be a reason for this.

If I am good enough or perfect, what I lost will come back.

Distractibility

Almost anything can remind me of my loss.

Coping protects us from reminders, but often fails to work—a sign that we're permitting ourself to be vulnerable, for the moment. Zach found it hard to concentrate after his wife died of cancer in her early forties:

I had to keep going. I couldn't concentrate. I tried to read, and my thoughts kept wandering back to her. Going to a movie helped for a while. Even then I kept having moments of painful awareness. When I have to pay attention, like when I'm listening to other people on my job, or when I'm with the kids, listening to them, it's okay. Sometimes it helps to look at old pictures and read over her letters from years ago, when we were young lovers. Sometimes it helps to think that sometime in the future, I will meet her again—in another lifetime, perhaps.

Assume total responsibility

I think I am responsible for this loss.

I feel I should have done something to prevent this
from happening.

A more personalized form of holding on is to assume more than our
fair share of the responsibility for what happened. Somehow we think that
if we were to blame, we wouldn't feel so helpless. The pain of our grief
would make sense—we are being punished for making this happen.

There are times we contribute to our loss. A doctor tells a patient that
she has cancer and will soon die—then later finds out that the patient
committed suicide. Or we drive the car in which someone else dies. We
can bear some guilt, some responsibility for the tragedy that follows. In the
process of our grieving, our task is to sort out how responsible we actually
are—and eventually, what we can do about our residual guilt.

Forgiveness and restitution are only possible when the amount of
responsibility assumed matches as closely as possible our true responsibility. *In holding on, that's not possible.* We take on too much. Arthur
struggled with his responsibility after his daughter Joanne died of Cystic
Fibrosis, a genetically inherited disease:

> *Every day, I feel so riddled with guilt. If only I had been there at the
> time. If only we had some warning. If only I didn't have genetic
> predisposition. There must have been something I could have
> done. Sometimes I feel that if I could suffer enough myself, Joanie
> would come back. I wish I was that powerful. I know I'm not.*

Omissions are also hard to reconcile. We replay "if only" records in
our heads—partly magical thinking, partly reviewing, partly taking on
responsibility. "I didn't know how bad she felt" was Vince's cry after his
girlfriend committed suicide. "If only I had asked her that evening. If only
I hadn't been so long in getting back to her on the phone." Being more
aware of and responsive to what's happening with the people around us
may be an eventual solution to our guilt. We may find we will dedicate
ourself to being more aware in the future—or we may discover that our
sensitivity may only have delayed the inevitable, not prevented it.

Focus on the past

I wish things were the way they were before this loss occurred.

The memories of the way we were before the loss happened are
precious. We spend hours recalling them because they tell us of what it is
we wish to cherish—the essence of what was. When we are holding on,
our memory of past times tends to be selective—focused mainly on the
positives. "I always thought Henry was a good person, only to hear Meg

talk, you'd think he was a saint!" was Mike's comment after spending time with the widow of his best friend. We wish things were the way they were before the loss occurred. We also wish to recapture the sense of innocence we had back then, the belief that everything was right with the world— or at least in our lives.

Emotional Aspects of Holding On

Fear, anger, guilt and a desperate need to control our feelings are dominant ways we respond emotionally when we're trying to hold on. We're angry about the loss. We're also afraid of what it means. We fear that we were responsible for what happened, or that we've been disloyal since. We keep our feelings focused on ways we can overcome the loss. Likewise, we struggle to find ways to avoid being overwhelmed by their intensity. In doing all this, we act to keep alive what has been lost.

Anger/frustration

I am angry about this loss.

Anger represents our desire to destroy the source of our loss or its threat, often to make someone else feel as much hurt as we do. If our loss involves someone else's actions, we may want revenge, not mere justice. Anger can also be more half-hearted in its attempt. It's more a matter of frustration over the loss than a rage against it. When no one escalates our initial anger by the way they respond, our anger often loses its steam and gives way to the sadness just behind it.

Anxiety and fear

I'm scared to share what I've been thinking, feeling and doing.

I am scared by how unpredictable my feelings are.

We fear the awareness generated by the loss. These are fears of loneliness, helplessness and hopelessness, of unending suffering, of being reminded of our own mortality, and our capacity (or lack of it) to effectively grieve so that we can get over the loss. We even fear that we might forget what was lost.

Loss deprives us of security and predictability, which increases our anxiety. When we recognize its source, anxiety gives way to fear of the unknown future brought about by the loss.

Guilt

I feel guilty or disloyal when I forget this loss.

I feel guilty thinking about enjoying myself.

Guilt results from thinking we are responsible for our loss. It is a painful emotion from which there is little relief. We feel guilt over what happened or didn't happen. We may feel a need to be punished. Or we feel guilty for coping too well—and not suffering enough.

Holding on to guilt usually serves two purposes: It deflects us from awareness of what we lost by focusing on ourself, and it allows us to believe that events are controllable.

By focusing on ourself, we limit feeling helplessness. If only we had been good enough, it wouldn't have happened. Sometimes we think we've done the unforgivable—no punishment could ever be enough. On the other hand, we may think we're totally guilt free and that even thinking about it is nonsense, a letting go strategy. We may even bounce back and forth as we search to determine how guilty we feel for what happened and for how we're dealing with it.

Mistrust

I'm not sure I trust the feelings I have about what I did and/or didn't do before the loss happened.

There is a myriad of feelings at the time of the loss. We may feel proud that we did everything we could, only to feel guilt that we're focused on ourself and not at how everyone else was feeling. We may feel shocked at how helpless and paralyzed we were—ashamed to let anyone know we were such a coward. We may have felt relief that Mom was dying, only to realize we didn't really want that. We wanted an end to her suffering, or to the battles we'd had.

As a result, we may not trust our reactions during these times. We are at the mercy of our own emotional intensity and of unresolved issues coming to the fore. It's only with time that we become more trusting of ourself—or reconcile ourself to being unpredictable for a while longer.

Fear of craziness/helplessness

My feelings are so unpredictable I wonder if I am crazy.

My feelings are so intense I'm afraid I'm losing control.

Being in control helps me feel less overwhelmed.

We may have too many feelings coming at the same time, or one right after the other. We laugh and cry at the same time. We are furious one moment and loving the next. Many of us wonder if the emotional merry-go-round isn't evidence we're "cracking up."

This commonly happens in grief. When we're holding on, we question whether all the other feelings—of wanting to run away, of profound sadness—are real. They *are*—only they represent the emotional yo-yo that is grief. We're not just holding on to the belief that we can overcome the loss itself, we hold on to controlling the way we react to it. We're afraid that if we lose control, we'll be overwhelmed by our feelings. Feeling helpless, we'll do things that can complicate an already complex and perplexing situation. We struggle between the intensity of awareness and the need to function and protect ourself and others.

Controlling our emotionality

I try to hold back the tears.

I can't control my feelings when I'm with those who share my loss.

Unless something happens soon to change this, I don't know if I can control my feelings.

We don't want anyone to see how we are feeling. Men in particular resist sharing tears and showing how helpless they feel. Women tend to suppress their anger. Holding on means not expressing feelings, so we will often avoid persons and situations which would encourage us to open up. For a brief period, this is adaptive. If suppression of emotions becomes a long-term strategy, however, it invites stoppage of the grieving process.

We need to feel safe to let go of our feelings of grief. Eleanor found this out when her husband finally left after years of alienation in their marriage:

I felt guilty that I didn't seem to need to cry when he left me. It was more of a relief. Maybe I didn't really love him that much after all. Maybe our love died years ago. I remember crying about it then.

Vindication

I want someone punished for this loss.

When someone hurts us, we want to strike back. We want them to hurt as much—if not more—than we do. When we experience a loss, we may cope by wanting whoever was responsible for the loss punished for it. It infuriates us if we see those persons seemingly unaffected by our loss, as happens when family members overhear the nurse or the doctor laughing in the hall after a loved one has died.

Vigilance and obsessing

I am afraid to think about anything else except my loss.

I'm afraid I'll forget my loss if I stop thinking about it.

Loyalty to the ones we love is an important part of the bonds we form with them. When a loss threatens or occurs, we can become so focused on it that everything else ceases to exist. We become vigilant for signs of reversal or disconfirmation—hoping against hope. We can't leave the bedside of a dying loved one, for fear they will die in our absence. We are hypersensitive to every twitch and ache in our chest after a heart attack, wondering if this is the end.

After the loss has happened, we often feel afraid that we'll forget it. In part that's because we'd like to ignore its existence. We know that eventually other things will demand our time and attention. We have to get back to work, to the kids, etc. It's particularly hard when others can't get away from their grief when we can:

Rod and Marlee lost their daughter Andrea at the age of ten. Rod had to go back to work the day after the funeral. Marlee stayed home. Rod talked about his fears of forgetting three months later:

Every day I can go to the office and get absorbed in my work. I like what I do. It requires me to think, to be assertive with other people. I enjoy it. I can go whole days not even thinking about Andrea. When I come home and see Marlee, who's spent the whole day being reminded of Andrea everywhere she goes in the house, in everything she does, I get scared. Didn't I love her? Why is it so easy for me to forget her? Will I forget her? It would be horrible if I did.

Sometimes I wish I could be the one to stay home, to have to face the memories day after day. Then at least I'd know how important she was to me—as painful as I know that would be.

Determination

Nothing is going to rob me of my feelings about this loss.

I'm not ready to let go of my feelings about what happen.

We often measure the significance of a loss by the intensity and length of our feelings. When we lose the love of our life, there is a part of us that wishes to hold on forever to these feelings. Our sense of devotion or loyalty seems to demand we *not* get beyond this loss, because no loss could be greater.

Determination protects us from the deepest pain of grief by keeping us focused outside ourself. We figure that we'd rather hold on to the past than risk moving forward to a life we fear will never have such love in it again. Indeed, it might not, especially if we can't let go of the past.

Others may be uncomfortable with our determination and with the feelings we keep on having. They wonder how much crying we need to do, how often we have to get angry about it. Sometimes we even catch ourselves thinking we should get over this, only to realize how many ways our life has changed, and how unfair it seems. Shouldn't we be getting over our rage about the incest, even though we've just become consciously aware of it thirty years later?

Sometimes it's not a matter of the length of time we feel as it is having *at least one opportunity to feel it fully*. It may not help much to beat on pillows if we're angry enough to kill someone for what they did to us. We need some way to safely express that rage fully, to the point of exhaustion. Our sense of integrity won't release our feeling until it's had that fullness of expression.

Physical Aspects of Holding On

Grieving is often a physically demanding and exhausting process. *By extension, holding on is the most intense coping strategy physically.* We will expend whatever effort it takes to overcome or control this loss, or to move on from it. Through intense exercise, sexual activity and other methods, we may be finding ways to "self-medicate"—releasing the body's pleasure sources, the endorphins and enkephalins.

Extend our physical capacities

> I've increased my exercise.
>
> I ignore the physical pain to keep going.

One coping technique is to find ways to physically express and prepare ourself for the stresses of grief. On one side, we'll let our bodies do the work of resisting awareness, a form of holding on. We won't let ourself stop and fully experience the emotional pain, which is a way to let go. We exercise like mad to muffle our feelings. Manny found relief from his divorce by exercising:

> *I knew on some level for years before divorcing Claire that it would be one of the most stressful periods of my life. Long before I left, I started running. I built up to ten miles a day. While I was running, I felt good. I didn't even think about Claire. They say exercise gives*

you an endorphin high—they're your body's "don't worry, be happy" fix.

When the divorce became final, I was up to running marathons. Here I was, in the most painful life experience I'd ever be through, and I felt as if I was on top of the world—floating along, seemingly without a care in the world. At least it gave me a break from what it was like the rest of the time.

We start that exercise program with a vengeance. We ignore pain so we can keep going. We use our bodies as a way to distract us from our losses—holding on to our bodies while letting go of our feelings.

Hypersexual or celibate

Sex gets my mind off the loss.

I keep myself from having sex.

I don't feel like I am a sexual creature.

In holding on, sex is either a great distraction or something we discipline ourselves to avoid. Like exercise, sexual release can give us respites of pleasure. Sometimes we can pretend that nothing has changed because while making love we feel the same. This is often when some people replace a lost partner with a new one "on the rebound."

Making love can likewise bring us too close to what we've lost, so celibacy becomes the coping strategy. "The one thing that was uniquely ours was our lovemaking," replied Charlene, discussing her late husband. "I would feel disloyal to him if I had sex with someone else—at least right now."

In addition to threatening feelings of loyalty, sex may be avoided because lovemaking would stimulate weakly suppressed sadness over the lost loved one. Celibacy can be the result of fear of new intimacies and the risk of more loss. If rejection or abandonment was involved in the loss, we may feel unworthy and unlovable. We may not be so much committed to celibacy as we are feeling asexual or unattractive. We may also feel virtuous by being celibate, another way to experience pleasure and distraction from our loss.

Breathing difficulties

I have times when it's hard to breathe.

I have panic attacks.

When we try desperately to stay in control, we may try to choke back the tears and the sadness. We may constantly feel a tightness in our throat as we hold back the wish to yell or scream. In so doing, we may alter our breathing and create a sense of panic and anxiety. It's only when we can allow expression of these feelings that our breathing stabilizes and our fear of repeated episodes diminishes. Often we have moments of panic when we are in public, or must otherwise control our feelings. Sometimes they come in the middle of the night, when our defenses are down. Matt described several instances of panic in the first six months after his daughter was killed in a car accident:

> *It usually happens when I am driving some place alone. I flash on Mindy, start to choke back the tears and then I can't breathe. It feels like I am dying. I've had to stop the car and pull off the road.*

"Keep breathing" is an important admonition to those in grief. During such a panic attack, it's helpful to have a friendly hand on the shoulder, encouragement to breathe deeply—and most importantly the permission and safety to cry, even sob uncontrollably.

Changed appearance

My weight has changed.

I don't eat as much.

It's obvious to others I'm upset.

I am sleeping less.

We can't engage in the high level of energy expenditure that holding on demands without it showing in a variety of ways. We work much too hard. We lose or gain weight without even trying.

Because our thoughts have been so active in trying to solve this loss, we often have trouble getting to sleep or staying asleep. We keep thinking about what's happened, and are afraid that if we let down our guard we'll lose control. We decide that giving up sleep is the lesser of two evils—being exhausted is better than being aware of our loss.

Spiritual Aspects of Holding On

The spiritual theme of holding on is *survival:* to overcome that threat, or to live until we can find a more effective way to deal with it. Our dreams may try to convince us no loss has happened. We maintain that the loss holds in it some inherent meaning or purpose, even if we have no idea what they are. We believe we can overcome the loss by our greatest virtues and beliefs, or that this loss merely is a test of our inherent goodness. We remain optimistic in holding on—that something good will come out of this. Or we believe that there is some higher spiritual power giving us a test, but we will survive after all. We search for this meaning and purpose like a student in a library—it's just sitting there waiting for us to find it if we use all the right methods.

Dreams

> I dream that it never happened.

> I dream that something has happened to reverse my loss.

Dreams often occur that involve seeing the lost person or object as if still alive or returning:

> *There were many nights for a while after our separation that I would have vivid, intense dreams that she was lying in bed next to me, or saying to me "I miss you." Some of these dreams were so vivid as to be called lucid—they woke me up, yet I could still feel her physical presence in bed with me.*

Looking for a rescuer

> It would help if someone could help me understand this.

Thinking that some people or ideals are better, stronger, or special can be a response to a loss. Someone or something can provide a way to avoid our grief. Perhaps by associating with these special people, religions or ideals, we will overcome our loss.

When the rescuer disclaims or betrays special status or powers, we're angry. People who have life-threatening illness, for example, may refuse to believe there is no cure. They may withdraw from mainstream medicine for unproven alternative treatments, looking for one that promises cure. Sometimes this is normal coping: When the illness can't be reversed, grief is the result.

> *I know my chances of surviving are slim, but I just can't lie down and give up. I have to try everything that has a chance. I keep hoping that someone will come up with a cure before it's my turn.*

When it becomes an avoidance of dealing with dying, however, grieving may stop.

Beliefs confirmed

> Life seems unfair.
>
> I believe if people could love each other, no one would have to suffer.
>
> I believe something good will happen.

The philosophy of holding on is optimism. Life may seem unfair, only deep down we're hoping it will even out in the long run. We're not giving up yet—not by a long shot. We remain convinced that:

- *we have the capacity to overcome any crisis*

- *we can outlast any intruder*

- *our hard work will overcome anything*

- *we can find and maintain meaningful and supportive relation-ships*

- *we can believe in people's inherent good and trustworthiness*

- *we will not be tested beyond our capacity to endure*

This optimistic system of belief can extend our capacity to overcome loss to include belief in the miraculous, hope for a rescuer, or that we can hold out long enough for someone or something else to save the day.

Cycles

> There are times it seems I am going through the same thing again.

This loss reminds us of some other experiences we've had, or perhaps ones we've heard about. Sometimes one loss produces repeated reactions and challenges to our beliefs. "I thought I'd already dealt with my issues about mortality," commented Jim after his dad died, two years after he lost a brother. "It seems I'm facing it all over again."

Beliefs challenged

> I wonder if I deserve what I have.

If we've lived our lives believing that effort gets rewarded and that sins get punished, it's logical at the time of a loss to believe that we're getting what we deserve—or that we've had it too good. Most of us can come up with some excessiveness in our lives to feel guilty about, especially at a time of a loss. Such wondering may distract us from our loss. They certainly don't bring much comfort.

Hold on/survive

I am not able to forgive those who contributed to this loss.

I won't give up.

I won't accept that this loss has happened.

Holding on wouldn't be holding on if it made it easy for us to let go, to move on, to accept what's happened. It's the part of us that fights change, resists integration and denies the comfort of forgiveness. We'll go on living, in spite of how bad things are.

"I've always known I was a survivor" is a comment often made by people who are coping by holding on. We keep going, sometimes wondering why we live a life devoid of meaning, pleasure and intimacy. We're waiting for something to happen—only we're not sure what it is anymore. We must make it to a time and a place where we'll feel safe enough, strong enough to fully experience this loss.

Seek justice

I will make those responsible pay for this.

It's a natural desire to see those who contributed to or created our loss be held responsible for their actions. It may be less a desire for revenge than it is an issue of justice and fairness. Revenge avoids grief by creating an "eye for an eye" mentality that invites further revenge in return—a cycle that can go on for generations. In normal coping, the purpose is to insure that this won't happen again to someone else, or to honor our responsibility to the loss.

Believe in the reversibility of the loss

I'm looking for a way out of this loss.

This loss must be changed.

From the time we were young, we believed that losses could be reversed. Indeed, sometimes they are—almost miraculously. When miracles are possible, our tendencies to hold on become reinforced. We'll continue to look for a way out. We'll try to reverse the loss—yet we'll not do so at the price of our integrity.

Presence of the lost person

I sense the presence of the lost person.

It's a common experience to believe we've seen or felt the presence of departed loved ones. "Ghosts" form the substance of many mysterious stories that seem to defy reality. Colin Murray Parkes (1969) found that over two-thirds of the widows he interviewed had felt some kind of connection with their deceased spouse.

Many people are reluctant to talk about these experiences, for fear of being labeled crazy or eccentric. For some, the felt presence of a loved one is a respite from the painful grief over their loss. Sometimes these experiences reassure the bereaved of some unfinished business between them—permission to go on living, to get into new relationships, reminders of special memories.

Grieving may stop, however, when the bereaved believes in the *real* presence of the departed, or that contact with the spirit world is preferable to dealing with the real one. Such approaches invalidate the need for grief because it is believed that nothing has been lost.

Letting Go: Flight or Escape

> *He died in exile; like all men, he was given bad times in which to live.*
>
> *—Jorge Luis Borges*

> *I felt like withdrawing from everyone. I was sure they would want to know, to even offer support, except every time I would end up helping them with their grief. I don't want to be reminded. I wanted some time out, some time away from helping <u>others</u> deal with <u>my</u> loss.*
>
> *—Marianne, fifty, after the sudden death of her husband.*

As a part of the natural ebb and flow of grief, letting go balances holding on. One uses energy; the other conserves it. One is overly optimistic; the other excessively pessimistic. One romanticizes our best self. The other denies its existence. Between them, they can maximize our capacity to grieve *and* survive.

Letting go is a way to conserve energy by prematurely releasing attachments—just the opposite of energy-demanding holding on. It is essentially a *flight from the reality of the loss* rather than a fight, which defines holding on. Like holding on, letting go is an early phase in grieving, often mistaken by others around us as a sign that we've "gotten over" the loss. In fact, we haven't really resolved the loss, as we shall see.

Basic to letting go/flight is our desire to be rid of attachments that no longer work. To do this, we deny or diminish the significance of the loss or else we continue in an unhappy situation lacking meaning or purpose.

In pulling away from our attachments, we believe that no matter how hard we try, fate, God, or powerful others will determine the outcome. "It's just the universe telling me I shouldn't be in this relationship" was the reason Jane gave for precipitously leaving her marriage. Such comments minimize our sense of responsibility, limit our guilt and permit us to distance ourself from the actual or potential loss.

Much in life cannot be controlled. By recognizing limits, we can adapt to change and limit our frustrations. We need to let go of unrequited love, unrealistic goals, unwarranted assumptions, and mistaken priorities. We need to protect ourself by not becoming too attached to transient relationships or to someone else's dreams. We might even need to explore the possibility that the lost relationships, roles or dreams weren't very important, to protect us from how overwhelming their loss feels at other times.

Eventually we'll find out the true meaning of what we've lost. In the meantime, letting go gives us a break. It allows us to pretend that we don't care so much about it, that it could have been worse, that there's no use worrying about it right now. It *validates* our helplessness and how hopeless it is to try to change what's happened. It gives us permission to conserve our energy, to withdraw, and to find some ways to feel good in the short run.

Letting go can also permit us to focus exclusively on the negative aspects of the loss so that we can distance ourselves from it. Unlike holding on, letting go allows us to admit the loss exists. It's just that we insist it wasn't so important after all. We look for reasons to ignore our grief.

Fear is a major motivating factor in flight or letting go responses to loss. We're afraid that if we try and fail to prevent the loss, we'll be consumed by a sense of incompetence, shame, helplessness and guilt. We're afraid that if we acknowledge the significance of the loss, we won't survive. We fear being trapped and paralyzed by our grief.

In our desperation to escape a loss, we may lack access to our best self. We may not see it in others. We look "realistically" at our world and ourself and conclude there is no such thing as heroes, virtue or truly good people as a way to protect ourself from expecting too much. While letting go, we note with satisfaction when some respected political figure is caught with his pants down or her fingers in the till. We see the hate, evil, lust and greed in human nature.

During these times, we may begin to build a case against the lost relationship. We develop a knack for seeing the negatives in everyone and everything. We also reinforce our rationalizations for our coping strategies as another way to avoid looking within and getting into the deeper issues behind the loss.

We look at ourselves and conclude we can't make it if we admit how much our life has been destroyed by this loss. So we escape from too much reality by distracting ourself or minimizing its significance. Or we may deny the dark side and seek only light—which becomes shallow and transparent. After all, we will all die—so what difference will this make?

Sometimes our ambivalence about holding on to a relationship or letting it go is so profound that we remain paralyzed until some event (the famous "last straw") frees us or else the ambivalence itself becomes the pattern of the relationship. Letting go can take place if after enough time, it becomes clear that the relationship no longer has growth potential or mutual satisfaction. Letting go validates that hope is limited.

Figure 4-2 lists some of the strategies that characterize flight-escape-letting go:

Figure 4-2: Dimensions of Letting Go/ Flight

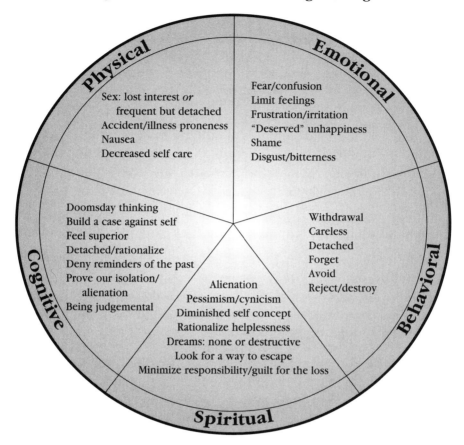

Behavioral Aspects of Letting Go

Although the purpose of flight is to conserve energy and avoid conflict, frequently we withdraw from self-care activities. We may stop exercise programs, eat improperly, neglect hygiene. We couldn't care less. We may withdraw from or reject our most significant sources of support. We indiscriminately withdraw energy from our world.

Withdrawal

I avoid telling anyone what I'm thinking, feeling and/or doing.

I avoid people who remind me of this experience.

I'm less patient with people.

I refuse to discuss this loss.

I don't see much of my old friends.

I don't spend as much time with my family.

Withdrawal can involve physical isolation, drugs, alcohol, aloofness, or indifference. We make sure the loss cannot affect us by not getting involved with anyone or anything. We hide from others the real impact that the loss is having on us. We're afraid of showing our vulnerability for fear no one will respond or we'll face further rejection.

The people we are most likely to avoid are those we associate with the loss. Parents avoid each other after a child dies, fearful of seeing the other's grief, ashamed of their own response. We don't want to talk with friends who are sympathetic—we even convince ourselves that they didn't care enough. Adam tried to drive away his friends after his wife left him with their three children:

> *I don't understand why I did it. I told my best friend to get out of my life, to stop bothering me, that I didn't need her anymore, that I didn't need anybody or anything. Thank God she didn't listen and hung in there with me. I sure gave her much abuse during that time—and she gave some of it back to me. I wasn't so fortunate with some of my other friends.*

Carelessness

I've been careless.

Sometimes we deliberately go out of our way to prove we don't care what happens to us. We drive without regard. We take unnecessary chances. We go to dangerous places, do risky things.

Detachment

I act as though this doesn't matter to me.

I avoid getting involved in anything.

To limit our vulnerability, we pretend we don't care. We may even develop an elaborate rationale for why it doesn't bother us. We act detached from everything.

Forgetting

I drink to forget my loss.

I use drugs to forget my loss.

I lose or misplace things that relate to this loss.

Unlike the forgetting characteristic of holding on, forgetting in letting go allows us to ignore our duties, commitments, anniversaries, and appointments. Forgetting reflects our desire to eliminate awareness of the loss. Examples of such forgetting:

- *Forget to make a will during terminal illness*

- *Not attend a funeral of a friend, spouse, parent*

- *Misplace letters, photos, etc. that are reminders of the past*

We may be good at convincing others that the loss is forgettable. We may not be so good with ourself. So we escape into addictions of various kinds—alcohol, sex, rescuing others, drugs—to mask reality. Ron sought such an escape:

When I found out I lost my job, I went out and got drunk. I figured, what the hell. I won't be able to make the house payment anyway, so why not have a little fun while I still can.

Alcohol and drugs can be temporary escapes during stressful times. They are dangerous when used too systematically. They can work too well in helping us forget.

Avoidance

I've put away anything that could remind me of this loss.

I avoid reminders of this loss.

I have kept secret what happened.

Not only do we avoid people, we avoid any reminders. We might drive blocks out of our way going to work, so we don't have to drive past a cemetery, an old rendezvous, the place where our "ex" works. We put away or throw away anything associated with the loss.

A part of this avoidance can involve keeping the loss a secret. This happens frequently when the loss involves something we're ashamed of. It also happens when we're unprepared to deal with others' responses. Sometimes we fear they won't believe us, or that they will judge us. Sometimes we hide what's happened because we fear the consequences and by hiding, we can delay the inevitable reaction a while longer.

Long-standing secrets take on a life of their own. People who have been sexually molested in childhood may keep it secret because they fear for their lives, and later fear that the perpetrator, often a member of the family, may die or be hurt if they let it be known.

We may be selective about who knows and who doesn't. For example, parents may not want their children to know they had an abortion, figuring that if they don't know, they won't experience a sense of loss—of a sibling or of their image of their parents.

Rejection/destruction

I can be physically abusive when others remind me of the loss.

I can be verbally abusive when others remind me of this loss.

Reminders of a loss can be so painful at times that we strike out at others. We feel cornered, unable to escape the reminder, so we react by trying to destroy the reminder. It's usually a momentary reaction, followed by regret and guilt. It's often an ineffective defense because it can create other losses in its wake.

Cognitive Aspects of Letting Go

We might use our thinking to help distract us from what happened, to diminish the impact of the loss and our response. Our goal is to delay having to do something about it. We may "build a case" to prove we don't have to grieve this loss.

Doomsday thinking

Something else is going to go wrong.

If I get too happy, something bad will happen.

I cannot imagine how anything positive could come out of this loss.

One way to diminish the impact of a loss is to convince ourself that it is one of many bad things in life. We convince ourself that the best way to prepare for life's disappointments is not to expect too much, especially not happiness or permanency.

In some instances, it's not that we *can't* imagine the positive while we're letting go, it's that *we won't*. We resist and reject suggestions that there might be something positive.

Building a case against ourself

This loss is evidence that I have failed as a person.

If a loss happens because we failed to do something, we usually feel guilt. Eventually, we'll feel moved to do something to address the extent of our responsibility. This represents coping by holding on and later restitution as a part of integrating our loss.

But when we are letting go, we tend to generalize our failure to prevent a loss as a sign of failure as a person—there is no restitution, no forgiveness without a total change of self, or personhood. Such thinking can temporarily be helpful in distracting us from a loss and give us a sense of control. In the long run, we need ways to refute its message, or to limit our sense of failure to our actions or inactions, not our personhood.

Feeling superior

> If I don't look out for myself, no one else will.
>
> I deserve a better deal than I'm getting.
>
> Very few people are worth my time and energy now.
>
> I'm better off without it/him/her.

"I gave myself a pity-party, and nobody came," smirked Laura, who had suffered through a job loss, battles with her oldest son and her husband's extramarital affair. "That's all right. I can take care of myself." Laura was looking out for herself by feeling superior—she didn't need anybody else. She was above it all.

It's not unusual to feel superior at a time of significant loss. We know something about life that others, in their naiveté and innocence, haven't experienced. We believe that those who do not share our loss aren't worth our time, nor do they appreciate what's going on. We convince ourself we're better off—we're so much freer not to have to concern ourself with them.

Detachment/rationalization

> No one can change what's already happened.
>
> No matter what I do, what will happen will happen.
>
> I lack the energy to make sense out of it.
>
> Even if I could understand why it happened, it wouldn't change anything.

Feeling superior, of course, is one way to detach ourself from others. Believing in fate, luck and powerful others also permits detachment and resignation. They are too powerful for us. We are helpless victims in a universe we had no hand in creating, in lives and bodies randomly assigned to us. From a letting go perspective, we think understanding is useless because it can't change anything—it can't bring back the loss. However, this is not to be confused with a deeper understanding and acceptance that comes much later in the process.

Avoid the past

It's best not to dwell on the past.

It's easier when I can forget what happened.

If understanding is futile in letting go, then dwelling on the past is worthless, too. What good does it do? We can't go back. All we have is today, so forget what's over and done with. Get the past behind us as quickly as we can—especially if it contains reminders of our own weakness or destructiveness.

Isolation/alienation

Nobody understands how this loss affects me.

Nobody cares how this loss affects me.

Letting go types of thinking are designed to demonstrate how alone and miserable we are in this world. We look for evidence that people don't understand us and don't care about how this loss is affecting us. Of course, we find it. We put people to the test and many, if not all, of them fail it at one time or another. We're distracted from our loss by the more controllable and soothing feeling of self-pity.

Being judgmental

My thinking has been critical and judgmental.

I've rejected others' ideas about the loss.

I've focused on the present.

Our thinking can become very self-centered, protecting us against letting anyone or anything be important to us. We focus on the present, with little concern or regard for the past or the future. We reject ideas that might help us understand the loss. We're critical and judgmental. We're out to prove that nothing can help; that nobody cares; that our best self no longer exists; that nothing matters anyway. We even set things up to prove that no one can profit from looking at the loss any more.

Table 4-1: Beliefs Supporting Letting Go

Eat, drink and be merry, for tomorrow may never come.

Why get involved? You just get hurt.

Don't rock the boat. You'll get noticed.

It's God's will. Learn to accept it.

Nobody cares about me. Why should I care about anyone else?

Why try? It won't make any difference.

Easy come, easy go.

There's no such thing as a free ride.

I'm better off without him.

The good die young.

Out of sight, out of mind.

What the eye doesn't see, the heart doesn't remember.

What did I tell you? You can't trust anybody.

It's best to forget it. There's nothing you can do about it.

Do your own thing.

If you're too happy, something bad will happen.

Fate is against me.

To succeed is to die.

Don't settle for less than perfection.

Emotional Aspects of Letting Go

The emotions of letting go are *distancing* and *protecting* emotions. They represent our attempts to limit the full impact of feelings like sadness, helplessness and loneliness. We're trying to keep from awareness how bad this loss is—how much it hurts. Fear, frustration, shame and disgust are a major part of the way we feel when we try to let go, if we feel anything at all. The feelings that do get through are ones that give us a sense of distance and control. We look down on others, irritated by their pettiness. We're disgusted—an emotion that puts us in the driver's seat. *Our* judgment rules the day. Even when we feel ashamed, it is a way to stay isolated from others' judgment. Or we are too busy judging ourselves, determining our own punishment—unremitting unhappiness.

Confusion

I feel confused and disoriented.

I feel overwhelmed.

If we're convinced that understanding what's happened is futile, we won't have to know a lot about our feelings. As a result, on occasion we are likely to feel confused, overwhelmed and unpredictable. Our worst fear is that we're going crazy.

Limit feelings

> I try not to let anything affect me.
>
> I avoid feeling too sad about this.
>
> I feel detached and separate from others.
>
> I feel dissatisfied with everything.
>
> I feel bored with life.
>
> I refuse to wallow in self-pity.

In letting go, we try to minimize. When we're effective at this, we feel distant from our feelings. We can limit our sadness. We aren't happy, either, and that makes us dissatisfied and often bored. Still, we don't want to be seen as being affected by this.

Frustration/irritation

> People irritate me easily.
>
> I get angry at myself.
>
> I feel frustrated.
>
> I'm fed up with spending so much time on this.

When we're defensive, we're easily irritated, for people can get too close to the truth and to our feelings for comfort. Like a porcupine, we send out messages not to get too close. We also want this "grief stuff" to be over. We're frustrated that it takes so long.

"Deserved" unhappiness

> If I let myself, I get so unhappy I can't stand it.
>
> I deserve punishment for what I contributed to this loss.

It's hard to be happy after a loss. When we're in a period of letting go, we may be convinced we don't deserve to be happy. We may even feel that being punished will make us feel better, clear the air.

Shame

> I get upset with myself for the way I have behaved.
>
> I'm ashamed of the way I've behaved.

Shame is a feeling we have in response to what we do, or fail to do. We may have contributed to the loss. We may have reacted poorly in the time since the loss. People may blame us, judge us, or shun us as a result. Friends may also be unable to break through our protective shield of self-blame. For example, Mary loved Joe, in spite of their numerous arguments and disagreements. He suffered from post-traumatic stress disorder, the result of being in an auto accident where his best friend was killed. Episodically he was explosively abusive, especially when he had been drinking. Mary eventually broke off the relationship, refusing to see him:

> *I couldn't let him know how much I cared about him. It hurt too much, knowing I could do nothing to take away his pain. So I pretended not to care. I was ashamed of myself for the way I treated him. I couldn't face him, knowing how much I hurt him.*

Shame may result from an inability to maintain an image of perfection in a role, a failure to complete a mission, being defeated in competition, or from not realizing our potential. Whenever our goals or dreams are known by others and we fail to achieve them, we may feel a sense of shame or fear ridicule. Men in particular aren't supposed to fail, or, in failing, show grief. They aren't supposed to mourn over the loss of relationships, especially ones with other men. Men bring further shame upon themselves by being a poor loser, a "sentimental wimp," or by showing vulnerability, sadness or helplessness. As a result, loss for men is often associated with failure, disability, impotence, helplessness—and shame.

Losses such as unemployment, poor school performance, being unable to provide necessities for family or not living up to role expectations combine powerful forms of loss and shame for men. It is often the helplessness that accompanies loss that creates the greatest difficulty for men. Showing helplessness in an environment that is hostile or competitive can be destructive, if not physically, at least to self-esteem by subjecting them to ridicule. In some cultures shame can become so extreme that suicide is considered an honorable recourse.

As stated earlier, shame itself can produce further losses by threatening our sense of self or destroying our curiosity and our feeling of innocence. Viewing ourself through the prism of shame, we may discount the significance of our grief process and poorly judge our intentions concerning the loss. In the most extreme case, accepting shame and failing to grieve, our will to live erodes.

Disgust/bitterness

> I am revolted by the way people have responded.

> It disgusts me to think of how it happened.

It's sometimes hard to distinguish disgust from anger. Both are feelings intent on ridding us of something we don't want to accept. Anger tends to see the danger as something external—eliminating it will solve the problem. Disgust sees the danger as something internal—we wish to rid ourself of the internal reminder of our loss.

Disgust is such a feeling of revulsion we can even feel nauseous with it. We'd like to throw up to expel the poisonous loss that is transforming our lives.

Bitterness is a lingering feeling of betrayal often associated with lost assumptions and beliefs. It reminds us of our naiveté that we once believed in something that didn't come true.

Physical Aspects of Letting Go

Changes in sexual frequency

> I am not interested in sex if it means getting involved.

> I've had more sex with more people.

> I don't want to be touched.

Sex without intimacy is an ages-old escape from loss. So is the decision to avoid sex, if it means intimacy.

We may even avoid being touched, for fear of the feelings it will arouse. Sometimes we associate sex and affection with a particular person or time of our lives. We don't want to be reminded of what's gone by being touched. "I didn't date during that whole time I was in graduate school," confessed Gale, who had broken up with his fiancee Eileen just before starting. "I didn't want to have to deal with all the feelings it would have stirred up about Eileen. I wasn't ready to deal with them."

Proneness to accidents or illness

> I get hurt more.

> I'm more clumsy and accident prone.

> I am sick a lot.

Physically, when we let go, we're wanting to eliminate anything that demands extra energy. We want to feel good in the present, at any price. If we're feeling pain, we'll do anything to our bodies to eliminate it. We get sick easily—our immune system isn't as alert and responsive to infections. We don't have the energy to expend.

Nausea/disgust

> I have felt sick to my stomach.
>
> There is a bitter taste in my mouth.

Nausea and bitter taste are the physical parts of the feelings of disgust and bitterness. They are the physical side of trying to rid ourself of something we believe is poisoning us—our loss.

Decreased self care

> I exercise less.
>
> I sleep more.
>
> I don't watch what I eat.

During times of letting go, we are less involved in almost everything. We don't care about our health. We can't be bothered with disciplining ourselves to exercise, sleep regularly, watch our diets.

Spiritual Aspects of Letting Go

If the attitudes we hold during times of letting go were all we had, we'd lack a desire to live. We wouldn't invest in anything. Love, meaning and hope would be empty. Without access to our best self, we'd give up easily. Yet we sometimes need the protection of pessimism and detachment. We've run aground from too much optimism in a world that does contain evil forces, where bad luck, fate and accidents take away our attachments. We have to pull back and divest ourself of the old before we can find out whether there is enough left worth living for. The spiritual theme in letting go is just that: *let go.*

Paul was forced to examine his own trustfulness after his wife was raped by his best friend:

> *I realize for the first time—if that could happen, what else? How naive to trust anybody or anything. Never again.*

After a loss, we would sometimes like to rid ourself of the ideals, beliefs and values that made us vulnerable:

> • *If we hadn't loved, we wouldn't be hurting now.*
>
> • *If we hadn't trusted, we wouldn't have been betrayed.*

• *If we hadn't hoped and dreamed, we wouldn't be disappointed.*

• *If humans didn't have these damned emotions, we'd be better off.*

Christine found herself letting go of hope—twenty years after her husband had been declared missing in action:

> *The image I had held—that there was light at the end of the long lonely path—the image was fading. I couldn't see the light anymore. There was no more hope.*

We're certain now that we see things as they are. For the first time perhaps, we see how shallow our lives have been. We criticize our church, family, job, country, educational system, neighborhood. We're convinced that there are no heroes or good people who do not have feet of clay; there are no values that endure. We are finally being "honest" with ourself and everyone else. We reject pledges of trust, commitment, hope or growth. Scott found himself bitter in the months after being forced into an early retirement at the university he'd served for thirty years:

> *I became a cynic in the months after they terminated me. After all I had done—all the hard work. I had been much too believing, much too trusting. Every chance I got, I showed my bitterness. I would put down with scorn and derision anyone who said anything positive about the university.*

Looking for a way to escape

I wish I could be saved from having to deal with this experience.

During letting go, we're always looking for a way out. We'll take any way out of this loss, to escape, even if it is temporary. We'll try drinking, running away, whatever promises us distraction or avoidance—almost anything to save us from the inevitable reality of this loss.

Pessimism/cynicism

I doubt that anything or anyone can give my life meaning again.

I wonder what point there is in going on.

I can't imagine anyone ever being as important to me.

No one could ever pay enough for causing this loss to happen.

I've given up believing that my life has any particular significance.

My life doesn't seem to have a purpose.

As we explore the extent of our losses, we may come up with very similar versions of these statements, wondering if life has any meaning. When we explore these possibilities from a letting go perspective, we're likely to be convinced that life has no meaning, that there is no point in going on, or that no one can ever be as important—it's not open for debate.

Alienation

It's hard for me to trust anybody.

Nobody cares how I am doing.

During times of letting go, it's hard to let anyone near us. Closeness can bring painful memories. We feel betrayed or so different from others that no one could possibly understand how we feel—or even care to try.

Rationalize helplessness

Nothing has made any difference, so why bother?

There's no sense thinking or worrying about what happened.

I've realized that nothing could have prevented it.

It's one thing to have tried to figure out a loss and to conclude that further thought and worry are futile, and quite another to conclude the same without any effort at understanding or any attempts at prevention. The latter is characteristic of letting go.

Diminished self-concept

I've lost respect for myself.

I wonder if I'm a disgusting, worthless person.

If people important to me knew my contribution to this loss, they would be shocked.

When we lose our internal sense of our best self, these statements may reflect an awareness phase of our loss. When these statements result from our direct response to an external loss, they are more likely to represent coping by letting go. We may not have acted when action could have minimized or avoided the loss. We may have burned some bridges after the loss. We may continue to push people away, drink excessively, be verbally or physically abusive. We can complicate our grief by the way we respond to it.

Seeing ourself in a negative light is also a way to limit feelings of helplessness and the depth of hurt. If we could attribute the loss entirely to our own doing or lack of worth, then the solution is simple: we must be punished for the rest of our lives. As Margaret said a year after her husband divorced her: "I've had my one chance. I've screwed it up. I'll never date or marry again." When such statements are made in times of letting go, they are often later revised. When they are followed religiously, they block the grieving process.

Dreams—none or destructive

I don't remember any dreams.

I've had fantasies of being dead.

I dream that I destroyed what/who I lost.

Dreams are supposedly a window to our soul. When we are letting go, we're in touch with our destructive tendencies. We either remember nothing, or we find ourself a part of destroying something—ourself included. Our dreams may be doing for us what we can't consciously admit—that our ties to the loss, to old ways of relating, are dying.

We may consider destroying what has taken our loss from us. We would consider killing or fantasize the death of the person who murdered our loved one or the spouse who abandoned us. We don't run from our fantasies. We consider that we'd even be willing to die in the process. Indeed, we often hear about people who act on suicidal or homicidal impulses resulting from a previous loss.

I certainly don't endorse people acting out their destructive fantasies and dreams. Such behavior isn't normal coping, but a pathological form of defending against awareness. Having the fantasies, however, can be an effective way to cope.

Minimize

It wasn't my fault this happened.

No one can blame me for the way it turned out.

In holding on, we tend to exaggerate contributions to a loss—our own and those of others. In letting go, we minimize them. The truth lies somewhere in between, though we won't discover this until later.

Avoid responsibility

I can't be expected to be responsible at times like this.

I deserve to be taken care of, after what's happened.

Sometimes a loss is seen as a badge. Other people assume we have suffered when we've had a loss, so they often exempt us from responsibilities. As kids, we delighted in finding some excuse that would get us out of class or a chance to miss that piano lesson. As adults, that permission comes rarely, though it can come after a significant loss. During letting go periods of time, we may find ways to get others to absolve us of responsibility and to take care of us.

Consequences of Fight and Flight

Strategies for coping delay and give us times of relief and respite from our awareness and our need to process the loss. As in everyday life, they are natural and essential parts of grief—our capacity to adapt to changing times and to maintain what we value. Delay can mean waiting until adequate safety and resources exist to explore the loss.

The outgrowth is *survival*. Some ways of surviving until we can grieve are less functional than others. Some merely prevent us from enjoying life, nevertheless allowing us to be competent, able to work, or live a seemingly normal life. Some are extremely stressful, as if we're driving a car with both the brake and the gas pedal simultaneously pressed to the floor. Our way of surviving can be so profoundly dysfunctional that it prevents us from meeting our basic needs. Sometimes we find we'll do anything to avoid being on our own. We may be unable to find meaning in anything. Our wounds may turn us against or away from other human beings.

It may take years, even decades, before we have what is needed to complete the memory of a traumatic experience and begin the journey to trust ourself again—to regain our integrity and wholeness. An unintegrated loss can be complicated by a loss of a sense of self and an inability to experience the world fully. Yet it is the starting point for many who survive until they can find the safety and courage to make their losses real.

When should we worry about our ways of coping? Chapter Ten will discuss some of the problems we can get into with coping strategies that don't work, or work too well. How do we know we'll eventually get to what's troubling us?

If it's been our pattern to come back and deal with things later, it's likely we will do so with any significant loss. If we don't feel safe with sharing our experience, we may be wise not to share it until we find someone or some place to help us. Chapter Ten will suggests what needs to be available *before* grieving can take place.

It's also a matter of trusting that we will be able to deal with and fully resolve this loss for ourself. That may not be something we consciously choose. We may believe we're doing it the wrong way, that we are going crazy, that nobody believes in us. We may *look* as if we've succeeded in letting go of a bad relationship that we thought needs no grieving, but we're still thinking and dreaming about it. Something feels incomplete.

It's that sense of incompleteness that eventually brings us back to our grief and, hopefully, the grief issues of our entire life up to now. We're motivated to know the fullness of our life experiences. We want to honor the memory of our pasts, our involvement, what's made our life meaningful along the way.

We will grieve, eventually, if what we lost truly has meaning to us. It is the only way we can maintain our integrity.

Facilitating Coping

Validation is the principle intervention during most phases of grief. Coping is necessary, even vital to existence and the meaning in our lives. Sometimes we need *not* to question, *not* to understand, *not* to communicate or feel. The delicate interweaving of holding on, letting go and becoming aware of our losses is the process we use to *discover the extent of our loss*. When any of the three is absent, we struggle.

Sometimes professionals who misdiagnose normal grief can interfere by challenging our ways of coping, treating them as if they were pathological defenses rather than supporting and expanding them. On the other hand, therapists typically confront clients' defenses because they aren't functional anymore or because they are resistances to awareness. This is necessary when grieving stops or never begins.

Such approaches aren't necessary in normal grief. *During a loss, coping plays a protective role by limiting awareness.* We may be habituated to too few ways of coping and need to learn more ways. Instead of attacking, analyzing or otherwise invalidating our defenses, we need to validate and expand our need for them.

It's important to feel that we have some degree of control and choice in the ways we limit our awareness. Anxiety about why we are doing what we need to makes it hard to feel safe and be able to trust. Such a lack of trust can imply that something has gone wrong other than the loss—we aren't doing it the right, socially acceptable, or best way. If we don't trust ourself, we'll look to other people's answers to our loss, and fail to validate our own approaches.

For example, shame leaves us vulnerable to the judgment, ridicule, punishment and shunning of others. It can render us so helpless that we are at the mercy of others. It's most damaging when we experience judgment coming from those who are trying most to help us. At a time when we need to feel safe to explore our shame, we can be distracted by the views of those supposedly able to suspend their judgment. It places another step between us and our grief over what we have lost in the process.

Sometimes we need an authority or significant person to tell us we're not going crazy or that our shame is not entirely deserved. It helps to be able to know the difference between grief and depression, to recognize when we have become addicted to a particular way of coping, or when we cannot get past the time of the trauma. We may need to hear from "experts" that coping is normal, that forgiveness is possible and no one way is the best.

It can be very helpful to read or hear the stories of others who struggle like we do with a particular loss. It's reassuring to know we aren't the only ones who do crazy things in response to a loss—and that people do survive and reach some peace of mind.

Summary

Significant losses can be overwhelming. We can't take in the entire meaning at one time. We need times of respite and delay when we can focus on other things, and maintain and rebuild our lives. We need to know how to cope, to eventually get back on our feet. Our ways of coping are characterized by strategies that limit our awareness of loss: we hold on (fight) and we let go (flight). In some ways, we try to live only in our best self (holding on) or totally without it (letting go). Eventually, our sense of integrity will bring us together, able to measure the full extent of what we've lost.

Chapter Five
Awareness of Loss:
It Is As Bad As It Seems

There is no sun without shadows . . .
it is essential to know the night.

—*Albert Camus (1957)*

I follow'd rest;
rest fled and soon forsook me;
I ran from grief;
grief ran and overtook me.

—*Quarles,* Emblems *(1635)*

There came times when I had nothing left. I was empty, a shell. I
could see no hope, no future-—just pain, exhaustion. I realized my
children's love for me and mine for them was no longer enough.

I looked at death. For the first time I didn't fight it. I wasn't afraid.
A little disappointed, perhaps. Only a few months before I had so
much hope for me, for the future. The light at the end of the path
had gone. I saw only blackness right now. Death seemed almost
like a friend who would release me from my burden.

—*Michelle, 38, recently widowed.*

If we are to discover the light—what we have left and what we can do
with it—then discovery of what we have lost must precede it. Awareness of grief is joy's shadow. It measures the depth and breadth of our
attachments. During this time we comprehend that we will die someday.
We observe what is gone without the benefit of accomplishments or the
distraction of leading a meaningful life. Loneliness seems to have no limit,
no end.

We struggle against this cruel reality, fight it, and question its
fairness. Does anyone care? Can anyone know our grief?

The awareness phase of grief is:

• *A time of reckoning.*

• *A time to accede to limits.*

• *A time of emptiness.*

• *A time to acknowledge how much of our life is over.*

• *A time to mourn.*

• *A time of sadness.*

The phase of grief that is central to mourning is awareness—the most painful, lonely, helpless, and hopeless of times we will ever face. Whereas we were not able to admit the depth of our loss previously—with our coping strategies of holding on and letting go—we are now entering a time of deepest pain and suffering. If there's a time when we choose to live or die, it's in the awareness phase.

With any loss, awareness comes and goes. It is unexpectedly triggered by a memory of our loss. And it relaxes as we take a deep breath, sigh, and go on, doing what has to be done.

Awareness begins when our coping no longer protect us. While a normal part of the larger process of grief, holding on and letting go as coping strategies are not defined here as part of *active grieving*. It is not until we enter the awareness phase that we begin active grieving. We then begin to learn the *full extent* of what is missing in our lives.

When we cope, we try to overcome or minimize our loss, so when awareness begins we feel overwhelmed by the extent of our loss. All life lacks meaning. During the moments, hours, days and weeks of awareness, nothing else exists. Flooded by our feelings, we act deprived. We see only the empty spaces in our lives. We understand what can never be. But as we become aware, we come closer to the truth about the empty spaces— in bits and pieces. That truth will eventually help us gain perspective, but for now, we can't see the forest for the enormity of the trees.

It's not possible to be in awareness without it being a total experience physically, mentally, emotionally and spiritually. Sadness, pain and emptiness are experienced on many levels. These are the "pangs" of grief, episodes of realizing how completely alone we feel. At such moments we don't feel hope for regaining the loss. We know we can't return to a time before it occurred. But we can't yet move forward to a time when the loss can be contained. *This is a crisis of being.* We are aware of the fragility of life, the emptiness of the present, and that death—our death—will happen. Frieda Fromm-Reichmann (1952) portrayed this in her book, *Loneliness*, with this poem:

No one comes near here
Morning or night.
The desolate grasses
Grow out of sight.
Only the wild hare
Strays, then is gone.
The Landlord is silence
The Tenant is dawn.

The pangs of grief can occur for a few minutes after a favorite team has lost a game. Conversley, these pangs can also occur for days, weeks, even years when the loss is more extensive, such as when a spouse or child dies. The measure of our grief isn't in a particular moment, for awareness is always total. It's in the number of episodes, the time, the extent to which it radiates through our lives.

The times of awareness have as deep a sense of aloneness as we'll ever experience. As Clark Moustakas (1962) wrote:

Sometimes I wonder what will become of me .
My heart yearns for permanence which never can be .
I do not know a real face any more
And my compassion is misplaced .
The spontaneity and joy and continuity are gone.
Where is the beginning which remains?
Where is the heart which speaks only truth?
No where, no more, will I find commitment to meet mine.
To live a lie, to die of life, to search in failure—
Is this to be my destiny?

At such moments, if it were only up to us, we might not go on living. It takes something beyond us to make living worth the risk. Sometimes it's not there. At other times it is. Here are some examples:

Marion lived in pain for two years before she died of cancer. It was an empty existence after her husband left her.

John kept going because of his dog—who would take care of her?

Anne kept going because her son Mike needed her.

Mark had his work as a doctor. People needed him.

Angie held Chuck's hope for him.

Marlene had people who believed in her.

Dolores felt the presence of God—a personal savior.

George was curious—what else could happen?

In awareness hope is not found internally—it needs to come from beyond us. Hope can be *held by others* as we explore hopelessness. Hope comes from a grace we didn't know existed. "It's like a spiritual transfusion," Marty, a physician-rabbi, told me. "We couldn't make it on our own, so we have to find the blood of life outside us." In Figure 5-1 we see the various dimensions of the awareness phase of grieving, which will be discussed in turn in the following section:

Figure 5-1: Dimensions of Awareness

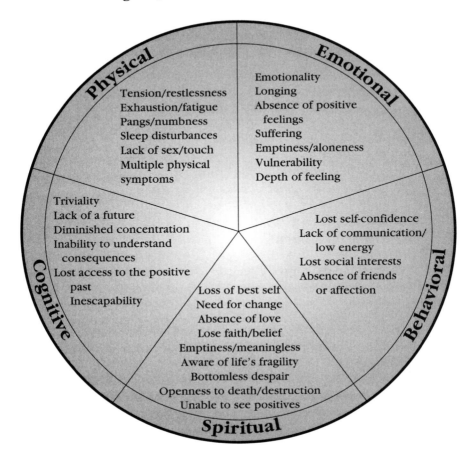

Behavioral Aspects of Awareness

Low self-confidence

> It's hard for me to make decisions.
>
> I never seem to know what to do with myself.
>
> I am less confident.

We have so little energy for the outside world. We are scattered and it's hard to do or decide anything. It's often the case that we're more competent than we think, because we're on "automatic pilot," doing what we do without having to put much thought or energy into it. Anything that requires forethought, judgment or planning doesn't seem to happen during awareness.

Lack of communication or energy

> I have very little to say.
>
> I talk about how it's been for me since the time of this loss.
>
> I've had no energy to do anything.
>
> I do less of the things I enjoyed before.
>
> I avoid being in new situations.

Because awareness is primarily an internal process, we aren't very active. We're silent and preoccupied. We make few attempts at casual conversation, preferring to be by ourself (although not isolated), and generally wait for others to initiate contact. We're uninvolved in the immediate circumstances around us or in current events.

Significant contacts during this phase often consists of a few sentences, many tears, holding hands, or being held and rocked—all with only the closest of friends and family. If we talk about anything, it usually focuses on how we have been since the time of the loss—the sense of losing ourself along with the loss.

Lost social interests

> I've not been interested in meeting anyone new.
>
> I avoid getting close to others.

In letting go, we may actively pull away from relationships and avoid new ones, for fear of being hurt again; or we may go about our business as if nothing had happened. In times of awareness, we aren't interested in investing the time and energy in someone new—especially if they don't already know about our loss. The thought of sharing our story with someone new and risking their rejection isn't worth whatever benefit might come:

> *"I'm sure he is a wonderful therapist," responded May to a friend who suggested she see a therapist after May's son had been murdered. "I can't see myself going over what happened again. I've done that with you and Clay. It helped—a lot. Bringing him up to date about me seems like an enormous task right now—not to mention how he might respond."*

We do avoid getting close to others, although we're not likely to push away if they are already there. We lack what it takes to invest in someone else. If they are willing to listen or sit with us, that's fine. But we can't give that much in return.

Absence of friends or affection

I lack love, affection and companionship.

My friends have been avoiding me.

I've lost friends.

My friends avoid talking about my loss.

We feel alone during awareness, and we're more likely actually to be alone. It's partly our own doing. In times of coping, we may push people away or demand too much. In times of awareness, we don't have much to give. And some friends may feel uncomfrotable with us.

When our loss involves a loved one who gave us love, affection and companionship, we feel deprived of their presence. We lack ways to express special feelings which relate to that relationship.

Sometimes we lose contact because others can't handle our loss. For example, people with cancer, or a contagious or sexually transmitted disease find that others avoid touching them.

Friends may avoid us because the nature of our loss produces strong feelings in them. They are frightened, saddened, angered or disgusted— and can't easily share their feelings with us. "Seeing you brings me to tears," sobbed Emily to her friend Joyce, recently diagnosed with pancreatic cancer. "Every time I pick up the phone, I can't make myself dial." Emily hadn't seen her friend in weeks.

Some friendships rely solely on having good times together. This clearly isn't one of the good times. Such friends may disappear from our lives. We are their reminder that life isn't always a bed of roses.

Cognitive Aspects of Awareness

Diminished concentration

> It's been hard to concentrate.
>
> I seem scattered and ineffective.
>
> I get so preoccupied that I forget where I am going.
>
> I forget to do routine, everyday tasks.
>
> My thinking has been slower than usual.
>
> I lose track of what's going on.

After times of awareness, we are surprised at how much time has gone by and how little we've done. Perhaps we've been reliving an experience and totally lost track of what's happening around us. Our sense of time feels slowed. "I've got a bad case of the 'stupids,'" claimed Jeff during a move from his hometown to take a new job. "I'm not able to concentrate or problem-solve the way I usually do. Too much has changed too quickly."

Lack of a future

> I am unable to find anything to look forward to.
>
> I can't imagine how things will get better.

The future looks totally empty from the viewpoint of awareness. We judge it only for what we have lost, not what's left. It can't get better from this limited perspective, because what we've lost won't be there.

Lost access to the positive past

> I forget how things used to be.

We can become so focused on the reality of the loss during awareness that we cannot recall what was going on before. We may find it extremely painful to even think of life before, because the pleasant memories are too starkly contrasted with the present sense of loss.

Triviality of everyday life

> I'm struck by how trivial everyday life seems.
>
> I'm struck by how other people go on with their lives while I can't.

No one else seems to be as affected by our loss—indeed, if they don't share the exact nature of it, they aren't. They go back to life as usual, perhaps a little shaken, nevertheless unchanged. We look at what they are doing, or what strangers or casual companions do with their time, and find it incredibly trivial. "If they only knew how they are wasting their lives, how fragile life is, they'd stop doing such meaningless things," Samantha observed of her college friends who were going out one Friday night after her boyfriend had been killed in the Gulf War.

Inescapability

I am overwhelmed at how real and inescapable this loss seems.

I know I cannot bring it back.

There comes a time in grief when we surrender to reality. Perhaps we've tried to overcome the loss. We've pretended it didn't happen. We've waited. We've run away. Something happens that convinces us there is no escape from the reality of a final, irrevocable, real loss. It is over. There is no escape.

Inability to understand

It seems hopeless to try to understand what happened.

There's no way I can fully understand why it happened.

There are times when we try to convince ourself that if we could only understand our loss and why it happened, it wouldn't be so bad. Perhaps understanding has helped, at least to narrow our focus on what we have lost. It's a rare loss that we can so fully understand that it doesn't affect us anymore. Usually we reach a point where we see how futile our attempts at understanding are. Even if we could know why it happened, our understanding won't keep us from feeling the loss.

Consequences of the loss

I think about how my life has been changed.

I am aware of what is no longer a part of my life.

I'm reminded how little I control.

I think about what's missing in my life.

I think about the dreams that will never come true.

One of the major tasks of grief is to know the implications of the loss. We need to address questions like the following:

- *How bad is it?*

- *What is it I don't control?*

- *What can't be retrieved?*

- *What have I lost of myself?*

- *What will never happen because of this loss?*

- *What is missing right now?*

We may resort to such questioning when another fragment of our loss surfaces or when a new memory is aroused. In time, we get more focused with our questioning, less likely to distract ourself with holding on or letting go. It doesn't take quite as long to answer these questions as it did earlier.

Emotional Aspects of Awareness

Emotionality

The tears are hard to stop.

My feelings come.

Awareness is an emotional time. We can no longer pretend that the loss didn't happen or that it didn't affect us. Feelings come, we can't stop the tears. May Lynne found this happening to her after her multiple sclerosis progressed to the point that she could no longer work:

I couldn't stop crying when I realized my active work life was over. My job meant so much to me—and to no longer be able to do it . . . thinking about it still can get me very close to tears.

Longing

I long for what (whom) I've lost.

I miss it/him/her.

It's hard to express what I feel in words.

Longing and yearning can be a sign of *holding on* to the past or missing what's absent in the present. Awareness provides us with the experience of how limited words are to express feelings. Nothing comes close to conveying how we truly feel. We know what we miss and long for, realizing it's much, much more than that. Words escape us and feel trivial compared to the tears, aches, pain in our heart, and the loss of meaning we experience.

Absence of positive feelings

> I miss expressing my love.
>
> I miss feeling happy.
>
> Joy is missing in my life.

As our grief progresses and we discover what it is that is missing in our lives, we find that along with an external loss, we are no longer able to express a particular part of ourself. We can't be loving to the one we've lost. We miss that wonderful feeling of being totally, unreservedly happy. We can't remember when joy was a part of our lives. Even if we have such moments, they are quickly followed by sadness:

> *"I was watching a beautiful sunset, drinking in the glorious colors and the peacefulness. As I felt the joy of witnessing nature's glory, I wished that Gary could have been there," whispered Vanessa through her tears, a year after her husband had died. "Then I realized . . . Gary would never share another sunset with me. That sunset changed. I couldn't see anything except sadness in it then."*

Suffering, sadness and helplessness

> I feel a great deal of hurt and emotional pain.
>
> I feel sad.
>
> I feel helpless.

There seems to be a core of feelings that go with grief. They include pangs of emotional pain, sadness, helplessness, emptiness and loneliness. Sometimes we experience all of them at once, which is confusing. Or perhaps one feeling is stronger. Maurice felt helplessness after his divorce when he had the kids:

> *Even though I am relieved that we no longer are together, I often feel helpless. I am reminded every day how much I relied on her— to cook my meals, to do my laundry, pay the bills. It's particularly bad when I have the kids. I just don't know what to do or how to do it.*

Emptiness/Aloneness

> I feel empty, like a shell, as if I am just existing.
>
> I feel lonely and alone.

Any loss has the capacity to remind us that we can lose anything else in our lives. We frequently become aware that there are no relationships that can be counted on to endure for our entire life span. Combined with the actual loss, the awareness of the potential for other losses makes us feel lonely—cut off from others and from ourself. Clark Moustakas (1972) suggests that loneliness is missing a part of ourself—our best self:

> Loneliness is often evoked through feelings of guilt for not being who one is and not actualizing one's potentialities. It is associated with a new truth that suddenly shatters old perceptions and ideas; it is connected with feeling different from other members of a group, of feeling misunderstood and apart from others. It is frequently associated with broken relationships and separation experiences. Each experience of loneliness is unique and represents a significant moment of awareness and renewal. (p.36)

The loss of a loved one may produce intense, lonesome feelings. Heidi felt this after her husband Joe died:

> *Joe and I were almost constant companions for thirty years. His death cut deeply into me. The loneliness is beyond anything I imagined. It's as if my right arm had been cut off. It's worse when I do something, like go for a walk. I want to share—a new bird, a funny story I heard on the radio. But he's no longer there to share it with me.*

Sometimes, intense aloneness occurs when our beliefs are challenged. Karen was sure she could handle any challenge medicine could send her way. After all, she'd been a social worker before she went into medicine and her mentor had alerted her to the obstacles she faced. She'd taken good care of herself:

> *I had gone into medicine because I thought I could handle it. It would be different for me. I would not be dehumanized like I was told everyone was at some point. It wasn't until my internship, working in intensive care twelve hours on, twelve hours off, seven days a week, that it finally happened. I no longer cared—they were just a bunch of symptoms and bodies that I had to do something about. One night I let one die without even trying. My limits were exceeded. Ashamed? I guess some . . . humiliated . . . like I betrayed or lost myself. I felt cut off—a stranger to myself.*

Vulnerability

Music can stir up my feelings.

Being in certain places can evoke feelings unexpectedly.

Looking at old photos arouses painful feelings.

Certain odors (e.g. perfumes, old houses) can trigger feelings.

Many things can arouse our feelings when we've had a loss. Irene found this out after she'd had a mastectomy at the age of forty-five:

Why is it that everything seems to be a reminder? I can't see friends and how they look at me without being reminded. I can't go to bed with my husband without being reminded. I can't hold the children in my arms without being reminded. I certainly can't look at a full length mirror and see the depression where my breast once was and not be reminded! I wish I could turn it off. I can't.

We have fewer defenses against our senses than we do to protect ourself from our emotions. Feelings come when someone touches us or we begin to make love. We hear a piece of music and we realize the last time we'd heard that was when our son left home. We smell the fragrance of a particular flower or perfume and we're reminded of a long lost love. Denise had such an experience in her job as a social worker with the elderly:

In the home of the elderly woman I visited, I noticed a familiar smell about the place. It reminded me of my grandmother's home. I hadn't been there since she died. I felt sad. I'd forgotten how much I miss her.

Depth of feeling

I feel as if I would rather die than go on experiencing this.

I am at the lowest point I have ever been.

At this time in our grief we feel more emotional pain that we have in our entire life. We're suffering. We're not sure we can handle any more. We're exhausted.

Then it gets worse. We feel more pain. There's no relief. We've never felt lower in our life. We entertain the thought: death would be a relief. We don't run from the idea.

Physical Aspects of Awareness

Tension/restlessness

> I feel restless.
>
> I feel tense.
>
> I use up much more energy than I did before.

Without even reflecting about our loss, we're using up tremendous amounts of energy. We're restless, we feel tense. When we stop to reflect, we realize we've been dealing with this loss every waking and sleeping hour for days, even weeks. No wonder we feel drained!

Exhaustion/fatigue

> My body feels heavy.
>
> I am exhausted by any effort.

It's not so much that any effort will exhaust us. We're already exhausted when we reach awareness. Sometimes we have done so much to try to overcome the loss, we have nothing left. Depleted, we no longer can defend ourself against awareness—or recognize how exhausted we are.

Pangs/numbness

> I feel strong emotional pangs.
>
> I feel numb.
>
> I cry or sob.
>
> I sigh.

There are clear physical counterparts to the feelings in awareness. Pangs often center in our chest or stomach as expressions of pain. We feel physically numbed by all the feelings and all the intensity. We cry, sob, and sigh out of sadness. We ache to be with the ones we love. Felipe felt his loss of Rosie physically:

> *My back ached. I could feel hot spasms between my shoulder blades. I knew it wasn't physical. That's where I store my memories of her—my body's way of telling me how much I miss her.*

Sleep disturbances

> I wake up feeling stiff and ache, as if I'd been tense all night.
>
> I have difficulty getting to sleep.

I wake up during the night.

I am more tired than usual.

My dreams remind me of my loss.

I have trouble getting up in the morning.

Our sleep is rarely left undisturbed by grief. Sometimes we're awake, trying to figure a way out of this loss. Sometimes the quiet of bedtime takes away our distractions. In the twilight of falling asleep or in our dreams, we're doing the grief work we didn't have time for during the day. "I work all day and I grieve all night," Soren, a train driver lamented six weeks after his train ran over a man. "When will it ever end?"

Lack of sex/touch

I lack a sex life.

I lack touching, holding and hugging.

When someone touches me, my feelings come to the surface.

We are never more vulnerable to the power of touch, and its absence, as we are in grief. When we're touched, we are defenseless against our feelings. We're also very aware of how little we are touched and how comforting it would feel if we could be touched. We may engage in lovemaking, though usually not from our initiative. But we aren't as interested in sex as we are in being held. If we've lost our love partner, making love with someone else isn't likely during awareness.

Multiple physical symptoms

It's like I've been hit in the stomach.

I feel sick.

I feel tight in my throat, as if there is a lump in it.

My stomach churns.

I hurt all over.

I have aches and pains that remind me of my loss.

I don't know if I can stand the physical pain for one more day.

In awareness, we are buffeted by the thoughts and feelings that focus on the loss. We're reminded of a loss, it hits us in the stomach. We feel sad, a lump in our throat makes it hard to eat, drink, or even breathe. We feel sick, hurt all over, aching to hold a loved one.

Spiritual Aspects of Awareness

The spiritual theme of awareness is *honesty*. We don't soften the blow or ease the loneliness. We admit what's gone. We are inconsolable. We find out how extensive this loss is.

In that honesty, we can make a choice—to live or not. We consider the full extent of what we've lost. Is it worth even trying to find what we have left, what can be restored, how we can build new meaning? Do we have the resources to get us through?

If we weigh the pros and cons of living through awareness, we rarely *consciously* choose life. The deck is stacked against us. We've only been focusing on what we've lost. We have yet to evaluate what we have left.

We may have a religious belief that has previously sustained us but now seems irrelevant. We are no longer certain there are things we consider meaningful.

Emptiness/meaninglessness

No amount of money could ever replace my loss.

Everything else seems trivial and meaningless.

The future seems empty.

There is a great emptiness in my life.

Priorities get reordered after a significant loss. It's often the case that we wish that what we lost could be our top priority. It can't. Almost anything else seems trivial by comparison. A future without our loss seems meaningless.

Unable to see positives

There is nothing positive or redeeming about this loss.

What I value most in life has been destroyed.

There are no protective features of a loss while we are in awareness. We are convinced that nothing of value remains or can be restored. When others try to tell us to look for the silver lining, we feel even more alone— for we can't find it.

Lose faith or beliefs

My beliefs don't give me the comfort they used to give me.

I question the existence of the God I used to believe in.

My faith has been shaken.

Significant losses are powerful threats to our beliefs and religious faith. We assumed they would protect us from such devastation. We now doubt the validity of our beliefs. Martin had this experience at eighteen when his father died suddenly:

> *I'd always believed that my religious faith would see me through any crisis. I believed that life was orderly, fair, meaningful, and that virtue would be rewarded. I guess I believed that God would protect me and those I loved from pain and suffering. When my dad died last year, all of these beliefs went out the window. It wasn't fair. I wasn't protected. I could find no meaning in his death. I couldn't accept it as quickly as everybody wanted me to. I felt empty, in a vacuum, without direction or purpose.*

Need for change

> I cannot continue life the same way as before.

Life can't continue as usual. Even if we could go on, to attempt to do so would dishonor the significance of what we've lost. Something has happened that causes us to reassess the most basic of premises about our lives.

Absence of love

> I don't have the kind of love I had.

We lack the kind of love we had, whether it was the love of friends, family or pets. We wonder how life can go on at all without it. All we know is that it is missing.

Awareness of life's fragility

> I realize my life will never be free from pain and suffering.
>
> I realize how fragile life is.
>
> I know I will lose things and people important to me.
>
> I've lost my sense of innocence.

We may hope that someday we'll get beyond this loss. Yet we'll never have that sense of protection and innocence we once had. Bad things can happen to good people. Effort doesn't always pay off. Life isn't fair. Death does happen to those we love. Regardless of how wonderful life might be in the future, we now have an acute awareness of life's fragility and lack of protection.

Loss of best self

There are parts of me that are missing.

My belief in myself as a good human being has been shaken.

I am not the loving, caring, trusting person I was.

We lose a part of ourself during grief—through pain, being destructive, losing what defines who we are. We may lose our best self as we respond to the loss with feet of clay. The loss may have taken from us the object of our love, the person who brought out the best in us. When parts of self are missing, we feel lonely, less capable than we are. We're convinced we'll never get that part back again.

Bottomless despair

When I'm convinced things can't get any worse, they do.

As empty as our life seems, we're convinced it can't get any worse. But sure enough, there are times when it does get worse. We think we've reached the lowest part—only to have the bottom fall out again. We are tested once again.

Open to death or destruction

It is easier to realize that someday I will die.

It seems as if I have lost my desire to live.

I've lost my fear of dying.

The awareness phase can be our worst nightmare—only we don't wake up from it. It keeps on going, day after day.

Some pain can get so bad that we question if living is worth it. Our will-to-live is challenged in ways we may never have experienced before. Harold had this happen about six months after his wife died:

I've never thought about being dead before, you know? Now I can. In some ways it would be a relief from all this pain and loneliness. It's not as frightening to think about as I used to believe it would be. I wonder what it would be like.

Isadora reached that point two years after her divorce:

I reached that point of despair and emptiness. Life didn't seem worth living. I tried twice within forty-eight hours to kill myself. Both times the doctors said I took enough to die. I didn't. So . . . for some reason I can't kill myself. I guess I'm going to have to learn to live.

We go on. Or will we? Our experiences in awareness give us reasons not to.

We lack the energy in awareness to do anything about dying. It's a time when we might succumb to an infection or illness. We wait.

With perspective, we begin to find out what we have left. We discover *why* and *if* life is worth living. For now, going on is an *act of faith* in something or someone beyond us.

When we fail to find the strength to go on, parts of us do begin to die. It's not necessarily active or conscious. We know the moment it starts. Perspective will give us time to remember why life *was* worth living—and why it might or might not be any more.

Self-Validating Awareness

There are places in grief only we can go—alone. Awareness of our loss is one of those places. We are the only ones who know what our loss means, what our contributions were, whether there is enough left. We are the only ones who can validate the fullness of our own loss.

Awareness is a gathering of moments of honesty. Eventually, we see a pattern emerge from self-confrontations with our loss, freed from others' views and our own coping.

The truth shall make us free, so we're told. However, at first it makes us miserable. Honesty is that agonizing pathfinder to the truth. This is the miserable time. Freedom will come from what we do with the awareness.

Validation and honesty require safety—safety to explore the unimaginable. Safety comes from letting someone else hold our best self as we explore the full extent of our gloom. We need to know that others aren't judging us as we look honestly at what we've done or neglected.

Self-validation is essential in grieving if we are to make choices. The most basic choice we can make is whether or not to go on living. Even that may not be a choice, for we have obligations and religious dogmas that tell us we must go on. Then we decide *how much* we will live. The time we can devote to healing, gaining perspective and integrating our loss will determine how fully we will live in the future.

When living is preferred, we discover that we can't make it on our own. If we want to live, we need help. Something or someone more powerful than ourselves needs to lift us from this valley. It can't be just anyone. It needs to be someone who believes in us, in our self-healing, in our lovableness.

Facilitating Others Through Awareness

Even if we wish to confirm what has happened to us, to a loved one or to a person we're helping, a part of us wants to believe that the suffering of awareness is not necessary. A part of us wants to believe that we'll always want, and choose, to go on living. But suffering does exist, sometimes in such horrible forms that death or destruction are preferable. There can also come a time, if for no other reason than our own aging process, when we recognize that we've lived long enough. There's not enough left to keep us going.

As a professional caregiver, if we've never experienced a powerful loss, we may be reluctant to accept the necessity of delving so deeply into oneself as occurs in the awareness phase of grieving. If we have not found benefits ourself from such explorations, we may not have the wisdom as a friend or helper in grief to let others do what they need to do. We'll try to go with them to the places they need to explore, not realizing that our presence and our actions may be a source of distraction, inhibition and self-doubt for the bereaved. Likewise, if we haven't fully explored our own grief issues we may feel tempted to abandon the grieving person at this phase.

Early in my career as a psychologist, I did not want to let my clients face their awareness alone. I eventually "bailed out" when they reached awareness. I was effective at helping them cope, even at the start of their active grieving. My father's sudden death had prepared me for that. I could stay with them for a while, but finally I would get impatient, anxious about feeling so helpless, worried about their potential for suicide. Then, one of my intensive psychotherapy clients committed suicide out of depression, not grief. A few years later, I twice came close to death myself. Next, I went through a divorce. I left for Denmark, determined to reject what others needed from me. Then, overseas, I was shunned so completely I lost faith in myself.

After each of my personal losses, I became a little more honest about myself and my limits. Paradoxically, I became more capable of staying with people through the coping phase and of respecting their need for privacy in awareness. I became more humble about advocating the growth potential in loss. I recognized what *I* needed—which sometimes didn't match what they needed for themselves.

Finally I realized that none of us can make it alone. We need to believe in something greater than ourself to go on. I could have chosen to die—

not by suicide, but by a lack of will to go on. My body would have stopped functioning, probably by a heart attack.

Instead of dying, I found the love and hope I needed. I felt my own forgiveness and eventually believed I deserved to be loved. I recognize now that I'd been transformed each time I had a loss—from the time I lost my dog at the age of four, to adulthood, changing my career, moving away from friends of twenty years. I know the future holds more transformations for me, although I can't know the form they will take or when there won't be enough left for me to live for.

My admissions may feel uncomfortable to some, too intimate to share with strangers. By extension, I expect this chapter to be difficult for many to read. But helping others through the phase of awareness is an intimate time. It is our ability to share such intimacy that eventually allows people to know they aren't alone—there is nothing they can think or feel that will drive us away. We need to learn to live with such intimacy if we are to help rather than judge it, fear it or try to change it.

We can be present for others when our own life experiences have softened our defenses, taught us humility, given us patience and helped us recognize how important it is to experience awareness, to feel the full extent of being lonely, empty or helpless. Again, Clark Moustakas'(1962, 1972, 1974, 1976, 1977) writings about loneliness can give us a sense of intimacy with ourself at such times:

> Being lonely is a time of crucial significance, an entering into an unknown search, a mystery, a unique and special moment of beauty, love or joy, or a particular moment of pain, despair, disillusionment, doubt, or rejection. (1962)

Being attentive to our own loneliness and grief enables us to respect when others experience it. We can be there when they question the value of living. We can confirm the courage it takes to face such a basic issue and witness the direction life then takes.

Summary

"You've got to walk that lonesome valley. You've got to walk it by yourself. Nobody else can walk it for you. You've got to walk it by yourself" go the words of Woody Guthrie's song. He certainly knew what the awareness aspect of grief was about. It is a lonesome walk, finding out how much our lives have been changed by this loss. It is an honest walk, filled with all the valleys, pitfalls, briars and barriers that characterize our loss. It can pervade every niche and corner of our lives.

When we know how extensive our loss is, we have a choice to make. Will we go on with life? If we choose to go on, how fully can we live? What assets do we have to help us make it?

If there is any solace in grief, it comes from knowing how universal and necessary a process it is for anyone vitally involved in life. Out of the depth of our awareness emerges the potential for transforming our lives in ways we could never have imagined or have willingly chosen. We gain courage by grieving so we can do what we need to do. We find strength we didn't know we had because we have to. We face our limits and find new options. We face dark parts of ourself and know that forgiveness is necessary for continued life. We discover we can't make it all on our own.

Helpers are there to witness this time of transformation, to believe in us, provide comfort, and remain present. No one can take the burden from us. They can help us find the best in ourselves to carry that burden. They can help us realize we can't make it without love and hope—and hold it for us while we cannot.

Chapter Six

Healing and Perspective:
What Remains After a Loss?

The lowest ebb is the turn of the tide.

—*Henry Wadsworth Longfellow*

One morning I woke up and I heard the waves lapping at the shore. I couldn't remember when the last time was that I heard anything. I noticed the sun coming up, how beautiful it was. I don't think I'd ever noticed either of those since I lost my job.

—*Harry, 56, a year after being forced into early retirement.*

There can come a time when grief doesn't feel like a crushing burden. The light we see in the darkness isn't another freight train rushing towards us—there is an end to the tunnel! We cross some invisible barrier that allows us to rest and heal.

These are times when we can step back and see our loss from a distance. "It's as if I'm on the other side of the river," noted Gene, a little over a year after his wife died:

My grief is still all there, clear as ever. Somehow it can't quite touch me as deeply. I can separate from it. I'm exhausted, but I feel OK. The worst of it's behind me. It's scary to say that—I've hoped that was true many times in the past year. It feels different this time. I know I'm not over this. I think I can make it now. For the first time, I feel as if I am beginning to heal from her death.

For so long we couldn't get away from our loss. We did our best to cope, sinking in it like it was quicksand. We couldn't feel separate from it. Then a morning comes when we see the sun rise—and wonder how long it had been since we'd last observed that everyday miracle. We marvel at how sweet and tart the blueberries on our cereal taste. We hear birds singing. We smell the flowers. We're hugged and we hug back. Something stirs in us.

Our senses reawaken to experiences other than our loss. We may still slip back into awareness, but when we do, we aren't so frightened or exasperated. There's simply more to explore.

When we reach the true bottom of awareness, we stop struggling. We let be what will be. We get off the roller coaster and feel the peace of accepting our loss for what it is. Our searching ends.

We can now open to *what we have left*. For one, we have *ourself—* our senses, our feelings, our values, our competencies. We look around. We see who is here—perhaps they have been here all along.

We can again feel pleasure without guilt or sadness immediately following. Loneliness isn't painful or frightening anymore. Sadness begins to sweeten. Helplessness feels more peaceful. Hopelessness doesn't last. Pain measures the import of our loss.

The honesty of awareness gives way to the truth of *perspective*. We take a step back and see more than what we've lost. Perhaps there is more to the picture than the loss . . . .

How does this transformation happen? We've all seen people who don't make such changes in their grief, year after year. Are they doing something wrong? Is their loss so much bigger that they can't get beyond it? Is their transformation still to come?

These are impossible questions, but they highlight the fact that *the process of grief is a highly individual experience.* Yes, there are losses so overwhelming we can't seem to get beyond them. It's impossible to know what may keep us from crossing over. Biological depression can block it, requiring medical treatment. Lack of safety, not exploring the full extent of the loss, not enough time, too few ways of coping, a worn-out body, a will-to-live that is broken—all can explain lack of progress.

The right times and circumstances may take many years—for enough safety, for the right person or message to come along, for enough healing to have transpired, for all the levels of awareness to emerge.

Yet we can heal from loss. What makes it possible? Those who have succeeded identify several things that helped:

- *Over time, they explored the full extent of the loss.*

- *They hit bottom—often more than once.*

- *They had people who believed in them, who held their hope for them.*

- *They felt safe to explore whatever they needed to explore.*
- *They realized they weren't totally alone.*
- *They accepted that they couldn't make it by themselves.*
- *They rediscovered their best self.*
- *They kept going long enough.*
- *They possessed a body capable of handling stress long enough.*

On some level, we make a choice to go on. "God knows why I did," sighed Kevin, long after his family was murdered:

There certainly wasn't anything I could see to live for. There simply came a time when I knew I wouldn't die or give up. Since then I've been building a new life.

"The first year I spent surviving," Tracy remarked, years after her divorce:

The second year I began to make sense of what happened. I see things differently—things I couldn't see when I was being tossed and turned every which way that first year. I thought I was getting somewhere. It was so temporary—and sometimes far from the truth.

It does take time before we can make sense out of what happened to us. We finally accept that our life is changed. How is it different? What is there left to build on?

Our grief has entered a healing phase. We have enough protection from the pain to be curious—did anyone get the number on that freight train that ran over us? We can smile, sometimes even laugh at how devastated, frightened, desperate, lonely and empty we felt. We're able to remove ourself from it now, at least some of the time.

For the first time, being "depressed" may not fit how we feel. "Yeah, I still have sinking spells," Martha conceded fourteen months after she lost her job and went through a divorce:

It's not depression. Depression was when I didn't know if I'd make it. Now I know that whatever comes out of this, I'll be OK. It's hopeless to think I'll get back what I lost. But I'm not hopeless.

Martha's perspective on her loss limits her hopelessness. She couldn't get back her job and the security and beliefs that went with it. She discovered she was more than a role—she hadn't lost herself. During much of that first year she couldn't find the limits to her hopelessness. She felt depressed. Once she could limit the hopelessness, her depression lifted.

There can be setbacks. Anniversaries and significant dates bring back feelings in full force. This can happen many years later, as happened to Walt, whose father had died suddenly of a heart attack when he was sixteen:

> *I had been having chest pains most of the day. I felt uneasy. I was too busy to stop and pay attention to it. Occasionally, I let out a deep sigh and found myself wanting to cry. Finally, I noticed on a calendar that today was October fifteenth. Suddenly, I realized it was the anniversary of my father's death from a heart attack— fifteen years ago.*
>
> *Now the chest pains made sense. I went to my room and sat quietly for about a half hour, thinking about him, savoring his memory. At the end, I felt much better. The chest pains were gone.*

Sitting quietly, remembering . . . that's all it takes sometimes. We need time to heal. We need to let perspective emerge.

Healing and Solitude: Discovering the Essence of Ourself

Awareness and holding on are exhausting parts of the grieving process. We need all the self-love we can muster, and to receive what others have to give. As awareness pangs ebb, we rest and heal the scars of what is missing. It is not an active time. It is time spent quietly, in solitude, listening to soothing music and reading reflective poetry or comforting books. A massage feels great. So does a trip to the lake. We stop trying to figure out our loss. We take a break.

We enjoy the simple things of life again—swimming in that clear, refreshing lake, listening to children at play, absorbing the rays of the late afternoon sun, or walking quietly in the woods. It can be a peaceful time, when obligations and responsibilities can be put aside. Such healing can take place with a trusted friend who is comfortable with silence, willing to be present, who appreciates the comfort and pleasures of a held hand or a massaged shoulder.

Healing requires rest and recuperation. The time it takes to do so is a luxury in our "hurry-up" society. Too often we rush back to our work, family, and commitments the moment we can set limits on our awareness, only to find ourself easily exhausted, with no energy and even less enthusiasm. It is as if a cast had been removed from a broken leg and we now expect to immediately resume running! Healing is a natural, time-consuming process.

The time of healing is also a time for turning outward our energies that have been so long focused inward on our loss—to search, examine, and fully experience the loss. We emerge from our cocoon, the protective isolation necessary for grieving. As we heal, we regain awareness of the outside world through our senses. We rediscover there is life around us.

Healing can also involve finding our best self again. During awareness, with our focus on what we've lost, it's all we can do to get through the day. As we heal, we find old strengths and develop new ones. "It's been so long since I even tried to go anywhere on my own," beamed Sylvia, an ex-pilot who, after her husband of forty years developed Alzheimer's Disease, took lessons and made a trip back to her hometown:

It was wonderful to discover I could still fly a plane. I could even find my way back to the old place.

Times of solitude are healing. We sort out what remains. We find the remnants and restore what we can.

Early in grief, we insist on understanding why this loss happened. We search. We read. We investigate. Our hope is that understanding will reverse the loss or, at the very least, soften its impact. When we do understand we're ready to accept the fullness of our loss. Acceptance doesn't require work, searching, reading or investigation. It comes to us.

We can't rush perspective. When we struggled between holding on and letting go, we had many brilliant, seemingly penetrating insights about the importance of the loss. We found the "true" significance of our loss. What we'd actually found was one possible way to look at the loss—one that protected us from its full impact. Relieved, we temporarily closed our minds to other possibilities.

Faith in our best self and in the process we are in is necessary. Someday it might be possible to find more than one purpose for this loss, but for now we'll settle for what we've got. Openness and endurance of ambiguity permit a wider range of possibilities to emerge. Figure 6-1 shows the many experiences that become available to us when we reach the perspective phase in grieving. This is the first step in discovering what remains after a loss:

Figure 6-1: Dimensions of Perspective

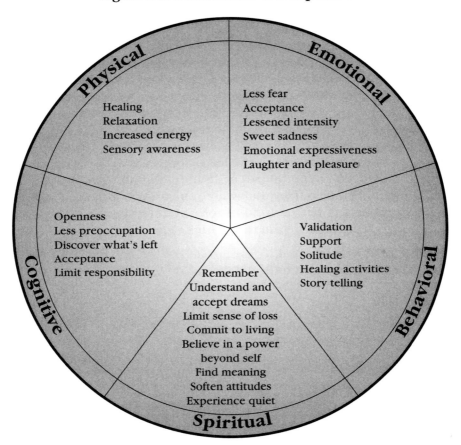

Behavioral Aspects of Perspective

Validation

Hearing about others' experiences with similar losses helps.

Friends who know what I've been through have validated my grief.

During the first few stages of grief, we may find it helpful to be with people who have endured a loss similar to our own. We look to them for hope and for ways to make it from one day to the next. But we don't need that kind of support forever. We may eventually be the one to offer support to others. What we may want later is to share with others our memories, good and the bad, that go beyond how the loss happened. We want to be with those who don't feel guilty for letting something other than their loss exist. We enjoy friends who know what we've been through but don't have to talk about it, or avoid it.

Support

> There is at least one person I can count on for support.
>
> It helps to be with a friend who accepts me as I am.

It's a risk to let someone know how we feel as we pass through grief. It frightens us how furious we've gotten, how judgmental we can be, how often we've wanted to throw in the towel. To have even one friend listen, put up with our ambivalence and come back after we've sent them away is a treasure. Perspective is a time during which we can appreciate their presence and what we've put them through.

Sometimes that "friend" is in our fantasy life or in our religious faith. We can tell it all to our diary or to God. We feel respected, validated not by any individual in our lives, but by some force or power beyond ourself.

Solitude

> Being by myself has been healing.
>
> It's easier to let myself experience this loss.
>
> It helps when I don't have anything to do.
>
> I take long walks and daydream.

We'd do anything to escape being alone when all we can do is hold on. We scorn the ineffectiveness and the untrustworthiness of relationships when we let go. During awareness, we find out how separate and alone we are. When we accept aloneness in grief, loneliness can be transformative. It can become solitude, the experience of wholeness within ourself.

We need time alone in grief. We already faced our fears of being alone during awareness. We now realize the loneliness can be a way back to ourself. Out of loneliness comes appreciation of our best self and the potential richness of life. Without other people, obligations and demands, we can eventually be freer to creatively express ourself. We will know we are all that we have in life.

When we realize it is us—our memories, our feelings, our freedom to think and to act—that we miss, we can do something. We can take back ourself and what we've temporarily lost, restore what we can, acknowledge how we've changed and develop what is still possible.

Moustakas (1973) suggests that transformation of loneliness comes from shifting from the honesty of the moment to the enduring truths of our lives. Perspective is a time when we begin to resolve the contradictions that befall us in earlier stages of grief. Our emotional extremes begin to relax and shift to ambivalence—we can both love and hate, yearn and despise.

We can see both good and bad traits, things we'll continue to miss and things we're happy to never have to deal with again. The wholeness that comes with solitude allows a diversity of honest responses to coexist.

Truth in the perspective phase endures the test of time, whereas honesty is often momentary. Truth and honesty form the essential parts of integrity and wholeness, our desire to both accept reality and explore our dreams. During the perspective phase, the loneliness of the unfinished gives way to the solitude of feeling whole.

Healing activities

> There is a special place that is healing for me.

> Activities like getting a massage, painting or music are soothing.

> I've found ways to enjoy myself.

Early in grief, we need protection from the demands of everyday life while we explore our loss. Later, we still need some of that protection, though not for exploration. We need soothing activities. We're often amazed at the capacity of the simple things in life to give us pleasure. "If I was rich, I couldn't have enjoyed myself any more than I have these past few days," smiled Mel, after a week's camping, eighteen months after he'd lost the remainder of his lottery winnings in an IRS audit.

Story telling

> Telling or writing my story about this experience helps me feel relief and release.

When we first told our story about our loss, it had a fullness and a reality. Our story was one way to convince others we shared a common loss. There were times when we couldn't say or write anything because it was too painful—it would have validated the immensity of the hole in our lives, how close we felt to giving up.

Now that we have some distance from the loss, some things seem clear and stable. Living isn't as painful. It feels good to remember the good times as well as the bad. We aren't so focused on the loss itself. We're more engaged with what we have.

Cognitive Aspects of Perspective

Openness

> I can take what comes.
>
> I can let things turn out the way they will.

When we are holding on or letting go, we try to solve the loss, or prove that it didn't matter. In awareness, we consider how comprehensive this loss is. When perspective emerges, we're less concentrated or preoccupied. We take what comes. "Hey, my brain is Swiss cheese," remarked Cal, two years after he'd returned to his home country after losing his job:

> *For two years, I've been trying to make sense of this mess. What happened, happened. I can accept that now. I wish it had been different. It wasn't.*

Less frequent preoccupation

> I can think about other things than this loss now.
>
> My imagination has returned.

Without the intensity of coping and awareness, we can think about other things—fantasies and daydreams that don't involve the loss. We can return to conversations we left as our minds wandered to our loss.

Accept what's left

> I realize that I've lost a lot, but I haven't lost everything.
>
> What I have left in my life is enough to keep me going.
>
> I think about how I have changed, what is different.
>
> There are some things I will never understand about this.

The essence of perspective is the transition from the focus on what we have lost to what we have left. There may not be much—or there can be a lot. Our willingness to keep going is different from times of holding on, when keeping going was something we had to do, regardless of what happened. In times of perspective, to keep going is more fragile, for another loss may weaken our resolve.

As the emotions of our grieving process soften we can consider how our lives have been changed without having to select only those that proved a particular point. We're more interested in the implications, positive and negative, of the loss. For example, we may discover how the loss of a loved one frees our time to do what we want to do.

We may not have all the answers for this loss. We've done what we can. New information helps. But it's not worth the search.

We anticipate how our future will be influenced. Instead of the immediate implications, we examine long-term consequences.

Claire had lived with a severe allergic condition for several years when she had to give up her job, became dependent on her husband and even her children. It was some time before she could see beyond the routine unpredictability of her illness to other patterns in her life:

For a long time, I could only live a day at a time. My allergic reactions were so unpredictable that I couldn't count on anything. Eventually, there were several good days in a row. Then, it gradually got longer. I began to see how I had fallen into a pattern of not planning anything and then being bored a lot. I realized I wanted to have a future again—a career that took into account my disability. I also realized my marriage couldn't continue on a crisis basis. I could see it not lasting unless we were able to change.

Jim deserted Jayne shortly after the birth of their child. It was five years before she could stop to reflect:

I've found out I can take care of myself—something I was frightened about before. I've also found I can see that not all men are like Jim, and even Jim is not like Jim anymore. I'm still very cautious. There are even times when I wonder if I'm not better off because he left—even in the way he left.

Betty took quite a while before she gained perspective on selling her home and moving:

Marrying and moving to Evanston had been the fulfillment of all my dreams. It was the perfect place for the children and for me at that point in our lives. It was that way for years. It was devastating when we had to move again. Nothing could compare to the old place. Everything we looked at seemed to have so many deficits. In exasperation, Bob finally decided to buy a place that at least he liked. I complained a lot, I guess. Even some of the new neighbors got tired of all my negative comments about living here and how great the last place had been.

Well, things have a way of growing on you, and eventually I began to realize there were some good things about being here. It is a place with some memories now, too. I guess part of all my nostalgia for the old place was missing my friends. Now that I have friends here, it's not so bad. I guess going back last year helped me realize you can't live in the past. The old house somehow didn't look quite as perfect as I thought it would be.

Limit responsibility

I'm not as responsible as I thought I was for what happened.

I wasn't the only one who contributed to this loss.

When we hold on, we exaggerate our responsibilities, or someone else's, for our loss. When we let go, we reject the notion that we had any responsibility. When we reach perspective, we're some place in between. We're probably not as responsible as we once thought, nor are we totally free either. The same logic applies to others' responsibilities as well.

"I realize the doctor made a mistake and it's left me crippled for the rest of my life," Madeline reflected three years after corrective surgery following a car accident failed:

I was the one who had the car accident. It wasn't his intent to leave me in this state. He was doing the best he could to help. He screwed up. I put myself in the position of needing his help. It wasn't that I wanted this to happen either. It simply turned out this way.

Madeline had gone through times in the previous three years of blaming either herself or the doctor for what happened. Now she could consider both—and put limits on just how responsible they each were.

Every time we get new information about a loss, we question: "Can I accept this as one of the ways my loss has meaning for me?" Earlier in our grief, we either quickly rejected new information or exaggerated it. When we have perspective, we can entertain new ideas, not just how it affects our loss. Monty had such an experience five years after he had lost a client through suicide:

For years after Cleo died, I felt that she must have been furious with me to kill herself. I couldn't even entertain the possibility that she was so desperate that nothing I could do could have made a difference. I needed to hold on to the illusion that I could have made a difference. There came a time when I didn't need that illusion any more. I could see her desperation then—and feel a sense of freedom and acceptance of my limits. That realization was a peaceful one for me.

Emotional Aspects of Perspective

Lessened fear

I have already passed the lowest point.

My fears about dying are less.

With so many ups and downs in grief, how do we know we've turned the corner? We may not know immediately, not until we realize it's been a while since we've felt the pangs. We can still feel the loss, but we also feel other things.

Awareness lessens our fear of dying; when we reach perspective, we feel less trapped by life and by our loss, and our fear of being helpless is reduced. We have a choice around living and dying—a choice that can deliver us from pain that goes on too long. Our strength returns. We have turned a corner.

Emotional expressiveness

My feelings make sense when I think about them.

I am able to express my feelings about the loss.

When we are aware of a loss, we may lack words to express what we feel. Perspective allows us distance to express feelings with or without words. We find expression in playing the piano for the first time in years. We write a poem that captures a moment of our grief or paint a portrait of our loss. We express or validate feelings trapped inside.

Emotional acceptance

I don't need to struggle to accept what has happened.

My feelings still catch me by surprise, but they don't last as long.

Perspective lessens our need for coping. We need not protect ourself from being caught unprepared by a devastating awareness. There are moments when our feelings are sharp. We've been there before—we know we'll survive. The more accepting we are, the quicker our own emotions relax.

Lessened intensity of feelings

I still hurt, but the pain has lessened.

My guilt has lessened.

I'm not so sad.

My feelings of anger are not as strong anymore.

My disgust over what happened has lessened.

Once we've felt the full impact of our feelings about a loss, the intensity can begin to lessen and we can find distance from them. Things begin to brighten—with a few setbacks, as Angelina experienced nine months after ending an affair:

My life got to the point where I was beginning to enjoy each day again. I found myself looking forward to things, and getting up in the morning was a lot easier. Then one day, nine months after I broke up with him, he sent me a bouquet of flowers. I didn't even know he was in town. The feelings all returned, as if I'd been hit in the stomach. I knew I couldn't go see him—not yet. I was still too close to those painful feelings. I found myself thinking about him a lot, and after the first shock, it wasn't so bad. The intensity left.

I was finally able to see him. It was sad. I knew that what we had was over.

Sweet sadness

My feelings can be ones of "sweet sadness."

I realize that sadness and peacefulness can coexist.

Sadness can be a barometer of grief's intensity. We may keep it as a way to remember our loss. But sadness can lose its intensity and its sharp edges. It can also become a sweeter emotion. It can be a peaceful feeling. Dee was two and a half years past her daughter's death before she noticed a change:

There came a time when it wasn't so painful all the time. One day I thought, "Hey, it's been a while since I thought about my little Katherine." I still get sad when I think about her. Now it seems a long time ago.

Laughter and pleasure

It feels good to be able to laugh again.

I can enjoy simple pleasures of life again.

Friends have been telling us to cheer up, look on the bright side, laugh and the world will laugh with us. Finally we can. We're surprised at how much easier it is now. From monumental issues of life and death, we're able to relax and watch a ball game, plant some flowers, listen to some old favorites on the radio.

Physical Aspects of Perspective

Healing

My body is healing from the stresses of this experience.

The aches and pains I used to have with this loss have lessened.

We've already spent enormous amounts of energy in our grief. We've been shoved and yanked in every direction. "It felt as if I was the Raggedy Anne doll I had as a kid," Rae observed of the first year after her house was destroyed in a flood:

We spent all that time and energy searching. It felt as if I'd been hit in the stomach when we'd find a ruined picture or piece of furniture. Now there aren't many surprises left—nothing to search for, nothing that can clobber us. We can relax now—for the first time.

Aches and pains can be the result of exertion—searching, trying to overcome the loss, staying vigilant. Sometimes pain is symbolic, for example, the chest pain on the anniversary of Dad's heart attack. Sometimes we're stiff because we were inactive for so long. Our muscles atrophied while we sat, immobilized. Now we have the energy to move again. We're aware of what our body has been through, or how we've neglected it.

Relaxation

I'm able to relax.

I enjoy being touched and held again.

When we can limit our vulnerability, it's a lot easier to relax. When every touch isn't a reminder of our loss, we can enjoy it. We don't outgrow relaxing, touching and hugging.

Increased energy

My energy level has improved since the time of the loss.

It takes less energy to do things than it used to.

Our energy had to be focused to respond to the loss. "It amazes me," confessed Bob, six years after losing his job and only three months after settling the lawsuit:

I haven't had energy for anything else for all these years. It wasn't until the suit was over that I could do anything else. I had to be ready to respond, to stay loyal to my feelings about the loss until that was over. Now I can get on with the rest of my life.

When we're not bouncing between the extremes that coping and awareness carry us, we can be more efficient. We expend less energy to accomplish things, not having to assess everything for its significance to the loss or deny it, which leaves us with more energy.

Sensory awareness

I am more aware of myself physically than I was before the loss.

I notice how things smell and taste again.

The fullness of our grief means we pay attention to ourself more. That includes the physical. "I never paid attention to my appearance, sleep, what I ate before the accident," Jerry admitted two years after a car accident left him a paraplegic:

I sure have since then—mainly in very hard ways. I've had a lot of pain. I couldn't sleep. I lost my appetite. Now I find myself feeling great when there is no pain, when I get a good night's rest. Food tastes so good sometimes now. I never would have stopped to notice that.

Sometimes it takes a good knock on the head before we come to our senses. Loss can do that. Few things have more clarity than our senses. Paradoxically, they are also the cradle of our imagination. We experience through our senses. We can remember the past and imagine new sensations, too. When we are no longer directly tied to our loss, we find the pleasures of our senses again.

Spiritual Aspects of Perspective

The spiritual theme in perspective is *truth*. We can see a bigger picture than we could in awareness. This larger picture takes in what we have left as well as what we lost. We can look farther into the future and deeper into the past than we could when our focus was only on the loss and the way it happened. We may not yet be ready to do something about it. We're less certain we know exactly how it happened and who's to blame.

Spirituality emerges during perspective as a more central factor in our grief. Transformation relies on this spiritual aspect. To reach perspective, for example, we need to decide to go on with life, knowing it won't contain what we've lost. We need to have faith that our lives can transform themselves without knowing how that is possible.

There is more to us than a combination of a mind, a body and a cluster of feelings. We thrive on being loved, and feel diminished by hatred and shunning. When others believe in us, we believe in ourself. When we have faith in God, or a higher force in the universe, we rely on our interconnections to help us through or to alter our isolation.

Limit sense of loss

I have learned to accept that losses and changes are a part of life.

There are limits to what I lost.

We step back and look at what we've been through. We listen again to others. We realize our loss isn't so unique. There is something left, or something to live for. "This past year has been terrible," sighed Bonnie after contracting AIDS. "If it wasn't for Agnes, my cat, I wouldn't have made it." Bonnie at that moment realized there was something left to live for—Agnes. There were limits to her loss.

Commit to living

My life will continue.

I've decided to go on living.

We'll go on living, at least for now. Something deep down has changed—a commitment to give life one more chance. No guarantees, mind you, but from the way things look right now, it's worth a try.

Understand and accept through dreams

My dreams seem to help me understand and accept what happened.

While we are holding on dreams tell us the loss can be reversed or that it never happened. Letting go dreams are often dark, destructive of what or whom we lost. Awareness dreams tell it like it is. Perspective dreams are more benign. They are often gifts of wisdom, often transparent. "I've never had a dream that was so clear, so easy to understand," exclaimed Vera, a little over a year after her parents were killed during a terrorist attack:

> *My parents were standing in my living room, just as I remembered them. They said they had forgotten to tell me they weren't coming back. They said they loved me, and that they'd be OK. I woke up crying. I felt better about them. I knew I could go on.*

Believe in a power beyond self

Someone or something powerful and loving has helped me make it.

My faith or spiritual understanding helps with this experience.

"One of the hardest steps for me was to admit I couldn't do it myself," confessed Mac, a recovering alcoholic:

> *That first step in joining AA was a huge one. I know now I wouldn't be here today if it wasn't for a divine source that kept me from dying that night. I was killing my family as well as me. It took a supernatural force to save me from demon rum.*

Sometimes we have a ready-made context within which to place our most recent loss. We've learned a life philosophy that includes loss. For many people, a religious faith is such a context. For others, our life philosophy results from growing up in an environment where death, illness, starvation, crime, incest, abuse, war and torture are real, not something read about in a newspaper—something that allows us to accept the fragility of life without giving up too easily. We put ourself in God's hands and accept that whatever happens will happen.

Find meaning

Something good could come out of this.

My life does seem to have meaning.

In awareness, it was impossible to feel that anything good could result from our loss: No meaning existed. Now, without anything changing, so it seems, we've begun to believe in higher purposes, that we're here for a reason even if we have no idea what it is. In spite of what we've lost, there are places in our lives that have meaning. We can make a difference. We can contribute.

Soften attitudes

No one is to blame for what happened.

Whatever I contributed to this loss, I did not want it to happen.

I believe there is some good in every person.

We soften our attitudes during perspective. We're finally willing to give ourself and others the benefit of the doubt. Don't ask us yet to get specific about the good in every person, or to speak or act in a forgiving way. We're only willing to *consider* not blaming or feeling guilty all the time. We can look back and accept we were doing the best we could—as Peter did after his divorce:

> *I finally got over my rage and fear of having to give up any opportunities to be free from my marriage until the children were older. I realized I had kicked hard at many of my friends who had supported me in my search for independence. I had refused phone calls and sent letters saying never to write or call again. I even sent back the books they had sent that focused on the wonderful possibilities in independence and solitude. These were reminders of what I couldn't take for myself right now. I know in my rejecting them I hurt them, too. It was necessary. I could see no other way. Eventually I accepted that I was doing the best that I could at the time.*

Experience quiet

Life seems more fragile and precious.

There are quiet places in my life now.

From the moment we consider that death isn't the worst thing that can happen to us, life takes on a fragile and precious quality. No longer will we avoid death at any cost, nor will we go to the other extreme, not caring if we live or die. For now, we prefer life with all its uncertainties. It took Tina a year and a half of chemotherapy and counseling before she could appreciate life again:

> *When they first diagnosed my cancer, I wanted to scream out, "It's not fair!" I was bitter for a long time. I couldn't even tolerate my friends coming over. That's long in the past. Sure, I'm still frightened of dying. I've also gained a lot by this illness. I'm closer to Bob now than I ever was. Now I stop and enjoy life more than I ever did before. Each day is precious.*

We stop struggling. The internal noisiness of coping fades. We get away from constant reminders that blast us out of moments of composure.

We find and keep times and places of quiet in our lives because they exist inside us.

Remember

> My past will always be a part of me.
>
> A part of me will always be connected to what/who I lost.
>
> The fond memories are there along with the painful ones.
>
> What I've lost will always have a place in my life.

We've had restful times early in grief, but they were to escape the reality of our loss. Now we have no need to escape what's happened. We're relieved to realize we won't forget our loss—nor do we want to:

> *"How silly I was to think I could forget the most important person in my life," smiled Channing sheepishly, years after her mother died. "She was such an essential part of my life—for better and for worse. Recently, I've realized how much of her there is in me."*

Facilitating Perspective

Perspective begins the process of transforming the bereaved and those who help them. It is also important to remember that perspective doesn't begin one day and finish the next. What we can do now is validate the needs of those who are grieving for time, patience, openness, and faith.

For the bereaved, finding truth, safety and honesty requires more time free from external demands and for periods of reflection. Perhaps the best help caregivers can provide during this phase is a place or sense of *sanctuary*. It is a place we can go where our journey inward won't be interrupted or ridiculed. It could be a communal or spiritual place, like a church, temple or a chapel. Or it could simply be a room where we control who enters and why. At other times nature provides sanctuary in places of solitude and beauty, by the natural healing sounds of water, the vistas of mountain tops, the color changes that sunsets bring, or the awesome expanse of the universe on a starry night. The awareness of eternity and peace lends strength in times of stress. It is in such solitude that our loss event becomes part of our life story.

We need to celebrate the transformations that occur between awareness and perspective, but quietly, for who has the energy for anything more during this phase? We know how far our friend, loved one or client has come to reach this point. We know people who rarely make it this far, so it's cause for celebration when they do. We've witnessed the transformation and can validate how profound the change has been.

Summary

We need distance from our losses to acknowledge and accept their full reality and consequences. Perspective takes three forms:

- *We discover the balance of the positive and negative, how we have changed as well as what is permanently gone.*

- *We discover the extent of and the limits to our loss.*

- *We want to know the truth about our loss and our lives.*

Perspective represents acceptance—what's done is done. We are at peace with the existence of our loss. We no longer need to fight or flee from it. We take time to heal, remember and savor in order to discover the enduring truths about ourself.

Our journey is not yet over, but we know we'll make it. We feel connected again to people and powers beyond us. Most importantly, we have a renewed sense of inner strength and integrity. We're beginning to make sense of this mess.

Is it enough? For now, yes.

We grow restless with grief. Once the burden of awareness has lifted, we want to get back to business as usual. People offer us new relationships, new work, new alternatives to being alone. Yet we still need time alone, quiet time before we strike out in new directions. We need to savor, remember and restore what we can before trying on the new.

Chapter Seven
Integrating the Loss:
Remember, Restore, and Recreate

I have got my leave.
Bid me farewell, my brothers!
I bow to you all and take my departure.
Here I give back the keys of my door—
and I give up all claims to my house.
I only ask for last kind words from you.
We were neighbors for long,
but I received more than I could give.
Now the day has dawned and
the lamp that lit my dark corner is out.
A summons has come and
I am ready for my journey

—*Tagore, from* **Gitanjali, XCIII**

I t's time to move on. Still, it's no easy walk to freedom. For grieving to lead to growth, our life must come back together. We need to put aside our preoccupation with our loss while finding a place and space for it. There is more to us than this loss. We need to move on, to say good-bye, to forgive but not forget. It's time to feel whole.

Easier to say than to do!

As we have seen, the most shocking aspect of grief comes when grieving begins. The most stressful parts of grief lie in our limited ways of coping—holding on and letting go. It's most painful and lonely in awareness as we discover there are fates worse than death. Peacefulness comes with healing and perspective. But the most time- and energy-consuming aspects of grief involve *integrating our losses and moving on.*

The Process of Integration

What makes integration such a demanding process? We are reconciling the paradoxes inherent in who we are and what we've lost. We come to acknowledge parts of ourself we have despised or denied. Integration means giving up protection, the kind afforded by avoiding conflict or choice, denying reality, or staying too long identified as a survivor or a victim. It means challenging and sometimes relinquishing beliefs, assumptions and roles—questioning our basic values. When we integrate our losses, we relinquish the comfort of our sadness, the support for our loss, and the power of being rightfully indignant. We move on—to an unknown future that lacks the familiar focus and predictability that living in our loss afforded us.

Integration can create new losses through our own actions. We don't know what's ahead, yet we're willing to take that conclusive step to shut the book on the past. Moving on can mean taking the steps necessary to complete our life—to find the resolve to implement decisions about living or dying made during awareness.

Resolve means that we decide to go on living, knowing as fully as we can the meaning of this loss. I used to think that we resolved our grief at this stage, permitting us to move on. I've since realized, based on the experiences of myself and others, that "resolution" doesn't apply to the loss itself. That implies that we can somehow "finish" the loss, put it away, and never explore it again. At this phase resolve means having the determination to go on *in spite of* our loss.

By the time we integrate a loss, we know we can't retrieve the form of what we've lost, but we can't move on unless we've retrieved or maintained the *essence* of what we lost. Sometimes the form is so battered or worn out that we have to let go of it, hoping that what's essential about us will live on. We can't always overcome illness, poverty or the effects of aging.

To integrate a loss, we need to believe that the important aspects of what we've lost won't be forgotten and will remain a part of us. We need to accept that we've done everything we can to restore or recreate what was lost or destroyed.

Integration and moving on involve an *acceptance of and participation in transformation*. We take an active step toward pulling the pieces of our life back together again, to make a coherent whole of ourself and what we're about. We need to "own" every aspect of ourself, to harmonize mind, body and spirit. Barry Stevens (Rogers and Stevens, 1972) summarized this step:

But understanding alone is not enough. When I understand some-thing and do not put this into action, nothing has been accomplished either in the outside world or within myself . . . . when I was being my own therapist I hit on something that was blocking me and kept telling myself that as long as this was clear to me, as long as I understood how it had come about, I didn't need to do anything about it. "It's all right." It wasn't. Nothing happened until I acted on what I knew. It seems to be one of the follies of . . . intellect that it can think that what I know, I am, and that words take care of everything.

In some instances, acceptance is all that's required, or possible, as we grieve. People who are unconscious, embattled, in extreme pain or dying, for example, may be able to do little more. Once acceptance has been reached under these circumstances, integrating the loss can only come by taking whatever opportunity is left to pull all the pieces together and unite oneself as a whole. Sarah was terminally ill, trying to say good-bye to her family. Her husband Sam didn't want to hear it because he knew what it meant:

Sarah had been in such pain in the last month of her life. Yet all of us, particularly the children, couldn't face the inevitability of her death. As I look back now, she was for a long time asking us for permission to give up on living. Of course, we refused to even acknowledge her request. I remember so vividly that last day when she said to me, "Sam, whether you're ready or not—I have to leave you. Please tell the kids I love them, too." That was the last thing she said. Two hours later she slipped into the last coma before she died.

"Getting it together" was Matthew's battle at forty-three:

I had believed life had reached its lowest ebb. Each time I struggled with the pain and went on. I couldn't believe it could ever get worse. It did. I lost my job, my wife, my children, my home. A few weeks later my mother died. In a desperate attempt to keep my family, I had already rejected my support system. Now I had nothing. Nothing to live for.

I realize that it would be easy to die. In a way, I think I did die at that time—not physically, but psychically. All my illusions and beliefs evaporated, too—particularly those about working hard, about being a good person, putting the needs of others ahead of my own. Where had it gotten me? I felt as if I was dead.

I also felt building in me a determination to live. It took me awhile to realize it. On some level, I must have believed I have a purpose in being here. Despite everything, I believed I had something to contribute to my world. I resolved to go on, to seek meaning, to take new risks. "Keep breathing," a friend told me. I did. I had nothing more to lose.

Yet I couldn't just say that to myself. After all that had happened, there were too many things left incomplete for me. I had to recontact those people who had been supportive, the ones I had rejected. I told them where I was, what I had been through. I didn't ask for their forgiveness. I guess in sharing with them, I was in a way forgiving myself. It was a wonderful gift to find that one of them, Christine, accepted me. She told me she never lost faith and love for me. It freed me to move on.

We have to empower the past again. Our lives get fragmented at times of loss. We have to put the pieces back together. It's not enough to remember what we have left. We need to do something with our memories. It may mean taking back the rituals and identities of our ancestors. It may mean telling others of our significant life experiences.

We restore what we can of the damage we may have caused. Or we make up with old friends, compensate for what we've destroyed, forgive those who have suffered.

We may have to recreate a part of ourself damaged beyond repair. This psychological "plastic surgery" allows us to activate our best self. We can't change what happened, but we can change ourself. Such recreation may involve placing ourself in situations we had trouble with before—and have the fortitude now to respond to as a whole person.

To remember, restore and recreate are the necessary components for us to move on after significant loss. Yet integration requires something more—curiosity, patience, firmness, and forgiveness.

Integration is both a phase in grieving and an essential ingredient in the entire process. We actually begin to integrate our loss from the time we become aware of what we've lost. We face choices while coping—will we face the pain, go as deeply as it takes us, accept the necessity of suffering and loneliness? Can we get back the parts of ourself we lost when we split our minds from our bodies?

At this phase we stick around to better understand what has happened to us. Like a puzzle, we begin to put the pieces together, eventually recognizing patterns within the whole. During the perspective phase we figured out what our loss looked like, but we had not finished grieving it. In order to connect the pieces of the puzzle we must move into integration, otherwise we'd see coherence, pattern, and meaning in our loss, but not be sure what to do with them.

During integration the process may look very different than we thought it would. It can take on an air of excitement as both old and new parts of self become apparent. *We begin to discover what's possible.*

Integration takes time. Picking up fragments can be a long process. So can the time it takes to get back on our feet, to take care of our daily responsibilities. Other losses can occur before we integrate the first one, adding extra dimensions and complexities. It's not unusual to be integrating a significant loss for as long as fifteen years after it occurs.

It takes courage to integrate our lives. We must face our pain or shame and remain open, for who knows how a piece might eventually fit into this puzzle? That also means continued vulnerability, that we'll feel helpless sometimes, and often sad and lonely. We aren't as satisfied with easy or convenient explanations for what happened as we used to be—especially those that cast us in the role of helpless victim, the "bad guy" or as permanently bereaved. Eventually we accept some responsibility for the loss, as small or as large as that might be. To grow, we must risk the unknown. Growth requires us to face our fears and go beyond them.

Patrice, at thirty-eight, found the nerve to leave a destructive marriage two years after Janine, one of her children, was killed in a house fire set by her drunken husband Frank:

> *People thought I was courageous when I tried to save my children from our burning house. That was nothing. I didn't even think about it so focused was I on Janine. What's taken courage is facing myself, rescuing me from the burning building that was my marriage. I was never more afraid than I was the day I left Frank. I knew he would try to find me and kill me if he could. I had to conquer my fears and recapture the best of myself to make it. I realized there were things worse than dying—living in the hell he created certainly was worse. I still fear that he'll find us—but now we can live as human beings instead of frightened animals. Each day I celebrate the gift of life, for the kids and for me.*

Forgiveness is another piece of the integration puzzle. It can be an act of surrender, but not one of defeat. Giving up an old identity means absolving ourself of the guilt for being disloyal, for growing, for being more than we used to think we were. We have to relinquish our desire to get our full pound of flesh in revenge or payment. We need to release the intense grip our feelings have had in the time since the loss.

We may have already tried forgiveness while coping through letting go. Usually it doesn't work, for we are not yet aware of what it is we are surrendering. It's not possible to let go of something unless we *have it* first.

We need a sense of mastery of our roles, our identity, our losses. We need to be sure that we won't forget. What needs to precede this kind of "letting go" is time to acknowledge the true importance of our loss and the associated feelings.

For example, we can't give up being bereaved parents unless we've had the time to know the significance of that part of our self-identity and done what we needed to remember our lost daughter—not only the way she died, but how she lived. We need to cherish the meaning her life brought to ours. Without time to value our loss, we lack recognition of what it is we're giving up and the security and confidence for moving forward.

Figure 7-1 outlines the various aspects we encounter once we have reached the integration phase in grieving. We have not completed our grieving, but the fragments of our life, like pieces of a puzzle, are beginning to fall together into a recognizable new form:

Figure 7-1: Dimensions of Integration

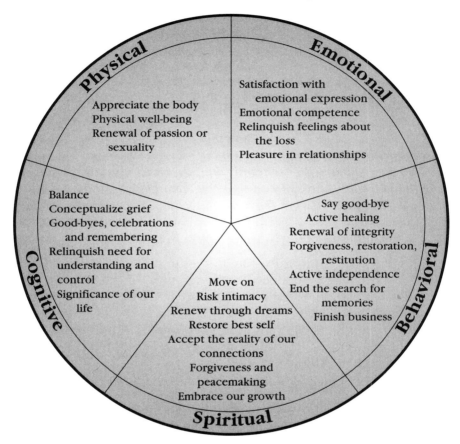

Behavioral Aspects of Integration

It's often the case that we know what we want to do long before we can do it. It's especially true of integration. We can't make the changes until we've worked through everything else. Early in grief, our behavior was the easiest to change and we may have looked better than we felt. Like the perspective phase before, integration is principally an internal process.

Renewal of integrity

> I've found ways to get back my integrity.

We take little steps back to ourself. We embrace both our best self and our "worst" self. We acknowledge our role in the loss and the limits of our responsibility. We make friends with our pain, our illness, with the disengaged child within us. We let others know how we are feeling and thinking, even though they may not approve or agree. These can all be steps toward regaining a sense of our integrity—toward pulling ourself together. Carmen recognized these steps with two near-death experiences:

> *It was five years ago that I had the breakthrough, when I realized I could die at anytime. I almost did, twice in the preceding year. I began to look at life differently then. I wanted to get as much from it as I could. I made some major changes in my diet, exercise, times for relaxation, and in the time and way I worked. It's taken a lot to keep up the discipline at times. I know I won't let myself go back. Besides, I'm enjoying life so much more now than I ever did!*

Getting back our integrity can be the hardest and most courageous thing we can do. In the past, perhaps as a survivor of childhood trauma, we gave up a part of ourself in order to survive. We may have stopped fighting back, knowing that our persecutors wouldn't kill us if we let them have their way with us. We were ashamed that we took the easy way out, may have derived some pleasure from incest and were afraid to admit it. We felt guilty afterwards, because we knew that we made a choice to live rather than to die defending our integrity. It may have been a wise choice, although wise choices don't always mean fearless, shameless, guiltless ones. We may have added to our burden by denying that anything was happening to us. We relinquished attachments to our bodies, minds or values because they attracted unwanted attention and assault. To survive, we may have fallen into addiction, mental illness or spiritual indifference.

Reconciliation within ourself may be life-threatening, for the danger and the threat may still be present. It could mean loss of face or death of the persecutor whom we still love and hate. It can mean losing a family, a job or career, friends—everything outside of us that has significance. Is our integrity worth it?

Abraham Lincoln once wrote that he chose to live his life in such a way that at the last moment he could look up and if all he had left was himself, that would be enough. He could accept the loss of everything else except his loss of self.

Perhaps the pieces we lost along the way weren't quite so enormous. We lied, cheated, hurt others, manipulated. We convinced ourself we didn't *mean* to do it, that we weren't being ourself, that it was the stress, the alcohol or the drugs that made us act so crazy. Unless we've done something to reclaim that piece, to own our self-betrayal, to admit our guilt and responsibility and grieve the loss of self that resulted, we won't be able to restore or integrate that particular loss.

Active independence

> I've changed.
>
> I don't depend as much on others.

We're not the same person we used to be. We're also not in the same place emotionally as we were in the midst of our grief. We don't need or depend on others as much as we once did. We're not as controlled by their opinions. We've found ways to demonstrate this transformation. Perhaps we're quieter—or more outspoken.

Active healing

> I've experienced this loss in ways that were healing.

We're beginning to integrate after a loss when we can realize we've been healing for quite a while—that even the most painful parts of the process were necessary parts of our healing. We had to go to those dark places to find ourself and the resources we needed. Acknowledging our rage and anger was necessary. So was accepting our despair, helplessness and loneliness.

End the search for memories

> I've remembered what I want to remember about it.

We haven't remembered everything, but we don't need to now. We're aware of the essence of what happened. When we're integrating, we're not devoting energy to new discoveries, but if they come, all the better.

Finish business

> I've done everything I can do right now about this loss.
>
> I've finished things related to my loss as completely as I can.

"I know there are things I could still do about the divorce," confessed Tom ten years after his marriage dissolved and he lost a close friendship:

> *But they involve people who aren't willing to engage with me on the issues—including my ex-wife Jeannie. I'd love to talk with her about the abortion, forgive each other for what we did. I wish I could tell Sam I still love him in spite of the hurtfulness and misunderstandings around the divorce. I've done everything I can do right now.*

At this time, we need to tie up the loose strands of our loss. Although we can't do everything, we can sometimes do more than we thought. Even if we can't finish business directly, we can still follow through for our own sense of completion by writing a letter we don't send, role-playing what we want to have happen, talking to an empty chair as if our ex-wife was there, listening receptively.

Finishing things about our losses can mean we're ready for a total transformation of our life, which can include dying. In awareness, we may have discovered there was nothing holding us to life anymore. In perspective, we appreciated the past for what it was, but saw the present as not having enough to keep us going and imagined the future to be in another dimension. Integration can mean taking the final steps necessary to move us into that new dimension. Sometimes that means initiating the process of "active dying."

Luke reached the point where he was ready for the transformation of death. He found a way to participate in that process dynamically:

> *I've lived with multiple sclerosis for twenty-five years now. It hasn't all been tough. I've had good periods and not so good ones. I've made friends with my illness, recognized what it's done for me. It's made me a more sensitive and appreciative person.*
>
> *I've known for a long time that eventually I would die. I've been exasperated many times by this illness. I wanted to give up, escape from this body. I've been suicidal. Each time I came back, aware that I wasn't ready to die. There was more to me than this illness. I was still curious. After all, if the Berlin Wall could come down, what else could happen? I'm too damn curious for my own good!*
>
> *I'm ready to die. I don't have the energy to fight on anymore. There doesn't seem any reason to do so. I am so handicapped now that I am a burden to Judy, not a husband.*

So I've learned how to use imagery. It's a tool I've used for many years to help me with the pain and with my grief. I intend to use it to help me die. I think about it, about going toward the light. I feel out of my body at times, held back only by a slender thread. I need to say good-bye to Judy and the kids. I want to finish writing this. Then it will be my time.

A week later Luke died, peacefully.

Acts of forgiveness/restoration/restitution

At least one person knows that I've forgiven myself.

I've taken steps to forgive those involved.

I've restored relationships that were disrupted by it.

I am making restitution for my contributions to this loss.

Forgiveness is a powerful act of integration. It takes a deeply wounded part of ourself and restores it to a place in our life. Forgiveness can demand every ounce of courage, compassion and humility we can muster. It is an action we take, with witnesses, and a spiritual leap of faith.

Early in grief, we may have concluded that pardon was impossible. "I can never forgive him for what he did to me" is a common resolve as we realize how devastated we are by the actions or neglect of others. We may say the same about ourself—we feel unforgivable.

At the time we made that resolve, we also didn't know where our own process of transformation would take us. We had no way of knowing how strong and resilient we are, or what we'd learn about ourself as a result of our grieving. As we discovered within ourself our capacity to be destructive, we became less comfortable with externalizing total responsibility for what happened. We were the victim, to be sure, an innocent child taken advantage of by an adult who should have known better, but didn't. As we experienced our rage and anger, we also found strength so great we know we can protect ourself and even destroy our persecutors.

It is from our strength and confidence that we see the fear and weakness that were there before—in us and in those who injured us. We understand our life is much richer now than theirs have ever been or probably ever will be.

Acknowledging our inability to forgive can be paradoxical. It can be forgiving in and of itself. Bob noted about himself as he thought about a long-lost friendship:

I can forgive myself for not forgiving Ken. I can then let go of that and allow forgiveness to come from another source, a higher power, my best self. I have to separate from my emotions, my physical capacity that says I can't forgive, and give it to my spiritual self, which can. It's like that line in Born on the Fourth of July when Slovik tells the wife of his soldier buddy, whom he accidentally killed in Vietnam, that he had done it. She says to him: "I don't know if I can ever forgive you. Perhaps God can."

Forgiveness can require overlooking the need for retribution, equal suffering, unending guilt. It is a transformation of energy from dismissal and shunning to openness and inclusion. When we pardon ourself, we are adopting a lifestyle that not only admits what we've done but determines never to put ourself in those impossible circumstances again.

Forgiveness can also involve making restitution. Usually we cannot bring back what we lose, but we can take what we've learned and apply it to others. Restitution may involve more than a single action, taking years to complete, perhaps the rest of our life. That we are engaged in the *process* of reparation is what gives us a sense of integrating our responsibility for the loss, not necessarily the *completing* of that process. Mark, who had sexually abused his three children and served time in prison for it, became an advocate for incest survivors. He was a survivor himself:

I can never reverse the damage I've done to my children. Whatever I do now will not be enough to compensate them for what I have destroyed. I have to do something. I couldn't live with myself otherwise. I'll go on doing this as long as I can. It's the least I can do.

Forgiveness is also a restorative process. "We can never be friends and lovers the same way we were," smiled Henry through his tears after reuniting with his ex-wife Lucy and her new husband at their daughter's wedding. "I know I still love you and want the best for you. I always have. I let my feelings get in the way." What Henry restored was his sense of connection with Lucy even though a return to the old relationship was no longer possible.

Say good-bye

I've finished my good-bye to the loss.

It can require an act of will to turn and leave behind what we've lost. Moving on and saying good-bye is also a loss, independent of the original loss—only this time we have a choice.

Recently, my daughter Betsy left behind four children she had taken care of for seven years. The youngest, twins, were three when she became their nanny. Now it was time for her to move on with her life—to move to Czechoslovakia:

> *I can't believe I won't be seeing them again every day. I feel good that my sister Anne will be with them along with Martha, their mom. I won't be there. I've known for a long time I would be leaving. We've done much grieving together about that, and it's really OK. The other day when I was feeling sad, I questioned why I was doing this."*

> *Adam, who is thirteen, said "Betsy, this is a great opportunity for you! We're all proud of what you're doing. We'll miss you. This is what you need to be doing."*

> *It's helpful for me to remember that they will never forget me nor will I ever forget them. I was there during seven years of their growing up. No one else will ever do exactly the same, not even Anne, who may see them through much of their adolescence. I'm giving up the form of our relationship. I can do it because I'm not their parent. I'll always keep the love, the memories, how meaningful their lives have been to me. I'm confident they will keep me in similar ways.*

Betsy's good-byes triggered new grief. She'd already grieved the loss of her role as a nanny for these children, but she knew her impact would continue. Had she not discovered *what she had left*, the good-byes could not have taken place in a way that truly allowed her to move on.

Cognitive Aspects of Integration

How we think about our loss shifts again during integration. We're putting things together. We see a bigger picture beyond the loss. We begin to consider the possibility that we haven't lost as much as we once thought we had.

Balance positives and negatives

There are ways that I have both gained and lost.

Perspective is a time when we see both sides of a loss, the positive and the negative. Integration takes it a step further into an active acceptance of the changes in us that have resulted in gains and losses. The loss is no longer something "out there" that happened to us—it is a part of who we are, for better *and* for worse.

Conceptualizing our grief

> Putting my thoughts into words has helped me recover.

There was a time when our grief defied words, as during the awareness phase. During perspective, we could begin to express the thoughts, feelings and images of our grief, often in the form of drawings, movement, music, or something symbolic. It often was helpful to talk about the bits and pieces of the loss. Integration can involve putting the bits and pieces together in words and symbols, not only to identify the significance of the loss, but to appreciate its meaning in a much broader and more inclusive context.

Acknowledge importance of good-byes, celebrations and remembering

> I realize how important it is to say good-bye to what's (who's) gone.

> I understand why it's important to have times of celebration and remembrance before it's too late.

We can wait too long to say good-bye, to celebrate and remember with someone we will eventually lose. "I appreciate even more the chance to be here for your eightieth birthday because I never had that chance with Dad," confessed John to his mother. "I never could tell him how much I'd learned from him as I can with you—and celebrate how happy I am to still have you in my life."

Relinquish need for understanding and control

> I have as full an understanding as I can right now.

> I don't need to be so much in control of things.

When we can truly understand why things happen, it's amazing how much our need to be in control lessens. For one thing, we've discovered how little of what's important to us can be controlled. For another, we discover that the more we focus on a single thing, the less able we are to see the broad picture. Relinquishing control or direction enhances our capacity to understand the whole of what this loss is about.

Acknowledge the significance of our own life

> My life has more to it.
>
> I know my life is important.
>
> This experience has meaning for me.

During times of awareness, we assure ourselves there is nothing more to us than our loss. As perspective emerges, we rediscover parts of ourself and parts of our world. As we begin to reintegrate our life, we actively begin to make more of our life than we could before.

Integration also means we realize that our life has importance, at least to ourself and often to others. We need not discount it, as we did in letting go, exaggerate it as we did in times of holding on, or be unable to see it as we did during awareness. We can imagine what the world would have been like without us, much as Jimmy Stewart's character did in the classic movie, *It's a Wonderful Life.* We take the steps necessary to discover the impact we've had now. We look back at past accomplishments and relish them, as Teena did about college:

> *Graduation came at the wrong time for me. It seemed so empty, so trivial. I guess I was still angry about all the exams, the hurdles, the rites of passage. I only went to it because of my parents. I knew it was important to them. Their last child had grown up and I guess they needed a ceremony to mark the occasion. Six years later, I had the urge to go back for a visit. I'm glad I did, although at the time it surprised me. I didn't belong anymore. A significant part of my life was over. Many years have passed and you know—I'm glad I went to graduation. It seems more meaningful to me now than it did at the time.*

Emotional Aspects of Integration

Satisfaction with the fullness of our emotional expression

> I've had many feelings.
>
> I've felt all I can feel about this loss.
>
> I've experienced the loss as fully as I can.

By the time we have the capacity to integrate, we've already dealt with many feelings. We've gone about as far as we can with these feelings. We've experienced the loss as fully as we can— not because we are limited in ways to express the loss, but as a result of completing what needed to be experienced.

Emotional competence

> I've found effective ways to express my feelings.
>
> I've learned a lot from my feelings about this loss.

The reason we can say we've felt as much as we need to about this loss is that we have found effective ways to express our feelings. That can mean finding creative ways to express what we need to, as Charity did by writing a letter to her mom, who had died years before:

> *Mom died so suddenly I never had a chance to say good-bye to her, much less tell her a whole bunch of things I wanted to say to her. For years I carried around that feeling that I had been cheated out of that last good-bye. Years later, on the anniversary of her death, I wanted to write a letter to her—knowing, of course, she would never receive it. I felt kind of foolish. I did it anyway. In it I told her what I'd wanted to say, wanted her to hear, some of what I had learned in the many years since, some of what I'd wanted to share with her since then, but couldn't. Once I finished the letter and signed it, I felt more at peace with myself than I can ever remember. It's as if I'd said my last good-bye to her after all these years.*

There is no residual emotion lurking, waiting to catch us unaware. We know what our feelings signify about this loss.

Relinquish old feelings about the loss

> I no longer feel shame.
>
> I've let go of the guilt.
>
> I've let go of my sadness.
>
> I've let go of the anger.
>
> I no longer feel disgust.

When we finally accept our feelings as necessary components of our grief, we lose our fear of them. We may even get comfortable with them, or at least resigned to their presence. Their presence in a steady predictable form, however, can limit our capacity to move on. If our sadness is the same each time, or if it overwhelms us every time we think of the loss, we can't move forward. If we're not ready to let go of our anger over what happened to us, a part of us stays split off and suffering, unable or unwilling to overlook.

It is our willingness to surrender the comfort or predictability that the now familiar feelings of grief give us that is essential to integration. As hard as integration is, we need all our energy focused on the present to accomplish it. Energy tied to feelings anchored in our past can make it impossible to move forward.

This doesn't mean we'll never have feelings again about the loss. We will—the feelings will be new ones, with new voices, colors, moves and tastes. They will be more likely to empower us than deaden or mollify.

Pleasure in relationships

> I like being with people again.

Awareness and perspective are largely internal parts of the grieving process. Although it helps to have others there, we need to go deep inside. When we reach integration, we no longer need to be so preoccupied or alone. We have a better understanding of our feelings and don't feel nearly as vulnerable to being misunderstood or judged by others. When we're not afraid that a chance remark will trigger some feelings, we can genuinely look forward to being in someone else's company. We can take risks in reaching out to others.

Taking risks doesn't ensure results, at least not at first. It takes energy to overcome the inactivity and atrophy of social skills that occur during earlier phases of grief or after long-term relationships end. Sometimes, the social skills that we discover became dormant long ago, or we never developed them. Penny returned to her early-adult dating issues when she divorced at forty-three, after twenty years of marriage:

> *Two years after the divorce, I thought I was ready to start dating again. The past few years had been both painful and isolating. I discovered in the twenty years of my marriage, they had changed the rules about dating! Women take the initiative now. I thought that would be wonderful! Only one of the first times that happened, I couldn't get up the nerve for it. I couldn't make the phone call.*

> *When a guy asked me out, I didn't know what to say. I felt like a schoolgirl—awkward, too eager, too horny. On that first date, I must have turned him off by talking too much. All I got was a handshake at the door!*

Integration can have its times of savoring and satisfaction. We've found ourself again, especially our best self. We've found a purpose again. Even our loss makes some sense. We can think about things other than our loss. We can be the listener and the initiator. The resulting joy is something that we want to share, especially with those who have seen us through the process. We look forward to their fellowship.

Physical Aspects of Integration

Many of us have gone a long way in life without paying much attention to our bodies and how they respond. Before we can integrate our losses, we need to make our bodies a part of the process. That may mean a whole new learning process and time to learn effective physical self-care.

Appreciate our body

I can make sense out of the messages from my body.

I don't neglect my body.

I don't push my body beyond limits.

During integration, what comes together is often a combination of intellect and body. We realize one has something to say to the other. That chest pain wasn't a random ache—it was a reminder of an anniversary of dad's death. That lump in the throat was some unspoken words that needed to get out—an expression of love, a word of good-bye.

When we finally begin to listen to our body's messages and needs, we realize we can't so readily neglect them to meet external demands. We're more reluctant to push ourself beyond limits, in part because we get in return the renewed ability to experience pleasure and competence.

People with life-threatening or chronic illnesses are expected to be frustrated by and disappointed in their bodies. After all, they are being let down by this vessel designed to allow them to remain vital and alive. The messages of the body are either frightening, for they say we are dying, or the pain is intense and unremitting, discouraging in their reminders of what we can't do, or confusing in their disconnection with what else is happening to us.

What people with life-shortening illness learn in the process of integrating their bodies is to respect their limits, to appreciate that sometimes the messages from their bodies are clear. Some discover they can't will themselves to die because they are frightened, their lives lack meaning, they have pain or frustration—or because they still believe the mind can control the body. Some can.

Sometimes these messages challenge us to decide again whether life is worth living. When we know, accept and respect the messages of our bodies, it is amazing what we can do. Life can be lived fully. Death can be a graceful passage, facilitated by our capacity to relinquish basic life functions.

Physical well-being

> I have the energy I need.
>
> I relax.
>
> I feel better.
>
> I sleep well.
>
> I exercise.
>
> I eat sensibly.
>
> I take care of the way I look.

The consequence of respecting physical limits and practicing self-care is a sense of well-being. We have more energy available. We can relax, sleep well, generally taking care of our needs and appearance.

In the past we may have used our bodies as protective covering against being abused. Perhaps we gained weight so that no one would see us as sexually attractive or so we couldn't be pushed around. We may have lost weight to avoid sex as well. We may have used our bodies in ways to postpone dealing with our feelings. We may have overeaten to avoid feeling sad, or ran marathons to dissipate anger. When we integrate a loss, we begin to allow the body to resume its more natural functions, letting go of the need to protect or suppress our feelings. Somehow, it's not enough to say, "Well, I know why I did it and I can forgive myself for doing it." We need to take action to reconnect our body with our mind and emotions. That can mean taking the long road to losing or gaining weight, and to regaining optimum health.

Renewal of passion or sexuality

> I can be sexually or romantically interested.
>
> Passion is a part of my life.

When our senses awaken, so may our sexual interest, our sense of adventure and excitement. We're willing to try new relationships again, perhaps in a way that reflects our learning and our values. "I have discovered passion and the joy of being with others for the first time," smiled Joyce, a former nun, five years after leaving a cloister and three after her mother died:

> *If I wasn't a celibate, I'd probably be ripe for an affair. As it is, I find my senses peaked, looking for a way to express this urge to create, to express myself and to be with others in nonsexual ways.*

Spiritual Aspects of Integration

The spiritual theme of integration is *resolve*. This loss is not the end, we will keep going. We're committed to bringing together all the resources we have to move forward.

We have moments now when we're able to do better than before. We like ourself more. We have peak experiences, times when we surprise ourself with our capacities for nurturing, self-care, wisdom, love, creativity. We rediscover our best self, the spiritual integrator.

Spirituality is the adhesive force in integration. It consists of accepting our values, balancing our minds and bodies, and putting all the pieces of this loss and previous losses together into a whole. Without this resolve, we'd lack motivation to finish what we need to do or to take a chance on living fully. There is no guarantee that this will last any more than the present moment. It is our opening to our spiritual self that permits us to forgive and to commit ourself to what it takes to reconcile or restore. Part of what makes integration such a hard aspect of grief is the need for our best self—our spiritual self—to be fully alive and well. Without it, we lack the necessary belief in ourself.

Renewal through dreams

My dreams are restful, playful and helpful.

Some of my dreams have survived this loss.

Dreams can be reminders of enduring truths in our life. During times of integration, our mental images can be restful, playful and often obvious reminders of what's important to us. "My dreams used to be so dark and frightening," observed Tracy, several years after her best friend's suicide:

> *I was afraid to go to sleep for fear of what would come up. Now my dreams are a pleasure. They're not something I wouldn't think about while I was awake—it's that I don't think about them with all I have to do. The other day I found myself talking to Marsh, like he was still alive. We laughed and talked about some of the good*

times. He reminded me that I didn't need to wait for him anymore.
I knew that. It was very helpful to hear it—you know what I mean?

Tracy got permission from her dream not to feel disloyal to Marshall for going on with her life—a permission she didn't know she needed until her dream gave it to her.

Restore or regain best self

I've restored or regained part of what I had lost.

I am finding ways to fit this experience into the rest of my life.

There's an active element to our spirituality in integration, which calls upon our best self. Anne struggled for a long time with the relationship with her father—the loss of his being the way she wanted him to be. Eventually she found a way to free herself from the way he was:

I've tried many times to tell my father how I felt about him. He never lets me finish. He never listens to me. It wasn't until I was in a women's group where the therapist encouraged me to talk to the empty chair as if he was there—and then to take his position and hear what I had to say—that I finally could let go of my anger at him. He's still the same, but I no longer feel bound to try to change him.

In times of integration, we can both take action and accept things as they are. We make restitution when we can. We restore friendships when possible. We actively work at making these experiences a part of our everyday life. What better way to remember a loss than to weave it into what we do each day without making it the focus?

Accept the reality of our connections

I feel the presence of what/who I lost.

Feeling the presence or the influence of someone or something we've lost is often an early sign of a spiritual connection after a loss. Early in our grief, we may have desperately sought to give that sense a form, to try to communicate with it. At other times, we may have attempted to discount it as our overactive imagination. In awareness, we may not have even sensed it. During integration, we may feel that presence inside us. "I know she is there when I feel that warm, soft pressure over my heart," admitted Lee, ten years after his affair with Lindy ended:

Perhaps she is thinking of me at those times. I know we had such times before we broke up when we could confirm it. Now I don't need it. It feels good to feel that it's her, that I still have within me the love we shared.

Risk intimacy

This loss has opened me to love and friendship.

"I'll never fall in love again" is a resolve many of us have after we've gone through the loss of an intimate relationship. It is a protective, healing stance that allows us to mourn what we've lost without distraction from a new relationship. It protects us from getting hurt again at a time when we feel very wounded.

By the time we're in a process of integrating our loss, we're willing to reconsider being closed down to opportunities for love and friendship. We remember more than the painful ending now. We're ready to take the risk again to have the benefits that love and friendship bring to our life—something we've missed for quite a while.

Active forgiveness and peacemaking

I have forgiven myself for what happened.

I have been forgiven for what I contributed to this loss.

I have forgiven others for what happened.

I've made peace with those involved in this loss.

Forgiveness and peacemaking are the ends of a long process that involves both spiritual and behavioral components. As was noted earlier in this chapter, we began with the shock of betrayal (the beginning of grief), our struggle to overcome, reverse or protest it (holding on), our denial of its significance or even its existence (letting go), the painful and lonely descent into awareness of how devastated we are by it. Gradually, sometimes grudgingly, we discover there is still something left of us and our relationships when we reach perspective.

Many of us stumble and falter over our values and spiritual self when it comes to active forgiveness. We ask if we or the other deserves clemency, if enough suffering or restitution has taken place—indeed, if enough can ever take place. We often have considerable support and justification for not forgiving. Some religions and cultures define certain actions as unforgivable. Revenge-based wars whose origins are centuries and even thousands of years old reflect views that mercy is not possible even for our children and their children. Spiritual integration is not found.

On the other hand, we may try to forgive too quickly as a form of coping. We know the person didn't mean to injure us—they did not know what they were doing. We don't want to lose them as a part of our life. Even if the hurt was intentional, we're afraid of the recriminations if we don't let go of the sense of injury and betrayal we feel. We'd rather not feel the full force of the guilt that comes with exploring how extensive the damage to our best self was. Martin, a therapist, recalled the results of such an attempt with one of his clients:

> *"I'm gonna sue that bastard," stormed Clay as he entered my office. A year before this meeting, Clay had lost his daughter Emily in a car accident at the beach when Emily was hit by a car. The man driving the car was a minister, rushing on his way to a family whose son had just committed suicide.*
>
> *Clay saw the minister immediately after the accident. He came to Emily's funeral, upset and overwhelmed with guilt. Clay embraced him, told him it was OK, that he hadn't meant to do it—it was one of those things that happen.*
>
> *Over the course of the year, Clay had gone over the incident many times. The paper reported the incident as if Emily had darted in front of the car, and that Clay had neglected to warn her. Yet he had. She had looked both ways. The car had been speeding. The investigating officer confirmed that, but hadn't issued a ticket because the minister was so upset and had truly been rushing on an errand of mercy.*
>
> *Still, the impression left was that it was Clay and Emily's fault she was killed. After a year, he couldn't accept that responsibility. He couldn't let Emily's integrity be marred by being seen as the child who carelessly ran in front of cars.*
>
> *Clay realized he had forgiven the minister much too soon. He had never expressed his anger for what had happened.*
>
> *"Well, that's one thing you can do," I replied, caught off guard by the anger in this normally gentle man, in response to his determination to sue the minister.*

"I suppose you're gonna tell me I should go over and get this thing off my chest with him man to man," Clay snarled at me. Without waiting for a response, he snapped, "Well, I'm not gonna do it. The bastard deserves to be sued—and don't you try to talk me out of it!" He stormed out of my office, long before his scheduled session was over.

The next day Clay called me on the phone. "Well, I did what you told me to do." Puzzled, I did not remember telling Clay to do anything. "I called up that minister and told him I wanted to talk to him. He said, 'Thank God you called.'

"I went over and saw him last night. I told him what I'd been thinking and how angry I was at him. He started crying. Rob— that's his name—he told me he had been paralyzed this whole year. Rob knew he didn't deserve my forgiveness when I gave it. He wanted to do something to make up for what he'd done. He felt totally paralyzed because I'd already forgiven him. He wanted to see me, to see how I was doing. He felt so guilty he couldn't pick up the phone.

"I told Rob I had been thinking of suing him, and he said he understood. When I heard what he said, something happened inside of me. My anger disappeared. I saw Rob, another human being, hurting so much about Emily's death. I knew Rob would never forget her and what happened as long as he lived. I knew I couldn't sue him. I told him so.

"I'm not ordinarily the hugging type—especially not with people I don't know very well—and definitely not with men or with ministers.

"I hugged Rob as I left. I think there were tears in his eyes. I can't be sure, because I wasn't seeing so well myself through my own tears."

We may also try to overlook things too quickly when we're afraid of the intensity of our own anger. "I have to let go of this," cried Mandy, panicked by her emerging awareness of the incest that had taken place with her father since she was six months old. "If I don't, I'll kill him." Mandy's rage at the violation, humiliation and pain her father had inflicted on her throughout her childhood, that resulted in her obesity and inability to enjoy sex as an adult, was so intense she wanted to pretend it didn't matter. She tried, unsuccessfully, to forgive her father without going through the rage to get there. It was only after a series of rage reduction sessions with her therapist and several friends that she felt safe with her anger. It took a long time to forgive him.

There are religions and cultures that recognize how hard it is to forgive—and how essential it is. "Christ died for the forgiveness of sins" is an often-quoted rationale in Christian teachings—an acknowledgment of how hard it is for mere mortals to give and receive forgiveness. Rituals exist to help us discover within us the best self that is capable of rising above issues of whether it is deserved, too soon or too late.

Embracing our growth

I would not want my loss reversed if it meant giving up all my growth from it.

Before this moment in integration, we might be willing, even eager to give up anything we had gained to get back what we had lost. We need to recognize that to be willing to give up what we've gained to get back what we lost is another way of holding on, the ultimate bargain, an impossible and totally unfair test of our loyalty. When we accept that growth probably could not have resulted without this particular loss or one of equal severity, *we can understand that our growth cannot be equated with our loss*. We can't go back to the past. We won't fall into the trap of thinking about reversing the past with present thoughts, deeds or actions. We won't relinquish what we have. Many years after leaving her husband and children, Angeline reflected on her growth and her losses. She had grown up in a culture where women had few rights:

One thing I still like about my ex-husband is that he is a good devoted father. Being a father was more central in his life than being a mother was to me. I had a career and a desire to be on my own. I had married so young—sixteen—I'd never had time for me. Despite getting an education, there was little permission for me to have any independence. In my country, I couldn't drive a car or go out after dark. I would have been stoned if I appeared in public without a veil covering my face

Yet it took being at the edge of death before I realized I had to leave, to give up everything, even the children. To stay meant I would die, and I would lose everything anyway.

One stormy April evening my husband and I fought physically— to the point that he threatened to kill me unless I left. Later, I realized he helped me do something I could not have done otherwise—leaving, knowing I was also leaving the children.

I moved to another country, far away, where women have more opportunity and more rights. I write to the kids. They never respond. It has not been easy. I have never felt so lonely, so desolate—ever. I cried every night for years for my children. My arms still ache to hold them. I miss seeing them grow up. I often wonder what they must be like, how they miss me, or if they have forgotten me, the mother who abandoned them.

The man I love now understands the depth of my grief. He accepts the love I have for him, and the need I have to be alone much of the time. He let me be the terrible person I believed I was. He fought with me to get me to express my rage at fate, my husband, myself, even at him for loving me. He held me those long nights when I hurt so much for the children.

Forgiven myself? Occasionally I realize it was the only way I could have survived. Sometimes, I even feel it was an act of love for myself that allowed all of this to happen.

My forgiveness comes in what I do routinely. My life now involves caring for others. I don't neglect myself—and there is much love in my life. Sometimes, I believe that what I could not give my children, I am giving to others wounded by life as well.

Move on

Life is worth living again.

I feel confident enough in myself to move on to other things.

It's time for me to get on with life.

It's an act of faith when we permit ourself to move away from a focus on what we've lost. We need to believe that we won't forget what we've lost. We are confident that we've learned what was necessary and possible from this loss. For us to go on, we have to accept there is more to us than what connected us to this loss. Sasha took that step eight years after she lost a child:

Timmy died from SIDS (Sudden Infant Death Syndrome) when he was three months old. It was the worst day in my life. I don't remember much about those first few weeks afterwards. Eventually, we found a group of bereaved parents, who met a couple of times a month. It was a tremendous support. We could talk and realize we had experienced the worst possible kind of loss. "There is no death so sad as the death of a child" was the motto of this group—and it helped us to know that.

Much of our life has focused on that group now for the past eight years. I'm not sure what we'd have done without it. In a way, it helped keep Timmy alive for us. I can't forget him. The group reminded us that our lives will never be the same again. I know we will spend the rest of our lives with our memories of him.

In the last year or so, I've stopped going to the group. They're still doing important things for the newly bereaved. I got a lot out of helping others for many years. It's been a long time since I've needed the group for me. I've been there for others. I don't need to do that anymore.

Now I feel a need to focus on other things. Timmy would have been nine now, becoming independent from his mom. I need to have back the kind of life I would have had if he had lived. I need to have other things, like music and square dancing—things entirely unrelated to Timmy and SIDS.

We think we are at the point of moving on many times before it actually happens. We wish we could be here long before it's possible. At times, we believe it will never be possible. It is the culmination of our integration of a loss. In his thirties, Charlie realized this about his home town:

The last time I went back to the town where I grew up, I knew it was over. I no longer belonged there. My home was in Greensboro, a thousand miles away. I realized I was saying good-bye to the place. I sold the land, said farewell to the few people I still knew. I no longer feel the need to go back. That part of my life is over, even though I'll never forget it. Much of who I am right now has it roots back there. I don't need to go back anymore to remind me of that.

Facilitating Integration

Helping others in the process of integration involves finding ways to help with completing and acknowledging the split-off, or dark, parts of self. It also involves bearing witness to the forgiveness that takes place, to the necessary restitution, and to the resolve to move on.

Helping With Restitution and Forgiveness

Some of us are fortunate to belong to groups that recognize the frailties of the human condition and the need for forgiveness as a part of growth and transformation. Some religious communities have rituals and sacraments for reconciliation which at their best encourage and permit spiritual reintegration. Gestalt therapy and psychosynthesis focus on the importance of completion by confronting the ways we've split ourself off and by recognizing the need to reintegrate—saying good-bye, owning our responsibility, and safely confronting our persecutors in ways that permit us to alter the decisions we made way back when.

There are a host of careers and volunteer organizations that permit people to provide some form of restitution to those injured. Many people in helping roles are consciously or unconsciously dealing with a sense of guilt or responsibility for a significant loss: Some have been victims who help others by validating their losses and give others permission to grieve.

Much of the energy that I devote to bereaved people and to trying to understand grief comes from my sense of responsibility in many of the losses I have experienced. My process of integrating the lost parts of myself continues. A key part of this is having close friends in this field who support me despite being a normal human being with complex motivations.

Perhaps all we have is a friend or a therapist who recognizes our struggles with gaining integrity and is willing to travel on the path with us. There's no easy road to integration, but it helps to have someone along.

Help With Completion and Conscious Dying

"I can't say what I need to say to my dad. He died three years ago." Hugh felt stuck with his unexpressed feelings for his dad because he couldn't do it directly. What he needed help with was that he still could express what he needed to, even if his dad couldn't receive it. He could talk to his father through role-playing, talking to an empty chair, or by writing him a letter. Through these techniques

Hugh discovered what he most wanted from his dad and begin to integrate this into his life.

When we don't have access to the lost person, we feel incomplete. We have to use our imagination. We need to find ways to express what's inside us. Sometimes the other person may be available, but it may not be safe to do it directly:

> *"I could never talk to my 'ex' the way I want to about what's happened to us," admitted Marcelle. "I'd resigned myself to having to keep it inside of me when I went to this bioenergetic type workshop where they had us act out physically what we were feeling. I screamed and pounded my fists until I saw them bleeding. Then I said what I've needed to say to her for so long. I cried afterwards because she hadn't heard it at all. At least I'm not carrying it inside me anymore."*

Max, a therapist whose client had committed suicide seven years before, found help in facing his anger and saying good-bye at a workshop:

> *I don't know if I would ever have been ready to let go of my anger at his suicide if Marianne hadn't helped me to say good-bye to him. At first I was furious. Then, as I played his role with me, I accepted this as what he had to do. I was then able to let him go, to say good-bye. Suddenly, I realized I was free of his curse. I could go on living. I could take risks again. I didn't need to wait any longer for his forgiveness—or my own.*

Helping others with their grief when there is potential for growth, renewal and continued life. Helping people complete their physical existence is much more difficult. Hospice came into existence expressly for this purpose because the dying process can be lonely and painful. It is often perceived as a sign of failure by the medical profession. Teaching people how to use their consciousness and their imagination to facilitate dying has been the focus of approaches called "deathing" (Anya Foos-Graber, 1990) and "conscious dying" (Steven Levine, 1984). To help under these circumstances means we accept that death is inevitable and that our role is easing and witnessing that passage. For those of us in helping roles, it can mean challenging some of the assumptions we have about our role:

> *"It amazes me how people respond when you acknowledge their right to determine their own life," mused April, a psychotherapist friend of mine. "Several times a dying person I was seeing wanted*

me to be there at the time. We said our good-byes, which helped my closure. I've also had people so miserable in their grief and pain they wanted to die. I've told them that all I wanted was a chance to say good-bye. Every time they've broken down in tears and said they couldn't do that. I guess they realized their decision wasn't only theirs—that it would have an impact on me. Perhaps they realized they weren't quite as alone in this world as they thought. I'm not always sure. I am sure that it was OK had they died—as long as I said good-bye."

April had to challenge some of her basic issues about being a therapist. Was she obligated by her profession to stop people from killing themselves? Was asking for a good-bye a ploy to make it too hard to do it? Was her belief that people have the right to make this most basic of choices—to live or to die—a way that enhances the capacity to go on living.

Overcoming Assumptions

Overcoming the limits imposed by our beliefs may be necessary for integration. Challenging assumptions is a major source of loss and grief, especially in the early adult years. Some of those presumptions keep us in passive or victim roles. For example, if we accept that there is no death so sad as the death of a child, we may assume that it is impossible to ever move on. We may find ourself feeling hopeless because we assume nothing can be done without seeming disloyal, that we didn't love our dead child, for example. Unquestioned beliefs can paralyze us.

To challenge assumptions, it often takes help from someone with a similar loss whom we consider credible. Recovering alcoholics, for example, may need to hear from another alcoholic in recovery that forgiveness is possible for the horrendous things done under the influence.

Bearing Witness

There are times in grief when we've needed some help to take the next step. We needed to tell someone our story, often a number of people. We needed to have our ways of coping validated. We needed to know that we weren't totally alone as we emerged from the lonely vigil of awareness. The presence of others helped us as we began to heal. Now others can witness our resolve to step forward even if they may not approve. We need to *demonstrate* our commitment to growth.

It helps to have someone witness our completions and good-byes, especially if we can't say them directly to the person involved. It helps to go with a friend to the cemetery to say good-bye.

Summary

It is often the sense of incompleteness that motivates us to begin the integration phase of grieving. Grieving builds integrity and the restoration of our best self. Integrity comes by restoring the splits of mind, body and spirit, and healing the incompleteness that keeps us from functioning fully.

Integrating loss may be the most difficult phase of the grief process. It requires a clear definition of responsibility and admissions of self-betrayal. We relinquish or revise cherished assumptions, the familiar, the comfortable and the safe. We make choices that friends may not support. We commit to our best self, and conclude that there is more to us than just this loss. Integration involves acts of courage: We confront persecutors, make restitution, show mercy, and acknowledge our humanity. We reach beyond what we know and undertake what we once thought was a hopeless journey. We risk perceptions of disloyalty by moving on, looking for fewer external rewards. With the synergy of mind, body and spirit, we can fulfill this once seemingly impossible task.

Chapter Eight
Reformulating Loss:
What Is Possible?

> *This life is not concerned with health*
> *but with healing.*
> *This life is not about our being*
> *but our becoming.*
> *This life is not about rest*
> *but about exercise.*
> *We are not yet what we shall be*
> *but we are growing toward it.*
> *The process is not yet finished*
> *but it is going on.*
> *This is not the end*
> *but it is the road.*
> —*Martin Luther*

At this point in grief, we are not yet what we shall be, but we are getting there. We've gone beyond what we have left to consider possibilities and connections that defy our senses and sensibilities. To contemplate possibilities, however, we must abandon our search for the right answer. There is no single way to help us through the rest of our lives. *Reformulating loss emancipates us from our focus on limits.*

Peter Marris (1974) considered the process of reformulating loss to be an essential aspect of growth from grief. Earlier, while losses were viewed as either tragic (e.g., that there can be no death as sad as this one), limiting, or something we have to accept or as the end of a meaningful life, growth could not be consolidated.

Reformulating is a way of finding significance. We relinquish old ways, authorities, and external sources that provide us answers. Who can tell a blind person that blindness is a gift? We cannot tell a homeless or bankrupt person how freeing their new lifestyle may be unless we have been there ourself. We can't tell an abused spouse that giving up her predictable, dependent relationship could eventually be self-fulfilling.

Each of us must discover this for ourself from our own losses, from our own process of reformulating.

How important is reformulating? At the time of a loss, reformulating is almost impossible. It is the *worst* thing someone else can encourage us to do. At the time of a loss, to say that it might be a "blessing in disguise" or that there is a silver lining can leave the impression that we need not grieve. When we first experience loss, we are offended by people who tell us we didn't lose anything or worse, that taking time to explore the extent of our loss is a sign of incompetence, self indulgence or moral weakness. Attempts to reformulate the loss too soon, however well-intentioned, make it difficult for us to be around them until we feel much stronger— empowered by our *own* process of experiencing, integrating and reformulating.

Reformulating loss originates with the decision to live—to go on in spite of the emptiness and hopelessness we felt during awareness. With perspective, we are also reformulating our original conceptions and assumptions about the loss. Reformulating is a source of power when we've integrated the loss and accepted that there's no going back to the past—that it's time to move forward.

Reformulating or reframing a loss is an imposing task. Life events, once traumatic, tragic, disheartening and disillusioning, can now have positive effects. We can now consider that perhaps the loss was beneficial to our growth. There are more consequences we can tolerate when we feel greater self-trust. We no longer need to search for the right answers because many possibilities exist.

We may find ourself saying: "I didn't have a choice in this loss. Yet, as I look back, I'm not sure I would ever have awakened to who I am without going through it." My friend Lee shared this perspective with me, many years after she lost a child and had several miscarriages. She is now director of a successful hospice program and has become a respected presence in her community:

> *I was just a farmer's wife—married at eighteen, raised two kids, shared the toils of planting, harvesting, taking care of the livestock. If it hadn't been for losing those babies—they were all babies to me—I'd still be doing the same, not aware of anything else in life.*
>
> *Those losses, and the time I had to think and feel, led me to open to a bigger world, one that acknowledged suffering and death in a way that made living worthwhile. At some point, I stopped looking at those bales of cotton and those turkey feathers and saw*

there was more for me in life—and it was up to me to find it. So I went to nursing school, got a degree, practiced for years until I saw a way to get hospice going.

David's never quite understood what got into his wife, that naive little country girl he married. What got into me was a vision born out of stillbirth and miscarriage.

Reformulating is essential during times of rapid change and significant losses. We can't afford to take things only on faith, or to ritualistically remain in traditional roles, careers and relationships when to do so risks inertia in the face of attack, withdrawal when engagement is needed, or combativeness when a peaceful solution is possible. We need to be active in our appraisal of the circumstances of our life.

With a new sense of security, we can let appearances, rituals and habits change naturally during reformulation. We can challenge the assumptions and beliefs of everyday living and seek a new path, as Henry David Thoreau aptly stated:

If a man does not keep pace with his companions,
perhaps it is because he hears a different drummer.
Let him step to the music which he hears,
however measured or far away.

When our personal world disintegrates during a loss, we cannot go on living as we'd like: We are forced to stop and question the very basis of our life. The reformulating that occurs now forms the basis for considering other possibilities.

One such reformulation involves our notions of time. In our early years we dreamed of living forever and of having unlimited time ahead. If we don't have many years left, as with a terminal illness, we treasure the *fullness* of our remaining time, not necessarily its length.

Reformulating our losses is paradoxical. We can reduce active grieving because we know we'll never forget. We feel freer and more deeply connected to life than ever before. We become more passionate, yet less consumed by any particular emotion. We have more to offer, yet we may possess less. We feel stronger, yet more vulnerable.

"Strange," observed Elissa several years after becoming suicidal in reaction to a series of losses:

I wasn't afraid of dying back then. After all, I had very little else to lose. Now, with life as exciting and challenging as it is, I am afraid of dying. I don't want to die now. Life is full and beautiful. I know how fragile it is.

Elissa had created a new life—something to live for. It wouldn't be effortless for her to go back and face death or any other significant loss. Yet she is less likely to fight it than she was the first time around.

The capacity to reformulate reduces our desire to fight loss. We're willing to let go of the unrealizable, able to give up finding the "right way." And, paradoxically, we invest more in possibilities, dreams, and the improbable.

Reformulating doesn't eliminate the need to mourn new losses, but we won't resist change as readily as we once did. We believe more firmly in our abilities to grieve and to choose.

An important dynamic of reformulating loss is our capacity for *acceptance*. We can let go of attachments to ways that are no longer functional, and to relationships that lack give and take. We yield our righteous indignation and the power of any particular role. There are fewer things we can't live without. There is less worth fighting—or dying—for.

Eleanor, who had been blind since birth, was able to surrender her self-perception as a victim of her blindness:

For many years I resented being blind. I thought of it as a punishment—unjust and cruel. Eventually, I accepted it and could even see there were some benefits to being blind. One day, even that changed. I thought to myself, "Suppose I had lived before, and had chosen to live this lifetime as blind to test out something. Perhaps I even chose my parents to help me with it."

Since then, I've been unable to go back to seeing my blindness as a handicap. I'm not its victim. Now it is something to explore—and to even help others with. I can help others "see" what they take for granted, what there is to appreciate in our other senses. It has been a joyful discovery.

Reformulating a loss is an active phase in grief. It involves turning some possibilities into probabilities and some dreams into realities. All we have to do is accept the risks that sometimes the dream won't become a reality and that taking chances doesn't always pay off. If we've learned anything from our losses by this point, we can accept those risks. Grieving, as distressing as it can be, gives us the autonomy to empower the choices we eventually make, for we know that we will grow regardless of what we lose along the way. Self-empowerment emerges when we realize we have real choices about our inevitable death and how fully we can live the interlude.

By the age of thirty, Karla had lost both of her parents in a car accident. More recently, her husband died of AIDS. HIV-positive herself, she recognized that she'd never have a child, or a long life:

> *The first thirty years of my life were filled with loss—both parents, my husband, many of my dreams. Yet I realized that, as bad as life has been, perhaps I had spent all those years grieving so that now I can appreciate what I do have. Except for my own life, everything I once valued is gone. So why not take some risks? I know I can manage and even grow, no matter what happens.*

When grief guides us to growth, there are pauses, periods of rest, and patience for the unfolding of new discoveries. Growth cannot be hurried, no matter how much we desire to end the extended cycles of pain and doubt. When we transform loss we can provide closure to this process. Our internal search declines. We reach out to others. We open and amplify our view of self. Clark Moustakas (1972) noted:

> The self that does not reach out to encounter and include others is, indeed, still mourning, still split, and suffering. To come back to the human community, one must know the agony of broken communications, of unanswered doubts and questions; one must know the clear visions of loneliness and solitude and the joy of being born again. One must also know the depths of loving unconditionally and being unconditionally loved, of forming new bonds with others that cancel out pettiness, misunderstanding, meanness, and incomprehension; one must know the feeling of genuine communication and unity. (p. 36)

We extend ourself, get involved with a cause, or embrace others during the reformulating phase. This shift requires challenging previously learned and valued ways (e.g., "I have searched everywhere and found nothing," which rejects all that was found). It can involve relinquishing the protected and expected. It can mean grieving a loss without pursuing replacements.

Reformulating loss and self-empowerment go hand in hand. Our self-confidence frees us to think about an ever widening range of possibilities. By reformulating limits, we produce choices. Our experience with loss empowers us to create choices *and* to make choices, for we know the present may be all we have—we can accept whatever outcome results.

Reformulating can also force us to face some important issues we've feared. We look at our dark side, knowing we won't abandon ourself in the midst of this exploration as we might have when coping was all we could muster. We reconsider the cost-benefit of some friendships and family entanglements, and withdraw our energy from ones that are limiting or destructive to us. We can be self-seeking, perhaps for the first time, and live with the guilt.

Reformulating can create further losses. If confronting a "fair weather" friend about their unavailability during our grief ends that relationship, well, we can take that. If insisting that a spouse stop beating or abusing us leads to divorce, we accept it—we will not allow fear stand in the way of our growth.

Being a victim or a survivor of an illness, of a brutal childhood, poverty or war may not be enough to keep us going any longer. Learning to survive demands that we reformulate our beliefs. That means letting some dysfunctional ones go, at least for now. For example, abusive and incestuous parents may love us, but to focus only on that love desensitizes us at a time when we must escape their hate, wrath or lust.

Reformulating begins early in grief, but does not come to the forefront until integration has been experienced. The reformulating aspects of integration come when we can move on with life regardless of the loss, a situation unimaginable earlier in our grief. Reformulating can consist of finding ways to make restitution for irrevocable or inexcusable things we have done.

Integration enhances our discipline for facing or renewing whatever aspect we've neglected previously. Integration shifts into reformulating when we reconsider the importance of being a whole person by granting neglected aspects of ourself their due. Instead of asserting "that's just the way I am," we allow the neglected, mistrusted or feared parts of us to grow and make a positive contribution. We become more active in changing ourself.

Tim had never been athletic. He had been quite sickly as a child. As an adult, he was very kind, meek and non-aggressive. A friend took him to a men's workshop on grief, with drumming, dancing, yelling and sharing feelings:

For the first time in my life, I'm not ashamed to be a male. I am no longer afraid of my strength or my aggressiveness. For so long I've neglected my body—I guess because I was so sickly—and later because the women in my life found my softness and femininity so appealing.

Now I want to develop that part of me—the physical. I've always thought I was hopeless when it came to sports or any other physical expression. Maybe I'll never be good. Still, I want to find out what it is I can do with my body. Arnold Schwarzenegger has nothing to worry about!

I don't want to neglect the masculine part of me anymore.

Here, Tim is moving from an integrative understanding to an active reformulation phase by contemplating actual behaviors and activities that will move him to a new identity. He is willing to risk the loss of or change in some of the feminine characteristics that others found appealing, because he realizes that he needs his masculine side in order to grow. Reformulating creates opportunities to test our confidence, discover possibilities, create flexibility and alter what previously seemed fundamental to our self-definition. We reorder priorities to reflect our values even if that leads to further losses.

There are no guarantees that the additional losses will be easy. Divorce may follow the serious illness of a child, for example, when one parent is unable to deal with it but the other can. Janet recognized, in the wake of her son's life-threatening surgery, that her marriage could not provide strength under those circumstances:

Todd would never go with me to the doctor's office with Keith. He fought me about getting a second opinion, claiming Keith wasn't all that sick. He went to work the day of surgery and only came to the hospital once in the month Keith was there. Afterwards, he never spoke of Keith's illness. I had to go outside our marriage to find support.

It took me several years before I had what it takes to act on what I'd known from that time—that I deserved more in a relationship than I was getting from Todd. Todd was a good provider. Until Keith's illness, he had been a great lover. I saw much potential in him. That's all it still is—potential.

Five years after Keith's surgery, we divorced. It wasn't so hard. Oh, I'll never have the life style I had with Todd. I certainly couldn't blame him for what I needed to do, so I couldn't see alimony or *even an equal split of possessions. Material things aren't as important to me as my freedom. I'm still going to school and working part-time. But I have me. I have relationships where we can talk about anything. I have support <u>when</u> I need it.*

What I came out of Keith's illness with was a sense that material things weren't so important anymore. Nor were appearances.

I need to be able to love someone. I need to be loved. Neither were possible in my marriage anymore. So I had to radically alter my view of what I was about so that I could free myself. I have—and I am determined never to go back to neglecting what I consider essential to being me, even if I die or starve in the process.

I don't think I will.

Reformulating can result from the greatest suffering we have endured. Somehow, awareness opens to hope, growth, freedom, and new choices. If the greatest tragedies in life can be transformed, is there anything that can't?

Reformulating is a seed we plant when we accept that there is no real alternative to grief, in spite of our capacities to cope. It germinates when we can face our pain, darkness, suffering, emptiness, loneliness—and still go on. It blooms as we heal and gain perspective. It ripens and matures when we integrate our resources. We harvest its benefits when we consider previously nonexistent possibilities.

In understanding the various dimensions of the reformulating phase of grief, it is important to acknowledge that the distinctions between the physical, emotional, behavioral, cognitive and spiritual aspects begin to blur. As Figure 8-1 demonstrates, the transition to a more active phase deepens integrity and enhances wholeness:

Figure 8-1: Dimensions of Reformulating

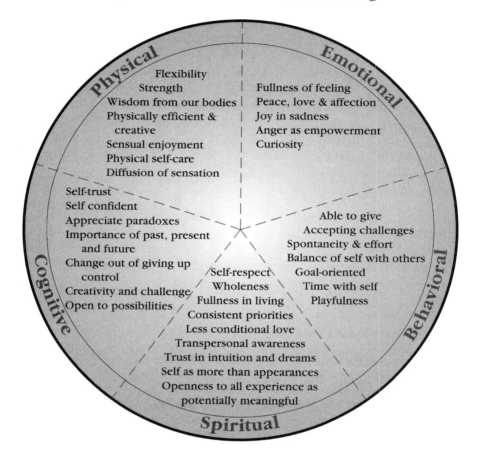

Behavioral Aspects of Reformulating Loss

Maybe we can look good when it comes to the behavioral aspect of growth after a loss. Our real tests come when we are challenged to reformulate: Do we have the strength, energy, flexibility, effectiveness and choices now to act—or to defer to new grief? Can we be spontaneous again, cope again?

Spontaneity and effort

> It takes less effort and thought to do what I need to do.
>
> I do things on the spur of the moment.

We discipline ourself while integrating losses. Reformulating gives us a break. After all, we need not be compulsive about everything. We look for an easier way, a more playful and pleasurable one. In the process, we may find a more efficient and effortless way. We can be spontaneous, for we are less frightened by what could happen when we are.

Time with self

> I enjoy being alone.
>
> I spend time by myself.
>
> I'm nicer to myself.

It's remarkable how freeing the actions of grief can be. By spending time alone, we learn to appreciate its importance and to even find ways to enjoy it. Being with people or being alone have equal legitimacy. Being alone becomes spending time with a special friend—ourself.

Playfulness

> I can laugh at myself.
>
> I'm not as serious a person.

The natural course of any intense life experience is to first validate it by taking it seriously, *then* understand and master what we can and grieve what we cannot. When we are confident with our sense of mastery and our grief, we can resume being playful. We can laugh at our previous seriousness.

Accept challenges

> I'm more assertive.
>
> I'm able to take risks again.
>
> I like being challenged.

Nietzsche declared that powerful events that do not kill us make us stronger. He could have been thinking about reaching this point in the grieving process. We are stronger now, perhaps stronger than we've ever been. It's a strength born from challenge and risk, without the assurance that we'll win or even survive. We may face hazards that can kill us. We also know that we have the strength to go on, to make something of this new experience. We can enjoy challenges to go beyond our self-imposed limits. We have fewer limits as a result of testing them.

Goal oriented

> I'm more self-disciplined.
>
> I discovered what I want in life.
>
> I don't place limits in front of myself as readily as I did before this loss.

Reformulating may increase our options, but it must also empower us to rearrange our priorities. We develop the self-discipline necessary to change careers and find new relationships, if they are necessary to grow.

Making such decisions doesn't mean we won't feel pain and sadness when significant parts of our lives change. It's that we know that we can't do everything, that we don't have forever, and we need to take care of ourself. We may outgrow our job, some of our friends, and the pledges we made long ago. We may no longer wait for a loved one to fulfill their part of the covenant.

Self-discipline keeps our lives from becoming chaotic. We may create new losses but are open to the repercussions of knowing what we want in life and of reaching for it. Unlike the more compulsive phase of coping, when we had to control and limit awareness, the self-discipline of reformulating is more spirited and gratifying. It also contains sadness, for we won't always be successful in getting our way.

For example, we start to lose some of our self-defeating beliefs, especially if an activity can bring us enjoyment or a new way for self expression. Mary Sue found such potential after her husband's sudden death of a heart attack:

> *As long as I can remember, I would always say to myself, "Well, I'm not good at that," "That's the way I am," or "That's just not me." I didn't realize what I was doing to myself. I became more constricted as I found more things in life that I couldn't do—at least not to my standards of perfection, or that I was frightened to do. It wasn't until I had to do a lot of things after Joe's death that I realized how I had trapped myself with all these self-defeating statements.*
>
> *I got a good therapist. You know, I realize now that I can do many things and not worry about how good or bad I am at doing them. The way I am can change. I'm still scared to try new things, but I don't use those old excuses anymore. I'm playing the piano again.*

I gave it up years ago because I didn't think I was good enough to play for anyone else. Now I love playing for me.

Life is a lot more exciting now. I never would have chosen having Joe die to find myself, but I realize it might not have happened otherwise, at least not for quite a while.

Able to give

I've started new relationships.

I am more able to give to others.

Our experience with our own grief, renewal and forgiveness can open us to be more giving. By the reformulating phase we have faced our fears to risk new relationships. We give more because we're less concerned that the "well might run dry" or that we'll be unable to limit what others take from us. At the same time, we aren't as likely to get into relationships that are one-way. "I still have an eye for potential," admitted Terry after leaving a depressed partner. "I don't invest as readily unless the other is open to challenge."

Balance of self with others

I can care for me and for others.

I have time for my family and friends <u>and</u> time for me.

When we learn to reformulate, we are less constrained by obligation and responsibility, although we won't tamper with what's basic to our integrity or our values. We are freer to give when we know we don't have to and that giving doesn't exclude self-care.

We discover ways to have more time for those who matter most to us—our loved ones and ourself. "It doesn't desensitize me when I do things that are just for me," confessed Marilee, who had struggled with taking time away from her marriage and her husband Tom:

And I'm more resistant than ever to doing things that involve me giving up what I want to do to please Tom. I've become much more creative in finding things for us to do that we both get something from.

Cognitive Aspects of Reformulating Loss

Reformulating involves inclusive and elastic thinking. It can include feelings, sensations, values and the actions that help us seek choices and think about possibilities. We can recognize paradoxes and not see them as contradictions or irreconcilable polarities.

Appreciate paradoxes

I can appreciate the paradoxes and seeming contradictions in my life.

The shift from integrating loss to reformulating is also a shift from being self-centered to inclusive. We give up our need to be self-sufficient, the center of a personal universe. We also open to paradox.

It can seem contradictory to see the death of a loved one as a liberation from a suffering or destroyed body while we acknowledge our personal grief. We can feel sad when our children no longer need us and, at the same time, feel happy for their growth, for by relinquishing control, we may find connections to others on an even deeper level. T. S. Eliot (1960) stated such incongruities:

In order to arrive at what you know
You must go by a way which is the way of ignorance.
In order to possess what you do not possess
You must go by the way of dispossession.
In order to arrive at what you are
You must go through the way in which you are not.
And what you do not know is the only thing you know
And what you own is what you do not own
And where you are is where you are not.

Open to possibilities

I'm more open to possibilities.

If something as grievous as the death of a child allows us to reformulate our priorities and discover untapped talents, is it possible that other life experiences can have that potential? Can we emerge from grieving and question the limits placed on ourself and the world we live in?

Reformulating literally means to *re-form*, to alter the form we started with. We go beyond a particular loss and investigate how it fits with other aspects of our lives. In the process, we may remodel what we say, do and believe. We may also affirm what matters for us—the basic nature of our affiliations, of who and what we are.

We may go beyond our usual reasoning and communicating. An example is Swami Rama's observation that "all of the body is in the mind, but not all of the mind is in the body." This notion of a non-local mind is a powerful perspective to consider.

We may be reformulating when we are aware of someone's death by seeing a vision or hearing the person's voice, even though the dying person was thousands of miles away. We may find that our dreams contain prescience of things to come, some of which happen.

We may connect with past lives or loved ones who have died. We may no longer need to reject the possibility of such occurrences. We don't need to give credence to them as "proof" of an afterlife or of our powers as a healer or psychic. Perhaps we can communicate without words or by simply being in the physical presence of the other. What's more significant when reformulating is that we are open to the possibility, not that we prove its existence.

Self-confident

> I feel more confident.
>
> I'm more patient.
>
> I've grown.

A life event that shattered our confidence, tested our ability to tolerate the time it took to grieve, and seemed bereft of any saving features is now a source of hope and confidence. We survived this loss—and more. We have more faith in ourself.

Transformation out of giving up control

> I've changed in ways that would not have happened otherwise.

Growth is a product of how we respond to loss, when we concede that we can't control outcomes. Darcy discovered this after an accident that killed her mother and her daughter—two years after her dad and brother died in a hunting accident:

> *For two years I wouldn't let my children out of my sight. I was convinced that if I could only keep them within reach, they wouldn't be injured or killed like my dad and Joe were. Then came the accident. I was driving. Shawna was sitting right next to me and she was killed. My myth about protecting them by controlling them didn't help.*
>
> *I'm not so protective anymore. Sometimes my kids wonder if I still care about them because I'm not hovering all the time. I do care.*

*It's that I know I can't control life. I have to live life as best I can—
and accept what happens.*

Significance of past, present and future

I see the past as just as important as what is happening now.

I don't spend as much time thinking about the loss.

Past, present and future are equally important.

Our energy is no longer centered in the loss, although it can still be
something we think about. We see how it's affected us over time and how
it fits in the context of our life story. We have a sense of continuity between
the past, what's happening now and what lies ahead.

Creativity and daring

I'm more creative in my approach to life.

I feel challenged to keep on going.

I enjoy dreaming as much as I do reaching for them.

Reformulating is a process of creating new possibilities that tap our
potential, that challenge us to use our dreams and our imagination as fully
as we can. "I figured, what else could I lose?" shrugged George, age fifty-
five, in the years after having a heart attack, losing his high-powered,
prestigious job with a law firm, having both his parents killed in a car
accident, being divorced by his wife and having his oldest son die of AIDS:

> *There was nothing else of importance to me left to lose. Everything
> was gone—my parents, Carla, Jack, job, home. I had faced my own
> death. It wasn't the time. So I started moving again. Since then, I
> can't look at life in terms of loss, limits, or problems. Now what I
> see and feel are opportunities, potential, and challenges. I want to
> know—what's possible?*

Emotional Aspects of Reformulating Loss

Self-trust

I trust my ways of thinking.

I know what I need to do to move my life forward.

Fewer things can feel more solid than surviving the tests posed by
loss. We have a greater degree of self-trust that goes beyond respect for our

limits. We consider what we want out of life—and how to get it. We look at what's happening in our life and appreciate the implications. Judy, in her late forties, was able to do this after her husband's death:

> *There are so many losses that radiated from Charlie's death. New awareness springs up just when I think I've finally gotten it resolved and put behind me. Just the other day I realized that with our youngest son Tom leaving for college, I will be alone—and without any excuses for not getting on with my own life. If Charlie had lived, I probably would have continued staying home. I'm comfortable there. It's frightening to think of going back to school or to work. It's exciting, too. I guess for the first time, now that all the kids are gone, I realize I lost the freedom to be out of the rat race when Charlie died. I miss being "just a housewife."*

Fullness of feeling

I don't avoid my feelings.

I believe my feelings are valid.

I've found new ways to express my feelings.

Emotions don't run amok when we reformulate loss. They don't disappear either. There are many ways we've tested our emotional reactions while grieving. We can find additional ways to express and be aware of them, to validate their fullness.

Peace, love and affection

I am at peace.

I feel loving and affectionate.

Being at peace with our feelings is not the same as accepting reality, nor does it mean we stop having reactions to things we consider cruel, unjust or tragic. We limit our internal wars over whether to validate a feeling as legitimate or to decide which feeling is more dominant. We feel at peace within ourself. That sense of peace can free us to be loving and affectionate.

Joy in sadness

I can feel both joyful and sad.

Sadness reminds me how important this loss was to me.

At one time in our grief, joy and sadness couldn't coexist, though one might have triggered the other. In the process of experiencing one, we'd lose touch with the other. Now they can be a part of the same feeling.

Sweet sadness, a part of perspective, has an even softer, gentle radiance in reformulating. We know what we're missing. Sadness does not take our energy as it once did—it can activate our exploration of what it is we miss.

Anger as empowerment

I can get angry.

Sadness isn't the only feeling we empower while reformulating. Anger is also cleaner and crisper, a source of energy for creating options. We can develop creativity in expressing anger if we don't need to deny it.

Curiosity

I am curious about many things.

It's hard for me to be bored.

What is curiosity if it isn't an openness to surprise, to finding things we don't expect or can't anticipate? Reformulating involves active investigation of our internal and external world. There's much to consider, detect, sense, feel, examine. If we have access to our curiosity there's less time for boredom.

Physical Aspects of Reformulating Loss

Wisdom from our bodies

The messages from my body make sense.

I listen to what my body tells me.

Early in grief the messages from our body may be incomprehensible, something to be disregarded, suppressed or apprehensive about. They may have coincided with special days or special events—a source of remembering. Throughout our grief, we may have discovered that our physical sense meant we were grieving our losses.

Bodily messages become clearer. For example, illness may represent our body healing itself. Physical aches and pains, pressures and flashes may signify unresolved issues from our past, both individual and transgenerational. We may be experiencing physical symptoms of unresolved grief handed down to us over several generations.

Our bodies are much more than a machine that requires fuel and a little maintenance. Our cells have memories and store them for us, to be recalled later. Our bodies make sense of feelings and give us ways to express them. We can't focus without our bodies. We lack energy to act when we deplete ourself physically. We learn to appreciate the wisdom of our bodies, pay more attention to them.

Physically efficient and creative

> I am efficient and creative at doing things.
>
> I take my time.

"For someone who's been a klutz all her life, I am amazed at how easy it is now to draw," observed Sandy, two and a half years after having a cancerous breast removed:

> *I've given up being so worried about doing things right. I do it to express myself—and I love what comes out!*

Sandy found how freeing it can be to lose the self-consciousness that cramped her physically. She internalized the criteria for what was good about her art. It freed her to draw as she felt.

Sometimes freedom and efficiency come because we take our time. We're less pressed by deadlines. Time seems to lose its linearity. We feel less of the need to follow it. Zach noted this shift as he recovered from bankruptcy:

> *I find myself these days doing some curious things. I'm in much less of a hurry to get back to work after lunch and I've rediscovered or discovered for the first time some amazing and beautiful things enroute. Do you know I've been traveling that same route to work now for fifteen years, and I never before noticed or explored the arboretum? It's beautiful—with all sorts of plants and animals once you stop to look at them. I've wandered through there several times now and keep discovering new things—like that duck pond or a bald eagle!*

Sensual enjoyment

> I enjoy making love.
>
> I enjoy touching and being touched.

We sometimes escape from sexual urges during grief by ignoring or avoiding them. We don't have the energy or interest. At other times, we use sex to escape from everything else. When our sexual impulses contributed to or created the loss, it is something we learn to control, contain or more effectively express. When we lose a lover, we may feel guilty or disloyal in making love with someone else.

Our sexuality may need to be reformulated after a loss. We may have had assumptions and beliefs about sex that we no longer consider valid. We may find a fullness in making love that wasn't there before. We can be frisky, sensual, free from guilt, able to mutually gratify in ways we weren't free to accept before. "I never thought about how wonderful it is to make love with someone you love," beamed Tibbs, a year after the start of his second marriage. "It is such a full declaration of how we feel about each other."

Sexuality can also be an energy we use to create, empower and enjoy our senses in other ways. "I'm not so interested in sex these days," admitted Mark, two years after his wife of thirty years died:

> *I remember how marvelous it was with Marion. I get my gratification now from making pots and playing music. They are a way of making love for me now.*

Strength

I feel strong.

Pliability gives us strength. Oh, it may not mean we'll win at arm wrestling, but we can blend energies with someone to do something neither could do separately. Strength through reformulating is also in our fantasies. In a study of terminally ill cancer patients, Jeanne Achterberg and Frank Lawlis (1977) found a very high correlation between the use of particular types of imagery (as an adjunct to medical treatment) and a positive course of the disease two months later. They found seventy-five percent of those using effective imagery had no further progress of the disease or a remission. At the other extreme, all (one hundred percent!) of those whose imagery showed the cancer to be a more powerful force than the immune system became worse or died in the next two months. In a series of studies based on Jeanne and Frank's approach, my colleagues and I (Schneider, Smith et al., 1990) have examined the relationship of imagery to the functions of white blood cells, particularly neutrophils, in healthy volunteer subjects. We've found strong correlations between imagery and the cell's ability to migrate, adhere and extricate itself. This work suggests that it is possible to alter the functions of cells in the body.

Imagery involves fantasy, an essential component of reformulating. It is also an integrative activity of mind and body that we can't do when depressed or highly stressed. When we're capable of reformulating, we have the strength to do so.

Physical self-care

> I am active in caring for myself physically.
>
> I get the exercise I need.
>
> What I eat is healthy.
>
> I make sure I have time to relax.
>
> I listen to music.

We can go overboard with exercise, as we can with sex. We can also restrict it just as thoroughly. "I used to say that I had the urge to exercise every day," smirked Bill:

> *So I'd go sit down until the urge passed. These past two years of sudden unexpected success has changed all that. I realize I need to care for my body as much as the rest of me or I won't make it.*

Marshall shifted his view of physical self-care as he approached his fortieth birthday:

> *Three years ago, I was thirty pounds overweight, rarely got more exercise than an occasional game of tennis. I was coming out of a very stressful three years in which, among other things, I almost died. I realized that no one else could take hold of my life and give it meaning. I had to. Part of that was getting myself back in shape. As I approached my fortieth birthday, I kept telling myself, "It'll never be easier than it is now." I've lost a lot of weight, and if more than a day or two goes by without running, biking, or tennis, I feel guilty that I'm neglecting myself. Until three years ago, the opposite was true—I felt guilty when I paid attention to me!*

We may reframe what it means to be healthy after grieving a significant loss. We become aware of what it takes for both short-term enjoyment and longer term health habits. We're less likely to ignore warning signs of stress or go for long periods without relaxing and enjoying what we like about our lives.

Flexibility

> I can express myself in many ways.

Flexibility is a key element in reformulating loss. We aren't as likely to rely on only a few ways of self-expression that may later be needed for coping with other losses. We may need to develop new ones, pertinent to our present circumstances.

Diffusion of sensation

I feel warm all over.

When we have difficulty remembering a loss, we may need to have a spot in our body that holds that memory. When we have grieved that loss and find other ways to remember, it may lose its need to be localized. Earlier in grief, for example, we may have felt a heaviness in our chest, a weight on our heart, a coldness in our stomach, a pain in a particular place that stores the memory or a lump in our throat for an unexpressed feeling. Reformulating can mean that the sensations we're aware of when we consider the loss are diffused, and may be experienced as warmth throughout our body.

Spiritual Aspects of Reformulating Loss

The spiritual theme of reformulating a loss is *wholeness*. Spirituality pulls mind, body, feelings and actions together in reformulating a loss. We want to find those principles that harmonize our world and our response to it and to test them in the context of each change we meet.

Openness to all experience as potentially meaningful

I'm no longer searching for answers to everything.

I have what is meaningful within me.

I act on what I believe and understand.

Peter Marris (1974) suggested that reformulating is a process of separating what is fundamentally meaningful from the loss and rehabilitating it. This is a primary point of gaining perspective and integrating a loss. There comes a time when searching is no longer necessary nor advantageous. We understand what we can and leave it at that. We also act on that knowledge. We express the meaning, not simply recognize it.

In reformulating loss, however, the end of searching can mean an opening to other experiences. When we explore and seek, we expect to find something in particular. Perhaps one of our more developed illusions is that there is meaning in everything if we look long enough or in the right place. Anne Morrow Lindbergh (1955) saw this as the "dredging of the sea bottom to find the treasures of the ocean." Searching implies impatience, a lack of faith in ourself, a "greediness" for meaning. When we reformulate, we let it emerge.

Self-respect

> I've learned to respect myself.
>
> I am not as hard on myself when I make mistakes.

Reformulating can help us understand the differences between honesty and truth. We have many moments of honesty in response to loss that seem to take us in all directions—approach and avoidance, hope and despair, sadness and joy, to mention a few. It's only when we can step back and look at those moments of honesty that we can see patterns in our responses to a life-transforming event. Reformulating allows us to respect our grief process and its unfolding. We need not to be so hard on ourself when we make mistakes. There may be something beyond the honesty of the moment in our response. *In reformulating, we validate the wholeness of our grief, not simply the elements of it.*

Wholeness of self

> I feel like a whole person.
>
> I like the way I am.

This reflection on the whole process also helps us to feel complete. This is also a product of having gone through the integrative process, of bringing together mind, body and spirit. By allowing the process to continue, we can find ways to truly care for ourself and others.

Self as more than appearances or roles

> I've discovered that there is more to me than meets the eye.
>
> I feel a part of something much bigger than myself.

There is more to us than what others can see. We've only begun to appreciate how complex we are, filled with paradoxes and images that sometimes contradict each other. We are more than what anyone else can appreciate.

When we see that others grieve as we do, that loss is a common condition of living, we appreciate how we are a part of something bigger than ourself. We consider patterns and connections beyond our individual capacities.

Trust in intuition and dreams

> My dreams make sense.

I trust my intuition to let me know what I need to know.

Slips of the tongue may divulge more about us than we care to know. Our dreams may be nightmares that a horror writer would love. Believing in ourself may get us in trouble—and may even have caused our loss. The tests and trials of grief can change all that. We face our dark side as we reformulate our loss. We admit our splits from reality, sincerity and integrity. We realize that authority can't help us choose whether or how to live. That's up to us.

When we're able to accept ourself as a whole person, we have less of a need for an unconscious that has to scare or embarrass us to get our attention. That doesn't mean we can't have slips of the tongue or pen, but their messages are more obvious and less frightening. We're more playful and can find some humor in our unconscious.

"How dull my dreams are these days," sighed Clarence, who struggled for years with his nightmares and behavior during and after the Vietnam War:

No more nightmarish visions, cold sweats in the middle of the night that I dread and can't understand for weeks or months. Now it's like a conversation with myself—things I already know only I didn't take the time to appreciate.

It also took May Lee a long time before her dreams were clear after the death of her daughter:

The dream I had is still clear to me. I was shackled in a deep, dark, cold, and damp dungeon. The chains were broken. I finally stopped waiting for someone to come and rescue me. I began climbing the stairs. I reached a huge door. I peeked through the keyhole and could see the sunshine and the green lush valley beyond. With strength I didn't know I had, I unlatched the door, pushed it open, and stepped forward into the blinding sunshine.

It was the beginning: I was filled with childlike excitement, in awe of the beauty of the countryside, curious about exploring every pebble, tree, and mountain, amazed at its magnificence. I stepped out and began a new journey. My fantasy was like reality—I am starting anew. It's been ten years now since June died, and I'm ready to go on.

Fullness in living

> I live as fully as I can.

Living fully means accepting that we may endure more cycles of loss and grief, that life has both positives and negative times.

Margaret discovered that she had cancer shortly after her forty-third birthday. It was well advanced because the lab results of a test a year before had not been sent to her family doctor—results indicating a mass in her lung. Now she would have a lung removed, with no assurance that it would contain all the cancer. She had ten days before the surgery. On the evening before surgery, she reflected on what she had done with that time:

> *I've lived my life taking care of everybody else. It's only in the past few years I've begun to find ways to do things for me. I've taken some risks. Some have led to disaster financially. I've traveled—to Ireland, my ancestral home. I've learned to love me.*

> *The cancer, I know, is my anger. I'm an incest survivor. I've never been able to express that anger toward my parents. They deny anything ever happened. Even now, they can't appreciate what's happening, that this could kill me. My mother complained when I called her that she was feeling awful too, having the same symptoms as me, except no basis. For the first time I realized that she doesn't get it. I can accept her limits. She will never be the mom I wanted and needed. I have that mom within myself.*

> *If I get through this surgery, my life will have to change. These past ten days have been full. I've done what I wanted for me. We all went to Disneyland for three days, enjoyed the time as a family. I've borrowed money—if I don't survive, it will be paid for out of my life insurance. My best friend has flown in to spend three days with me. We ate all the things I know aren't good for me—the best chocolate I could find, prime rib, lobster. We stayed up all night talking. She went with me to see my therapist. We did imagery together, for healing, for connecting in the times when we're apart. My husband and I had a wonderful dinner together. We made love—and for the first time in my life, I didn't have to leave my body during it. I made a tape for my five-year-old Timmy. Someday, he'll know his mom through that tape—at least my hopes and wishes for him.*

I worry a lot about my nineteen-year-old son Mike. Yet I need to let him go, whether I survive this surgery or not. Tomorrow, before surgery, I'll tell him: "Mike, I can't take care of you anymore. You'll have to take care of yourself. I know you can do it."

I have every intention of surviving this surgery. I have a lot to live for. Still, if I don't, I've had these ten days. If this is all I have of living fully, it has all been worth it.

Margaret died three weeks after the surgery, never fully regaining consciousness. Those ten days were all she had. How striking it is for people who are living fully that the completeness in life can be in the moment, not in how long we live.

Consistent priorities

I am more consistently aware of what's important to me.

What is important to me has changed.

Grieving challenges us to look at what's important. At one time, we are convinced that anything that could be important is gone. Over time, grieving gives us many opportunities to confront and reshape what is meaningful. As a result, we become more aware of what is important—so much so we're willing to alter priorities to sharpen our values.

What is important does change after a loss. We reorder priorities, in part because what we lost was one of the things important to us. By reframing other assumptions, we find that some things we thought we couldn't do without, we can—and vice-versa.

Less conditional love

I can love and be devoted to another without losing myself.

I have fewer conditions on my love.

Mature love is an inclusive emotion, a spiritual connection that not only feels extraordinary, it empowers. We feel related. We love even when we can't touch, hear or see the object of our love. We appreciate and contemplate how much people are a part of us. When we truly love ourself, we'll want to share.

Love, like joy, thrives on expression. During the reformulating phase, we seek ways for love to increase our options, test our courage and keep us open to those who share it. Relationships that pose no challenge and test of shared ideas, mutual respect and feelings of love become boring and restricting. At the same time, we become more open to who others really are during this phase, needing less from them to sustain ourself.

Accept role in death, separation and destruction

> Death is only one of many transitions I'll make in life.
>
> I realize I can do destructive things.
>
> I have some degree of control over how and when I die.

Reformulating loss involves death, separation and destruction. A loss destroys. So does death. We need to accept that we can be destructive—that creativity itself sometimes destroys old ways. We need to understand the common bonds between death and life, destruction and creation. We may have some control over when a loss might happen, including death or abandonment. Maria, at the age of thirty-five, found freedom from fear in the process:

> *From the time I realized I couldn't give up on life and somehow found the strength to go on, my life has changed. I no longer feel trapped—by anyone or anything. I no longer fall into my husband's games, designed to make me feel responsible for everything that happened between us. His desperation did not need to be my desperation. His threats no longer intimidate me. I have lost my fear of dying.*
>
> *When he left, I had to face my fears of being abandoned. I realized I still have myself.*
>
> *It's remarkable how my thinking, my outlook on the world, has changed. I have faced my worst fears—of dying, being aban- doned—and I've come through both. If I no longer need to fear either of <u>them</u>, what do I need to fear?*

Lovable

> I feel lovable.

We may have considered that one reason for our loss was that there was something wrong with us. We were being punished for a wrongdoing. We were worthless. We felt ugly, unlovable. We never should have been born. Nobody loved us. Yet, here we are, embracing life. We *feel* loved, by individuals or by a higher power. Our ability to bring together mind, body and spirit gives us a solid basis to love ourself. We know we are lovable, capable of giving a great deal to a relationship that can give something back to us.

Transpersonal awareness

> Some kind of "inner" wisdom has been guiding me.

From the utter aloneness of awareness, we believe that there is something more to us and to the world than this individual body, ego and collection of limits and talents. We couldn't have made it this far totally on our own. That was perhaps the most radical reformulating we'll ever make—from seeking total uniqueness and aloneness to the acceptance of being part of something much greater than our personal being. That transformation represents a paradigm shift, from the *personal* to the *transpersonal.*

Someone or something guided us in spite of our protests to the contrary. An inner advisor, or a guardian angel, exists that remains a part of us. "Sometimes when I talk, I am surprised at what I say," commented Bob. "I'm not sure I know what I'm saying or if something is coming through me." Sometimes the wisdom that comes out of our mouths has mysterious sources.

Challenge basic beliefs

> I've challenged and altered some of my most cherished and long-standing assumptions and beliefs.

In grief, we reexamine the premises underlying our lives, especially if those assumptions didn't prepare us for our loss. We test, revise or discard beliefs we may never have challenged otherwise.

Diane reexamined the beliefs she'd held about her birth mother. At the age of two, Diane was taken from her mother, who had given birth to five children in five years following her fifteenth birthday. Her husband at the time was dying of tuberculosis. Desperate to survive, Diane's mother turned to prostitution, and to drinking. Abuse and neglect of her children resulted.

At the age of thirty-nine, Diane began looking for her mother, and discovered that she was dying. They met twice. They acknowledged the painful past and said good-bye. Diane had a profound sense of having been reborn through facing her own death—at the hands of her mother and more recently, during her grief, at her own hands. She found herself reformulating her notions about love:

I realize now, with some sadness, that my mother really did love me. She even loved me when she tried to kill me, either to save me from a horrible life of neglect and abuse or to give me the gift of learning very early to fight for my own survival. On some level, she knew that if I was going to make it in life, I would have to know how to survive. As it has turned out, she was right.

Perhaps her greatest gift was her self-love that led her to give me up. It was killing her <u>and</u> me for her to keep my siblings and me. Her only chance for survival was to be free of all us children. As it turned out (as I discovered thirty-seven years later), she has been able to start a new life. She had never forgotten us. From what her new husband said, she cried herself to sleep many, many nights, worrying about us—wondering if we were OK. For thirty-seven years, she didn't know.

My sadness? I didn't realize the extent and the depth of her love and her wisdom while she was still alive. I am alive now because of her love—in ways I would have never experienced otherwise.

Reformulating can help us choose how to live our lives. When we experience the fullness of a loss, we can choose: Is life worth living, given the extent of our loss?

We may chose to go on—even conditionally. We could chose to give up. We may decide to live within the limits our losses imposed on us. We may dispute beliefs that limit our options.

We don't simply surrender or revise old beliefs. We form new ones, especially while we reformulate a loss. Some reformulating is based on our experiences while grieving and what we've discovered helps us to ease our way through the process. These include some suggested in Table 8-2:

Table 8-2: New Beliefs Commonly Formed During The Process Of Grieving

I believe different things about life than I did before this loss.

Understanding sometimes helps.

Pain is inevitable.

Accepting pain doesn't guarantee anything.

Helplessness is sometimes avoidable.

Death is one of many transformations we can experience.

Life is fragile, something to appreciate while we have it.

Loneliness can mean missing a part of ourselves.

Life is precious.

Feelings are ways of knowing ourselves.

Hopelessness is a necessary part of finding hope.

No experience in life is completely good.

No experience in life is completely bad.

Perfection isn't possible.

Creativity can also be destructive.

Heroes can inspire us or they can diminish what we've done.

We can't have anything unless we are willing to let go.

Letting go doesn't guarantee that we'll get what we want.

Everything can be enriched if we question it.

Questioning does not guarantee answers.

Terror and dread can be a beginning.

Self-awareness is both freeing and painful.

Facilitating Reformulating

What can caregivers offer those who need to discover the power of their helplessness, the creative potential in their dark, unintegrated side, and the joy in relinquishing old ways? When people aren't ready to reformulate, such paradoxes seem like nonsensical gibberish, offensive to their sensibilities and reinforce the desire to remain safely fixed in their grief process. We can't usually extend to others this gift of wholeness, of comprehending paradox, of expanding knowledge beyond the boundaries of the body and senses. They might seek us out, provided that we are open.

We all need help in reframing and relinquishing assumptions at one time or another. We rarely recognize our blocks until someone points them out, or a loss hits us hard. After a loving and passionate, abruptly-ended affair, Chet struggled to understand why it happened:

I had thought I had considered and accepted almost every possible reason for her precipitous ending of the relationship. There were many possibilities, such as finishing the business at hand, i.e., her marriage, before being available to me. I considered the possibility that she was not ready for our relationship. I could even consider the possibility that I might never see her again.

I didn't let myself look at some other possibilities until a friend, over several weeks, pointed them out to me. Each time, I realized I hadn't wanted to examine those possibilities. Each one was a new loss—a new way of looking at the relationship. My friend would quietly say, "Suppose she is deciding to die—can you accept that as possible? Suppose she is deciding to give up her children to be with you? Suppose she is giving up on her own growth—so that you can make up your mind if life is worth living without any hope of having her in your life?"

Painfully, I considered each possibility, realizing what it would mean for me—what would have to change, be grieved, how my self-image would change, how it would affect my desire to go on with life. Each time, I gained more freedom to be myself, even though it felt as if a part of me was dying.

Posing alternatives is one way to reformulate loss. Being present as people consider unpleasant options is another. It is important not to become too attached to any particular outcome. We must trust that the bereaved person will do what's best for them, even if it doesn't correspond with what we'd like them to do. If considering suicide, for instance, is a result of alienation, then our ability to stay with them as they consider that option may help them feel less isolated. If dying is made more painful and less graceful by fear of abandonment, then being present when someone dies can lessen that fear.

To help in reformulating loss, we profit from our own experiences. Sometimes we have to say something to get it out of our system. We may not need an argument or even a validation. We're more likely to discern someone else's timing and readiness for facing an issue when we've been there ourself.

Since reformulating is a self-empowering process, our fumblings or lack of empathy may be more helpful than not. "I realized my therapist wasn't always right about me," commented Teresa. "I have to rely on my own inner wisdom."

Sometimes it's our ability as a caregiver to keep ourself from going too deeply into a loss, to keep distance and to simply permit others to look at it that's most helpful. "Focusing" (Gendlin, 1985) is a therapeutic technique that can allow someone to clear away other meddlesome issues, keep some distance from their loss, and get a "felt sense" of it—a process of reformulating the way someone has experienced their loss at sensory and feeling levels.

Summary

Reformulating loss revitalizes us. We're more likely to recognize the potential in our lives for growth, challenge, self-discipline. We let go of seeking a place where loss will no longer concern us. We open to those few principles that will calm us in the face of loss. We can shift from a person-centered existence to a transpersonal one. Reformulating eases the paradigm shifts we make—including the transformation of death itself.

Chapter Nine
Transforming Loss:
Fully Living the Interlude

> *The most beautiful and most profound emotion we can experience is the sensation of the mystical. It is the power of all true science. [Those] to whom this emotion is a stranger, who can no longer wonder and stand rapt in awe [are] as good as dead. To know that what is impenetrable to us really exists, manifesting itself in the highest wisdom and most radiant beauty which our dull faculties can comprehend only in their most primitive form—this knowledge, this feeling is at the center of true religiousness.*
>
> *—Albert Einstein*

The awe-inspiring nature of wisdom is the result of the kind of spiritual transformation that Einstein describes. Consummating the full cycle of transformation is joyful and liberating, and reaches far beyond our senses to the mystical. We affirm how deeply we are related to others. Nothing can take from us the substance of who and what we are, or the love that links us to others, living and dead, present and missing. In those instances when we undergo transformation of loss, we exceed the separateness of detachment and the finiteness of death. Advancing full cycle after a loss creates new paradigms for time and our senses. New connections shatter old conceptions of possibilities.

We may not look, act or perceive the same way as we did at the start of our grief. Everything seems different now. We've moved to something inconceivable before the loss—or impenetrable earlier in grief. We trust our capacity to endure, to open to powers beyond self and complete transitions. What is meaningful to us remains. We alter only form and appearance. *Our essence remains intact.*

We are free from appearances and external demands without the loss of the memories or the resulting wisdom. Still, we're more than spiritual travelers, observers and students of life—we're participants, vibrantly alive. We value friendships, dreams, and loves. We fear and grieve death and loss—but on a different level than before. It's not so much physical death we fear now—it's the spiritual ones.

On the public radio program *Fresh Air*, Wilbert Rideau, an African-American man serving a life term in a Louisiana prison for a murder he committed at the age of eighteen, was being interviewed. At the time he was in his fifties. Wilbert had lived for eleven years on death row before his sentence was commuted to life. After getting off death row, he had wanted to do something productive with his life and started writing. After some opposition and problems with segregationist prison policies, he became quite successful as editor of the prison newspaper, which now has an extensive circulation outside the prison. In the interview, he talked freely of his crime, the awful thing he did. He had been abused much of his life, as a black man in the Deep South. At eighteen, he struck back, killing a police officer. He realizes now that he could not bring the person he killed back to life, that there was no restoration of substance he could make.

The life he leads now includes restitution—an apology for what he did to another human being, and what he did to himself in the process. Wilbert continues to rehabilitate from it; he is no longer a danger to anyone. He intends to live out his life peacefully.

The years on death row forced Wilbert to face himself. He only had time with other people twice a week for fifteen minutes during those eleven years. His punishment was the almost total deprivation of contact with other humans. He realized how much he needed others, and searched to find some way to gain contact with others again. His vehicle became writing. He is respected, has earning praise from *The New York Times* and other publications. Many people write to him, often people with similar histories of crime and self-betrayal, people living with shame from their pasts.

Wilbert, like many other people, lived with an event in his life that had radically altered his acceptability in society. He was ashamed of what he had done. His shame, however, and society's response to him have not stopped him. He has grieved his loss of freedom, the circumstances that led his dark side to kill, the permanence of his punishment. Within the context of his resources, he lives as fully as he can. He has transformed his loss and his sense of shame into a new way of living.

We can treasure the liberation that transformations bring, the opportunities for both new and deeper attachments. Wilbert touches many people's lives, even though he rarely, if ever, touches others physically. We desire a full life—a new abundance that reaches beyond material wealth, exclusive love, peak experiences. We'd rather *be* than *have*.

Grief's transformations can be personal, transpersonal and transgenerational. We can be different from the way we were. We open doors for people we barely know, or don't know at all. We may end cycles of despair that radiate through untold generations in our family.

When transformations happen, we relinquish certainty, authority and empty ritual. Our lives regain a spiritual openness. We connect—to previous lifetimes, to future ones, to people we've never met, to loved ones long gone, to a purpose for living that goes beyond our individual existence.

Transformation can be something much more than simple modification. The prefix "trans" means "across" or "beyond." Our transformations may take us beyond—beyond change, beyond the adaptation and coping so necessary in a world based on the senses and the material, beyond the personal loss we encounter with change. In transformation, optimism may have no basis in reality, only in the spirit, in the empowering of our *best self.* In the breakdown of our crusty old egos that never wanted change in the first place, in how our lives influence other lives we, in return, are transformed. For example, Marshall found a new love relationship, six years after a divorce:

> *One day I recognized I wasn't the only one who had ever experienced a tragedy, grieved it, and grown from it. I simply was living a life story experienced many times in the history of humanity. After that, I no longer needed to see myself as so special. I found I was connected—to the past, and to those who will do the same in the future.*

> *I questioned for years if I would ever commit to someone again— be in love, let myself be vulnerable, open, patient, put aside my own needs. Now, I give myself fully, feel a part of a whole when I am with her, and feel complete myself. I'm no longer afraid—of myself or anyone.*

When we cope with loss, we fear change, hate it, hide from it, analyze it, try desperately to understand it—and in so doing, change ourselves into someone who lives a seemingly untransformed life. We try to live without transformation. We have our personal ego, while losing our connections—or the opposite: maintain attachments but lose our sense of self. We may survive and possess things while losing the capacity to share and experience.

In his novel *Shoes of a Fisherman*, Morris West saw the implications of transformation:

> It costs so much to be a full human being that there are very few who have the enlightenment or the courage to pay the price. . .

> One has to abandon altogether the search for security, and reach out to the risk of living with both arms. One has to embrace the world like a lover. One has to accept pain as a condition of existence. One has to court doubt and darkness as the cost of knowing. One needs a will stubborn in conflict, but apt always to total acceptance of every consequence of living and dying. (p. 117)

What *remains* from a loss is pivotal to the transformative experience. Remnants survive changes in structure—the result of our aging, moving, loss of friendship, job, home, and goals. The process of grieving, with all its mutations, allows us to learn what is substantive about ourself. We see who we are.

Who are we? What is our basic nature that moves through time and space, that constitutes our life story? Sometimes it is a gossamer-like thread, sheer and delicate, hidden by our initial response to a loss. It appears broken, only to emerge later, linking our loss to our story. That tough, delicate fiber is our legacy, the reason for our existence that we may never completely discern. This is what a "lifetime" is about. It is the unbreakable strand that weaves through many lives, conjoins us in the tapestry of our transgenerational family, our multicultural links, the times in which we live, the themes of our civilization. It allows us to accept kindness, love, healing, hope and peace as enduring human qualities.

Transformations originate in loss and in our choice to experience life fully. Survival only measures how much we can miss in life and still be alive. We arrive at the point when we know we can't keep going as before. Something has to change—and the environment is finally right to make that happen. We give up predictability and open to the modifications that grief brings. All we have for this journey is hope—hope for a mending of what we've lost and for a new vitality.

Each loss involves unique experiences. *By admitting what no longer is, we can find what remains and what can grow from it.* It may be something momentous—a deeper devotion, less dependent on formula, character or reason, or it may be something minute, a reminder to appreciate what we have.

We don't outgrow our need to grieve, for living involves form—our body, our relationships, our lifetime—which can die or change at any moment. Most transformations we experience are, as a good friend tells me, "quiet whispers" rather than peak experiences. Many common events are only remarkable from the perspective of many years. Only at the moment of death may we fully comprehend the magnitude of a lifetime of transformations.

We terminate legacies of incomplete sorrow, from our own lifetime and before. We may break transgenerational patterns of abuse and incest or cultural programming for addiction or victimization. We welcome the best of the traditions and rituals of our ancestors and discover roots much deeper than recorded family history. We encourage our children to go beyond, to find their own way. Perhaps we can become role models for people to complete losses from other lifetimes. Considering possibilities can create a wider range of potentialities.

We are transformed whenever a meaningful loss happens, never to be the same again. There is no going back to the naïveté or the predictability of our past. Like the old adage, once aware we can never go back to sleep. There is no way to know the future. Life isn't the way it used to be, nor will it ever be. Still, loss that is grieved liberates us. We are more than we were before, despite having less.

Fundamental principles are not only reformulated but transformed in the process of grieving, including the supposition of simple solutions to complex lives. Bit by bit, piece by piece, we discover a new life, one that weaves loss into its fabric. We live abundantly, not just in fleeting moments on mountain tops or watching spectacular sunsets. We consider possibilities rejected earlier in our grief. We open to the mystical with a healthy questioning. We're more inclusive.

Transformation and Growth

Transformations astonish and fascinate us. They tap hope in the face of despair. Transformations are restorations of the human spirit, the throwing off of the burden of fear and loneliness. It defies our understanding when we recognize forces beyond the individual ego.

Transforming loss into a fuller life is a gift. Gifts often come without search or wishing. When we grow from a loss, we begin to have hope that the energies determined to destroy the world through greed, envy, war, environmental destruction and disease can be transformed. If *we* can change, aren't other transformations possible?

Looking at Figure 9-1, we see that the five dimensions of loss merge or blur in distinction during the transformation phase. There are still themes characteristic of this phase, but these are less important than the whole:

Figure 9-1: Dimensions of Transforming Loss

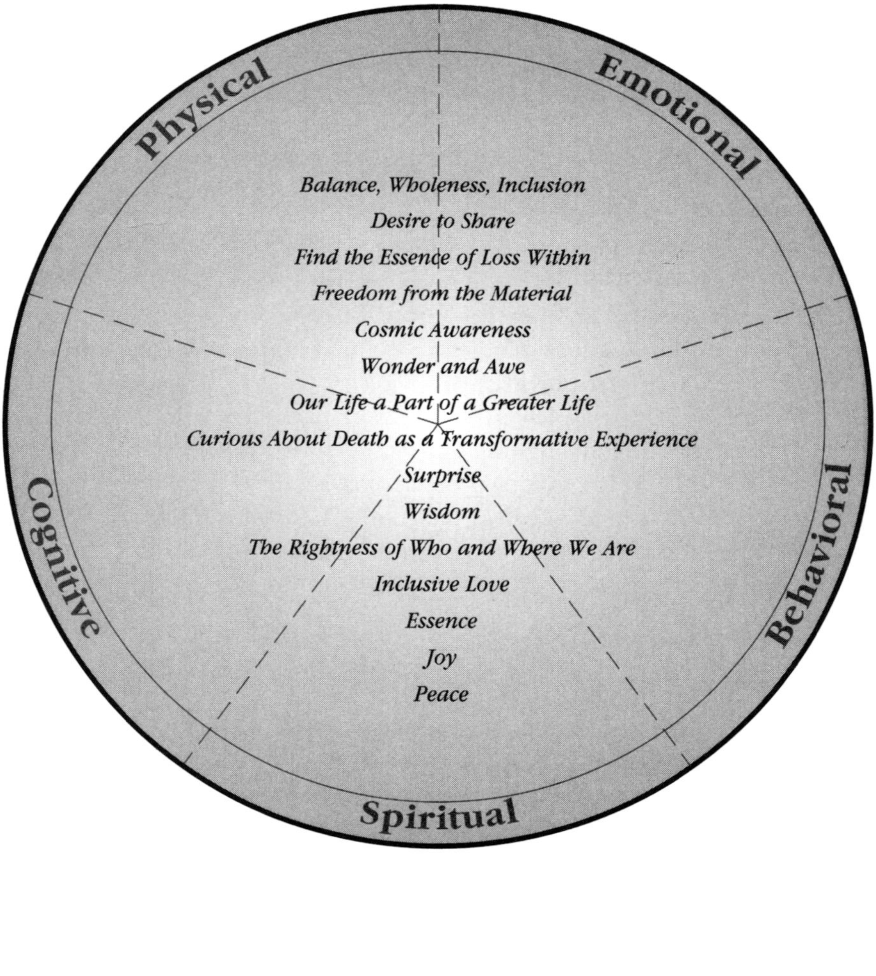

Physical

Emotional

Cognitive

Behavioral

Spiritual

Balance, Wholeness, Inclusion
Desire to Share
Find the Essence of Loss Within
Freedom from the Material
Cosmic Awareness
Wonder and Awe
Our Life a Part of a Greater Life
Curious About Death as a Transformative Experience
Surprise
Wisdom
The Rightness of Who and Where We Are
Inclusive Love
Essence
Joy
Peace

Balance, wholeness, inclusion

> I've found a balance between devoting energy to my personal growth and to my relationships.

> I know I want other people in my life.

When we experience transformations, we make a place for others in our life, regardless of the form those relationships take. People offer us a way to express ourselves, to give and receive, to love and be loved. Solitude and communing with nature offers much the same reward in a different form. We find a balance between solitude and love.

Desire to share

> I have something important to share with others.

> I want to share with others who have these life experiences.

What is unique in our life story we want to share. We empower and inspire by telling our story, and in listening to others'. What constitutes our life experiences becomes a road to the experiences of others. Early in grief, that connection was limited to those with very similar losses. By now, our empathy and our wisdom may have opened to the universality of loss, grief and the potential for transformation that any life story might contain.

Find the essence of loss within

> I've discovered that the most important parts of my loss remain alive inside of me.

When we discovered that we would not forget our losses, we knew that inside of us was an important part of our connection to our loss. During the process of integration of the loss, we found ways to anchor and internalize its essential qualities. Now it's possible to feel the aliveness of those qualities in us. "It's more than an internal dialogue with my mother," remarked Kathy. "She is so much a part of who I am now. It's as if I carry the best of her spirit within me."

Freedom from the material

> What I own isn't as important.

> I can get along with less than I have needed in the past.

What we own is a matter of form rather than substance. In the long run, we know it's an ephemeral part of our lives. Knowing that, we enjoy what it is and stop pushing to make it more than it can be—a defining part of us or a reflection of our importance. Loss and grief help us learn to do without and at the same time expand ourself. "The best thing that ever happened to me was getting divorced from Clyde and all his wealth," smiled Grace, years later:

> *I was so caught up in a material world I'd lost touch with my personal resources, who I really was. I've been forced to see who I was without all the trappings—and I've grown to love the me I've found.*

Cosmic awareness

> I know the cycles of life have times of birth and death.

> I feel a deep connection to people who are no longer alive.

In grief we may struggle with the death or disappearance of someone we loved. Did it mean there was nothing left? Without being able to touch, hear or see them, we were convinced there was nothing. We confirm the transformation when we feel that connection in the absence of physical presence, and that the association is deeper. John affirmed this link many years after his father's death:

> *My dad's death when I was eighteen was a transformation of our relationship. For a time, I was angry at him for deserting me. For awhile, I deeply missed him. I still do. Watching the movie "Field of Dreams," where the ghost of a man's long-dead father gets to meet his grandchild released a well of tears for me—my father had never met my children. All this, over thirty years later.*

> *Over the years, I have discovered bits and pieces of him—in my dreams, in things I said, in remembering what we'd done and said to each other. Eventually I realized that had he lived, I would have struggled with him much more than I've had to. Our relationship is both deeper and more superficial because it lacked the form it would have taken had he lived. I can't imagine what it would have been to see him age, to have taken care of him as he died, or to have fought with him over the differences in our values that I discovered as time went by. We would have struggled to find ways to express our love for each other—with many hurts and misunderstandings getting in the way. Our relationship is much more internal because I've not had to struggle with him these past thirty-four years.*

We become attached, physically and spiritually, in ways that go beyond genetics, family or culture.

Wonder and awe

> I am sometimes surprised by what I know and say.

"Sometimes it feels like something is coming through me rather than from me when I talk," marveled Eric, a well-known and respected lecturer and poet:

> *Sometimes I am embarrassed when others credit me for what I've said or written. I feel like a vessel for something much bigger than me. I get in the way by trying to close it down. When I'm open, what comes forth amazes me as well.*

Our life a part of a greater life

> I believe there is something much more than any single human being.

> I feel connected to the world and to nature.

Conventional religious dogma may distract us from our personal affiliation with something beyond us at various times in our life. Such frameworks may not be as distracting when we've been able to transform a loss. We realize that form is just that: dogma and ritual are for our use rather than a source of constraint. Rituals may again resonate with something within us that is cross-generational. Form and ritual may be a vehicle to help us express our wholeness and spirituality.

Wisdom

> I don't have to have all the answers for why I am alive.

> I know that things in my life can change and life can still be meaningful.

When we honor our transformations, we also recognize that *search* to discover why we were alive can limit us. Reasons for living are often beyond human capacity to comprehend. Worse, such searches can constrain our capacity to experience. Our lives are still unfolding as long as we're here. Perhaps such meaning has yet to come forth. Perhaps our lives provide inspiration or an example for others.

Life continually transforms what has meaning for us. We aren't as excited by the social causes and the personal relationships we had as a youth, or perhaps even those of a few years ago.

Curious about death as a transformative experience

I am curious about my death.

I am curious about what will happen after I die.

Transformation can involve a deeper curiosity about death. The shift from a personal to a transpersonal focus makes death more a transition than a terminal event. How could death be any greater a change than what we've already experienced? Richard Moss (1981) found such transpersonal wisdom in many dying people:

> Whether (a) disease progresses rapidly to death, goes into remission or is cured, one cannot help being struck by the transformation fostered by the process. I have been with individuals so powerfully eroded by the cancer process. . . that profound energy and (formerly unexpressed) wisdom radiated from them. . . It is as if the disease provides the final empowering through which they attain new levels of consciousness.

Death can be an enemy, to be avoided at all costs. It is the final, humiliating evidence that we are mortal humans. Depending on our developmental process, how integrated we perceive our lives to be, death can also be an partner—a release into new forms of life we can only suppose exists. Eventually, as an enemy or as a friend, death is our final opportunity to transform in this lifetime.

It is the nature of that shift that intrigues and frightens us. How will our passage from life to death take place? Do we have any say in the matter? Do we want to?

If we live fully, accept transitions, losses, joys and sorrows, then dying is one more journey whose outcome we cannot know at the start. But when do we ever know what's ahead?

The rightness of who and where we are/inclusive love

I know I am in the right place for me right now.

I realize that I can't live without loving myself.

"My life has led to this moment and place," April declared. "Each piece of what's happened to me has its place. I don't know what I'm supposed to do. I do know I am to be here now."

Five years earlier, April had survived a car accident when her daughter and husband were killed. She tried to punish herself for over two years after the accident by not wearing makeup, socializing or enjoying anything. To enjoy life would trivialize the significance of her loss:

> *I was searching for the meaning in it all—and I didn't find it. I found significance only in what I do with my life, knowing how fragile it is, how arbitrary death can be. I was hating myself for surviving. I had to feel the pain of grieving over them, even being angry at them for having it so easy by dying. It's only been recently that I've learned that I do love myself—and that love is essential to going on with life.*

Love that is inclusive and not bound by structure can be a discovery and a loss. Carl Jung (1937) observed that alteration in the nature of loving:

> Above all we have achieved a sense of real independence and with it, to be sure, a certain isolation. In a sense we are alone, for our "inner freedom" means that a love relation can no longer fetter us; the other sex has lost its magic power over us, for we have come to know its essential traits in the depths of our own psyche. We shall not easily "fall in love," for we can no longer lose ourselves in someone else, but we shall be capable of a deeper love, a conscious devotion to the other. (p.17)

Gentle surprise

I feel connected to what I've lost in ways I never expected.

Some relationships remain amorphous, their basic qualities hard to recognize. Some relationships turn sour when formal commitments are made, though some also deepen and strengthen from them. The transforming of grief may allow us to actualize our love, abandon the rotting framework it once had, and explore what new shape it might now take. Donna reflected after her son died of cystic fibrosis at the age of twenty-one:

> *When Matt died after so many years of near-death, it was almost a celebration of the release of his spirit from the poor, battered body. Long ago I had grieved losing him—many times during his childhood, I was reminded of the fragility of his life.*

> *We commemorated his death as he had celebrated his life. I felt his presence during that service. He also made a tape for us to play— he always did like to have the last word!*

It's not simply a matter of talking to him as if he were still alive.
I did that. Now I realize he lives inside me.

At one time, I started experiencing a great deal of pain in my wrist.
I realized it was Matt telling me he was angry—that I hadn't been
awake when he died, angry that we hadn't shared those last
moments. He spoke to me through my own body and there was a
release, no more pain. Yet he remains a part of my life—sometimes
comfortably, sometimes not.

Essence

I discovered essential parts of me.

We may not discover important parts of ourself unless we're tested.
Grief gives us a better sense of what we need in life. Perhaps we need to
admit responsibility for ourself. We may need to give up being a victim, let
go of formulas or the predictable. Marion reached this understanding
many years after multiple losses involving incest, adoption and chronic
illness:

Psychotherapy helped me to realize I no longer needed excuses,
such as my parents, the way I was raised, the breaks I didn't get.
I didn't need to be a victim anymore, to seek the predictability that
comes with being righteously angry, finding someone else to
blame for my misfortune. I take responsibility for my life. I feel at
peace, alive, and eager to get on with my life.

Yet, I find myself feeling sad and down, realizing the years it had
taken me to reach this point. I am still indignant that it took incest,
adoption and illness for me to learn about forgiveness, about how
precious life is. I can accept, although I certainly don't like that
there were not other ways for me and others to learn such lessons.
I hope I never lose that sense. What I've lost is my sense of shame,
my rage, the energy I no longer invest in just surviving.

For a while I believed I had wasted the better part of my life,
surviving. Now I realize I couldn't be where I am without the
struggles along the way. Now I use what time I have. It's a solid
feeling, a fullness of life I savor.

Joy/peace

> I have peaceful moments.
>
> My life has times of joy.

When transformations near realization, we feel peaceful. When we experience transformation, joy is a natural part of it.

Summary

When a significant loss actualizes its transformative potential, it is a joyful and peaceful time. Such transformation can be both personal and transpersonal—it is ours and it is everyone's who is inspired by it. It can reach back in history and alter the course of our family's grief and growth. Transformations of grief can reach forward and liberate unknown future generations.

One transformation of loss may cause other cycles of loss and grief—other opportunities for transformation. We're challenged to find new strengths, new linkages, new depths of love. Wisdom measures lifetimes of transformations, love of life and curiosity about death. We value uniqueness, and honor attachments. We share the love, losses and opportunities for joy of this lifetime, respect and lament the legacies of our collective past, and appreciate the power of prayer and meditation that joins us all. Transformations allow us to remain open to what's ahead—and beyond.

Section III
When Others Call:
Ways to Respond to Loss

> *If we could read the secret history of our enemies,*
> *we should find in each person's life*
> *sorrow and suffering enough to disarm all hostility.*
>
> *—Henry Wadsworth Longfellow*

Change and the human capacity to respond to it at any age are essential parts of living. Some people don't survive change. Significant change can and frequently does break the will, the integrity and the life story of its "victims." At times, coping and surviving from day to day are all that can be managed when the impact of the loss floods one's awareness. Only later can we make sense of it and begin to adapt. We struggle with the traps and pitfalls of seemingly perpetual grief. Often much later we discover ways to thoroughly alter our view of the loss, abandon the roles of victim or survivor, feel empowered and make the loss aspect fit into the rest of life. Lives are transformed at each step in grief, with each change.

These issues can be viewed from the ways loss is responded to by professionals, families and friends, suggested in Table III-1:

Table III-1: Approaches to Loss Within Various Models

Model	Focus	Major Concern	Time Applicable	Available Resources
Denial of Loss	Avoid loss	Self-protection	As long as possible	Limited or accidental
Victims of Tragedies	Overwhelming loss	Loss of reason to live; Post-traumatic stress	As long as one is a victim	Foundations, agencies, social services, funeral homes, crisis teams
Pathological Responses to Loss	Stress; mental illness	Breakdown of health or functioning	Life-long	Medical and psychiatric; psychotherapy
Adapt to or Survive Catastrophes	Normalize grief and loss	Effective coping	Zero to life-long	Self-help groups
Existential	Face the full extent of the change	Awareness	As long as necessary	Grief groups; counselors, friends
Reformulate Loss as Growth	Grow; self-empower	Choice	Usually years after the loss	Humanistic psychology
Transformative	Inclusive of all of the above	Inclusive	Depends on time since the loss	Transpersonal psychology

Denial of the Loss or the Need to Grieve

We may deny the existence or significance of a loss. We naturally look for alternatives to grieving. We pretend it didn't happen. We forget where it happened. We "bury" the evidence. "I don't think about the past. What's over is over. It doesn't do any good."

Denial is a mechanism we all use at one time or another. It gives us time to delay our response or recover from the shock. We use denial until reality overwhelms us, until something unexpected shatters our protective walls.

Denial can also go too far. It can be so effective we never admit what really happened. It can lead us to distort reality, attack others who remind us of our avoidance, fall into ever deepening depressions that have no acknowledged origins.

At first, denial seems like a wonderful defense. We get away with not having to grieve while those around us are suffering. We don't have to change—at least not at first. Its immediate price can be in a distortion of reality and in attacking those who remind us of our loss. Its cost over time can be the accumulation of unrecognized losses, with more energy devoted to avoidance than to experiencing. Denial is a stress-filled way of living. The body often records denied memories of what is lost in inconvenient, uncomfortable and even life-threatening places, such as the heart.

Victims of Tragedies

There are times when the magnitude of the trauma or catastrophe is so extensive that denial is impossible and it's not reasonable to expect recovery or adaptation. We use the word "victim" to describe the person who needs to be helped or rescued, who is no longer to be held responsible for their behavior because of the extreme circumstances they face.

The feeling that grieving "doesn't do any good" is a logical conclusion to being a "victim" of a loss. The loss is too extensive to overcome. Our lives seem over. No one expects us to recover. We may even be excused from trying.

Denial and the role of victim eliminate or reduce the need to experience the full impact of change. They protect us from what we fear—

that too much has changed and very little remains. When we deny, we conclude that nothing—at least nothing of real importance—has changed. We may be fine as long as there are no reminders and our sleep remains undisturbed. While in the victim role, we accept that meaning as we knew it is gone. Grieving seems futile at best, dangerous at worst.

These stances are often taken during the immediate periods of time after a loss. We need to realize that grief that is not experienced is what Shakespeare said about unspoken grief—it is like an "oven stopped that burns itself to ashes from within." We need to be sensitive to how stressful the avoidance of grieving can be and how critically important safety and normalization are. There are times it isn't possible to find such support directly following a loss, as discussed in Chapter Four about coping.

Protecting the Victims

When people are clearly helpless in the face of traumatic circumstances, we are eager to help. As long as we are convinced that someone didn't "ask for it"—consciously choose the circumstances that created their loss—we support their being treated in a special way. They are "victims" and we find resources to be their "helpers," if not rescuers.

A dilemma is created in how to respond to such people over time. Is "victimhood" a life-long condition indicating permanent incapacity to regain normal functioning and choices, or is it a temporary condition, a necessary step in healing and transformation?

Some people relish being a victim. It gives them a freedom they may never have had before. "For the first time in my life I don't have to take care of everybody else," smiled Carol, recently diagnosed with breast cancer. "I'm not sure I want a cure. That would mean going back to being the caregiver." For some it means a protective identity that entitles them to membership in a group of commiserating fellow victims.

At a certain point, some people object to an indelible label they now see as limiting and allows them *only* to be a victim. They insist on having choice in how they define themselves. They find such a designation demeaning, restricting and hopeless. They don't want to be called, for example, "an AIDS victim": they are "people with AIDS." There is a difference between being a Holocaust *victim* and a *survivor*. There may also be a time when our relationship to the traumatic event no longer defines the wholeness of who we are.

Consider the objections of some young adults with Muscular Dystrophy (MD) being referred to as one of Jerry Lewis" "kids" for the purpose of fund-raising. They were trying to be accepted in society as productive adults, get jobs for which they were qualified not by their MD, but in spite of it: "As long as people view us as victims of a disease, we aren't going to be seen as whole people, just as capable as anyone else in the jobs we want to do."

There comes a time when some "victims" need to be challenged to discover what there is for them that goes beyond their identification with the loss. The transformation from victim to fully functioning human being begins with facing the fullness of the loss and ends with letting go of the primacy of the loss. "Everyone has limits," noted Tom, an adult survivor of Cystic Fibrosis:

> *To focus only on what I can't do, on my victimhood, is depressing. I want to focus on my competencies and my relationships like most people. I want to live as fully as I can as long as I can.*

In so doing, Tom became more than a victim of disease; he was a vital, alive human being.

Pathological Responses to Change

Denial and victimization as ways of responding to change are common concerns for professional healthcare workers. Our training demands we look for *problems*, for inabilities to integrate mind, body and spirit after a traumatic loss, when the shock effects can be life-threatening and when people are unable to self-correct in the months, years and even decades that follow. Post-traumatic stress is a major problem for survivors of war, torture, rape, natural disasters and accidents. So is biological depression and panic disorders. People can be vulnerable during the remainder of their lives unless intervention and eventual awareness takes place.

Fear is common at times of profound change. We fear loss of control, helplessness and going crazy. We are moody and irritable. We can't sleep. We keep reliving a traumatic event over and over again. Friends and loved ones urge us to get back on our feet, to be our old self—only we can't go back. It hurts too much to laugh, feel joy, love again. There are too many sounds, smells, places and people who can make us remember and cry. At some moments we'd rather be dead than feel so awful, empty, lonely and unlovable. Unless we open to these fears and admit our suffering, the resources won't be there to help us let go of the restrictive shell of our personal ego. We'll remain alone, imprisoned by shame, obsessed by uniqueness and accomplishments, searching in the wrong direction for positive transformative possibilities.

Traditional mental health care in the US reflects our dilemma with change. Normal responses to extraordinary circumstances, for example, are too often categorized as a deficiency of the individual. Visiting a mental health professional during times of personal transformation could result in being given a diagnostic label. We might feel inadequate in our ways of responding to the change. We feel guilty, fly off the handle or cry. Life may not always seem worth it when we've had a significant loss. We may have our sanity questioned by these professionals instead of feeling validated for our struggles during tough times.

Major change is a challenge and a stressor. It poses significant risk for health and growth as well as for illness and stagnation. Numerous studies highlight the danger of depression, abusiveness, major physical illness, the loss of a zest for living. For example, few would disagree that major losses were sustained by the Vietnam soldiers. Many have been diagnosed and treated for Post Traumatic Stress Disorder (PTSD). It has been widely reported in the news media that more veterans have committed suicide (well over 65,000) after the Vietnam War than died in combat (about 55,000). Even more are homeless (over 250,000), unable to adapt to life as usual in the aftermath of the trauma of their time in Vietnam.

Colin Murray Parkes, a prominent physician and an expert on bereavement, has conducted one of the few long-term studies on grief (1969, 1981, 1987). Parkes has found lasting effects of widowhood in Boston and London. The majority of those with sudden losses of spouses, for example, are usually not even dating ten years or so later. George Engel (1958, 1961, 1967, 1971, 1977), a psychiatrist who, in the 1960s, raised the question whether grief ought to be considered a disease process, has also documented the potential devastation of sudden loss: it can contribute to sudden death.

Teresa Rando (1984, 1986, 1988, 1993), a psychologist, has exhaustively documented how complicated grieving can become and require profession intervention. Along with many self-help books on the market, Rando suggests strategies to limit the potential devastation of change in our lives. She states that the complications of mourning can rarely be overcome without the help of a professional trained in grief counseling, post traumatic stress or "critical incident debriefing" (Ramsay, 1977; Mitchell and Bray, 1990), or in the management of depression.

A by-product of this research focus is the professional training in traditional settings that emphasizes distance and objectivity. It encourages professionals to put distance between the phenomenon they observe in others and their own personal life experiences. As a result, less attention is given to normal reactions to change, loss and stress, to validate that some life situations are indeed overwhelming or especially to note that we are fellow humans. Co-dependency, poorly defined boundaries, dual relationships and counter-transference are terms used to alarm professionals about getting too close, of risking sympathy or identification with those we serve.

The majority of research is conducted on the negative *individual* outcomes of death, stress, loss, abuse and trauma—a result of policies by government funding agencies and private foundations. Fewer studies are made of healthy transformations, familial, systemic and spiritual approaches to health, the exceptional cancer patient, "eustress" and transgenerational liberations. Such positive and holistic foci are often relegated to "alternative" treatment approaches concerned with "life quality."

Even less attention is paid by most professionals to the spiritual and the communal—those qualities which transcend the normal human response, that empower our best self and which help us find resources and meaning beyond ourselves. Few studies exist, for example, on forgiveness as it relates to mistakes made by health professionals; how healing involves an embracing of those injured; and an acknowledgment of collective issues of shame, guilt and violated expectations. Ironically, litigious responses to professional mistakes is a huge cost that demeans the providers and frequently defrocks the victims of their right to grieve.

Traditional Mental Health Approaches to Change

Traditional training prepares one human being to help another by diagnosing and intervening in a process that is destructive and lacks potential for self-correction. Diagnosis is intended to refine the treatment process. Unfortunately, in this day and age, it is often a political and social labelling which permanently brands people as victims.

For example, some traditional, psychodynamically-trained therapists focus on how the past is mirrored by current reality. During my years in training and beyond, I have been struck by how many of my teachers were themselves survivors of World War II, the Holocaust, or else of American prejudice, abuse, incest or oppression. Some had survived bouts with drugs, alcohol, illness, or attempts at suicide. Many learned that spontaneity and an unexamined life were dangerous: such behaviors could be life-threatening if they led them to act impulsively, if they gave free reign to their imagination. Allowing any patient to consider suicide was considered a sign of failure in the essential duties of a therapist. I've been told many times that grieving is a luxury in their theoretical orientation, a private matter, not a legitimate focus for therapy or analysis.

Behavioral or cognitively-oriented therapists focus on the risks to health that change poses. Controlling stress, thinking and acting in a healthy way is the most important issue, even if it is not felt, thought or valued. People could think about suicide, as long as they didn't do anything about it. A client, Sue, for example, found that others thought she was doing fine even a few months after her son's death. She had learned how to hide her feelings of desperation and grief, to keep her thoughts and questions to herself, to ignore her physical symptoms. To her behaviorally-oriented therapist, she was doing fine.

So dominant are these models of pathology, coping and adjustment that that normal bereavement is excluded from mental health reimbursements for insurance coverage. In order to be reimbursed, the practitioner must diagnose reactive depression, post-traumatic stress, panic or adjustment *disorder*—all classifications within the Diagnostic and Statistical Manual. As a colleague of mine says:

> *You don't get reimbursement unless you can put a diagnostic label on [patients]. "Uncomplicated bereavement" doesn't make it in our system. Adjustment disorders will still only give you five sessions. If you're going to have enough time to treat somebody, you have to use the depression diagnosis.*

A psychiatric diagnosis is a stigma. It can affect careers, self-confidence, the ability to believe we are doing the best we can under trying circumstances. A diagnosis is often perceived as a professional judgment that the way a person is responding to their world is deficient. "Depression," for example, implies that we are in some way not reacting correctly to a loss. Diane was given such a label after a prolonged legal battle awarded custody of her adopted son Timmy back to his biological parents:

> *When my doctor told me I was depressed, I felt defeated. I knew I was sad, cried a lot. I was devastated to realize Timmy would not be in my life anymore—that he wouldn't even be named Timmy. Physically I was OK. I just haven't snapped back mentally. Now I am told I am depressed. It's like adding insult to injury. How should I be reacting at a time like this? I've had to spend five sessions dealing with my "problem" in accepting my diagnosis!*

Adding to the burden of a psychiatric label is the failure to validate the attempts of people facing major change. "All I needed to hear was that it must be a tough time for me," sighed Jim a year after his child died of SIDS (sudden infant death syndrome):

> *I realized they had to question me about how Holly died. After that, all I ever heard from my doctor was that it wasn't my fault; there was no reason to be upset; it shouldn't prevent us from having another child; I shouldn't get morbid about this. When I cried in my therapist's office, she gave me a prescription for an antidepressant, which told me I shouldn't be doing such things.*

> *I expected that from my friends, not my doctor and my therapist. No one admitted that losing a child, regardless of how it happened, was a devastating loss that would lead me to question the very basis for my being alive. No one encouraged my hope while I struggled with the meaninglessness of my life in those first years after Holly's death.*

Is the picture of how inadequately we respond to loss as bleak as many professionals seem to think? When we sustain a major change, do we always need professional help, especially help that considers our response to loss to be a sign of illness? Are we *all* victims at risk at some time or another for depression, traumatic disorders, cancer or some other diminished fate? Does this psychopathology-oriented perspective contribute an iatrogenic millstone to the "illness" of grief?

Paul visibly bristled when I was introduced to him as a psychologist at a party recently. "Are you one of those kind who analyze everything?" he challenged. In the next few minutes, Paul shared the basis for his hostility:

> *My wife developed breast cancer two years ago. She was told that it would be a good idea for her to go into therapy, so she found an analyst here in Denver. She went for therapy three times a week for the next year and a half, right up until two weeks before she died.*

> *She got in touch with how much she hated her mother, what an awful childhood she had as a result. She refused to see her mother during the last six months of her life. At the end, she was angry and bitter with all of her family, including me. We never did have a chance to work it out.*

She told me during that last week that they hadn't discussed her illness in therapy. Whenever she had to cancel a therapy session because of her illness or treatment the analyst confronted her with her "resistance." When she was bedridden or hospitalized, the analyst refused to see her, stating that the illness was merely a manifestation of Meg's early conflicts with her mother. She didn't even come to Meg's funeral.

I'm no psychologist, but it seems to me that it's the human thing to help someone with the crisis, not to just mess with their past. I am bitter at that therapist. She took my wife away from me and my family in those last precious moments we could have shared.

Maybe if they had five years for the "full" analysis, things would have gotten better. She died in the middle of all that "transference" crap. Maybe her illness was a manifestation of her conflicts with her mother. Damn, we never got a chance to say good-bye. We never talked about the kids and what their future would be like without her. We never even discussed the good times we'd had.

There are many wounded people among helping professionals. Wounded people are often very self-centered, attempting to heal and understand themselves. Ironically, by focusing on the needs of others and on illness, some caregivers and professionals have less time, energy and disposition to profit from their current life circumstances. Paul's wife's therapist, perhaps due to unrecognized wounds around her own family's way of dealing with dying, had lost the sensitivity necessary to see what people need as they are dying. Coping with a major loss had become "resistance," dying a way to avoid dealing with deep psychological issues.

Adapt or Survive: Normal and Systemic Reactions to Change

Professionals are expected to focus on the ten to twenty percent of the population that responds to stress and change in maladaptive ways. "That would not be a problem if people who sustain normal life changes and respond accordingly would stay away from these professionals," scoffed Tom, a humanistic psychiatrist colleague of mine who is also sensitive to this issue. "Let me tell you about Donna":

Donna was a psychiatry resident who had been in supervision for several months with a particular faculty member. She approached him one day crying and upset. Her husband had just left her, only two months after the birth of their first child. She asked for some time off to figure out what she was going to do in terms of child care and even continuing the residency. The supervisor refused her request, saying that now was as good a time as any to learn how to cope with life's blows and to begin to examine how this event related to difficulties she had earlier in her life with her father, who had rejected her.

Donna was stunned and angry. She felt that her current situation was dismissed as unimportant, or was interpreted as a vulnerable moment to get her to examine her earlier life issues. "That may be true," she said to the supervisor, "right now I couldn't care less. I don't know how I am going to stop crying, find a baby-sitter for my child, make house payments, or even find out why this happened, much less work things out with my father. I am learning how to cope. I can't do everything you think I need to do."

Donna is not unusual in her response, despite her training. She was going through a time of profound change: a new child, the loss of a spouse and a way of life. What is striking about her experience is that her psychiatry supervisor sees her resulting vulnerabilities as an opportunity to get her to face long-standing life issues. How she was coping with the current circumstances is not of interest; how it related to early issues with her family of origin was. An opportunity to validate her grief was lost.

When I told Marlene of my interests in grief, she responded:

Ten years ago my husband left me with three children under the age of ten and no means of support. I joined a divorce group. I remember a psychiatrist coming to speak to us. He said that grieving was a natural process that lasts about six months. By that time, life should be pretty much back to normal.

I became anxious. Here I was, five months since he left, declaring bankruptcy and being on welfare. I was supposed be over this in another month! I went into therapy. It took three years before I could look at myself in the mirror and see the person I had become. It was not the same one as I had seen before. Even today, I'm not sure that I shouldn't have been over that loss sooner. Was there a way?

In the course of three decades working as a psychotherapist, teacher and researcher in medical school and residency settings and with hospice programs, I have encountered many Donnas and Marlenes, many psychiatrists, therapists and supervisors who have difficulty validating the reality and the extent of normal grieving. They, like myself, are often unwitting proponents of the American mythology that denies loss and grief. We are part of a health care system that is desperate to adapt and afraid to transform.

The Self-Help Movement as a Response to Change

The self-help movement and the development of hospice programs are, in part, efforts to bypass mental health professionals who often do not help with "normal" life crises such as illness, divorce, accidents or dying. Many programs have arisen since the 1970s, I believe, because of this tendency to see pathology under every rock and in every psyche regardless of the realities people face. Hospice programs, for example, initially reflected grassroots desires to normalize the dying process, to make palliation and support for grief the focus rather than the futile, dehumanizing, crisis-oriented attempts that permeate approaches to hospital-based death.

"We spend a lot of time bitching about our doctors," Madeline, a woman with AIDS, told me about her support group. "Every one of us has had at least one kind of horror story or another about the insensitivity, prejudices or fears we've encountered from the professionals who are supposed to be helping us." Such "professional-bashing" story-telling is common in support groups. Professionals, unless they have life experiences of their own that help them understand what it's like to be victimized by a loss, are often objects of suspicion in these groups, as I was twenty years ago:

> *I was a young professional who was a self-proclaimed expert on depression and grief. A colleague invited me to attend a meeting of a group of terminally ill individuals he had started with a thirty-year-old woman, Sandy, dying of leukemia:*

> *I was convinced that the members of this group must all be depressed. After all, I would be if I had what they were facing. Depression was something I could help them with—confronting their resistance, their faulty way of thinking, encouraging them to try antidepressant medications, discover what in their life had led them to "choose" illness.*

It didn't take more that five minutes for me to feel so uncomfortable that I wanted to leave. I had discovered they were not depressed.

They were enraged at the way professionals treated them—as specimens, symptoms, a bed in a room, an object to burn, poison or mutilate. They were lonely, often abandoned by friends, family and physicians. They were scared—of dying, pain, being humiliated. They wanted to know how to say good-by to loved ones who didn't want to talk about their illness, much less the reality of their impending deaths. They wanted to keep some semblance of control over their lives, to stay independent as long as they could, to avoid the dreaded trips to the hospital. They wanted dignity in dying.

I felt helpless. There was nothing I had to offer them. I listened, saying nothing. I cried as Sandy talked about the hardest times being after wonderful experiences, knowing they may never happen again, as she spoke of going to a friend's funeral with her two boys, six and eight. They wanted to know if she was going to have a party after her funeral and whether they'd have to go live with their dad, her ex-husband.

Afterwards, members of the group came up to me and asked me if I would return. I was surprised. All I had done was listen. Marilyn French in The Women's Room perceptively observed that the essence of listening is to let people, without blinking or flinching, be whatever horrible creatures they think they are. That I had done. Many years later, after seeing the movie "Black Robe," in which the Jesuit priest cried in response to the diseased and decimated Huron Indians' challenge for why they shouldn't kill him, I knew what else led to my invitation, just as it had for the priest. "We see by your tears that you have a human spirit. We can trust you," was the chieftain's response. So must my tears have been for the dying people in that group.

I have been with groups since that time that weren't so accepting. I've been asked to "facilitate" cancer groups, widowed or divorce groups, AIDS survivors, parents with terminally ill children and those who have lost a child, pet, house, homeland or way of life. More often than not, "facilitating" meant unlocking the doors of the meeting rooms, fixing the coffee and keeping my mouth shut. Occasionally I would be challenged to share just what in my life had led me to be there. "We've met too many bleeding-heart professionals who get off on our suffering and feel good because they are so wonderful to be with us," sneered Ted, a recovering alcoholic. "You get the feeling they come to demonstrate what caring people they are."

When asked, I share the losses in my life and how they have affected me. I was profoundly affected by my contribution to the loss of our pet Dalmatian when I was four, by my father's sudden death at eighteen, the suicide of a client, two life-threatening experiences of my own in my thirties, a divorce, moves, job loss and early retirement in the time since then. I may say that I don't understand their loss, but I know something about suffering. Some people accept my unique story of loss and the common nature of our grief.

I've had to transform my professional training to be responsive to my own grief and to validate other people's losses. In my twenty-seven years in medical school settings, I've found a few professionals who shared the notion that grief involved something more that treatment, distancing and looking for problems. Those exceptional people are often prized by colleagues and patients alike.

Groups which normalize grief find it important to identify the uniqueness of the losses that form them. In my naiveté about the differences between the death of a spouse and divorce many years ago, I help organize a "loss of spouse" support meeting. It lasted one session. Participants could only see their differences and how much more of a loss theirs was than the others. Instead of validating each others' losses, they focused on diminishing or exaggerating the others. It was not a safe environment for sharing. Death and divorce, at least at that stage of their grief, involved losses that were too diverse.

The result of seeking such safety has been a proliferation of support groups, each with their own emphasis, from suicide, violent deaths, life-threatening and chronic illness conditions, to lost pets, adult children of incest, alcohol, abuse; singles, men, women, war vets, elderly—to mention just a few. These groups have an important role in dealing with the trauma of the event, with debriefing and defusing the emotional intensity. They begin to develop a new social support based on *accepting* the changes their loss provides them. People often need the accepting and loving support such groups provide.

Membership in such groups seems to have a natural course. Most who find it helpful attend some time during the first year or so after the loss or a diagnosis. Individual friendships may blossom and the group frequently fades as a needed safety net. Sometimes the group turns into a social gathering of people bonded by a common loss.

Some find that such groups become central to their lives. They relish the opportunity to tell the story of their loss over and over again, often to new and appreciative audiences. Some even get on television talk shows because their group has a wrinkle that no one else's has. Some, however, are disturbed by the long-term involvement:

> *Lennie lost her twenty-eight-year-old son in a fire. She went to one meeting of Compassionate Friends. She decided not to return. "I was greeted at the door by a woman who had been in the group for fourteen years," she confessed later. "During the sharing time, she sobbed as she told of her daughter's death as if it had just happened. It scared me. Am I going to be feeling my loss of Charlie just as intensely fourteen years from now? Will I be a life-long victim?"*

Recent times have brought a greater willingness to examine systemic and spiritual aspects of change in families and communities. Such words as "love," "courage," "wisdom," and "spirituality" are appearing as legitimate parts of "healing." "Choice" as a response to loss is gaining favor beside the more deterministic, pathology-oriented approaches. People are challenged to see themselves as their own healer, not dependent on some powerful external force. Helpers are often necessary at crucial times in grieving, but must realize that they play only a partial role in the process of transformation.

We all need to know that we're doing our best in spite of the stressfulness of change. Our moodiness, crazy thoughts and actions result when what we've lost means so much, not because we are going insane. We'd like be taken care of. However, we know we need to find out for ourself what this potential transformation is about. We need self-affirmation.

Coping and adapting is necessary during the first year or so after a change as we get back on our feet and resume daily living. It is a way of balancing times of awareness with times of respite. It helps to recognize that *remembering* what was lost and its role in our lives is the goal, not forgetting or at the other extreme, to exaggerate its significance.

Surviving change means living long enough to understand its meaning. *But just surviving the loss is not the same as grieving and finishing the process.* To fully grieve, more steps must be taken.

Existential Issues: Facing the Full Extent of the Change

Grief is a process of coming to grips with all the ramifications of a change, both loss and gain. We may not realize its full extent for years. We need to experience whatever loneliness, emptiness, challenges to meaning, invalidation of our myths, assumptions and beliefs this event or process may initially produce. When we have fully confronted the change, we can make informed choices about living. Awareness endures, often in symbolic or physical form, until we've found the time to face it.

Elizabeth Harper-Neeld, in her book *Seven Choices* (1990), eloquently demonstrates that facing our losses fully is essential in grief, and that under the appropriate conditions, it is a choice. Feelings of helplessness, hopelessness, loneliness, emptiness and a loss of meaning characterize the central core of grief.

People who have not personally experienced grief in this way are naturally frightened by the prospect. There is no assurance going in that they will emerge on the other side. During the deepest times of awareness, in fact, we believe there is no other side—all that remains is the blackness of the present. Suicide becomes a realistic alternative. Once that awareness is reached, however, we are no longer trapped into living only with what we lost; we can now discover what remains. Our life force, similar to the changing of the tide once it reaches its lowest ebb, builds once again.

It is striking how many people attribute their creativity and growth to the way they have handled major change. Their lives have been transformed by these losses.

Peter Marris, a sociologist mentioned previously, studied the effects of young widowhood and urban renewal in the late sixties and early seventies. In his Pulitzer Prize winning book *Loss and Change* (1973), Marris saw common issues of loss in those whose spouse had died and those forced to move because of housing changes. He found that those who were able to reformulate their loss into a new context of meaning often did very well, and were increasingly capable of handling other changes. Rollo May, Eugene Gendlin, Clark Moustakas and Elizabeth Harper Neeld are among many who have made similar observations about how people's openness to face life's existential challenges fully can empower them to choose healing and lead transformed lives.

Ed Eisenstadt, an epidemiologist, has conducted a fascinating set of studies which compare the age at which the most creative and productive people lose a parent to death to that of other groups. Eisenstadt found that the 400 most creative people of the last several hundred years (for example, Van Gogh, Einstein, Beethoven, Edgar Allen Poe) lost their first parent on the average at the age of twelve. Comparable "normal" individuals lost a parent on the average at the age of eighteen. Eisenstein and his colleagues went further and discovered that political leaders, alcoholics, schizophrenics, juvenile delinquents and drug addicts shared with the creative types a similar age of early parental loss. They concluded that a loss such as that of a parent during the critical early developmental years radically altered the life path taken from what would be considered "normal." Many times that path was destructive; other times it was highly creative or productive: the loss of a parent forces the issue.

As attractive and hopeful as human potential approaches to loss can be, they also have their shortcomings. Challenge can come too soon, before we have had the safety and unquestioned support needed to acknowledge the full extent of the loss. Many of us would like to bypass facing the fullness of our loss. We get caught in the American dream that gain, growth or overcoming potential loss is possible *without* full awareness; when we cannot bypass it, we attribute it to weakness or illness. Suggesting that choice is *always* possible after a loss means ignoring circumstances that lack safety, or verification of reality and support, or where people's ego strength, lack of resources or age limits their options. Some might suggest that choice exists and believe that only *one* choice—growth—is the *right* choice, thereby invalidating someone's choice to die or stay within an abusive relationship as the lesser evil, or healthier of several difficult options.

When friends, family and even professional helpers have yet to experience the fullness of their own grief, they will try to keep us from experiencing ours. They will likely see such opening to fullness as dangerous, a risk of going too deeply and never re-emerging. They lack the life experience to believe in our best self while we descend into that empty space.

Those who have yet to be in this place are unaware of how healing the experience of full awareness is. Physically, it is like telling our immune system exactly what is self and what is not. Our immune system responds, getting rid of that which is no longer (or never was) part of ourself, and provides healing and soothing endorphins and enkephalins to the wounded remainder. The recognition of what is no longer part of ourself allows us to let go of it and begin to nurture what we have left.

To Reformulate Change: Limit or Alter Its Tragic Nature

When the intensity of awareness lessens, we're no longer so vulnerable. When we've been able to fully explore how much life has changed, find what's left, remember and integrate the past, then we begin to explore what we can now do. Instead of providing comfort and safety, reformulation challenges the ways we have understood our loss and increase our options. Paradoxes and new priorities cause us to shift.

The Human Potential Approach to Change

In addition to those who see pathology in every response and those who wish to find normalcy in any change, there are those who challenge us to see potential for growth in *any* life event. In contrast to the motto of Compassionate Friends, "there is no death so sad as the loss of a child," others believe that *any* loss can give us the motivation and opportunity to choose to grow. Human potential groups emphasize the *choice* to move on.

An emphasis on human potential is a time of challenge when loss is no longer raw and the greatest intensity is already in the past. It comes when people *can* choose to go on living and when they have found ways to remember the loss and its meaning. Many consider their challenges to be a result of having faced the worst nightmare they could have experienced.

Growth from loss can be suggested long before the grieving person is ready to hear it. For some, it suggests that they can just skip over all the pain of grief and immediately get to the "good stuff." For others, it feels insensitive to the healing process that grief involves. When we are deep in the awareness of how extensive this loss is, we cannot hear that something good could possibly result. Poorly-timed suggestions about growth invalidate the necessity of experiencing the fullness of the loss and the resulting healing:

> *"If I had a broken leg in a cast, he wouldn't be telling me to get up and run on it," observed Margaret, infuriated after her pediatrician asked her if her son's death three months previously was still "100 percent tragedy." "Why can't he let me grieve as long as I need to?"*

Transformation: Accepting the Full Scope of Change

The notion that loss transforms us incorporates all of the previous models. Each way acknowledges that something significant has changed. In denial and victimization, it is the external world that has been transformed. In the others, it is one or more aspects of the internal world of the individual that has shifted.

These ways of responding to change involve quite different approaches:

- *Do we have to grieve the loss? Deniers would say no. Victims would not see it as possible without facing the loss of meaning in life; that would be unthinkable. Growth to victims is an impossibility.*

- *How do we know we're not going crazy when we have so many ups and downs? Those looking for pathology may find depression instead of normal grief. Supporters of coping would defend these ups and downs as normal grief.*

- *Can we truly face the full implications of loss or death? Some would say we cannot. Existentialist philosophers would say it's essential that we try, regardless.*

- *Can we heal from every loss? Sometimes we can only survive and keep going. The safety and support is not available at the time. With safety and support, however, we can heal from many losses.*

- *Is growth possible? Only for small, minor changes, some declare. Others believe that any change has possibilities for growth.*

Some differences posed by these approaches are a matter of timing and vulnerability. Someone at risk for heart disease or depression will need special support and treatment at times of change and for months thereafter. We need to know we aren't going crazy as a result of our lives being turned upside down and inside out. We need someone to hope for us and believe in our capacity for love and our best self. We can heal, provided we choose the choice to go on living and find time, solitude, love, and forgiveness. We make new attachments, often in more inclusive ways. We eventually see the world through different, wiser eyes.

In this section we will explore what happens when grieving stops, as well as what can help facilitate the transformative process.

Chapter Ten
When Grieving Stops:
Losing Our Way

*The mind is always prone to believe
what it wishes to be true.*

—Heliodorus

*In such cases, show no mercy; the punishment is to be a life
for a life, an eye for an eye, a tooth for a tooth, a hand for
a hand and a foot for a foot.*

—Deuteronomy

It's a common belief that we won't be tested beyond our capacity to respond. This is helpful during times of normal stress and strain, when our ways of coping are good enough to make the necessary adjustments. This belief is not so helpful, however, when the loss we experience is so overwhelming, the hurt so painful that our limits are exceeded. We may cross over a line that separates normal coping from avoidance, grief from depression, self-protection from distorting reality. Crossing that line into a pathological response to loss can add to our sense of humiliation and failure when we cannot live up to our standards of behavior. We lose ourself. Our grieving stops, never begins or never ceases. The way back is a long and difficult journey. We are a lost soul, wandering in the wilderness of unexplored or unfinished grief.

Years ago, while living in Denmark, I was a consultant on a study of Danish sailors who had served on convoy duty during the Second World War. Denmark was a noncombatant; those who served had to leave their country and serve under a British or American flag. In this study, done by the Danish government, they found that these men had significantly higher rates of illness than other Danes their age. Over 75% of them had significant mental or physical illness by their mid-fifties. Their suicide rates were seven times higher than their non-combatant cohorts. While interviewing these men, an interesting trend was found. Those who were considered healthy could talk of their war experiences, including some tough experiences they had. They were animated, sometimes sad, and many seemed at peace with what had happened.

A significant portion of those who were considered ill admitted that they had never discussed what happened during the war. Some related, *for the first time*, experiences during the war where they had been forced to do something they were ashamed of doing. For example, one had been forced by his commanding officer at gun point to shoot the men on the bridge of a torpedoed companion vessel completely surrounded by a burning oil slick. The victims were slowly dying from the heat and had no apparent escape. To hasten their deaths, the commander ordered them machine-gunned. A second sailor was a helmsman who, under orders, took evasive action from torpedoes that forced him to run over sailors in the water.

Both men returned from the war, never mentioning their experiences. The memories of those times were still as vivid as the day they happened some forty years before. Repeatedly they woke up in the night, reliving those horrible experiences in their dreams. They showed the classic signs of post-traumatic shock—they felt detached from the people they loved and the lives they were living. Shame prevented them from sharing their nightmares. They had lost a part of themselves in the war, and lived without grieving it ever since.

There are instances when grief is not possible at the time. Sometimes loss produces such trauma that we are shocked and paralyzed by a reality so harsh that we are caught between two worlds, neither one seeming real. We try to prove that what is lost is not gone.

Differences Between Normal Coping and Defending Against Loss

What are the differences between normal coping and defending against a loss?

- *Coping allows time for respite and delay while we grieve.*

- *When we defend against a loss, we attack, distort or avoid the experience and reminders of grief.*

There is risk involved in defending—we may burn bridges, alienate others, or destroy or avoid reminders or messengers, making it that much harder to regain a sense of wholeness and connection. We can become prisoners of our own defenses if we use them so well we can't find our own way out.

Defending against loss creates and reflects our desperation, depression, fear, rage, or detachment. The intensity of a defensive response exceeds the magnitude of the loss. Defensive responses are primitive and childlike—they attack, deny, give up, distort, avoid, shun.

In the process, we may add to our loss by the way we respond to it. We may lose those who would have otherwise supported us, adding injury to what's already gone. The response of many post-traumatic stress-disordered war veterans, for example, is to strike out at others when reminded of the initial trauma by a dream, scream or sudden noise. Many lead lives of isolation or commit suicide because they fear their own combat-trained responses which could injure those they love.

What can cause us to react with violence, despair, passivity or distortion? Sometimes no one is available to validate our loss and support our grief; at times real danger exists in the external world if we let ourself be preoccupied internally with our grief. Perhaps we are ashamed of what we did or didn't do.

If our defending against grief goes on long enough or if what we do in our immediate response is destructive, we may *lose the thread of our life story*. We can lose sight of who we are and why we started defending in the first place. We may convince ourselves that grief is no longer possible or that we don't deserve it. We may revise the past and believe it never mattered in the first place. We may give up hope.

The cost of defending against grief is incredibly high. It can cost us our sanity, our integrity, our zest for living and our health. We lose our humor, optimism, playfulness. We can be frozen in a moment in time, while unable to acknowledge the events surrounding that moment to anyone. We believe no one or nothing else is important to us. We accept the role of being a victim or a perpetrator, and become incomplete because of what we've lost or how we lost it. We create a fantasy world where the loss never happened and things are as they were before.

The vast majority of the research on grief and its complications has focused on the consequences of unresolved grief, post-traumatic stress, depression and other complications of the grieving process, a focus in *Stress, Loss and Grief* (Schneider, 1984) and in the more recent works by Catherine Sanders (1989), Colin Murray Parkes (1987), Ken Doka (1989) and Teresa Rando (1993). The consequences are physical in terms of illness, pain and premature death; emotional in terms of anxiety, panic and depression; spiritual in terms of a loss of meaning and hope; intellectual in terms of preoccupation and rigidity; behavioral and social in terms of alienation or over-socialization, lack of accomplishment and destructiveness. Table 10-1 suggest some of the ways grieving can stop after a loss:

Table 10-1: Normal Coping Vs. Defending

Normal Coping	Defending
Holding On/ Fight: Anger Denial Guilt Loyalty	Attack or Cling: Blame Prejudice Revenge Distortion Destroy evidence or messenger Persecutor/perpetrator Obligation Worship lost person as hero or saint
Letting Go/ Flight: Withdrawal Shame Forget Disgust	Avoid or Abandon: Depression Detachment Permanent victim identity Amnesia Abandon or shun Vilify the lost person as evil, persecutor or criminal

Attacking or Clinging Instead of Holding On

Blame/prejudice/revenge

Losses can involve gross injustice, inhuman behaviors and deliberate destruction as well as incompetence, insensitivity and a lack of foresight. We may react as much to the intent or failure of others as a means to protect ourself as we do to the loss itself. When a loved one is murdered, a drunk driver maims, or a prank gets out of hand, we are outraged. Our sense of justice demands punishment. When justice is served—as when a murderer is convicted—this can help the victim's family put anger aside and continue grieving. But it can also lead us to focus more on our system of justice than on our grief, delay grieving for so long that appropriate support is no longer available.

> *The lawsuit against the hospital and the doctors following Mike's son's death took six years to settle. He had testified several times concerning its impact on him and his other children. "Each time was a reliving of the event, just as painful as before," he reflected. "I couldn't let go of that pain. It would have shown them that I could get over Tony's death. Now that it's over and we won, I feel like I don't deserve to grieve or that it's too late. I don't know what to do with the money either. Spending it on enjoying life seems wrong. We just wanted to make sure those doctors didn't get away with what they did."*

Sometimes it's not clear who or what caused our loss. Seeking someone or something to blame is a way to limit or avoid our helplessness. If we could place the responsibility on a single source—even ourselves— we would have a sense of control over the arbitrariness of such things happening. When blaming becomes an end in itself, a way to avoid helplessness, its projective nature prevents grief from reemerging later:

> *It's one thing to be irritable every once in a while, especially after losing your husband as Mary did. But I can't remember a time in the ten years since then that she wasn't always picking out someone's defects or limits. Heaven help us if we ever talked politics. It was as if she saw the president as the devil incarnate! Her children could do nothing right. She was always looking for someone to blame for anything that went wrong in even the slightest way.*

The desire to blame, combined with a craving for revenge, can be less spontaneous and more calculating. Someone rejects us. To avoid our grief, we seek ways to reject them, or to hurt them as badly as we have been hurt. We may distort reality in order to enhance our chances to gain revenge. Our motivation? *To keep ourselves from having to face what we have lost.*

Denial, distortion and isolation

There are also times when we want desperately to believe that a loss didn't happen. We believe that grieving can be avoided altogether; we can pretend nothing has changed. All we need to do is eliminate evidence of that loss in our lives. We need to forget and get on with our lives.

Sometimes that works—what we lost wasn't that important or essential to who we are. But sometimes it doesn't, and we live with the resulting regrets, depression, denial and isolation:

> *In the five years after Jane's son was killed in a car accident, she kept his room exactly as it had been the day he died. She continued to talk about him in the present tense, as if he were still alive. Friends, uncomfortable with her denial, gradually stayed away. People said they were not surprised when she committed suicide on the anniversary of his death.*

It also can happen that we violate our limits. As a result, we act in ways that are not consistent with our self-image, engage in acts of rage, desperation, greed, fear or lust. If no one else knows, we'll hide it. If others do, we'll struggle to keep them from telling, adding to our shame and loss of best self. We cannot admit what happened. Without that admission, we have no access to our sense of loss or to our grief.

In Western culture, grieving is usually a private process. Beyond the first few days or weeks, we are expected to show no outward signs of emotion. This has two implications for grieving. One, already discussed in Chapter Four, suggests that the normal and healthy part of the grieving process is to deny the loss in whole or part, to *hold on* while our lives stabilize and gradually allow more open grief to continue. I am suggesting a less healthy implication for denial of loss when it effectively *stops* grieving—a way of avoiding it altogether.

It is an adaptive function of coping with a severe loss to try to keep from grieving too much, too soon. But there is a difference between *coping with* a loss and *defending against* it so well that we don't experience its impact. It is equally true that it's hard to know the difference between normal coping and defending against grief at the time. Still, "I can't talk about it right now" is clearly coping, while "Don't *ever* mention what happened in my presence" can represent our defensiveness.

Denial is a defense when it distorts or destroys reality. *Denial that distorts is the most primitive way of defending*. Distortion can prevent us from realizing our need to adapt. For example, we may ignore chest pain for hours even after having one or two heart attacks, continue to smoke heavily after developing emphysema, engage in unprotected sex or share needles with a partner known or likely to be infected with AIDS.

Destroy evidence/messenger

We can also believe that our loss only exists because someone knows about it. If we could magically eliminate their knowledge, our loss or guilt would not exist. Sometimes it is the evidence that needs to be done away with. Sometimes it is the messenger or those who remind us of the loss. Sometimes our behavior toward the messenger becomes another source of guilt that we avoid by further abusing or attempting to destroy the messenger.

Persecutor or perpetrator/transgenerational patterns

It's been observed that an abuser or incest perpetrator is someone who is likely to have been abused or victimized as a child. The losses involved in their own childhood were never resolved. As a result, they respond as they were responded to—a transgenerational liability, often going back many generations:

> *Bill's mother died in her forties of leukemia, hating her husband. He was abusive of her for years, as he was everyone in his family. Even though she died so long ago, I know how she felt, because Bill is the same to me as his dad was to her. Now I see signs in our ten-year-old, who has been beaten a lot by his dad, of doing the same— mostly to animals at this time. He's killed a couple of the pets we've had when they wouldn't obey him. How many generations of his family have been this way?*

Obligation

Choice does not exist when grieving stops—at least not choice when it comes to things associated with the loss. Responsibilities become obligations and work becomes a way of life rather than a means for living. What must be done, *has* to be done. There is no freedom to stop and question it.

The result is people who are married to their jobs, who have no other role in life other than caring for others, who are unable to feel playful or flexible in their everyday lives. Grief creates options; the failure to grieve creates obligations.

Worship the lost person as a hero or saint

When John Kennedy was assassinated, the names of streets, space centers, libraries and the like were changed, almost immediately, to honor this American hero. We wanted to keep his memory alive. For many years, very little negative was said of him. We did not want to let in the full impact of what his loss meant.

It's often the case when someone we love dies suddenly that we want to look only at the positive memories and ignore the more painful ones. When this behavior is carried to the extreme of creating a special status for that person that was not humanly possible (i.e. that of a hero or a saint), the need to go on with life is diminished. Everyone else suffers in comparison, as June discovered after marrying Mike:

> *Mike's second wife Rose died of a heart attack in his mid-forties. She had a special place on the mantelpiece and a whole wall of her pictures. I never heard him say anything but praise for Rose. He quoted her often, continued to tell the same stories about her after we were married. When I tried to kid him once about Rose's "sainthood" he got really angry. How dare I say such things!*

> *There were lots of times we didn't make love, times when Mike was thinking about her—their anniversary, her birthday, the birthday of their children, holidays. In addition to my own periods, I had to keep track of his "special days with Rose" on a calendar!*

> *A lot of the time, he's not really here. When I ask, he'll often say he was thinking about Rose.*

> *I left Mike after three years. I don't know if he even really noticed my absence. He's still living with Saint Rose.*

Avoiding a Loss Rather than Letting Go

In order to avoid a loss, we pay the consequences. What we lost no longer exists as a significant attachment. We relinquish who we are, splitting our consciousness, our mind living in a different world where there is nothing associated with the loss. For instance, we forget our pain-filled childhood and avoid going home.

Depression

Depression may include all of the ways already discussed of avoiding or defending against grief. When depressed, we believe that grieving will, at best, do no good and, at worst, lead us to a worse fate than we have now. As a result, depression represents the hopelessness of regaining meaning and enjoyment in our lives.

The term "depression" is often used interchangeably with grief. We often say "I feel depressed" when in reality, we are temporarily down-hearted or sad or the weather or our biorhythms are gloomy and gray. It is quite a different matter when professionals use the term "depression" when in reality it is grief they are observing. Grief requires validation and support, safety and encouragement to trust oneself. Depression, on the other hand, requires intervention and treatment. Challenge and confrontation are necessary when thinking has gone awry. Pharmacological and somatotherapies are necessary when biological factors are so stressful they can lead to physical and mental disease. Friends and family can help with grief. Depression requires professionals.

Depression refers to feelings of suffering and the loss of hope that do not fit the circumstances of a person's life. Depression cannot go untreated without risk to the health and well-being of the individual. It often includes such signs as awakening early, fatigue, weight loss or gain, the absence of pleasure, a sense of impending doom and feeling worthless. When a loss has been present, these signs are considered symptoms of depression when they persist beyond a reasonable length of time or without periods of feeling better. Professionals also sometimes use the term "depression" to represent the inability or unwillingness to grieve or the hopelessness of grief as a way to make sense of the loss.

Table 10-2 was adapted by Diane Deutsch (1992) from an earlier article (Schneider, 1980) and suggests some of the ways that grief and depression differ from each other:

Table 10-2: Differences Between Grief and Depression

Issue	Grieving	Depression
Loss	There is a recognized loss.	A specific loss may or may not be identified.
Cognitive Schemas	Focus is on the loss. Preoccupation with deceased, implications of loss, the future.	Focus is on the self. Persistent, distorted and negative perceptions of self.
Dreams, Fantasies and Imagery	Vivid, clear dreams—sometimes of the loss; dreamer feels comforted	Negative imagery that contributes to negative thinking and to an intensified physical response.
Physical	Modulated physical response: The body is allowed to collapse and person admits to exhaustion.	Unmodulated response: Bodily damage and increased vulnerability to illness via lack of sleep, anorexia or weight gain, unnecessary physical risk.
Spiritual	A connection felt to something beyond, e.g., God; continued dialogue with emotions allows challenges to previously held beliefs.	Especially a year or more past the loss, a persistent failure to find meaning; focus on "why me" and unfairness of loss; no answers to questions.
Emotional States	Variable: shifts in mood from anger to sadness to more normal states in same day.	Fixed: withdrawal, despair; reports feeling immobilized or stuck; difficult to "read" emotions.
Responses	Responds to warmth, touch, reassurance.	Responds to promises and urging or is unresponsive.
Pleasure	Variable restriction of pleasure.	Persistent restriction of pleasure.
Attachment Behavior	Feels reassured by the presence of close friends or someone who will listen to their story.	Loss of connection with self and others.

There are biologically-based forms of depression that clearly differ from grief. When treatment of this type of depression is in the hands of a biologically-trained psychiatrist, treatment is and can be quite effective. The reader is encouraged to use Klein and Wender's *Understanding Depression* (1993) as a companion volume to this one when there is concern about depression.

Detachment

Detachment can be a way of coping, of minimizing the significance of a loss for a period of time. Detachment can also be *too* effective and becomes a way of defending against the loss. Denial, of course, is a way to feel detached from a loss—it's a popular alternative to grief. People may encourage us to forget about the loss, don't let it get to us and to get on with life—long before we've begun to deal with it. We can't do that without feeling detached.

When we burn bridges, keep secrets, eliminate reminders of the loss, or forbid ourselves and others from ever talking about it, we're using detachment to distort the reality of the loss, to invalidate its impact. We can't continue to do so without paying a considerable price in our integrity, in our health or in our relationships.

Elaine was raped by her older brother when she was sixteen. Consequently her mother took her to have an abortion. Her father refused to discuss what happened. Later, when Elaine brought it up, her father became enraged, demanding that she leave. Thereafter she was forbidden to enter the house or have contacts with her parents. In her own words:

> *It's as if I were the one who did the horrible thing. All I did was refuse to deny that something happened. That was the bigger sin in my father's eyes than what my brother did to me.*

As Elaine painfully experienced in her forced detachment from her family, her father avoided grieving by pretending the loss did not exist and added to it by shunning his daughter. What a price to pay! We can be robbed of our memories, positive as well as negative, and our sense of integrity. In denial and detachment, we can't stop to make sense of our lives. We need to be cautious about where we go, who we see and what we say and do, for fear we may run into reminders or inadvertently admit the hidden loss.

At first use, detachment can be selective and normal. But when it becomes pervasive in our response to loss, it darkens all parts of our lives. We realize on some level that if we lose one thing, we can lose others, so it is best "not to get involved with anyone or anything." Detachment then creates an inability to attach or bond. Others become objects. Such detachment is characteristic in people with massive psychic trauma or those denied the right to grieve their losses during childhood and later.

When we detach from a loss, we systematically block the pathway back to a fuller sense of growth and transformation.

Traumatization

When we are overpowered by factors beyond our control—natural disasters, accidents, wars, criminal acts, abusive or incestuous adults, to name a few—we are seen as victims. People generally respond to victims at extreme ends of an emotional gamut—they either feel sympathy or pity for us, want to protect us from further harm, or they want to blame us for being victims. We are either given permission to be exempt from the usual rules, or we are further punished, ridiculed, or shamed. Others will excuse our preoccupation, understand our ill health, respect our loyalty, let us be vulnerable and weak, or they will ignore or shun us.

We can be traumatized by losses. The violation of social norms and the total uselessness of our usual way of acting and reacting paralyzes us. We are frozen in that moment when the old reality was lost. Often what we lost at that moment was the capacity to believe in ourselves—that we could overcome anything with enough effort, that we'd never act destructively, that we'd never let our fear so totally control our actions. Or we may have lost our belief in others—that people don't do that sort of thing, that we have been betrayed, that our God wouldn't allow this to happen. We may hold on to anything that keeps our loss alive.

While we are in this traumatized condition, our usual problem-solving and reality-testing capacities can malfunction. We may be able to do routine activities, but we can't figure out how to respond to new circumstances. Our dreams become nightmares, so real that waking seems more dreamlike than our sleep. We confuse things, places, people, see danger where it doesn't exist, defend ourselves when we need not defend. Many untreated trauma victims isolate themselves, or stick to well-controlled tasks.

These are normal responses to trauma. It only becomes a defense against grief when we accept the identity of victim as defining *all* of who we are. We become no more than a parent who has lost a child, an AIDS victim, a survivor of the Holocaust, a Vietnam veteran. Nothing else in our lives comes close to representing who we are.

There is a difference between seeing ourselves as *being victimized by* a trauma or a loss and *taking on the role* of victim. Being victimized means we accept that for a period of time, we were unable to control our world, that horrible things happened to us, and that now our ways of coping can't stop the emotional flood. That response is necessary to gradually permit the grieving we need.

Being a victim implies a more permanent condition, that a particular trauma was so powerful we'll never recover from it, much less fully grieve its impact. Difficulties arise when the role of victim becomes central to our lives, eliminates the other roles we play and keeps us from exploring the ramifications of our loss. We are defined only by our weakness and vulnerabilities, not by our potential and strengths.

It's hard to get appropriate support for the true extent of our trauma when people see us as a victim. Some will exaggerate it:

> *"I can't imagine being able to go on with life if that had happened to me," Jane was told by a therapist shortly after her whole family had been murdered. The therapist's response frightened Jane. "I came away feeling so totally alone—that if I let in what had happened, I'd probably kill myself" was her response to a friend later. "It was as if she was saying there is no hope for me—what had happened was beyond the human capacity to endure."*

The intensity of the therapist's reaction to Jane's story served to frighten her, causing Jane to retract emotionally. *It is essential that professional caregivers learn to modify their responses appropriate to a client's needs.* This is how validation as a therapeutic tool becomes effective.

Alternatively, professionals will sometimes wrongly minimize the significance of a loss or the need to respond to it. They may know somebody with a similar life experience who brushed it off and is doing fine. They may try to persuade us to forget it, put it aside, rise above it, laugh it off. We'll get dozens of "how to" books that tell us exactly what we need to do to get on with our life and use our loss for our growth and well-being.

As a result, we may lack the validation for what we've experienced. When people around us cannot identify with our loss because it is beyond what they have experienced, we can be confused and frightened by their fears for and about us. We can lose hope because others can't hold it for us or believe in us.

Amnesia

It is not uncommon to have no memory of the time around a significant loss. This can be so extensive that an entire period of life is blocked. Instead, a false memory is often created—pleasant events, no disturbing actions, no loss, a happy childhood.

The extent of the amnesia is often related to the extent of the losses experienced. Single events can be forgotten, a blank in an otherwise intact life story. Extensive or repeated losses may mean suppression of all memories, even when some of them are positive. "I don't remember anything prior to the age of eleven" can indicate there were several losses prior to that time.

Traumatic experiences can result in amnesia. Survivors of rape, accident, torture, war and concentration camps often cannot remember what happened at such times. In the process of surviving, they may have discovered how to separate from their bodies, creating a sense of unreality and distance from the painful experience that was going on. Later, they recall what happened as if it were a dream. Often they only have access to those memories in vivid, often symbolic nightmares. The dream-like quality of their memories is often used by others to dismiss the reality of the experience itself.

Clinical experience has shown that remembering a profound loss or traumatic events is not safe as long as there is a dependent relationship with or influence by the source of the loss. That's why survivors rarely remember incest or abuse until they are clearly free of the influence, control and potential retribution of the perpetrator. Those working with incest and abuse survivors need to know that as long as the perpetrator can continue to influence the victim (beyond continued abuse), normal grieving stops.

In recent years, there has been a tremendous increase in the number of people openly discussing their incest experiences and seeking treatment. When courageous people begin to write or speak of their experiences, others are given permission to remember what they had previously dismissed as nightmares, bad dreams, or their imagination.

At the opposite extreme are people who have no memory of early traumatic events, but are led to believe in their existence by therapists who specialize in early trauma or whose theories insist that certain symptoms are inevitably connected to childhood abuse. We are all suggestible, at one level or another, especially in our memories of early childhood. Therapists must exercise great caution lest they falsely induce traumatic memories instead of validating real ones that emerge as a natural consequence of safety and the opportunity to remember unresolved losses.

Shun or abandon

Shunning is another way to defend against reminders of a loss. When we shun another, we won't have anything to do with them, including ignoring their presence or existence. Instead of destroying the evidence through aggressive behaviors, our passivity and capacity to ignore or exclude is used to eliminate them as a reminder of a loss. Some religious groups and cultures use shunning as a way to control behavior.

Another common way to defend against grief is to abandon others connected to the loss. Some people leave town, never to be seen or heard from again after the death or birth of a child or some other loss. Rather than deal with the grief over the loss, they let go of everything and start a new life elsewhere.

Vilify the lost person as evil, a persecutor or a villain

The flip side of sanctifying a lost spouse or loved one as a way to defend against loss is to vilify them. Especially in cases of abandonment or divorce, the partner left behind may defend against their sense of loss and embarrassment by seeing only negative characteristics in the one who left.

Such bitterness can prevent grief, for no real loss is acknowledged as worthy of grief. The energy involved in such a stance, however, can be just as consuming as its opposite, and just as destructive of new relationships which must stand in the shadow of the unresolved ones. It can also affect the capacity of children of divorce to grieve.

Consequences of the Inability to Grieve

Loss of the will to live

Grief that is not expressed erodes the human spirit. Instead of allowing ourselves to be aware of the full implications of a loss, we assume we've lost much more or much less than we have. When we assume it's much more, we may be unable to reconcile continuing to live. Without grief, there's no way to experience the ebb and flow of life and inimitable movement toward death. When loss cannot be explored, we may lose sight of why we are living:

> *Frances was a lovely woman who lived in her husband's shadow.*
> *He was a well-known pediatrician. He was loved by many people,*

and often helped parents who had lost a child. Frances was a librarian and lived a quiet life.

Early in their marriage, they had two children. When the youngest, Anna, was four, she contracted a virus. Karl was away at a meeting and unable to get home before she died.

Karl and Frances were unable to cope with their loss together. Frances was angry that Karl wasn't home at the time of the death, though she couldn't express it. Karl poured himself into his work, developing a special practice treating children with leukemia, at that time an almost certain terminal condition.

Thirty years had passed when I met Karl at a five-day workshop. During the workshop, we took several long walks in the woods. Karl told me of his daughter's death. He began opening to the grief that had been bottled up for so long.

In the year that followed, I visited Karl and Frances many times. Karl and I frequently conducted workshops together. In their home, Frances rarely spoke unless Karl or I directly approached her. She was very shy and reluctant to share her thoughts. We spent long hours listening to music, both classical and new age. I persuaded Frances to try to do some Tai Ji to Pachelbel's Canon— she loved it.

Slowly Frances began to blossom. She began to take courses on Tai Ji. She went to a women's support group. She mentioned occasionally in the support group Anna's death, only to note it had happened, and that Karl hadn't been there.

One day, after being away for several months, I called. Karl answered the phone. In his quiet way, he sadly said that it wasn't a good time for me to visit—Frances wasn't feeling well. This pattern continued for several months. I persisted with Karl, who finally explained that Frances was severely depressed.

She had been at a Tai Ji workshop. She looked at everyone else and suddenly felt old, out of place. "It's too late for me," she told herself. "I don't deserve to be here."

Over the next several years, Frances had the full range of treatment for depression—drugs, therapy, even electroshock. Except for a few days here and there, the depression wouldn't lift . She did admit how angry she was about what happened at the time of Anna's death, but she couldn't seem to get past it. By this time, I lived far away. I only saw Frances once and it was clear she was not reachable by my friendship.

Four years passed since my last visit. I received a letter from Karl. In it he told me that Frances had committed suicide six months before. She had tried several times over the intervening years. Life had no meaning for her, she said.

Karl wrote that he lived in dread of what he would find when he came home each night, for he had already interrupted several lethal attempts. Once she had been found nearly drowned in the bay. Finally it happened. She drowned herself in the bathtub.

"It was like a long terminal illness," Karl shared as we visited the cemetery six months later. "I knew it would happen someday. She was suffering so much. She never could find someone to trust to deal with her grief. She felt that her life had little meaning once she reached retirement age and could 'only' look back at her years as a librarian. She compared herself to me and to you, and found herself wanting. Perhaps if she'd had a therapist who could have made it safe enough, been confronting enough. She had the best and it didn't work.

"I'm glad she's out of her suffering. Those last years were so painful. I can look back at the good times again—past those years of depression. We shared a lifetime. I can go on. I miss her. I don't miss what we went through these past five years."

Frances had waited a long time to deal with her daughter's death—too long, perhaps. By her mid-sixties, depression set in, but as she began to emerge from her shell the internal and external resources weren't there to help her—in spite of a genuinely loving husband and the best of treatment.

One might also wonder if Karl had really dealt with his daughter's death. He had not openly talked about it until some thirty years later with me. Karl had found ways to move on from his grief over the death of his child. While he hadn't consciously dealt with Anna's death for those thirty years, his work with dying children with leukemia had given him opportunities to deal with his guilt and his sense of responsibility. His life, his work had meaning in light of his loss. Even after experiencing the five-year depression of his wife, he could grieve her death and her depression, knowing he had done what he could, that his life still had meaning.

Suicide is a major risk when we avoid dealing with loss. Our bodies, minds and spirits wear out from the stressfulness of defending against grief. Pleasure is a rare commodity for survivors who cannot grieve. Suicide can be a last desperate attempt to admit to ourselves how important this loss is to us, despite years of denial. Unfortunately, the consequences of a successful suicide produce transformations that we, the living, cannot comprehend or appreciate.

The inability to forgive

Combat veterans rarely speak of their experiences, especially if buddies were killed or if something happened to produce a sense of shame or guilt. "I did things I can never be forgiven for," was the comment of Doug, a Vietnam vet dying of a very painful form of pancreatic cancer, "This is my punishment." When asked if he wished to talk about it, Doug refused. "It wouldn't do any good," he stated. "I'm going to die anyway. It's too late. Let me have some peace these last days." Doug was living in shame, which prevented him from grieving.

Perhaps we're convinced our losses aren't forgivable because we were the ones to injure or act destructively. We made the choice to have the abortion, leave the marriage, quit the job, move away, have the affair. This is even more complicated when important people around us blame us for our actions. We have "done the unforgivable" and must "bear the consequences."

Tom, Mary and Sue were members of a support group that had met for years. They met two months after Marsha, a good friend and former member of the group, had died:

> We were surprised and saddened by how quickly and easily Marsha accepted her cancer. "I am at peace, for the first time in a long time" was her comment —two months before she died.
>
> Marsha had struggled for fifteen years after an extramarital affair. Her husband Ted never forgave her for it. But it wasn't something they ever talked about together, though she had shared it in our support group.
>
> At one point, she thought she could forgive herself and we were supportive. Self-forgiveness, she knew, meant she might have to leave her marriage, because she lived each day with the reality of being unforgiven by Ted. Each of us had been in similar straits. We

knew how painful it would be to leave. We knew it had to be her choice.

She made her decision—to stay in the marriage, to believe that there was nothing she could do to be forgiven. Divorce would simply add to her sins, not release her from them. She left our group. We rarely saw her.

Cancer and the prospect of dying was what it took. "I feel released. I am finally being punished enough" was her comment.

We weren't invited to be a part of her process of dying. Ted wanted only family. In a way, we could understand that. We would have wanted her to fight the disease, not accept it as a just reward for her affair. She saved us and herself the agony of struggling with what was a solution to her guilt.

Marsha lived to see her daughter graduate from college. Her death was her release.

The inability to tell the difference between reality and fantasy

The common theme of defending against loss is our inability to experience grief over loss. This inability comes from within and without. In the case of massive, multiple losses and severely traumatic experiences, the effects are overpowering. At the time, they seem unreal in their discontinuity with normal life.

We may be so traumatized by the experience that it seems unreal. "It's as if I were standing there, watching my body go through it. Even though it was painful, I didn't feel anything because I was outside of me" is a common reflection of someone going through a traumatic experience. It seems like a dream. We're not sure how we made it—although we often feel we didn't, for an important part of us is now missing. What happens at such times is the shock of the event splits us into emotional segments. Our thinking isn't connected with our feelings. Our body is on automatic pilot, going through the motions. We can do routine tasks, yet we don't remember doing them. For the time being, we've lost our sense of wholeness.

Since we are confused about what happened, we're all too vulnerable to how others respond to us. If they deny our reality, pretend nothing has happened or blame us for what happened, we're likely to question ourselves: Did I make it up? Was it a bad dream? Did I want it to happen, ask for it to happen? If our questions go unanswered, we're at the mercy of our imagination. We're frightened and vulnerable—what happens once could happen again. We'd like to pretend it didn't happen, because we know that to let it fully into our awareness will be painful. We're not sure how we endured the first time. We're even less confident we could survive going back to re-experience it.

The loss of our "best self"

There is perhaps no greater loss than the one that involves losing our belief in ourselves as a worthwhile person. When we do something that produces shame, we feel we no longer deserve what we have—even our normal identity. When we lose our sense of wholeness, we search outside ourselves for hope, because we no longer feel it internally. We wonder if life is worth living. We don't trust ourselves. We avoid the full impact of the loss.

When people lose their sense of their best self as a result of a shameful loss, they often push others away, become abusive and "burn bridges." This leads to self-fulfilling prophecies—that no one cares, that life stinks, that the best of life is over, that we have to look out only for ourselves. In this state, we keep secrets, ones we have to guard so closely that we don't even remember them ourselves, as happened for Tracy, years after she had been raped and given her infant up for adoption. Later, she married and had three children. She had never told them what had happened:

> *March is always a strange time of the year for me. I always seem to have aches and pains then. The past few years I have had incredible abdominal pains.*

> *Way in the back of my head I knew it was connected to something back there—back in my growing-up. I didn't want to admit it.*

> *I know it's connected with giving up that child. I gave birth to him in March. I've always wondered how he is doing. I wouldn't dare find out. I would never want my children or my husband to know. It would change their image of me.*

Living for an image can prevent us from having access to our grief by denying the reality of our loss, as happened with Tracy.

Another reaction to the loss of the best self is to live for others, denying our own needs. We become the "good servant," selfless, always helping others in need. We love too much—and others may despise us for it. We try to take care of others whether they need it or not. We do what we do very well because we have to, and because it feels good, in the midst of loss, to be doing something for someone else. Doing for others in the midst of loss is a natural way of maintaining control over our environment and our emotions. But it is often a means to avoid grieving. We never stop to question: Is what I am doing a waste of time and energy—not to mention a danger to my health and well-being?

The incompleteness of the experience

It is the nature of being traumatized that we can't take it all in at once. We can't quite believe it's happening because a part of us isn't experiencing it—only observing. Eugene Gendlin (1964) reasoned that a common theme in all psychotherapeutic approaches to problematic behavior is the incompleteness of experience. For example:

> *"If I had let it all in at that time, I would not have made it," observed Jack many years after his Vietnam war experiences. Jack had been diagnosed with a post-traumatic stress disorder that began during his tour of duty and included a series of events where women and children were killed, along with his best friend. Later, after severely abusing his wife and child and becoming an alcoholic, he subsequently lived alone in the Oregon hills for years.*

> *As he described it: "So I chose to survive. I became an animal except animals don't have nightmares like I've had."*

Jack had subsequently gone through an extensive treatment program at a VA hospital that gave him a chance to relive those war experiences and regain his sense of self. It took years, and much grief over the life he lost since the war.

Lack of energy for or attachment to new or existing relationships

Attack and avoidance are extreme ways of reacting. They also leave little energy, motivation or commitment to current relationships. No one does well when compared to a saint; it's hard to live with someone constantly bitter about their past. Their reactions often have little to do with us, more often it is a reflection of their unresolved losses. "I never felt like I could get through to her," or, "He would just get that glazed look in his eyes before getting violent" are comments one might hear from the partner of someone whose grieving has stopped or never begun.

It's not easy to live with someone whose grief has stopped. We may understand what it is that they have lost and what prevents them from experiencing the full measure of their loss, but understanding often isn't enough as time goes by and nothing changes. No relationship is likely to survive when one has to perpetually play second fiddle to a ghost, whether it be a saint or the devil himself.

Panic Disorder as Incomplete Grief

One dramatic and painful manifestation of incomplete expression of grief is seen in the repetition of panic attacks that lead to the diagnosis of panic disorder. So anxiety-provoking are these episodes, which feel like we are dying, that we may even lose sight of why they occurred in the first place. Medications may control panic attacks, but the cure comes in rediscovering their origins and completing the grief.

Incomplete Grief: Altering the Outcomes

For many people, there is a window of time during which intervention, support, validation and safety will allow them to more fully experience their loss. If this support is not available, some may become frozen in the incompleteness of the loss, subsisting until something happens to change what they cannot.

In extreme survival situations, however, detachment and suppression of feelings is often necessary, as in rape or torture. The situation may dictate denial: of the loss, the pain, the threat. A person being raped or tortured mentally leaves the body being ravaged because screaming or fighting back might get him or her killed, or lead to killing. Survivors later wonder if it happened because survival meant detaching their mind from what their body was enduring. A man in battle leaves his spirit, his best self, behind as he kills in order to avoid being killed. Later, he is not certain if it happened. The fear is that re experiencing the traumatic loss will recreate the same risk—the rape, torture or battle will be real, with its potential for death.

While these responses and fears are adaptive reactions to extraordinary circumstances, the consequences are so severe that professional intervention is often required to resume normal grieving. In this sense the person sacrificed the best self in order to survive physically.

As therapists listen to the horrors inflicted on their clients, they may need to put aside personal feelings in order not to be traumatized as well. They need to respect personal limits that create vulnerabilities. For example, I found it impossible to work with parents who had lost children when my own children were young. As a parent, I still avoid working with sex offenders, even though many are traumatized individuals dealing with profound losses. Especially in practices devoted to traumatized individuals, there is a risk of becoming deadened to life and less able to respond therapeutically.

Therapists need ways to deal with their own distancing and judgmental responses to people in such desperate need. I know of no one who can manage without a consultant or supervisor to help with the issues raised by grieving, or when it has stopped due to trauma.

When Professionals Don't Help

Traumatized people are often treated in ways that say they cannot be *helped*, only *maintained* in their present state. "You've got to learn to live with it" is a common response from professionals unable or unwilling to walk with them through the jungle of their experience. Professionals may give a diagnostic label—clinically depressed, adjustment, panic or post-traumatic stress disorders, to name a few of the more common terms. In our present health insurance system, reimbursable diagnostic labels do not include grief, coping, forgiveness, or how to become empowered. Hence bereaved people are often labeled as pathological, sick or crazy. Such labels from professionals deprive clients of hope, convince them of how alone they are, or how little they can trust themselves or anyone else.

Of equal importance, we must realize that those of us in helping roles aren't immune to our own losses. People in helping roles can be traumatized. I've come out of many sessions reeling from the power of the story I've heard. However, it is important that a therapist find a way to discharge strong reactions without violating confidentiality. Having friends within one's profession is critical to understanding the source of our reactions to client's stories.

Jeffrey Mitchell and Grady Bray (1990) have developed an extensive training program for emergency service personnel who are often the first at the scene of an accident or disaster. Their *critical incident stress debriefing* procedure contains all the essential ingredients of safety, validation and sharing the story. When a natural disaster happens, for example, a team of debriefers follows the emergency care workers to give them opportunities to discuss and relive the impact of their rescue work soon after or even during the operations. Such immediate debriefing often allows the worker to continue with the rescue, or not to lose time from work later.

When the Legal System Interferes

In this day and age, the US legal system may also attack the integrity of our response to loss. We are encouraged to blame, and to seek financial or criminal compensation for our loss. We're encouraged to extract our "pound of flesh" as revenge for what was done to us. In the adversarial legal process that results, our grief gets exaggerated and paralyzed.

We must remain victims for as long as the legal process continues, which often is many years. Grieving can jeopardize our case for permanent damages, for we will have healed and even grown as a result.

Also, the outcome of a lawsuit or criminal prosecution may not give us satisfaction or compensation. It may not bear any connection to our loss. For example, financial compensation for a death of a loved one may be experienced as "blood money"—an attempt to "buy out" our grief. If we get paid, if the offender goes to jail, are we still entitled to grieve the loss or have we received all that we deserve (or more)? The death penalty or life sentence for the murderer of a loved one may satisfy our sense of outrage, but it may not give us a chance to acknowledge the complexities of our loss or our need to confront and forgive. Only when the suit or trial is resolved in the way we desire is it possible to examine the extent of the loss and to begin to grieve. Unacceptable legal outcomes keep us distracted from our grief.

> *A colleague of mine joined me in consulting with an industrial firm a year and a half after an industrial accident killed thirty people. The firm had done a competent job during the first year of dealing with the trauma—debriefings, counseling and permitting time off for recovery. Sick time had almost returned to normal— until a lawsuit against them was settled for over a million dollars by a worker who later admitted (to his former co-workers) that he hadn't been injured in the accident—it was due to weight lifting. As a consequence, a majority of the workers then put in claims for injuries, and sick time reached an all-time high. The morale of employees who wouldn't resort to lawsuits plummeted. Greed interfered with grief.*

It seems the guilty go free, monetary compensation is paltry, and legal fees are exorbitant. Losing years of time to lengthy court cases or greedy family members—all these can stop grieving:

> *"After ten years of my practice, mainly on the side of the defense, I'm convinced that the legal and financial outcome is usually fair,*

but emotionally it never is," commented Dave, a lawyer who often provides support for the families in his practice well after the suit was settled. "People are wounded by the process—and no one is there to help them pick up the pieces."

Helping Those Whose Grieving Has Stopped

Can we accept that people who deny loss or avoid grieving are truly doing the best they can? Can we appreciate the courage it takes to keep going when life seems meaningless, when joy has disappeared from life? As caregivers we need to accept that it takes time—often years—to be considered a safe enough person for others to confide in. People don't usually prefer a life that is meaningless and without joy, unless the alternative is even worse. We can also help by telling others what we can handle and empathize with, and what our limits are:

"I've never lost a child," admitted Tara, a psychotherapist to a bereaved couple. "It's my worst nightmare that such a thing would happen. I know about grief. I know what pain is like. I know that it's important to feel safe. If it can help, I'm willing to listen." Tara gave the couple the choice of confiding in her. Her honesty convinced them that she was trustworthy enough to share the story of their child's death.

Perhaps what we can do is help others around the person unable to grieve—family and friends—to authenticate what's happened. We can suggest to them what helps and what doesn't, and validate their struggles with wanting to do more than can be done. We can help them get on with their own grief, or wait until it is their turn.

It's from our own grief that we discover what helps others. There's no substitute for having walked that mile in another person's shoes before attempting to validate their experience. Later we can recognize how similar grief is over many kinds of losses—and what remains unique to each one.

Distortion and Victimization: The Necessity for Confrontation

It is a common belief that all victims of loss need to be gently eased into awareness of the trauma. While this is true in many cases, as described elsewhere in this book, there are some times when dramatic intervention is required. In this instance we are unable to provide our own sense of safety; we need to have it provided, for we have already judged ourself too harshly. We need permission to care about ourself from someone powerful enough to grant it. And we need confrontation—of our distortions and passivity, of the unacceptability of our self-destructive behaviors, of the true nature of our loss. There are times when we need to be shocked into awareness of our loss, to literally have our noses rubbed into its reality.

Jan needed dramatic help a year after she had been diagnosed with multiple sclerosis but was nevertheless continuing with plans to become a police officer. We had agreed on five sessions of therapy at the beginning and set appointments for each one:

> *Jan had come in because she was angry at herself, and everyone else, about her multiple sclerosis. Her family doctor had almost killed her by prescribing a medicine 100 times the safe dosage. She was angry at her mother for trying to get her to give up the "ways of a sinner" which meant to Jan that she must have done something to bring this horrible disease on herself.*

> *Jan had spent the previous year focused on how everyone else was dealing with her illness. But she hadn't dealt with it herself. She was majoring in police administration but she hadn't looked at the implications of her illness on such a career. She'd claimed that she could hide its symptoms if she had to.*

> *Underneath this denial, Jan also knew that she had to deal with the illness. She was miserable and isolated. Its secret was something that was interfering with her friendships. She'd broken up with her boyfriend because she knew he wouldn't be able to accept it—yet she'd never told him anything about it.*

> *Early in the third therapy session, Jan was discussing what her plans for the future were—how she intended to become a police officer, play competitive tennis, have children. Exasperated, I interrupted:*

> *"Jan, how can you become a police officer? You have MS! Maybe you can play tennis for a while, though when the symptoms are active, you won't be able to do so. Have you discussed with anyone the risks of having children if you have MS?"*

> *"You insensitive son-of-a-bitch!" Jan shouted as she stood up and went to the door. "I don't need your fucking help!" She slammed the door behind her as she left.*

It was a week before her next session, previously scheduled. Jan came in.

"You were right," she admitted.

"About what?" I inquired.

"I wasn't being realistic. I wanted to blame everyone else for not dealing with the MS when it was me who wasn't dealing with it. I went home last week and started crying. I thought about not being able to be a police officer. I thought about not being able to play tennis. I thought about the possibility that I might not be able to have children. My future crumbled before me.

"But this week has been a good week. I went to my doctor and found out about the pregnancy risks. There are some. It's not impossible. I talked to my college advisor. I'm thinking now about rehab counseling as a career. It would let me do some of the things I'd wanted to do. I thought about tennis. I'll deal with losing that when I have to.

"I feel so much clearer about where I am. I was stuck, focusing on anything except what I needed to be examining."

Jan profited from the confrontation, although she didn't appreciate it initially. We need someone who will see us through times of anger and protest against the loss. We need opportunities to validate, or disconfirm, what we consider lost, then find out what we still have and what we'll do with it.

Psychotherapy can be a way to prepare us to grieve. What may be needed is an intervention in a process that is not self-correcting or healing. Safety, permission, confrontation, validation and love can all be parts of the therapeutic relationship that are hard to find in everyday life.

Jean was a forty-five-year-old social worker who came to therapy because he couldn't live anywhere but in sight of the capitol building in his home town—so he thought. "I left last year," he noted, "and got so depressed I had to return. My wife recently divorced me because I couldn't move":

As therapy progressed, Jean discovered that it wasn't the capitol building he was fixated on for so many years—it was a funeral home next to it.

In early childhood his biological parents died within the span of 18 months. His aunt and uncle adopted him. Assuming he had no memory for these early events, they never told him he was adopted. He was told that his aunt and uncle had died, and they frequently visited the cemetery where they, his biological parents, were buried.

He'd always secretly believed that it was his parents who had died. During hypnotic regressions, he remembered his mother being taken away in a white car with a flashing light when her "tummy got real big." He also remembered his daddy not waking up one morning when he came in to his bed. The last place he could remember seeing them was at the funeral home. Even as an adult, he believed they were still in that blue-brick building—he was waiting for them to come out.

It was important to find a way to confront Jean's beliefs that kept him from being able to move. Investigation of records from a local hospital in the early 1930's revealed that his "aunt" died of an "abdominal obstruction"—and that she had a year-old son. Other records indicated that her husband died of cancer at home—and that he had a thirty-month-old son. His memory was validated— the swollen stomach now made sense. So did the memory of his dad not waking. He was their son. It was his parents who had died.

Trips to the funeral home allowed him to explore where he had last seen them. He recalled accurately the way the building had looked, which was confirmed by the owner's review of blueprints—it had been remodeled two years after Jean's father had died.

Such authentication of the reality of his memories, in spite of the story his adoptive parents had given him, was having an impact. On a visit to the cemetery where his parents were buried, his therapist said, "They're dead."

Jean spun towards his therapist and, with a look of fury, shouted "NO!" Then his face dissolved in tears. "Yes," he muttered softly. "They are dead."

A few months later Jean started a new career as an artist. A year later he moved 3,000 miles away, to a place he'd always dreamed of living. He's only returned for family gatherings in the twenty years since.

Jean was frozen in space as well as time. This was partly due to his young age at the time of the death of his parents. It was also due to the invalidation of his memories by his adoptive family who reinforced the unreality of his parents' death. He needed the opportunity to confront these memories in order to make their deaths real. Once he did, he was able to grieve their loss and examine how it had affected his life—and move on.

There are times when the trauma isn't a single event, rather, a living nightmare. Henry Krystal (1968), working with concentration camp survivors, reported that long-term survivors could vividly recall many incidents from their traumas, although they were usually very reluctant or completely resistant to share them. They experienced what Krystal and others saw as *massive psychic trauma*, with so many events to recall that it takes months, even years for them to unfold and be re-experienced in therapy.

Survivors of traumatic losses often feel *survivor guilt*—they feel guilty that they are alive when others perished. Survival guilt, says Krystal, is based on a deep sense of shame over actions taken to survive. And by admitting to these behaviors, and to other experiences, survivors fear being severely judged as unworthy of living. Indeed, many survivors of massive trauma have died premature deaths, had high levels of illness and depression and frequently commit suicide.

Krystal has been successful in working with many survivors because he, too, was in a concentration camp. He had a credibility that gave them a sense of safety—that he would not judge them as they recalled what they had to do to survive the camps. He had empathy for what they had been through based on similar life experiences. He helped them find words for their experiences which validated the reality of what they went through. He found ways to help survivors meet each other. He also gave them hope, that sharing and reliving the pain of the past could free them from the depression and the burden of the repetitive images that plagued their dreams and lives.

Henry Krystal did what many of us can do for people who have had losses similar to our own. That's why alcoholics talk to recovering alcoholics; Vietnam vets confide in other vets; incest survivors support other survivors; parents who have lost children seek out other bereaved parents. Our loss may seem insignificant compared to others," so we need someone with a similar loss to *validate* what it's like to lose a pet, a brother or a sister, struggle with sudden success and fame. Kindred spirits give us safety to explore our experiences. They intuitively know the kind of support and the kind of challenge we need. Their very existence gives us hope that we too can survive.

If we are to be helpful to others, we need to know ourself and our limits. Pity and sympathy are not helpful feelings. When devastated by what others go through, we need to take care of ourself first. Perhaps we lose our sense of innocence, our beliefs about the world. Often our own unresolved losses get triggered. We must understand ourself first.

Validation

The absence of validation often means that we remain stuck until we can get it:

> *Maureen, a sixty-five-year-old woman, had hypertension for twenty years. She complained of "flashbacks" since her husband died twenty years before.*

> *When asked if she remembered what happened at the time of her husband's death, she reacted instantly: "Remember! It's as if it happened yesterday!"*

> *Maureen related, over a period of several hours, the feeling and experiences of the time around her husband's death. He had been admitted to the hospital a month before "for routine tests." He never left alive. She had never been able to say good-bye. The day of the funeral, however, her daughter gave birth to a child with severe birth defects.*

> *Maureen had immediately flown to her daughter's home. For the next six months, she cared for the older grandchildren. There was no opportunity for her to deal with her grief. When she returned home, her friends assumed she had "gotten over it."*

> *Not until this time, twenty years later, had Maureen related any one of her experiences. She reported feeling tremendous relief, and in subsequent weeks felt the memory had faded considerably. Her blood pressure was now normal.*

Validation can be a long time coming. When the time finally comes, we can grieve—not only the loss, but the loss of the years spent not being fully ourselves.

We also struggle when it comes to someone else's grief process. As Irvin Yalom asked as the therapist in *Love's Executioner* (1989), who wants to be the bearer of bad tidings—the executioner of the illusion that the loss doesn't exist? Sometimes we can turn over the responsibility of conveying the news to someone else. Sometimes we can't. We often conspire with others to "protect" a loved one from knowing what's happened, but we're actually protecting ourselves, unprepared to handle their grief, much less our own.

At the other end of the continuum is the concern we have that the person isn't facing reality. "What should we do about his/her denial?" is a frequent question about people with life-threatening conditions who go on about their daily lives as if nothing had happened. Should we pop their bubble? Are we limiting their time to work on and grieve their loss by agreeing that nothing has changed? It's not necessarily helpful to decide that denial has no place and to confront the person with reality. It is important to remember that denial has both adaptive and maladaptive functions in grief, depending on the situation of the person experiencing it.

Presence

When our own awareness of loss is new, we frequently feel vulnerable and, as a result, we can be highly critical of others. One insensitive statement, well intended or not, can lead to rejection ("I couldn't believe she would say something like that to me, that I should 'keep my chin up.' I've never forgiven her for being so insensitive."). Our need for things to be better gets in the way. Hopefully, later, the anger can be acknowledged and forgiveness can occur, especially when the bereaved considers their own instances of insensitivity.

On the other hand, we may place enormous trust in someone. What we think is minor or inconsequential can form the basis for trust, a close, enduring relationship (e.g., "I can't understand why I'm so important to him now—all I did was stay with him that first night," or "Dr. Jones is wonderful. She won my undying devotion when she cried while telling me about Joe's death.").

As hard as it is to think of the right thing to say, it creates images that are tough to overcome if we avoid contact during this time. For example, Mable and Art reported that their decision to sue a physician for malpractice came not as a result of a mistake ("We all make mistakes—we're only human"). It was because their physician avoided them after their son's death ("He didn't have the guts to face us. He was out having fun at the golf course. We didn't mean much to him.").

Sharing a crisis forms attachments. Not sharing a crisis puts distance between us. This is one reason why so many marriages dissolve following the death or life-threatening illness of children. Mandy was devastated when her husband Rolland couldn't leave his work when their daughter was having life-or-death surgery. Mandy not only lost her daughter on that horrible day—she also lost her husband:

> *When Rollie couldn't be there when Tawny was having his surgery and when the doctor told me she wasn't going to make it—well, that was the beginning of the end. I needed him then, and his work was more important. I knew we would eventually divorce.*

Challenge and Judgment

Because of our vulnerability and shame, we are very sensitive to anyone who might judge our actions, our feelings, or our loss. When we feel vulnerable, in shock, confused, disoriented, and without purpose, to hear someone else say we should not feel that way is almost certain to add to our sense of isolation, shame, guilt and helplessness. *This is true throughout the grief process.* Those who judge us add their fears of "doing it wrong" to what is already going on for us. It may lead us to stop talking about it. In some cases people stop grieving to avoid feeling ashamed of their grief.

Often it is not a caregiver's or friend's intention to stand in judgment. It is hard to see someone we care about struggle when we believe it isn't necessary. We may believe they need to "get on with life." We may not have had good support for our own grief. Much as an abused child often becomes an abusive parent, so do the judged become critical of others.

As the griever, it is also true that there are times when we need a challenge to move forward. We need someone to say to us that there's more to life than this loss—that there is a silver lining behind our dark cloud. The timing and the sources of such challenges are critical. We need to have had enough time to explore how extensive the loss is first. We need to hear challenges from someone whose integrity and openness to grief we respect.

The more powerful the person is in our eyes, the more likely their judgmental attitude is to affect our grief in those crucial, initial encounters. Mothers, fathers, ministers, physicians, and teachers are particularly powerful in what they tell us. So is the person who injured or rescued us. With others less powerful, their comments may simply annoy or anger us; they're not as likely to disrupt our grief. Then again, minor sources of annoyance can be helpful, since they provide a focus for our frustration and anger over the loss, as well as opportunities for reconciliation.

Those of us in helping roles that involve working daily with grief and loss can reach the point of insensitivity. We, too, struggle to survive multiple losses. Mike, for example, was a resident physician who lost eighteen children in his care in a single month:

Mike seriously considered giving up medicine altogether. He felt responsible in many of those deaths. "The only constant was me" he would say, even though there was no evidence that he was neglectful. As a result, he wasn't sensitive to what the many bereaved parents he met needed as he reeled from his grief.

During my years in Denmark, I heard that some people committed suicide by stepping on the train tracks at night, facing away as the train approached. About fifty people died that way each year. The driver of the train, who may only have had a momentary glimpse of the back of the person, was, by company policy, given the next day off, yet was expected back to work the following day. No debriefing of the experience was offered. Not surprisingly, one hundred percent of the affected train drivers were no longer in that job six months after the incident—and the vast majority were on permanent disability. Their grief over the event was not recognized—no opportunity was given to explore their perceived responsibility. The stress of the event paralyzed their lives. The only recourse open to them at the time was to flee. Fortunately, that policy has changed and debriefing and therapy are now available.

Summary

Grief waits for the time and place where safety and freedom from judgment exists, with someone who validates its reality and supports the time it needs to heal. Without safety, validation, support and hope, we lack the essential ingredients to move on when we are stuck in even the most common of life experiences. We need not to be judged. We need to be convinced that our story won't hurt or devastate the other. We need to anchor our experiences with words, drawings, sculpture, poems, songs. We need to discover other people who have had very similar, perhaps identical experiences to us—and have come through them.

Added to this external support is our faith in ourselves. We can make it through the painful, humiliating, emptying process that lies ahead, of grieving the full extent of what we have lost. We need to believe that we can forgive—and be forgiven—someday. We will laugh and play again. Someday we'll no longer be a victim or a survivor and become someone who is again whole.

In the meantime, we survive. We control what we can, avoid evidence of our helplessness and aloneness, eliminate awareness of our loss. We wait for the safety and resources and seek a path back to our transformative potential.

Chapter Eleven

Facilitating Grief's Transformations: Safety, Validation and Challenge

> *If someone comes to you asking for help, do not say*
> *in refusal, "Trust in God. God will help you."*
> *Rather, act as if there is no God, and no one to help*
> *except you.*
>
> *—Hasidic teaching*

Cheryl is an old friend. We have seen many good times and many tough times together. She's struggled, painfully, with many losses that involve family, friends and career. She's had chronic health problems that were painful, exhausting and even life-threatening. Yet she can be a loving, whole and joy-filled person. She sings, dances, writes, and delights in her fellowship with friends and in her work as a therapist. I asked Cheryl when things began to change for her:

> *Remember the workshop we did at the lake when I said I didn't feel I had anything to give—that I didn't feel I could love? I heard you say that you knew I was capable of loving. You said you would hold my love for me.*

> *I remember crying then. I remember a feeling of hope, a spark starting. That's when it began to change.*

Donna is another friend of many years. Years ago, she lost two children to cystic fibrosis. She went through a divorce and had to find ways to reconnect with her surviving son. Yet she, too, is a joy-filled person, living with her second husband, in a community with a voluntarily simplified lifestyle. Donna is a writer, publisher, distributor and storyteller. She, too, laughs, sings, dances, and enjoys her life as fully as she can. She remembers a time when things changed. She reminded me of my role some ten years before:

It was that time the year after Matt (her son) died—three years after he had left home. I had taken time to go off by myself. I felt hopeless, yet I was fighting it. I called you. You told me that you would hold my hope for me as long as I needed.

I felt an enormous relief when you said that. It was as if a burden of responsibility had been lifted from me. I could plunge as far as I needed to, knowing my hope was being cared for. Within moments, my feelings descended. I remember sobbing, feeling just how empty my world was without Matt. For three days I lived in emptiness. I stared with unseeing eyes.

I awoke on the fourth day, noticing the sounds of the birds, the sun on my window, I felt connected to my world again.

You held my hope for me. That's when everything began to change.

Others, including my wife Sharon, have held my hope, my belief in my competency, my love, my joy for me at times when I needed to let go of them, to live my grief fully. They held in the palm of their hand all that was good about me as I explored my dark, unforgivable side. I couldn't have done it without them—without someone to *believe in my best self* as I lived under my shadow. Without depending on something or someone beyond me, my grief would not have been transformed into new levels of self-discovery and growth.

When we grieve, what is the catalyst that leads to personal growth and transformation rather than to depression and stagnation? Obviously, having someone or something to believe in is an important element that holds us on the growth side of grief's chasm, even if only by the skin of our teeth.

This connection, however, isn't just anyone or anything. Some well-intentioned people can step on our fingers and cause us to lose our grip and our hope. Our religious faith or our family values may dictate that what we've done is unforgivable. Even therapists can convince us that we aren't coping well enough. They want us to forget, to move on more quickly than we can.

Who brings out the strengths in us we didn't know we had? Who is it we find helpful—and when are they beneficial? What is it they do or don't do?

In my experience, we are most often helped when others validate the reality of our loss and don't minimize its extent. They believe a "best self" exists within us. They may not be the source of our forgiveness, but they can believe in our forgivability. They may confront and provoke us at times we don't want to hear what they have to say, yet we know they care.

None of us is faultless. We can't expect to help others perfectly through grief. If we did, they'd never leave us and would depend on us more than themselves to make it through grief. But if we truly care for someone in this process, they often recognize this and forgive us for our inability to make the entire journey with them. Part of grief is forgiving, for which we may afford others ample opportunities.

I know some people have not found me helpful. I vividly recall Tina, who had been in a car accident a couple of years before. She had been unconscious for six months afterwards. Tina's fiancé had been killed in the accident. She had suffered brain damage. It was almost a year later before Tina was told of his death. When I saw her, it was two years after the accident. Her rehabilitation process had ended, but as often happens, it wasn't until then that the awareness of her multiple losses began to emerge.

I was eager to be of help. I was wanting to prove to Tina how much I knew about grief. I told her that what she was going through was normal, even though others around her expected her to be over it. I told her what was ahead in her grief—times of validating how extensive her loss was, perhaps a need to go back and find out what happened. I was supportive, encouraging, laying open the path ahead.

She thanked me at the end of the session, agreed to a subsequent session. She never returned.

Sometimes when people don't come back, it's because they have received enough in that one session to keep going. That wasn't what I felt with Tina. Something had happened to turn her off to seeing me.

I realized later that in my eagerness to help her, I had somehow trivialized her process, her need to discover her own grief. I probably conveyed that there was a right way to do this, even though I *usually* don't believe there is. I may even have frightened her about all the anguish that was ahead—after the long and painful struggle she'd been through during rehabilitation.

I hadn't helped—trying to be so helpful.

Something had been happening for me that day. I had received another rejection of my book manuscript in the mail. After thirty or so of those rejections, I had convinced myself it didn't mean anything (my own version of letting go). I could anticipate it happening many times more, that perhaps it never would get published. I was telling myself to accept this reality, not get too involved. I tried to minimize the impact the rejection was having. It wasn't until that moment that I realized I had then done the same thing to Tina! I had attempted to get her to face the reality of *all* the grief that was ahead. I had let neither Tina nor myself be where we needed to be at that moment—grieving the loss of that moment, that day, not all the future losses that would come or all the past ones.

People may not find us especially helpful in their grief and may look for support elsewhere. Sometimes they stick with us in spite of our faults and preoccupations. Whether it's because they believe in us or are simply desperate, many give us more than one chance to be helpful. They forgive us for being human. They help us to help them.

We also need to forgive ourselves. We aren't perfect, far from it, but we do the best we can. We can't ignore our own needs or our losses. Eventually we'll burn out as a helper if we don't learn to respect our limits and give ourself time for our growth. Inevitably we'll be traumatized if we don't respect the power of the life experiences others bring us.

But sometimes we are helpful as caregivers. Where do we get such a capacity? Did we have experiences with our families that allowed us see what helped and what didn't? As we go back to explore the losses of previous generations of our families and communities, sometimes we can understand how they reacted at times of loss. Familial and communal losses can help us understand why others could not support us or why they may have added to our burden—there was no one there for them. The way people handled their grief can make it possible for us to know what to do, to give what is needed at the time it is needed. By knowing what helped or hindered them on their journey, their ways of grieving, we may be able to validate our own process, our own pilgrimage, our links and our unique pathway.

Key Elements in Helping Others Through Grief

There are several key elements which help people find a transformative path through their grief:

- *The need to feel cared for, secure, protected and loved.*

- *The need for validation of reality at times of transition and loss.*

- *The need for challenge when a loss becomes our only important identity.*

- *The need for facilitative environments—places of sanctuary and therapeutic communities.*

- *The need for play and humor to have a role in the healing process.*

- *The need to ultimately find a source of nurturance, validation, forgiveness and adventure from within.*

Feeling Cared For

The greatest fears and attractions of being a helper involve both dependency and being indispensable. We want to be helpful—except we're afraid of making people too dependent on us. We want to give when others can't do it for themselves—or when they appreciate it when we do it for them. We don't want them hanging around all the time, however, creating the living nightmare depicted in the comedy movie "What About Bob?" when a client, Bob, drove his therapist crazy by moving in with his family on their summer vacation. We feel good about ourself when we can point to a way we made a difference in someone's life, when we truly rescued them or intervened at a critical moment to prevent a suicide, a beating, a death or permanent disability. We enjoy being champions of the underdogs, a spokesperson for victims, the one who understands what it's like to experience a particular loss. It doesn't have to be so decisive or noticeable, either. It can involve bringing some food to a family when someone is ill or has died or loaning them a car for visiting relatives.

Unfortunately, we go too far sometimes. We can be too good at taking care of others. We end up controlling or forcing our help on people who don't need it or reinforcing people who would rather depend on us than do it for themselves. Even worse, we sometimes frighten or intimidate them into believing they need us, then resent their dependency when we feel suffocated by them. Later we feel unappreciated when they move on without proper gratitude for our role in their growth.

Our own losses as helpers may keep us from realizing both the extent and the limits of what we have to offer. We get disturbed when people move beyond us in their own grief, when they seek out support from others to validate or encourage them. Like parents with children who grow and need their independence and separateness, we struggle with when to protect and when to revitalize autonomy and risk-taking.

Validation of Reality

Chapter Two discussed validation by recognizing and legitimizing losses. Validation provides us with the base for our experiencing and our self-trust, our willingness to mourn what we have to grieve. Validation is what gives substance to our loss and, later, to our growth.

As I experienced with Tina, the client who didn't return, it's not always clear what is validating and what is not. When we have an investment in getting people to master their denial, break through to awareness, and get moving again, we aren't validating their grief as much as we are *invalidating* their ways of coping. This is a crucial distinction to make.

To validate, we need to believe:

- *The person is capable of handling reality.*

- *They are doing the best they can at the present time.*

- *Their way of coping is appropriate to the complexities and stressfulness of the loss.*

- *Within them lies the strength for choices about their grief.*

Facilitative Environments

At the time someone experiences a significant loss, they need a safe place and non-judgmental people to permit them to see how far they can go in their grief and to help them discover the limits of the loss. As helpers we can rarely be all things others need during the process of grieving. The communities and the environment where people live are determining forces in their grief. Growth depends on safety and sanctuary. It involves people who can validate. These communities may encourage grievers to risk and to grow. In childhood, these make up what D. W. Winnicott (1986) called the *facilitative environment* that provides the nurturance, give and take, support, witness, humor, ritual and timely risk for normal development. In the adult years, this facilitative atmosphere may include places of sanctuary, individuals and groups separate from families of origin—people who share significant commitments, life experiences and values.

Places of Sanctuary

Grieving is an internal process rarely shared except at vulnerable moments or when someone is ready to risk or celebrate. To discover the extent, limits and possibilities that losses pose, it is natural to reach inside. Such internal journeys are best accomplished in places where someone is free to let go of concern for anything or anyone else.

A person experiencing a loss may be so bombarded by the demands, judgments and the dangers of their environment that they are unable to recognize the need for a protected space. A good example of sanctuary is the program called Commonweal in Bolinas, California, which provides a sanctuary of love, nurturing and creative expression for people with life-threatening conditions.

Safety is an important component of an effective sanctuary. Feeling protected, people can scream, cry, faint and beat their fists without shame or fear of admonition or constraint. Safety allows the bereaved to give a caregiver responsibility for holding their best self while they forage through the depths of guilt, shame, loneliness and fear.

Safety also means that survival needs have to be met, as well as basic comforts. It's hard to focus inward if people are freezing or starving. It's a lot easier when there are creature comforts like a down comforter, an inspirational book, a place by a lake or a spot to sit on a hill top.

Many of us identify the need for sanctuary with something spiritual. When a loss happens, and the safety to grieve is not experienced, there can be a spiritual crisis, a crisis of who one is, why one is here—is it all worth it anymore? The will to live can be a barometer of the safety bereaved people feel to explore this spiritual, internal self.

How do caregivers deal with such spiritual crises in clients? By creating a safe environment in which such issues are explored fully—especially being willing to discuss death in its many forms.

Therapeutic Communities

Contemporary times test the traditional values of family and church. Conservative ways can fall short when it comes to validating the many transitions and losses we now go through—changes other than the time-honored ones of birth, puberty, marriage and death. With a wide variety in lifestyles and beliefs, mobility in where we live, many custom-bound communities resort to shunning and judgment as a response to those not fitting their values. Families are important witnesses to our life changes. Yet they can be *too* invested in rapid restoration of our well-being to tolerate the time or the ways we may need for grieving.

Our mobility, careers and schooling may mean that the importance of community needs to be more global than ever before. Communities now go beyond neighborhoods, religion, ethnicity, national boundaries, sexual orientation or lifestyle preferences, since we are more than what is encompassed by any one of these groups. Work communities, for example, might be therapeutic if they recognize significant transitions: new membership, contributions, entrances and exits. Communities of friends and loved ones may be therapeutic both in their sense of outrage and their forgiveness, by celebrating commitments and achievements and by mourning loss.

Many professional communities could create services for facilitating grief for caregivers. *Therapeutic communities* come to pass when two or more people intentionally support each other during times of transition and validate each other's life experiences. We give to each other in times of need and permit each to take what they need. We need people who tolerate our questioning, withdrawal and anger. Therapeutic communities encourage play, humor and story-telling.

Communities become therapeutic if they help us learn how to give, take and receive. Today I may be the one with the need to lean on somebody's shoulder. Tomorrow or next week, it might be the opposite. There are times when nobody can know what I need, though they can be responsive when I ask or seek it. In the communities that are therapeutic to us, we are able to be a giver and a receiver, to open to the love of others, to love ourself and to feel the joy of having our love received.

These groups don't just happen. Reliance on traditional communities such as families, churches, work or neighborhood means taking on a real mix of people who may help with one aspect of our grieving but not with others. We may outgrow a group that was therapeutic early in our grief by giving us safety and sanctuary, but that we have to leave now to grow further. It may be up to us to find or even create communities that meet our particular needs. We need to develop support groups and fellowships who collectively empower members.

Play and Humor

Recreation, pleasure and humor are also an important part of therapeutic communities. Often we give each other support to escape at times when life seems overwhelming. We laugh away the tears of a few moments ago. We find that our triumphs and excitement are something we want to share with others. We may even allow ourself to look ridiculous in front of them.

Kinship, play and fun are important to the ebb and flow of life, the rhythms and cycles we all go through. There may be periods of time when we need to withdraw from our communities, only to return later, to be forgiven, to celebrate or to reconcile. We get love from one generation of a community: our parents, mentors and teachers. Instead of only giving it back to them, we pass it on to subsequent generations or to groups to which we belong.

At times, our therapeutic communities may consist of a single individual, or, in the absence of a person, an enduring belief that we are loved. Experiencing love can be a crucial lifeline as we hover on the edge of the wide chasm of grief:

> *Brenda had to reach the end of her rope before she realized that she was missing love, something she didn't feel she deserved after a childhood filled with incest and a rape when she was in her teens. No person could provide that love, for she was ashamed, did not feel deserving. She turned to God. In a Pentecostal church she felt her shame, that had taken the form of Lupus and chronic pain, disappear. She also felt it replaced by love. For the first time, as she neared the age of fifty, she felt herself to be a full person, free of illness, shame and the residual of unintegrated loss of a spiritual part of herself.*

The difference between one source of validation and love and none at all is enormous. Love that validates can get us through the darkest times, give us strength to mend and renew with our past communities or seek new, more loving ones. That one source need not be another person. It can be our relationship with God or an acknowledgment of powers beyond our individuality.

Communities can obviously inhibit as well as facilitate grief. Being excluded, rejected or shunned by a fellowship can have deadly consequences for our health and growth. So can community tolerance of abuse or neglect. Many groups, for example, lack mechanisms for forgiveness and reconciliation—or the opposite, confrontation and challenge. They may have no way to recognize transformations or spiritual growth. Communities may lack people within them designated as facilitators or validators when people need help during transitions. They may lack ways of giving, taking, playing and receiving, with the only available reciprocity involving loveless legal or financial channels.

The Role of Therapeutic Rituals

Some religious groups lack the rituals to acknowledge grief such as those of divorcing members or to embrace their children who are dying of AIDS. Cults may attempt to define members' needs only in terms of what the cult can provide, thereby forcing members to reject any other sources of support or ways of growing.

They ask us to give when we have something to give. Therapeutic fellowships develop rituals to acknowledge change, growth, forgiveness and dying. They witness our commitments to our loved ones and to our personal growth. They question when they see us violate those commitments. They remind us of our origins, our legacies and our potential.

Our Own Contributions to Transformation

As important as others are in our grief, it is still *our* grief. We are the ones who must make the necessary choices. We are the only ones to fully know what our grief is about. We are the only ones who will stay with us to the very end. What do we do to aid in transforming our own grief? We need to realize we have choices to make. To make those choices, we also need to find within ourselves nurturance, validation and challenge. The following outline some of our own contributions to the transformation of grief:

- *Choice and understanding*
- *Ability to laugh and play*
- *Legitimize the loss*
- *Rituals of recognition and commemoration*
- *Test limits*
- *Develop connections between the past, present and future*
- *Have witnesses*
- *Renew and forgive*

Choice and Understanding

Helplessness and passivity are a common consequence of a significant loss. What we need at some point is the opportunity to demonstrate that we can again act instead of react, sit or reflect. As Elizabeth Harper-Neeld (1990) has suggested, in order to grieve, we must choose to face this loss, accept the fullness, the suffering and understanding of what has happened. Eventually we can choose to move forward again with re-newed confidence in spite of our wounds.

In childhood, choice comes through validating the hurts, investigat-ing why they happened and in getting back on the bicycle we have fallen from, in going back to face the bully who pushed us. In early adulthood, choice often takes the form of meeting demands and of overcoming the obstacles posed in the rites of passage in various professions and trades. During grief, choice means to face our fear of death, of being helpless, lonely or devoid of meaning. *In choosing, we become master of the fears that have previously controlled our lives.*

Be Able to Laugh and Play

At times, grieving is a matter of life and death, hardly a time for laughter. Later, we can be playful with what was once so serious. This capacity to laugh and play often represents progression in coping or growth beyond a point of paralysis and stagnation. It validates our capacity to live with our fears and control the pervasiveness of our anxieties.

Legitimize the Loss

One liability of grieving comes from being so unpredictable and moody that we don't trust our sanity. Sometimes we need an opinion or authority we respect to tell us we have a right to be the way we are. What they can do is make our loss legitimate, when others may have dismissed its significance, validity or reality. They can help us accept our grief as natural when others may have considered it inappropriate or a sign of mental illness. Sometimes we need support when we forgive or say good-bye, when some think we lack the right to do so.

Early in life, members of our family of origin are frequently the legitimizers in our lives. As we grow older, it can be those whose views we respect, significant people—teachers, clergy, doctors, counselors, coaches, friends or mentors. When we are open enough to question, the legitimizers of our grief are those who encourage us to move on and reformulate.

Ultimately, it is up to us to legitimize our own losses. Unless external validation resonates with something internal or unless we resist the invalidations, we cannot believe in ourselves. It is our reality, sanity and meaning we must live with, while others can only guess at what it is.

Rituals of Recognition and Commemoration

Communities can facilitate grief when they provide witness and rituals for transitions. Many religious societies, for example, have rituals for birth, adulthood, marriage, and death, which can be times of loss. Schools have graduations. We need to develop our own rituals.

It's one thing for us to know we have changed due to facing our losses and grieving. It is something else for our process of growth and change to be witnessed by people who know, love and respect us. Parents, teachers and siblings witness the earlier parts of life, while friends, colleagues, children and grandchildren become important later.

Ritual at its best is a way to remember and renew by systematic reflection or behavior. At its worst, it is mindless, dull and perfunctory, deadening our sensibilities at a time when action is required. When accompanying loss and grief, ritual can bring together witnesses to remember a significant event or person or to give strength, renewal or power. It can be a way to overcome alienation.

Some rituals involve stimulating our senses (e.g., taste with food; smell with incense; hearing with music; speaking with chant; movement with drumming, dancing, marching; sight with pictures, sunsets, words). These sensory reminders help create the awareness sought.

Individuals and families can create their own rituals for remembrance, or adapt or expand on ones provided by their religious faith or by significant holidays or anniversaries. We can ritualize renewals of friendship by a regular meal together, playing tennis or getting together regularly on Friday afternoon for beer and popcorn. Work settings can have their rituals for celebration and sorrow, such as a yearly recognition of arrivals and departures, advancements and achievements.

Test Limits

There are contractions and expansions in grieving: a time to mourn and a time to dance, as the Biblical passage tells us. We need time to test our wings again after the hibernating winter of our grief. We often need to find out how far we can go. Grief can lead to the exploring of our potential. It is helpful when we can be supported while licking our wounds and challenged when we get too comfortable. It is up to us to know when to move from our protective cocoon and risk living fully.

Develop Connections Between the Past, Present and Future

Loss can dispute the continuity of the past with the present and the future. At various times in grief, it is only in the latter part of the process when we may recognize the thread of continuity that was not broken. We may need reminders of the way we used to be. Our own journals, photos and written or oral histories of significant events help with this remembering. So can genograms, trips to ancestral homes, or learning the language, rituals and history of our families and nationalities.

Have Witnesses

We often need others who were there when we went through our loss to validate as well as witness. We are the same person while at the same time, we are not. They can provide us with the sense of continuity that can, of course, go across our lifetimes and beyond. They can remind us of our best self when we have forgotten it, celebrate our growth by knowing our progression through grief. Often it is up to us to find or restore such witnesses by going to reunions or visiting elderly relatives or friends.

Renew and Forgive

There are times when we know what is gone is gone, that our loneliness is unending, what is done cannot be undone, what has happened is unforgivable or unredeemable. We are certain we will not survive, nor may we want to. We need to believe in our hopelessness or what holding a grudge feels like to later value renewal and forgiveness.

Renewal depends on the existence of moments of despair, condemnation, loneliness, and unremitting pain. It's only after these times that we can experience and appreciate the healing mysteries of forgiveness, love or restitution. When we discover within ourself the essence of our love after losing its external form, life has cause for celebration.

Forgiveness itself is a healing process, a mending of betrayals and insensitivities. It is something to give and to receive. The person who cannot forgive is still grieving, still split from that which will make forgiveness possible. The person who cannot be forgiven is likely to be depressed, unable to feel the wholeness of self that includes their best self. When we can experience forgiveness, it can be both a relief and a celebration of the joyful reunion of self.

Summary

Opportunities for recovery and transformation come when we believe in ourself and our health, and find the courage to honor our commitments. Transformation comes from forgiving and being forgiven.

It may not be easy, but it can be joyful. In childhood, the most powerful validators are our parents or relatives, teachers, siblings, and friends. As we grow and age, we replenish our strength and will to live with loved ones and therapeutic communities. We learn creative means of self-expression while grieving. Collectively, our communities of work and play, culture and meaning help us live the full measure of our personal transformations.

Addenda

References and Recommended Reading

Response to Loss Inventory

INTEGRA

Index

References and Recommended Reading

1979 Special Issue: Amnesty International Seminar, *Danish Medical Bulletin* 27:213-252.

Achterberg, J., and Lawlis, R, *Imagery of Cancer: A Diagnostic Tool For The Process of Disease,* Institute of Personality Assessment and Testing, 1978.

Achterberg, J., *Imagery In Healing*, New Science Press, 1986.

Achterberg, J., Lawlis, F., Simonton, O, C., and Simonton, S., "Psychological Factors and Blood Chemistries As Disease Outcome Predictors For Cancer Patients", *Multivariate Clinical and Experimental Research,* 1977, 3:107-122.

Agee, J., *A Death in the Family*, McDowell and Obelensky, 1957.

Ansbacher, H., and Ansbacher, R (eds.), *The Individual Psychology of Alfred Adler*, Basic Books, 1959.

Anthony, E, J., and Benedek, T., *Depression and Human Existence*, Little Brown and Co., 1975.

Aries, P., *The Hour of Our Death*, Random House, 1981.

Ausburger, D., *Caring Enough To Forgive: True Forgiveness/ Caring Enough To Not Forgive: False Forgiveness*, Herald Press, 1981.

Averill, J. R., "Grief: Its Nature and Significance," *Psychological Bulletin* 1969, 70:721-748.

Bartrop, R. W., Lazarus, L., Luckhorst, E., Kiloh, G., Penny, R, "Depressed Lymphocyte Function After Bereavement," *Lancet*, 1977, 1:834-36.

Becker, E., *Denial of Death*, Free Press, 1974.

Beckman, R., *I Don't Know What to Say: How to Help and Support Someone Who Is Dying*, MacMillan, 1988.

Beisser, A. R., *A Graceful Passage: Notes on the Freedom to Live or Die*, Doubleday, 1990.

Beisser, A. R., *Flying Without Wings*, Doubleday, 1989.

Berman, P. L., *The Courage To Grow Old*, Ballantine Books, 1989.

Bettleheim, B., "The Ignored Lesson of Anne Frank" In Bettleheim, B., *Surviving and Other Essays*, Vintage,1979.

Bloom, M., Ed., *Changing Lives; Studies in Human Development and Professional Helping*, University of South Carolina Press, 1992.

Bloom-Feshbach, J., S. Bloom-Feshbach et, al., *The Psychology of Separation and Loss: Perspectives on Development, Life Transitions and Clinical Practice*, Jossey-Bass, 1987.

Bly, Robert, *Iron John: A Book About Men*, Addison-Wesley, 1990.

Bordow, J., *The Ultimate Loss: Coping With the Death of a Child*, Beauford Books, 1982.

Borg, S. and Lasker, J., *When Pregnancy Fails: Families Coping With Miscarriage, Stillbirth and Infant Death*, Bantam, 1988.

Borysenko, J., *Fire in the Soul: A New Psychology of Spiritual Optimism*, Warner Books, 1993.

Bowen, M., "Family Reactions to Death," In P, Guerin (Ed) *Family Therapy*, Gardner Press, 1976.

Bowlby, J., "On Knowing What You Are Not Supposed To Know and Feeling What You Are Not Supposed To Feel," *Journal of The Canadian Psychiatric Association, 3*: 1979, 33-49.

Bowlby, J., *Attachment and Loss (Vol, 1)*, Basic Books, 1969.

Bowlby, J., *Attachment and Loss (Vol, III)*, Basic Books, 1980.

Bowlby, J., *Separation: Anxiety and Anger*, Basic Books, 1973.

Bradbury, R., *Dandelion Wine*, Bantam, 1957.

Branden, N., *Honoring The Self*, Bantam, 1983.

Briggs, D., *Celebrate Your Self.*, Doubleday and Co, 1977

Brody, H., *Stories of Sickness,* Yale University Press, 1987.

Brooks, A. M., *The Grieving Time: A Year's Account of Recovery From Loss*, Harmony Books, 1988.

Busgalia, L., *The Fall of Freddie the Leaf: A Story of Life for All Age*s, Holt, Rhinehart and Winston, 1982.

Caine, L., *Widow*, Bantam, 1974.

Callahan, M. and Kelley, P., *Final Gifts: Understanding the Special Awareness, Needs and Communication s of the Dying*, Poseidon Press, 1992.

Camus, A., *The Fall*, Alfred A. Knopf, 1957.

Capra, F., *The Turning Point: Science, Society and the Rising Culture*, Bantam, 1982.

Carkhuff, R. R. and Truax, C. B., *Toward Effective Counseling and Psychotherapy: Training and Practice*, Alsine Publishing Co., 1967.

Carpenter, L., *Getting Better All The Time*, Pocket Books, 1987.

Carr, A. C., "Bereavement As A Relative Experience," In B, Schoenberg, A, C, Carr, A, H, Kutscher, D, Peretz, and I, Goldberg (eds.), *Bereavement; Its Psychosocial Aspects,* pp, 3-9, Colombia University Press, 1975.

Carse, J. P., *Death and Existence: A Conceptual History of Human Mortality*, John Wiley and Sons, 1980.

Cassem, N., "Bereavement As Indispensable For Growth," In B, Schoenberg, A, C, Carr, A, H, Kutscher, D, Peretz, and I, Goldberg (eds.), *Bereavement: Its Psychosocial Aspects*, pp, 9-18, Columbia University Press, 1975.

Clayton, P. J., "Bereavement and Its Management," In E, S, Paykel (ed.) *Handbook of Affective Disorders*, Churchill Livingstone, 1980.

Colgrove, M., Bloomfield, H. H., and McWilliams, P., *How to Survive the Loss of a Love*, Bantam, 1976.

Colodzin, B., *How to Survive Trauma: A Program for War Veterans and Survivors of Rape, Assault, Abuse and Environmental Disasters*, Station Hill Press, 1993.

Cormier, L. S., and Hackney, H., *The Professional Counselor: A Process Guide to Helping.*, Prentice-Hall, 1987.

Cottington, E., Matthews, K., Talbot, E., and Kuller, L., "Environmental Events Preceding Sudden Death In Women," *Psychosomatic Medicine* 1980, 42:567-574.

Cox, P. R., and Ford, J. R., "The Mortality of Widows Shortly After Widowhood," *Lancet* 1964, 1:16-164.

Crenshaw, D., *Bereavement: Counseling the Grieving Through the Life Cycle*, Continuum, 1990.

Danto, B. L., Bereavement and The Widows of Slain Police officers, in: B, Schoenberg Et Al, (eds.) *Bereavement: Its Psychosocial Aspects*, Columbia University, 1975.

Darwin, C., *The Expression of Emotions In Man and Animals*, Murray, 1872.

Davidson, G. W., *Understanding Mourning: A Guide For Those Who Grieve*, Augsburg Press, 1984.

DeFrain, J., Martens, L., Stork, J., and Stork, W., *Stillborn: The Invisible Death*, Lexington Books, 1987.

DeFrain, J., Taylor, J., and Ernst, L., *Coping with Sudden Infant Death*, Lexington Books, 1982.

Deutsch, D., "Assessing the Grieving Process: Distinguishing Between Grief and Depression," Paper presented at Duet for One: Transforming Loss Conference, East Lansing, MI, May, 1992.

Deutsch, D., "The Development Reliability and Validity of An Instrument Designed To Measure Grief," *Unpublished Doctoral Dissertation,* Michigan State University, East Lansing, MI, 1982.

Deutsch, H., "Absence of Grief," *Psychoanalytic Quarterly*, 1937, 6: 12-22.

Dickens, M., *Miracles of Courage: How Families Meet the Challenge of a Child's Critical Illness*, Dodd, Mead, 1985.

Doka, K., *Disenfranchised Grief: Recognizing Hidden Losses,* Lexington Press, 1989.

Donnelly, K. F., *Recovering From The Loss of A Parent*, Dodd, Mead and Co., 1987.

Donnelly, K. F., *Recovering From The Loss of A Sibling*, Dodd, Mead and Co., 1988.

Dossey, L., *Healing Words: The Power of Prayer and The Practice of Medicine*, HarperSan Francisco, 1993.

Doyle, P., *Grief Counseling and Sudden Death: A Manual and Guide*, Charles C, Thomas Publishers, 1980.

Duda, D., *Coming Home: A Guide to Dying at Home with Dignity*, Aurora Press, 1987.

Edelstein, L., *Maternal Bereavement: Coping With The Unexpected Death of A Child*, Praeger Publishers, 1984.

Eisenbruch, M., "Cross-Cultural Aspects of Bereavement," *Culture, Medicine and Psychiatry*, 1984: 8 , 315-347.

Eisentstadt, M. A, Haynal, P., Rentchnick, P., De Senarclens, *Parental Loss and Achievement*, International University Press, 1989.

Eliot, T. S., *Four Quartets*, Faber and Faber, 1960.

Elmer, L., *Why Her Why Now: A Man's Journey Through Love and Death and Grief*, Bantam, 1990.

Elsass, P. and Schneider, J., "Application of Western Approaches To Grief Counseling To Non-Western Clients: Cases and Studies of Ethnic Grief and Bereavement," Unpublished Manuscript.

Elsass, P., "Depression As A Symptom of Poverty and Underdevelopment: A Case-Study of A Colombian Village," *Nordisk Psykologi*, 1988.

Elsass, P., *Strategies for Survival: The Psychology of Cultural Resilience in Ethnic Minorities*, New York University Press, 1992.

Elsass, P., "Symbols of Survival: A Social Psychological Study of South American Indian People," *Folk*, 1987: *29*, 53-75.

Engel, G. L., "Is Grief A Disease?" *Psychosomatic Medicine,* 1961, *23*:18-22.

Engel, G. L., *Psychological Development In Health and Diseases*, W, B, Saunders Co., 1967.

Engel, G. L, {Psychological Factors In Instantaneous Cardiac Death," *New England Journal of Medicine,* 1977; 294-664.

Engel, G. L, "Studies of Ulcerative Colitis: Psychological Aspects and Their Implication For Treatment," *American Journal of Digestive Disease,* 1958.*3*: 315-337.

Engel, G. L., "Sudden and Rapid Death During Psychological Distress," *Annals of Internal Medicine,* 1971.*74*: 771.

Epstein, G., Weitz, L., Roback, H., and McKee, P., "Research on Bereavement: A Selective and Critical Review," *Comprehensive Psychiatry,* 1975, *16*:41-72.

Erikson, S., *Companion Through the Darkness*.

Feinstein, D., Mayo, P. E., *Mortal Acts: Eighteen Empowering Rituals for Confronting Death*, HarperSan Francisco, 1993.

Ferguson, M., *The Aquarian Conspiracy,* J. P. Tarcher, 1980.

Fiske, M. and Chiriboga, D. A., *Change and Continuity in Adult Life*, Jossey-Bass, 1990.

Foos-Graber, A., *Deathing: An Intelligent Alternative For The Final Moments of Life*, Nicholas-Hays, 1989.

Frank, J. D., *Persuasion and Healing*, The Johns Hopkins Press, 1961.

Frankl, V., *Man's Search For Meaning: An Introduction To Logotherapy*, Alfred A. Knopf, 1963.

Fredrick, J. F., "Grief As A Disease Process," *Omega* 1977.7:17-31.

Freeman, L., *The Sorrow and the Fury: Overcoming Hurts and Loss from Childhood to Old Age*, Prentice Hall, 1978.

Freud, S., "Mourning and Melancholia," in: W, Gaylin, *The Meaning of Despair*, Science House, 1917.

Friedman, M., and Roseman, R. H., *Type A Behavior and Your Heart*, Alfred A. Knopf, 1974.

Fromm, M. G., and B. L., Smith, Ed, *The Facilitating Environment: Clinical Applications of Winnicott's Theory*, International Universities Press, 1989.

Fromm-Reichmann, F., *Loneliness*, University of Chicago Press, 1952.

Fromm-Reichmann, F., *Principles of Intensive Psychotherapy*, University of Chicago Press, 1950.

Frost, R., *The Collected Poems, Complete and Unabridged*, Holt, Rhinehart and Winston, 1969.

Fulghum, R., *All I Really Need To Know I Learned In Kindergarten*, Villard Books, 1989.

Gaffney, D., *The Seasons of Grief: Helping Children Grow Through Loss*, Plume/Penguin, 1988.

Gendlin, E. A., "Theory of Personality Change," in: A, Mahrer (ed.), *Creative Development In Psychotherapy*, Case-Western Reserve, 1971.

Gendlin, E., *Focusing*, Everest House, 1978.

Gendlin, E. T., "Client-Centered and Experiential Psychotherapy," in: P.A, Wesler and L, N, Rice (eds.), *Innovations In Client-Centered Therapy*, John Wiley and Sons, 1974.

Gerber, I., Weiner, A., Battin, D., and Arkin, A. M., "Brief Therapy To The Aged Bereaved," in: B, Schoenberg Et Al, (eds.), *Bereavement Its Psychosocial Aspects*, Colombia University Press, 1975.

Gilligan, C., *In A Different Voice*, Harvard University Press, 1982.

Gilliland, B. E., and James, R. K., *Crisis Intervention Strategies*, Brooks Cole Publishing; 1988

Ginsburg, G. D., *To Live Again: Rebuilding Your Life After You've Become A Widow*, J. P. Tarcher, Inc, 1987.

Glaser, B. G., and Strauss, A. L., *Awareness of Dying*, Aldine Publishing Co., 1965.

Glass, D. C., *Behavior Patterns, Stress and Coronary Disease*, Lawrence Erlbaum Assocs., 1977.

Goleman, D., "Positive denial: The case for not facing reality," *Psychology Today*, 1979, 13, 44-60.

Goodman, L. M., *Death and The Creative Life: Conversations With Prominent Artists and Scientists*, Springer Publishing Company, 1981.

Gorer, G., *Death, Grief and Mourning*, Doubleday and Co., 1965.

Gould, R., *Transformations: Growth and Change In Adult Life*, Simon and Schuster, 1979.

Greene W. A., "Some Perspectives For Observing and Interpreting Biopsychologic Relations and Doctor-Patient Relations," *Perspectives in Biological Medicine* 1958, 2:453-472.

Greene, W. A., and Miller, G, "Psychological Factors and Reticuloendothelial Disease," *Psychosomatic Medicine* 1958, 20:124-144.

Grof, S. and Grof, C., *Spiritual Emergency: When Personal Transformation Becomes A Crisis*, J. P. Tarcher, 1989.

Grof, S. and Halifax, J., *The Human Encounter With Death*, E. P. Dutton; 1977.

Grollman, E., *Talking About Divorce*, Beacon Press; 1975.

Hamachek, D., *Encounters With The Self,* Holt Rhinehart and Winston, 1978.

Hammarskjöld, D., *Markings*, Alfred Knopf, 1964.

Hansen, J. C., and Frantz, T. T., (eds.) *Death and Grief in the Family*, Aspen Systems, 1984.

Harper, J. M., and Hoopes, M. H., *Uncovering Shame: An Approach Integrating Individuals and Their Family Systems*, W. W. Norton, 1990.

Harper-Neeld, E., *Seven Choices: Taking The Steps To New Life After Losing Someone You Love,* Delta/ Dell Publishing; 1990.

Hofer, M., Wolff, C., Friedman S., and Mason J., "A Psychoendocrine Study of Bereavement: Part I," *Psychosomatic Medicine* 1977: 34:481-494.

Holmes T. H., and Rahe, R. H., "The Social Readjustment Rating Scale," *Journal of Psychosomatic Research* 1968: 11:213-218.

Humphries, D. and Wickett, A., *The Right to Die: Understanding Euthanasia*, Perennial Library, 1986.

Humphries, D., *Final Exit*, The Hemlock Society, 1991.

James, J. W., and Cherry, F., *The Grief Recovery Handbook: A Step-By-Step Program For Moving Beyond Loss*, Harper and Row, 1988.

Jewett, C. L., *Helping Children Cope With Loss*, The Harvard Common Press, 1982.

Johnson, K. and Ferguson, T., *Trusting Ourselves: The Source book On Psychology For Women*, The Atlantic Monthly Press, 1990.

Johnson, S., *Johnson on Johnson: A Selection of Personal and Autobiographical Writings of Samuel Johnson*, E. P. Dutton, 1767, 1976.

Johnson, S., *One Minute For Myself*, William Morrow and Co, 1985.

Jones, R. A., *Self-Fulfilling Prophecies*, Lawrence Erlbaum Assocs., 1977.

Jung, C., "The Stages In Life." In Campbell, J. (Ed), *The Portable Jung*, Viking Press, 1971, Originally Published In 1937.

Jung, C., *The Undiscovered Self*, Mentor Books, 1957.

Kagan, N. and Schneider, J. M., "Toward measurement of affective sensitivity: A report on the Evolution of the Affective Sensitivity Scale," *Journal of Counseling and Development, 65:* 1987.

Kagan, N., "Influencing Human Interaction: Eighteen Years with IPR," in: Hess (ed) *Psychotherapy Supervision,* J. Wiley and Sons, 1980.

Kagan, N., "Interpersonal Process Recall: Basic Methods and Recent Research," In Larson (Ed) *Teaching Psychological Skills,* Brooks/Cole Monterey Pub, 1984.

Kalish, R. and Reynolds, D. K., *Death and Ethnicity: A Psychocultural Study,* Baywood Publishing Co, 1981.

Kalish, R., "Some Variables In Death Attitudes," *Journal of Social Psychology,* 1963, *59:*137-145.

Keen, S., *To A Dancing God,* Harper and Row, 1970.

Klein, D. F., and Wender, P. H., *Understanding Depression: A Complete Guide to Its Diagnosis and Treatment,* Oxford University Press, 1993.

Kleinman, A. and Good, B., (eds.) *Culture and Depression, Studies In The Anthropology and Cross-Cultural Psychiatry of Affect and Disorder,* University of California Press, 1984.

Kobasa, S., Maddi, S., and Kahn, S., "Hardiness and Health: A Prospective Study," *Journal of Personality and Social Psychology, 112* 1983: 123-136.

Kopp, S, *An End To Innocence,* MacMillan, 1978.

Kraus, A. A., and Lilinfeld, A.M,"Some Epidemiological Aspects of The High Mortality Rate In The Young Widowed Group," *Journal of Chronic Disease* 1959.*10:*207-217.

Krystal, H., "Alexythymia and Psychotherapy," *American Journal of Psycho-therapy* 1979, *33:*17-31.

Krystal ,H., "Trauma," in: H. Krystal and W. G. Niederland, *Psychic-Traumatiza-tion,* Little Brown and Co., 1971, Pp, 11-28.

Krystal, H., *Massive Psychic Trauma,* International Universities Press, 1968.

Kübler-Ross, E., *On Children and Death,* Collier, 1983.

Kübler-Ross, E., *Death: The Final Stage of Growth,* Prentice-Hall, 1975.

Kübler-Ross, E., *On Death and Dying,* McMillan, 1969.

Kushner, H., *When Bad Things Happen to Good People,* Schoken Books, 1981.

LaFramboise, T., "Existential Issues of Native Americans," Conference On Intercul-tural Issues In Psychotherapy, Chicago, April, 1988.

Leonard, G., "Transpersonal Education", Lecture At The California Institute For Transpersonal Psychology, Menlo Park, CA, 1977.

LeShan, L., "An Emotional Life History Associated With Neoplastic Disease," in: E, M, Weyer (ed.) *Annals of The New York Academy of Sciences,* 1966, *3* P, 125.

Levine, S., *Meetings at the Edge,* Doubleday, 1984.

Levine, S., *Who Dies: An Investigation of Conscious Living and Conscious Dying,* Doubleday, 1982.

Levingson, P., "On Sudden Death," *Psychiatry* 1972, *35*:160-173.

Levinson, D. J., *Seasons of A Man's Life*, Alfred A. Knopf, 1978.

Lewis, C. S., *A Grief Observed*, The Seabury Press , 1961.

Lindbergh, A. M., *A Gift From The Sea*, Vintage Books, 1975.

Lindbergh, A. M., *Hour of Gold, Hour of Lead*, Signet Books, 1973.

Lindemann, E., *Beyond Grief: Studies of Grief In Adult Life*, International Universities Press, 1979.

Lindemann, E., "Symptomatology and Management of Acute Grief," *American Journal of Psychiatry* 1944, *101*:141-148.

Lord, J. H., *No Time for Good-byes: Coping with Grief, Anger and Injustice After a Tragic Death,* Pathfinder Publishing Co., 1987.

Lowell, J. R., *The Complete Poetical Works of James Russell Lowell*, Houghton Mifflin Co., 1925.

Lukas, C., and Seiden, H. M., *Silent Grief: Living In The Wake of Suicide*, Charles Scribner's Sons, 1987.

Lynch, J., *The Broken Heart: The Medical Consequences of Loneliness*, Basic Books, 1977.

MacDonald, J., *A Deadly Shade of Gold*, Ballantine/Dell Ray/Fawcett Books, Fawcett Gold Medal, 1965.

MacDonald, J., *The Turquoise Lament*, J. P. Lippincott, 1973.

Mahrer, A. R., *Therapeutic Experiencing: The Process of Change*, W. W. Norton, 1986 .

Marris, P., *Loss and Change*, Pantheon Books, 1974.

Maslow, A., *Motivation and Personality*, Harper and Row, 1954.

Maslow, A., *The Farther Reaches of Human Nature*, Viking Press, 1971.

Maslow, A., *Toward A Psychology of Being*, D. Van Nostrand, 1962

May, R., *Psychology and The Human Dilemma*, D. Van Nostrand, 1968

May, R., *Man's Search for Himself*, New American Library (Signet), 1953

May, R., *The Courage To Create*, Bantam, 1978.

May, R., *The Discovery of Being*, W. W. Norton, 1983.

Mayeroff, M. N., *On Caring,* Harper and Row, 1971.

McGovern, T. F., "Distinguishing between grief and depression in alcoholism: A Pilot clinical study," *Alcoholism Treatment Quarterly* 1986: *3*, 31-45.

McGovern, T. F., "Hopelessness in the Alcoholic Patient," *Alcohol* 1986: *3*, 93-94.

McGovern, T. F., "Loss identification in the treatment of alcoholism," *Alcohol* 1986: *3* 95-96.

McGovern, T. F., "The effects of an inpatient alcohol treatment program with two variations, on measurements of depression, hopelessness, loss and grief," Unpublished doctoral dissertation, Texas Tech University, Lubbock, Texas, 1983.

McGovern, T. F., "The effects of comprehensive inpatient alcohol treatment on measures of loss and grief," *Alcohol* 1986: *3* 89-92.

Miller, A., *For Your Own Good: Hidden Cruelty In Child-Rearing and The Roots of Violence,* Farrar, Strauss, Giroux, 1983.

Mitchell, J., and Bray, G., *Emergency Services Stress: Guidelines For Preserving The Health and Careers of Emergency Services Personnel*, Prentice-Hall, 1990.

Mitford, J., *The American Way of Death,* Simon & Schuster, 1964.

Montagu, A., *Touching: The Human Significance of The Skin*, Perennial Library, 1971.

Morgan, E., *Dealing Creatively With Death*, Jennifer Morgan (ed.) Celo Press; 1988.

Moss, R., *The I That Is We*, Celestial Arts, 1981.

Moustakas, C., *Finding Yourself, Finding Others*, Prentice-Hall, 1974.

Moustakas, C., *Loneliness and Love*, Prentice-Hall, 1972.

Moustakas, C., *Loneliness,* Prentice-Hall, 1962.

Moustakas, C., *Portraits of Loneliness and Love*, Prentice-Hall, 1974.

Moustakas, C., *Turning Points*, Prentice-Hall, 1977.

Nieburg, H. A., and Fischer, A., *Pet Loss: A Thoughtful Guide for Adults and Children*, Harper and Row, 1982.

Niederland, W. G., "The Problem of The Survivor," *Journal of Hillside Hospital* 1961.*10*:233-247.

Nouwen, H. J. M., *A Letter of Consolation*, Harper and Row, 1982.

O'Neill, C., and Ritter, K., *Coming Out Within: Stages of Spiritual Awakening For Lesbians and Gay Men*, HarperSanfransisco, 1992.

O'Toole, D., *Aarvy Aardvark Finds Hope*, Mountain Rainbow Publications, 1988.

O'Toole, D., *Bridging The Bereavement Gap*, Mountain Rainbow Publications, 1985.

O'Toole, D., *Helping Young People Grow Through Grief*, Mountain Rainbow Publications, 1989.

Olson, S., and Schneider, J., "The Nature and Nurture of Validation," *New Realities*, 1990, *1*, 22-25.

Olson, S., and Schneider, J., "Therapeutic Validation," paper presented at the Seventh Annual Congress For The Care of The Terminally Ill, Montreal, October, 1988.

Olson, S., *Into the Light: For Women Experiencing the Transformative Nature of Grief*, Colfax, WI: Seasons Press, 1993.

Olson, S., (ed.) *Your Gift: A Educational, Spiritual and Personal Resource For Hospice Volunteers*, East Lansing, MI; Spring Publishing, 1987.

Osherson, S. D., *Holding On or Letting Go: Men and Career Change at Mid-life*, The Free Press, 1980.

Osterweis, M., Solomon, F., and Green, M., (eds.) *Bereavement: Reactions, Consequences and Care*, National Academy Press, 1984.

Paine, T., *Common Sense and Other Selected Political Writings,* Liberal Arts Press, 1783, 1953.

Parkes, C. M., Benjamin, B., and Fitzgerald, R. G., "Broken Heart: A Statistical Study of Increased Mortality Among Widows," *British Medical Journal* 1969.*1*:740-743.

Parkes, C. M., *Bereavement: Studies of Grief in Adult Life*, International Universities Press, 1987.

Parkes, C. M., "Sudden Death and Its Impact On The Family," in: P. Pegg and E. Metze (ed.), *Death and Dying: A Quality of Life*, Pittman Press, 1981.

Parkes, C. M., "Recent bereavement as a cause of mental illness," *British Journal of Psychiatry*, 1964, *110*, 198-204.

Parsons, O. A., and Schneider, J., "Belief In Personal Control: A Cross-Cultural Comparison," *Journal of Cross-Cultural Psychology*, 1971, 1: 22-33.

Parsons, O. A., and Schneider, J. M., "Locus of Control with University Students from Eastern and Western Societies," *Journal of Consulting and Clinical Psychology*, 1974, 42: 456-461.

Patten, P., "Disaster," in: P. Pegg and E. Metze (eds.), *Death and Dying: A Quality of Life*, Pitman Press, 1981.

Peck, M. S., *People of the Lie: The Hope for Healing Human Evil*, Touchstone, 1983.

Peck, M. S., *The Different Drum: Community Making and Peace*, Touchstone, 1987.

Peck, M. S., *The Road Less Traveled: A New Psychology of Love, Traditional Values and Spiritual Growth*, Touchstone, 1977.

Pelletier, K., *Mind As Healer, Mind As Slayer: A Holistic Approach To Preventing Stress Disorders*, Dell Publishing, 1976.

Perls, F., *Gestalt Therapy Verbatim*, Real People's Press, 1969.

Pines, M., and Maddi, S., "Psychological Hardiness: The Role of Challenge In Health," *Psychology Today*, 1980, 13:27-38.

Plutchik, R., *The Emotions: Facts, Theory and A New Model*, Random House, 1962.

Rahe, R., and Arthur, R. S., "Life Change Patterns Surrounding Illness Experiences," *J. Psychosomatic Research* 1968.11:341-345.

Ramsay, R. W., "Behavioral Approaches To Bereavement," *Behavioral Research in Therapy, 1977*: 15:131-135.

Rando, T., *Grieving: How To Go On Living When Someone You Love Dies*, D, C, Heath and Co., 1988.

Rando, T., *Parental Loss of A Child*, Research Press, 1986.

Rando, T., *Treatment of Complicated Mourning* Research Press, 1993.

Rando, T., *Grief, Dying and Death: Clinical Interventions For Caregivers*, Research Press, 1984.

Raphael, B., *The Anatomy of Bereavement*, Hutchison Publishing, 1983.

Redman, L., *Surviving When Your Loved One is Murdered*, Psychological Consultation and Educational Services, Clearwater, Fla, 1989.

Rees, W. D., and Lutkins, S. G., "Mortality of Bereavement," *British Medical Journal* 1967, 4:13-16.

Riley, V., "Psychoneuroimmunologic Factors In Neoplasia," in: R, Ader (ed.), *Psychoneuroimmunology*, Academic Press, 1981.

Rinpoche, S., *The Tibetan Book of Living and Dying*, HarperSanFrancisco, 1992.

Rogers, C., *On Becoming A Person*, Houghton Mifflin Co., 1961.

Rollin, B., *Last Wish*, Warner Books; 1985.

Romond, J., *Children Facing Grief*, Abbey Press, 1989.

Rosaldo, M., "Grief and a Headhunter's Rage: On The Cultural Force of Emotions," in: R. A. Sweder and R. A. Levine (eds.) *Culture Theory*, Cambridge University Press, 1984.

Rosen, H., *Unspoken Grief: Coping with Childhood Sibling Loss*, Lexington Books, 1986.

Rosenblatt, P. C., Walsh, R, P, and Jackson, D, A, *Grief and Mourning in Cross-Cultural Perspective*, Human Relations Area Files, 1976.

Rosenthal, T., *How Could I Not Be Among You?* Avon Books, 1973.

Sanders, C., *Grief: The Mourning After*, John Wiley and Sons, 1989.

Sarason, I. G., Johnson, J. H., and Siegel, J. M., "Assessing The Impact of Life Changes: Development of A Life Experiences Survey," *Journal of Consulting and Clinical Psychology*, 1978, 46:932-946.

Saunders, C., and Baines, M., *Living with Dying: The Management of Terminal Disease*, Oxford University Press, 1989.

Schiff, H. S., *Living Through Mourning: Finding Comfort and Hope When A Loved One Has Died*, Viking, 1986.

Schiff, H. S., *The Bereaved Parent*, Crown Publishers: 1977.

Schleifer, J., Keller, P., McKegney, P., and Stein, J., "Bereavement and Lymphocyte Function," Paper Presented At American Psychiatric Assoc., San Francisco, 1980.

Schmale, A., and Iker, H., "Hopelessness as a predictor of cervical cancer," *Social Science and Medicine*, 1971, 5, 95-100.

Schmale, A., "Giving Up As A Final Common Pathway To Changes" in: *Health, Advancements In Psychosomatic Medicine* 1977 8:22-36.

Schneider, J., "Clinically Significant Differences Between Grief, Pathological Grief, and Depression," *Patient Counseling and Health Education* 1981, 3:161-169.

Schneider, J., "Men's' Grief: The Effect of Shame," paper presented at The American Psychological Association Annual Meeting, Washington, D, C, August, 1992.

Schneider, J., "Self Care Challenges for The Hospice Professional," *The Hospice Journal*, (1987) *4*.

Schneider, J., *Stress, Loss and Grief,* University Park Press, 1984.

Schneider, J., "The Transformative Power of Grief," *Noetic Sciencse Review,* Fall 1989, Institute of Noetic Sciences, Sausalito, CA.

Schneider, J., Smith, W., Minning, C., Hermansen, J., and Whitcher, S., "Imagery and Functions of The Immune System: A Summary of Findings," In Kutzendorpf, R.(ed.) *Imagery*, 1990.

Schoenberg, B., Carr, A. C., Kutscher, A. H., Peretz, D., and Goldberg, I., (eds.), *Bereavement: Its Psychosocial Aspects*, Columbia University Press, 1970.

Schoenburg, B. M., (ed.) *Bereavement Counseling: A Multidisciplinary Handbook*, Greenwood Press.

Schucter, S. R., *Dimensions of Grief: Adjusting to the Death of a Spouse,* Jossey-Bass, 1986.

Secundy, M. G., *Trials, Tribulations and Celebrations: African American Perspectives On Health, Illness, Aging and Loss*, Intercultural Press, 1992.

Seligman, M. E. P., "Chronic fear produced by unpredictable shock," *Journal of Comparative and Physiological Psychology*, 1968, 66: 402-411.

Selye, H., *Stress without Distress*, J. P. Lippincott, 1976.

Selye, H., *The Stress of Life*, McGraw-Hill Book Co., 1956.

Siegal, B., *Love, Medicine and Miracles*, HarperCollins 1987.

Siegal, B., *Peace, Love and Healing*, HarperCollins, 1989.

Sifneos, P., *Short-Term Psychotherapy and Emotional Crisis*, Harvard University Press, 1972.

Simon, S., *Negative Criticism—and What You Can Do About It*, 1978.

Simonton, G., Simonton, S., and Creighton, P., *Getting Well Again,* J. P. Tarcher, 1978.

Smeded, L. B., *Forgive and Forget: Healing the Hurts We Don't Deserve*, HarperSanFrancisco, 1984.

Smith, W. J., *Dying in the Human Life Cycle: Psychological, Biomedical and Social Perspectives*, Holt, Rhinehart and Winston, 1985.

Solomon, G. F., and Amkraut, A. A, "Emotions, Stress and Immunity," *Frontiers of Radiation Therapy In Oncology* 1972, 7.84-96.

Stack, J., "Spontaneous Abortion and Grieving," *American Family Physician* 1979, *21*:99-102.

Staudacher, C., *Beyond Grief: A Guide for Recovering from the Death of a Loved One*, New Harbinger Publications, 1987.

Stephenson, J. S., *Death, Grief and Mourning: Individual and Social Realities*, Free Press, 1985.

Stern, Z., and Susser, M., Widowhood and Mental Illness, *British Journal of Preventive Sociological Medicine* 1969: *23*:106-110.

Stevens, B., and Rogers, C., *Person to Person*, Real People Press, 1972.

Stoddard, S., *The Hospice Movement: A Better Way to Care for the Dying*, Vintage Books, 1991.

Stone, H. W., *Suicide and Grief*, Fortress Press, 1972.

Tatelbaum, J., *The Courage To Grieve: Creative Living, Recovery and Growth Through Grief*, Lippincott and Crowell, 1980.

Tatelbaum, J., *You Don't Have To Suffer: A Handbook For Moving Beyond Life's Crises*, Harper and Row, 1989.

Tillich, P., *The Courage To Be*, Yale University Press, 1957.

Travis, J., *The Wellness Workbook*, Wellness Center, 1978.

Uris, L., *Trinity*, Corgi Books, 1977.

Vachon, M. L. S., et al, "Stress Reactions To Bereavement," *Essence* 1976, *1*:23-33.

Vaillant, G., *Adaptation To Life*, Little, Brown and Co., 1977.

Viorst, J., *Necessary Losses*, Simon and Schuster, 1986.

Volkan, V., "A Study of a patient's 'regrief work' through dreams, psychological test and psychoanalysis," *Psychiatric Quarterly*, 1971, 45, 225-273.

Volkan, V. D., *Linking Objects and Linking Phenomena: A Study of the Forms, Symptoms, Metapsychology and Therapy of Complicated Mourning*, International Universities Press, 1981.

Wallerstein, J., and Blakeslee, S., *Second Chances: Men, Women and Children A Decade After Divorce*, Ticknor and Fields, 1989.

Walsh and McGoldrick *Living Beyond Loss: Death In The Family* W. W. Norton, 1991.

Wass, H., and Corr, C. A., *Childhood and Death*, Harper and Row, 1984.

Waters, F., *The Man Who Killed The Deer*, Pocket Books, 1941.

Watson, J. L., "of Flesh and Bones: The Management of Death Pollution In Cantonese Society," in: Bloch, M, and Parry, J. (eds.): *Death and The Regeneration of Life*, Cambridge University Press, 1982.

Watzlawick, P., *The Situation Is Hopeless, But Not Serious*, W. W. Norton and Co, 1983.

Weenolsen, P., *Transcendence of Loss Over The Life Span*, Hemisphere Publishing Co, 1989.

Weiner, H., *Psychobiology and Human Disease*, Elsevier North Holland, 1977.

Wennberg, R., *Terminal Choices: Euthanasia, Suicide and the Right to Die*, Grand Rapids, MI, 1989.

West, M., *Shoes of A Fisherman*, William Morrow and Co., 1963.

Westberg, G., *Good Grief*, Fortress Press, 1962.

Wilson, G., *Nyakyusa Conventions of Burial*, The University of the Witwatersrand Press, 1939.

Winnicott, D. W., *Home Is Where We Start From: Essays By A Psychoanalyst*, W. W. Norton, 1986.

Wolfelt, A., *Understanding Grief: Helping Yourself Heal*, Center for Loss and Life Transitions, Ft. Collins CO, 1988.

Worden, W., *Grief Counseling and Grief Therapy: A Handbook for the Mental Health Practitioner*, Springer, 1982.

Yalom, I., *Love's Executioner and Other Tales of Psychotherapy* Harper Perennial, 1989.

Young, M., Benjamin, B., and Wallis, A., "The Mortality of Widows," *Lancet* 1963, 2:454-456.

Zisook, S., and Devault, R., "Unresolved Grief, "*American Journal of Psychoanalysis*, 1985, 45(4) 370-379.

Glossary of Terms Used in This Book

Active grieving involves the times when our focus is on discovering the extent of what we have lost. It usually begins with a moving back and forth between awareness and coping by holding on (fight responses) or letting go (flight or escape responses).

Awareness the central core of grief. These are the moments when we experience fully the impact of our loss.

Best self is a term for that part of ourself which possesses the capacity to "rise to the occasion," to be more than we usually are as a response to challenge, crisis or loss. Some call this the "higher self."

Limiting awareness is coping, a normal response to loss that allows us to keep functioning and survive until we can take in more of the awareness of the loss, and gives us respite and a necessary delay in responding to our loss.

Defending against loss represents maladaptive responses to loss that prevent us from becoming aware of it and actively grieving. These responses involve denial and distortion of the loss, with many implications. When there are destructive consequences, or if defending lasts too long, professional intervention is often required.

Depression is a term frequently confused with grief. Colloquially, we often say we are depressed when we mean we are saddened, or haven't stopped to look at why our mood is down. Professionally, depression is a label applied to the inability to grieve or identify the losses which are connect with the feelings. Depression can be biological, cognitive or spiritual, and usually requires professional help in correcting or preventing further despair, desperation or illness. For a more formal definition of depression, the reader is encouraged to consult the Diagnostic and Statistical Manual, (DSM-IV) (1994 revision).

Developmentally disruptive losses are those which occur at the "wrong times" in our lives, or occur in ways that make it difficult to legitimize the resulting grief.

Dimensions of grief represents the aspects of our self that are affected by the experience of a loss. They include the following:

> *Behavioral:* the ways our actions and responses are affected.
>
> *Cognitive:* the way our thinking and problem-solving is affected.
>
> *Emotional:* the way our feelings are affected.
>
> *Physical:* the way our bodies are affected.
>
> *Spiritual:* the way our beliefs, values, assumptions, cultural and familial myths, as well as our will to live are affected.

Discovering what is lost is the first phase of response to a loss. It involves awareness and coping with a loss by holding on and letting go.

Discovering what is left is the second phase of response to a loss. It involves times of healing, the emergence of perspective and integration of the loss into the rest of our life.

Discovering what is possible is the final phase of responding to a loss. It involves seeing the loss in the broader context of life and being able to use the experience of grieving as a motivating force for growth and creativity.

Existential focus involves the universal life experiences that can lead to making basic choices. Such a focus happens during awareness of the extent of our loss and later, when we are able to experience the fullness of any life experience.

External losses are losses of something outside of our self that we have attachments to. These include relationships, objects and our environment.

Facilitative environment is a term for the external resources we need in order to have safety and support for grieving.

Grieving is the process by which loss is transformed into choices involving growth and finding new meaning. Grief is both a process and a state of being. Grieving is defined here as a process of discovering what was lost, what is left and what is possible.

Holding on represents one form of normal coping by limiting our acknowledgment of a loss. We attempt to overcome a loss by fighting, reducing its impact or by reversing its reality. It is an energy-intensive process.

Incomplete grief is a term for a grieving process that has yet to be fully experienced. Often, it refers to the absence of one or more dimensions of grief (i.e., behavioral, cognitive, emotional, physical or spiritual) in our process of grieving. Such incompleteness prevents us from fully integrating the loss into the rest of our life.

Integration is the process of completing grief by bringing together all of the resources of mind, body and spirit as they relate to a loss.

Internal loss involves losses of some aspect of our self: our identity, capacity to function or create, or our internal awareness of who we are.

Legitimize the loss is a therapeutic step that acknowledges that a loss really exists and is worthy of being grieved.

Letting go represents a second form of normal coping by limiting our acknowledgment of a loss. We flee or try to minimize the impact of the loss. It is an energy-conserving process.

Natural losses are those developmental losses which occur to almost everyone as a part of living in a particular culture or place. They are integral parts of normal development and maturity (e.g., learning to walk or talk, going to school, graduation, moving, getting a job, marriage, retirement, dying).

Normal coping defines the ways we have to protect ourselves from uninterrupted awareness of what we have lost. Normal coping provides us times of respite and delay in responding to our losses.

Perspective describes the phase in grieving when we can feel more distant and objective about what we have lost, and begin to consider what we have left or can regain.

Post-traumatic stress represents a response to traumatic loss that exceed our ways of normal coping, often with delayed symptoms. Without effective treatment, it can become a stressful condition producing exaggerated, unhealthy reactions, including destructive patterns of avoidance, distortion and denial.

Reformulation is a process of challenging our usual ways of thinking, believing, feeling and acting. Such challenges, when engaged in a timely fashion, can facilitate growth from a loss.

Self-empowerment is the capacity to find strength from our grieving process that would not have existed otherwise. It is often intimately connected with being able to reformulate loss.

Shared losses are losses that have an impact on others as well as ourself, even though the impact may not be the same.

Significant loss involves any change, gradual or sudden, that alters our attachments, behavior or what is meaningful to us. What constitutes a significant loss is different for each person.

Therapeutic communities consists of those people who affect, validate, support, witness or challenge our process of grieving.

Therapeutic validation is the intentional use of validation (see below) in ways that enhance the recipient's capacity to face life's existential moments.

Transformation means a significant alteration in the form of something has taken place—a moving across or beyond the old form to something unknown or unknowable before the change began. Grieving itself is the process of relinquishing our attachment to a particular form in order to experience the substantive nature of the attachment in a different, often more inclusive, form. Grieving then, is one transformative process. Responses to loss other than by grieving are also transformative in nature, although not usually positive or growth producing.

Transgenerational loss is a term used to identify losses that affect us but which occurred to others who have genetic, historic, cultural or familial connections to us, present, past and future. This is not a metaphysical concept, rather, an observable inheritance between generations that can manifest in both subtle and profound ways. For example, some members of the generation that lived through the Great Depression may have passed on unresolved grief issues to their children, who in turn react to them.

Transpersonal awareness: From the utter aloneness of awareness, we believe that there is something more to us and to the world than our individual body, ego and collection of limits and talents. This is perhaps the most radical reformulating we will ever make—from seeking total uniqueness and aloneness to the acceptance of being part of something much greater than ourself. This transformation represents a paradigm shift, from the personal to the transpersonal.

Validation is a process of accepting the full reality of our experience. Essential to validation is the following:

- What we are experiencing right now is real.
- Our reactions and methods of coping "fit" the stresses currently being experienced.
- We are doing the best we can under the circumstances.

Witnessing is an important part of validating life processes such as grief. We need to have others present at times of significant change in order to legitimize the change. Witnesses are sometimes most effective during rituals that memorialize the nature of a transformative experience.

Appendix I:

Life Change Inventory

©1994 John Schneider

NAME or CODE:_____

DATE:_____ AGE:_____ SEX: ☐ Male ☐ Female

LIVING ARRANGEMENT (check one):

    ☐ Alone   ☐ With partner
    ☐ With children   ☐ With parents
    ☐ With others

The following is a list of changes which people experience throughout their lives. These may include one or more which you have experienced. You are to:

   1) *identify significant changes and when they happened*

   2) *rate their current impact on you.*

First, identify whether a particular item applies to you. <u>Leave blank if it does not apply.</u> For those which apply, do the following:

- Indicate how long ago you were first aware of this event. (e.g. six mos.; ten years.)

- rate each item you have checked with a number between -5 and +5, according to the following guidelines:

-5 = this event is presently the most negative or equal to the most negative I've ever experienced.

0 = this event is neither positive nor negative at the present time

+5 = this event is currently the most positive or equal to the most positive experience in my life.

Example:

How Long?   Rate (circle)

How Long?		Negative Positive
_____	20.06 = decreased drug use	-5 -4 -3 -2 -1 0 +1 +2 +3 +4 +5
_____	20.07 = increased smoking	-5 -4 -3 -2 -1 0 +1 +2 +3 +4 +5
2 yrs.	20.08 = decreased smoking	-5 -4 -3 -2 -1 0 +1 +2 (+3) +4 +5
6 mos.	20.09 = increased drinking	-5 (-4) -3 -2 -1 0 +1 +2 +3 +4 +5

EXTERNAL CHANGES

0 = changes in relationships with spouse/significant other

How Long?		Rate (circle)	
		Negative	**Positive**
_____0.01 falling in love		-5 -4 -3 -2 -1	0 +1 +2 +3 +4 +5
_____0.02 death of a spouse		-5 -4 -3 -2 -1	0 +1 +2 +3 +4 +5
_____0.03 divorce		-5 -4 -3 -2 -1	0 +1 +2 +3 +4 +5
_____0.04 separation		-5 -4 -3 -2 -1	0 +1 +2 +3 +4 +5
_____0.05 prolonged absence		-5 -4 -3 -2 -1	0 +1 +2 +3 +4 +5
_____0.06 reconciliation		-5 -4 -3 -2 -1	0 +1 +2 +3 +4 +5
_____0.07 betrayal of trust		-5 -4 -3 -2 -1	0 +1 +2 +3 +4 +5
_____0.08 changes due to spouse's way of dealing with loss/grief		-5 -4 -3 -2 -1	0 +1 +2 +3 +4 +5
_____0.09 marital conflict		-5 -4 -3 -2 -1	0 +1 +2 +3 +4 +5

1 = loss of one's child:

How Long?		Rate (circle)	
		Negative	**Positive**
_____1.01 death of child		-5 -4 -3 -2 -1	0 +1 +2 +3 +4 +5
_____1.02 miscarriage		-5 -4 -3 -2 -1	0 +1 +2 +3 +4 +5
_____1.03 abortion		-5 -4 -3 -2 -1	0 +1 +2 +3 +4 +5
_____1.04 kidnapping		-5 -4 -3 -2 -1	0 +1 +2 +3 +4 +5
_____1.05 disappearance		-5 -4 -3 -2 -1	0 +1 +2 +3 +4 +5
_____1.06 placing for adoption		-5 -4 -3 -2 -1	0 +1 +2 +3 +4 +5
_____1.07 runaway		-5 -4 -3 -2 -1	0 +1 +2 +3 +4 +5

2 = other changes in relationships with one's children

How Long?		Rate (circle)	
		Negative	**Positive**
_____2.01 birth		-5 -4 -3 -2 -1	0 +1 +2 +3 +4 +5
_____2.02 starting child care		-5 -4 -3 -2 -1	0 +1 +2 +3 +4 +5
_____2.03 starting school		-5 -4 -3 -2 -1	0 +1 +2 +3 +4 +5
_____2.04 moving (as a family)		-5 -4 -3 -2 -1	0 +1 +2 +3 +4 +5
_____2.05 children leaving home		-5 -4 -3 -2 -1	0 +1 +2 +3 +4 +5
_____2.06 children's illness/disability		-5 -4 -3 -2 -1	0 +1 +2 +3 +4 +5
_____2.07 adult children living at home		-5 -4 -3 -2 -1	0 +1 +2 +3 +4 +5
_____2.08 becoming a single parent		-5 -4 -3 -2 -1	0 +1 +2 +3 +4 +5
_____2.09 loss/limitation of visitation rights		-5 -4 -3 -2 -1	0 +1 +2 +3 +4 +5
_____2.10 alienation		-5 -4 -3 -2 -1	0 +1 +2 +3 +4 +5

3 = loss or change involving one's parents

How Long?		Rate (circle)	
		Negative	**Positive**
_____3.01 parent death		-5 -4 -3 -2 -1	0 +1 +2 +3 +4 +5
_____3.02 leaving home		-5 -4 -3 -2 -1	0 +1 +2 +3 +4 +5
_____3.03 change in custody		-5 -4 -3 -2 -1	0 +1 +2 +3 +4 +5

_____3.04 reconciliation of parents
        with each other   -5 -4 -3 -2 -1 0 +1 +2 +3 +4 +5
_____3.05 being disowned/alienated   -5 -4 -3 -2 -1 0 +1 +2 +3 +4 +5
_____3.06 returning to live at home   -5 -4 -3 -2 -1 0 +1 +2 +3 +4 +5
_____3.07 change due to parental
        separation or divorce   -5 -4 -3 -2 -1 0 +1 +2 +3 +4 +5
_____3.08 parental illness   -5 -4 -3 -2 -1 0 +1 +2 +3 +4 +5
_____3.09 reconciliation with one
        or both parents   -5 -4 -3 -2 -1 0 +1 +2 +3 +4 +5
_____3.10 parental remarriage   -5 -4 -3 -2 -1 0 +1 +2 +3 +4 +5

4 = loss or change involving brothers and sisters/close relatives

How Long?   Rate (circle)

                                Negative   **Positive**

_____4.01 death of a sibling   -5 -4 -3 -2 -1 0 +1 +2 +3 +4 +5
_____4.02 loss of contact   -5 -4 -3 -2 -1 0 +1 +2 +3 +4 +5
_____4.03 living with sibing   -5 -4 -3 -2 -1 0 +1 +2 +3 +4 +5
_____4.04 estrangement   -5 -4 -3 -2 -1 0 +1 +2 +3 +4 +5
_____4.05 reconciliation with siblings -5 -4 -3 -2 -1 0 +1 +2 +3 +4 +5
_____4.06 sibling problems   -5 -4 -3 -2 -1 0 +1 +2 +3 +4 +5

5 = loss or changes involving friends

How Long?   Rate (circle)

                                Negative   **Positive**

_____5.01 friend's death   -5 -4 -3 -2 -1 0 +1 +2 +3 +4 +5
_____5.02 betrayal of friendship   -5 -4 -3 -2 -1 0 +1 +2 +3 +4 +5
_____5.03 friend moving away   -5 -4 -3 -2 -1 0 +1 +2 +3 +4 +5
_____5.04 other relationships interfering -5 -4 -3 -2 -1 0 +1 +2 +3 +4 +5
_____5.05 estrangement   -5 -4 -3 -2 -1 0 +1 +2 +3 +4 +5

6 = other external changes

How Long?   Rate (circle)

                                Negative   **Positive**

_____6.01 loss of a pet   -5 -4 -3 -2 -1 0 +1 +2 +3 +4 +5
_____6.02 loss of home   -5 -4 -3 -2 -1 0 +1 +2 +3 +4 +5
_____6.03 moving   -5 -4 -3 -2 -1 0 +1 +2 +3 +4 +5
_____6.04 loss of favorite mementos/photos -5 -4 -3 -2 -1 0 +1 +2 +3 +4 +5
_____6.05 leaving homeland/culture   -5 -4 -3 -2 -1 0 +1 +2 +3 +4 +5
_____6.06 unable to use native language -5 -4 -3 -2 -1 0 +1 +2 +3 +4 +5
_____6.07 living in unfamiliar environment -5 -4 -3 -2 -1 0 +1 +2 +3 +4 +5
_____6.08 natural disaster   -5 -4 -3 -2 -1 0 +1 +2 +3 +4 +5

7 = other external changes (please specify)

How Long?   Rate (circle)

                                Negative   **Positive**

_____7.01 = _____ -5 -4 -3 -2 -1 0 +1 +2 +3 +4 +5
_____7.02 = _____ -5 -4 -3 -2 -1 0 +1 +2 +3 +4 +5
_____7.03 = _____ -5 -4 -3 -2 -1 0 +1 +2 +3 +4 +5

INTERNAL LOSSES/CHANGES

10 = changes in self due to traumatic experiences

How Long?   Rate (circle)

		Negative	Positive
_____	10.01 imprisonment	-5 -4 -3 -2 -1	0 +1 +2 +3 +4 +5
_____	10.02 physical abuse	-5 -4 -3 -2 -1	0 +1 +2 +3 +4 +5
_____	10.03 torture	-5 -4 -3 -2 -1	0 +1 +2 +3 +4 +5
_____	10.04 being in combat	-5 -4 -3 -2 -1	0 +1 +2 +3 +4 +5
_____	10.05 rape	-5 -4 -3 -2 -1	0 +1 +2 +3 +4 +5
_____	10.06 witnessing a violent act	-5 -4 -3 -2 -1	0 +1 +2 +3 +4 +5
_____	10.07 injuring someone accidentally	-5 -4 -3 -2 -1	0 +1 +2 +3 +4 +5
_____	10.08 victim of prejudice	-5 -4 -3 -2 -1	0 +1 +2 +3 +4 +5
_____	10.09 incest	-5 -4 -3 -2 -1	0 +1 +2 +3 +4 +5
_____	10.10 verbal/mental abuse	-5 -4 -3 -2 -1	0 +1 +2 +3 +4 +5

11 = my own life-threatening illness/condition
(life expectancy less than six months)

How Long?   Rate (circle)

		Negative	Positive
_____	11.01 AIDS	-5 -4 -3 -2 -1	0 +1 +2 +3 +4 +5
_____	11.02 Cancer/Leukemia	-5 -4 -3 -2 -1	0 +1 +2 +3 +4 +5
_____	11.03 Heart condition	-5 -4 -3 -2 -1	0 +1 +2 +3 +4 +5
_____	11.04 Lung condition	-5 -4 -3 -2 -1	0 +1 +2 +3 +4 +5
_____	11.05 Diabetes	-5 -4 -3 -2 -1	0 +1 +2 +3 +4 +5
_____	11.06 Multiple Sclerosis	-5 -4 -3 -2 -1	0 +1 +2 +3 +4 +5
_____	11.07 Systemic lupus	-5 -4 -3 -2 -1	0 +1 +2 +3 +4 +5
_____	11.08 Environmental Illness	-5 -4 -3 -2 -1	0 +1 +2 +3 +4 +5
_____	11.09 Cystic Fibrosis	-5 -4 -3 -2 -1	0 +1 +2 +3 +4 +5
_____	11.10 Huntington's chorea	-5 -4 -3 -2 -1	0 +1 +2 +3 +4 +5
_____	11.11 Other: _____	-5 -4 -3 -2 -1	0 +1 +2 +3 +4 +5

12 = my own long-lasting illness/condition
(life expectancy uncertain or indefinite)

How Long?   Rate (circle)

		Negative	Positive
_____	12.01 AIDS (HIV **Positive**)	-5 -4 -3 -2 -1	0 +1 +2 +3 +4 +5
_____	12.02 Cancer/Leukemia	-5 -4 -3 -2 -1	0 +1 +2 +3 +4 +5
_____	12.03 Heart condition	-5 -4 -3 -2 -1	0 +1 +2 +3 +4 +5
_____	12.04 Lung condition	-5 -4 -3 -2 -1	0 +1 +2 +3 +4 +5
_____	12.05 Diabetes	-5 -4 -3 -2 -1	0 +1 +2 +3 +4 +5
_____	12.06 Multiple Sclerosis	-5 -4 -3 -2 -1	0 +1 +2 +3 +4 +5
_____	12.07 Systemic lupus	-5 -4 -3 -2 -1	0 +1 +2 +3 +4 +5
_____	12.08 Environmental illness	-5 -4 -3 -2 -1	0 +1 +2 +3 +4 +5
_____	12.09 Cystic Fibrosis	-5 -4 -3 -2 -1	0 +1 +2 +3 +4 +5
_____	12.10 Huntington's chorea	-5 -4 -3 -2 -1	0 +1 +2 +3 +4 +5
_____	12.11 Polio	-5 -4 -3 -2 -1	0 +1 +2 +3 +4 +5
_____	12.12 Other: _____	-5 -4 -3 -2 -1	0 +1 +2 +3 +4 +5

13 = job-related change

How Long? Rate (circle)

	Negative	Positive
_____13.01 being fired	-5 -4 -3 -2 -1	0 +1 +2 +3 +4 +5
_____13.02 retirement	-5 -4 -3 -2 -1	0 +1 +2 +3 +4 +5
_____13.03 promotion	-5 -4 -3 -2 -1	0 +1 +2 +3 +4 +5
_____13.04 being hired	-5 -4 -3 -2 -1	0 +1 +2 +3 +4 +5
_____13.05 reassigned	-5 -4 -3 -2 -1	0 +1 +2 +3 +4 +5
_____13.06 demoted	-5 -4 -3 -2 -1	0 +1 +2 +3 +4 +5
_____13.07 being passed over for promotion	-5 -4 -3 -2 -1	0 +1 +2 +3 +4 +5
_____13.08 responsibilities curtailed	-5 -4 -3 -2 -1	0 +1 +2 +3 +4 +5

14 = loss of physical function or ability to work due to

How Long? Rate (circle)

	Negative	Positive
_____14.01 injury	-5 -4 -3 -2 -1	0 +1 +2 +3 +4 +5
_____14.02 illness	-5 -4 -3 -2 -1	0 +1 +2 +3 +4 +5
_____14.03 accident	-5 -4 -3 -2 -1	0 +1 +2 +3 +4 +5
_____14.04 treatment (e.g. drugs, surgery)	-5 -4 -3 -2 -1	0 +1 +2 +3 +4 +5
_____14.05 aging	-5 -4 -3 -2 -1	0 +1 +2 +3 +4 +5
_____14.06 sexual orientation	-5 -4 -3 -2 -1	0 +1 +2 +3 +4 +5

15 = loss of sexual function/attractiveness due to

How Long? Rate (circle)

	Negative	Positive
_____15.01 injury	-5 -4 -3 -2 -1	0 +1 +2 +3 +4 +5
_____15.02 illness	-5 -4 -3 -2 -1	0 +1 +2 +3 +4 +5
_____15.03 accident	-5 -4 -3 -2 -1	0 +1 +2 +3 +4 +5
_____15.04 treatment (e.g. drugs, surgery)	-5 -4 -3 -2 -1	0 +1 +2 +3 +4 +5
_____15.05 aging	-5 -4 -3 -2 -1	0 +1 +2 +3 +4 +5
_____15.06 sexual orientation	-5 -4 -3 -2 -1	0 +1 +2 +3 +4 +5

16 = loss of mental functioning due to

How Long? Rate (circle)

	Negative	Positive
_____16.01 injury	-5 -4 -3 -2 -1	0 +1 +2 +3 +4 +5
_____16.02 illness	-5 -4 -3 -2 -1	0 +1 +2 +3 +4 +5
_____16.03 accident/trauma	-5 -4 -3 -2 -1	0 +1 +2 +3 +4 +5
_____16.04 treatment (e.g. drugs, surgery)	-5 -4 -3 -2 -1	0 +1 +2 +3 +4 +5
_____16.05 aging	-5 -4 -3 -2 -1	0 +1 +2 +3 +4 +5

17 = pain

How Long? Rate (circle)

	Negative	Positive
_____17.01 acute pain (less than 6 months in duration)	-5 -4 -3 -2 -1	0 +1 +2 +3 +4 +5
_____17.02 long-lasting pain (more than six months)	-5 -4 -3 -2 -1	0 +1 +2 +3 +4 +5
_____17.03 contained long-lasting pain	-5 -4 -3 -2 -1	0 +1 +2 +3 +4 +5
_____17.04 ending of long -lasting pain	-5 -4 -3 -2 -1	0 +1 +2 +3 +4 +5

18 = financial changes

How Long?   Rate (circle)

	Negative	Positive

_____18.01 significant indebtedness   -5 -4 -3 -2 -1 0 +1 +2 +3 +4 +5
_____18.02 winning the lottery
           (more than $40,000)   -5 -4 -3 -2 -1 0 +1 +2 +3 +4 +5
_____18.03 bankruptcy   -5 -4 -3 -2 -1 0 +1 +2 +3 +4 +5
_____18.04 significant increase
           in salary/income   -5 -4 -3 -2 -1 0 +1 +2 +3 +4 +5
_____18.05 significant decrease
           in salary/income   -5 -4 -3 -2 -1 0 +1 +2 +3 +4 +5
_____18.06 living on a fixed income   -5 -4 -3 -2 -1 0 +1 +2 +3 +4 +5

19 = change in status or prestige

How Long?   Rate (circle)

	Negative	Positive

_____19.01 graduation   -5 -4 -3 -2 -1 0 +1 +2 +3 +4 +5
_____19.02 becoming famous
           (award, publication, etc.)   -5 -4 -3 -2 -1 0 +1 +2 +3 +4 +5
_____19.03 being arrested   -5 -4 -3 -2 -1 0 +1 +2 +3 +4 +5
_____19.04 publically "losing face"   -5 -4 -3 -2 -1 0 +1 +2 +3 +4 +5
_____19.05 winning a lawsuit   -5 -4 -3 -2 -1 0 +1 +2 +3 +4 +5
_____19.06 losing a lawsuit   -5 -4 -3 -2 -1 0 +1 +2 +3 +4 +5
_____19.07 being cleared (exonerated)
           of an accusation   -5 -4 -3 -2 -1 0 +1 +2 +3 +4 +5
_____19.08 leaving a religious lifestyle
           or cult   -5 -4 -3 -2 -1 0 +1 +2 +3 +4 +5
_____19.09 sexual orientation made public -5 -4 -3 -2 -1 0 +1 +2 +3 +4 +5

20 = change in health habits (for longer than six months)

How Long?   Rate (circle)

	Negative	Positive

_____20.01 increased exercise   -5 -4 -3 -2 -1 0 +1 +2 +3 +4 +5
_____20.02 decreased exercise   -5 -4 -3 -2 -1 0 +1 +2 +3 +4 +5
_____20.03 stopped exercise   -5 -4 -3 -2 -1 0 +1 +2 +3 +4 +5
_____20.04 increased chances to relax   -5 -4 -3 -2 -1 0 +1 +2 +3 +4 +5
_____20.05 decreased opportunities to relax -5 -4 -3 -2 -1 0 +1 +2 +3 +4 +5
_____20.06 no relaxation   -5 -4 -3 -2 -1 0 +1 +2 +3 +4 +5
_____20.07 increased drug use   -5 -4 -3 -2 -1 0 +1 +2 +3 +4 +5
_____20.08 decreased drug use   -5 -4 -3 -2 -1 0 +1 +2 +3 +4 +5
_____20.09 stopped drug use   -5 -4 -3 -2 -1 0 +1 +2 +3 +4 +5
_____20.10 increased smoking   -5 -4 -3 -2 -1 0 +1 +2 +3 +4 +5
_____20.11 decreased smoking   -5 -4 -3 -2 -1 0 +1 +2 +3 +4 +5
_____20.12 stopped smoking   -5 -4 -3 -2 -1 0 +1 +2 +3 +4 +5
_____20.13 increased drinking   -5 -4 -3 -2 -1 0 +1 +2 +3 +4 +5
_____20.14 decreased drinking   -5 -4 -3 -2 -1 0 +1 +2 +3 +4 +5
_____20.15 stopped drinking   -5 -4 -3 -2 -1 0 +1 +2 +3 +4 +5
_____20.16 weight gain   -5 -4 -3 -2 -1 0 +1 +2 +3 +4 +5
_____20.17 weight loss   -5 -4 -3 -2 -1 0 +1 +2 +3 +4 +5
_____20.18 improved nutrition/diet   -5 -4 -3 -2 -1 0 +1 +2 +3 +4 +5
_____20.19 worsened nutrition/diet   -5 -4 -3 -2 -1 0 +1 +2 +3 +4 +5

21 = changes due to self-improvement efforts

How Long?   Rate (circle)

	Negative	**Positive**
_____21.01 counseling or psychotherapy	-5 -4 -3 -2 -1	0 +1 +2 +3 +4 +5
_____21.02 career counseling	-5 -4 -3 -2 -1	0 +1 +2 +3 +4 +5
_____21.03 education/retraining	-5 -4 -3 -2 -1	0 +1 +2 +3 +4 +5
_____21.04 other (specify):	-5 -4 -3 -2 -1	0 +1 +2 +3 +4 +5

22 = other internal (self) losses/changes. Please specify

How Long?   Rate (circle)

	Negative	**Positive**
_____22.01 _____	-5 -4 -3 -2 -1	0 +1 +2 +3 +4 +5
_____22.02 _____	-5 -4 -3 -2 -1	0 +1 +2 +3 +4 +5

Shared Changes

Communal: Change to someone other than self in a community/nation

How Long?   Rate (circle)

	Negative	**Positive**
_____30.01 death of a public figure	-5 -4 -3 -2 -1	0 +1 +2 +3 +4 +5
_____30.02 loss of a national/state/ community/religious image	-5 -4 -3 -2 -1	0 +1 +2 +3 +4 +5
_____30.03 catastrophe/natural disaster	-5 -4 -3 -2 -1	0 +1 +2 +3 +4 +5
_____30.04 war	-5 -4 -3 -2 -1	0 +1 +2 +3 +4 +5
_____30.05 recession/economic depression	-5 -4 -3 -2 -1	0 +1 +2 +3 +4 +5
_____30.06 connection to a community/ cause/collective goal	-5 -4 -3 -2 -1	0 +1 +2 +3 +4 +5

Familial: Change by someone other than self in a family

How Long?   Rate (circle)

	Negative	**Positive**
_____31.01 loss/death of a parent/ sibling/child	-5 -4 -3 -2 -1	0 +1 +2 +3 +4 +5
_____31.02 birth of an exceptional child/sibling	-5 -4 -3 -2 -1	0 +1 +2 +3 +4 +5
_____31.03 chronic illness/ disability of family member	-5 -4 -3 -2 -1	0 +1 +2 +3 +4 +5
_____31.04 adoption	-5 -4 -3 -2 -1	0 +1 +2 +3 +4 +5
_____31.05 abortion	-5 -4 -3 -2 -1	0 +1 +2 +3 +4 +5
_____31.06 divorce/separation/ abuse/incest	-5 -4 -3 -2 -1	0 +1 +2 +3 +4 +5
_____31.07 leaving home/staying at home	-5 -4 -3 -2 -1	0 +1 +2 +3 +4 +5
_____31.08 retirement	-5 -4 -3 -2 -1	0 +1 +2 +3 +4 +5

Transgenerational loss: Change by a generation prior to our own
How Long?   Rate (circle)

	Negative	Positive

_____32.01 incest   -5 -4 -3 -2 -1 0 +1 +2 +3 +4 +5
_____32.02 abuse   -5 -4 -3 -2 -1 0 +1 +2 +3 +4 +5
_____32.03 alcoholism   -5 -4 -3 -2 -1 0 +1 +2 +3 +4 +5
_____32,04 family secret   -5 -4 -3 -2 -1 0 +1 +2 +3 +4 +5
_____32.05 early death   -5 -4 -3 -2 -1 0 +1 +2 +3 +4 +5
_____32.06 leaving homeland   -5 -4 -3 -2 -1 0 +1 +2 +3 +4 +5
_____ 32.07 losing connection to
                land/ship/farm   5 -4 -3 -2 -1 0 +1 +2 +3 +4 +5

Appendix II:

Response to Loss Inventory

Note to reader: The Response to Loss inventory has an extensive history of development and validation. Anyone interested in using this inventory or in the research conducted on it, please contact the author:

John Schneider
Rte. 2 Box 75 Sundown Trail
Colfax, WI 54730
(715) 235-1724

This is an inventory of ways people respond to losses in their lives. All of the questions reflect the <u>normal</u> process of grieving, although, of course, none of us reacts in <u>all</u> of these ways to any given loss. Responding to this Inventory may help you identify your current reactions to significant changes in your life, particularly losses. You may find responding to this questionnaire difficult because some questions may bring up memories or feelings which are painful. <u>You may not wish to finish this inventory</u>. You are not required to do so.

- Since this inventory asks you *only* <u>how you are doing right now</u>, you may find that you have changed from how you would have responded even a few days or a few months ago.

- It might be helpful to discuss your reactions with someone. You are invited to record your thoughts about taking the inventory at the end of your answer sheets.

- When possible, respond to only <u>one</u> particular loss or change in your life. The *Life Change Inventory* may have already helped you to select your most recent and/or most significant loss. Please note in the answer booklet which loss it is that you are considering.

- When it is not possible to focus on a single loss, please indicate <u>all</u> the losses which were involved in your response.

- As you read each question, ask yourself if the statement is true about you <u>right now, or in the past few days or weeks</u>. You can indicate the degree to which you are having these responses according to the following scheme:

0 = *this isn't accurate about my current response to this loss.*

1 = *occasionally this is true about my responses to this loss.*

2 = *some of the time this is true about my responses to this loss.*

3 = *most of the time this is true about my responses to this loss.*

4 = *this definitely is accurate about my current responses to this loss.*

NOTE: If a statement is true about you, but is <u>not</u> a response to this loss, leave it blank.

Please read <u>all</u> questions, even if you leave some of them blank. You may find it helpful to take one or more breaks while you are filling out the questionnaire. It does not need to be filled out in one day, but within a few days. If the loss you are considering has occurred recently, or if filling out these items provokes strong feelings, you may wish to postpone filling out this questionnaire.

HOLDING ON
Behavioral

1. Keeping active and busy helps me feel less anxious about this loss.

2. I've been the one to make the necessary decisions.

3. I am smoking more.

4. I keep busy to avoid thinking about what happened.

5. Taking care of others distracts me from thinking about my loss.

6. Until it is proven this loss is real, I will keep looking for it/him/her/it.

7. I want/need to tell others what happened.

8. Winning at something helps distract me from the loss.

9. If I tried hard enough, I can bring back what I lost.

10. I've been able to do things I ordinarily could not.

11. I'm looking for who made this loss happen.

12. I keep reminders of my loss (e.g. pictures, mementoes) around me.

12a. I remain involved with friends and family to stay connected to my loss.

13. I avoid being alone.

13a. I haven't given up the rituals and habits that connect me to my loss.

14. I would do almost anything to get back what I've lost.

15. I look just as good as I always did.

16. I find myself talking or acting as if nothing has changed.

17. I've found someone or something to replace what/who I've lost.

Cognitive

18. This whole thing seems unreal.

19. I don't believe that this loss really happened.

20. I hope I am dreaming and I'll wake up and find out it never happened.

21. I keep thinking something could be done to bring back what I lost.

22. I think that if I am good or perfect enough, what was lost will return.

23. I try to figure out how it could have been different.

24. Something could have prevented this loss.

25. I try to figure out why this loss happened to me.

26. If I could find the reason this loss happened, I wouldn't feel so bad.

27. If I don't concentrate on remembering what has happened, I'll forget it.

28. If I work hard enough, nothing bad will ever happen to me.

29. If I'm good enough, nobody I love will ever die.

30. Cheer up—things could be worse.

31. It will all work out in the long run.

32. If I can just understand why it happened, everything will be alright.

33. Every cloud has a silver lining.

34. It's God's will. He has something better in mind.

35. People get the respect they deserve in this world.

36. Don't question it. Just accept it. You have to go on.

37. The show must go on.

38. I've got to learn to accept it.

39. Idle hands are the devil's workbench.

40. There must be a reason for this.

41. If I am good enough or perfect enough, what was lost will come back.

42. Almost anything can remind me of my loss.

43. I think I am responsible for this loss.

44. I feel I should have done something to prevent this from happening.

45. I wish things were the way they were before this loss occurred.

Emotional

46. I am angry about this loss.

47. I'm scared to share what I've been thinking, feeling and doing.

47a. I am scared by how unpredictable my feelings are.

48. My feelings are so unpredictable I wonder if I am crazy.

49. I feel guilty or disloyal when I forget about this loss.

50. I feel guilty just thinking about enjoying myself.

51. I don't remember what I did and/or didn't do just before the loss happened.

52. My feelings are so intense I'm afraid I'm losing control.

53. Being in control helps me feel less overwhelmed.

54. I try to hold back the tears.

55. I can't control my feelings when I'm with those who share my loss.

56. Unless something happens to change this, I don't know if I can control myself.

57. I want someone to be punished for this loss.

58. I am afraid to think about anything else but my loss.

59. I'm afraid I'll forget my loss if I stop thinking about it.

60. Nothing is going to rob me of my feelings about this loss.

61. I'm not ready to let go of my feelings about what happened.

Physical

62. I've increased my exercise.

63. I ignore the physical pain just to keep going.

64. Sex gets my mind off the loss.

65. I keep myself from having sex.

66. I don't feel like I am a sexual creature.

67. My weight has changed.

68. I have trouble breathing.

69. I have panic attacks.

70. I don't eat as much.

71. It's obvious to others I've been upset.

72. I am sleeping less.

Spiritual

73. I dream that it never happened.

74. I dream that something has happened to reverse my loss.

75. It would help if someone could help me understand this.

76. Life seems unfair.

77. If people could just love each other, no one would have to suffer.

78. I believe something good will happen.

79. I have the capacity to overcome any crisis

80. I can outlast any intruder.

81. Hard work will overcome anything.

82. I can still find meaningful and supportive relationships.

83. I still believe in people's inherent good and trustworthiness.

84. I know I will not be tested beyond my capacity to endure.

85. It seems like I am going through the same thing all over again.

86. I wonder if I really deserve what I have.

87. I am not able to forgive those who contributed to this loss.

88. I know I won't give up.

89. I won't accept that this loss has to be.

90. I am determined to make those responsible pay for this.

91. I'm looking for a way out of this loss.

92. This loss must be changed.

93. I sense the presence of the one I lost.

LETTING GO

Behavioral

94. I avoid telling anyone what I'm thinking, feeling and/or doing about this loss.

95. I avoid people who remind me of this loss.

96. I'm less patient with people.

97. I refuse to discuss this loss.

98. I don't see much of my old friends.

99. I don't spend as much time with my family.

100. I've been careless.

101. I act as though this doesn't really matter to me.

102. I avoid getting involved in anything.

103. I drink to forget my loss.

104. I use drugs to forget my loss.

105. I lose or misplace things which are related to this loss.

106. I've put away anything which could remind me of this loss.

107. I avoid reminders of this loss.

108. I have kept secret what really happened.

109. I can be physically abusive when others remind me of the loss.

110. I can be verbally abusive when others remind me of this loss.

111. I am not interested in getting involved.

112. I've had more sex with more people.

Cognitive

Since the time of this loss, I have thought:

113. Something else is going to go wrong.

114. If I get too happy, something bad is bound to happen.

115. I cannot imagine how anything positive could come out of this loss.

116. This loss is evidence that I have failed as a person.

117. If I don't look out for myself, no one else will.

118. I deserve a better deal than I'm getting.

119. Very few people are worth my time and energy now.

120. I'm better off without it/him/her.

121. No one can change what's already happened.

122. No matter what I do, what will happen will happen.

123. I lack the energy to make sense out of it.

124. Even if I could understand why it happened, it wouldn't change anything.

125. It's best not to dwell on the past.

126. It's easier when I can forget what happened.

127. Nobody really understands how this loss affects me.

128. Nobody really cares how this loss affects me.

129. My thinking has been critical and judgmental.

130. I've rejected others' ideas about the loss.

131. I've focused on the here and now.

In light of this loss, I believe:

132. I should eat, drink and be merry, for tomorrow may never come.

133. Why get involved? You just get hurt.

134. Don't rock the boat. You'll just get noticed.

135. It's God's will. Learn to accept it.

136. Nobody cares about me. Why should I care about anyone else?

137. Why try? It won't make any difference.

138. Easy come, easy go.

139. There's no such thing as a free ride.

140. The good die young.

141. Out of sight, out of mind.

142. What the eye doesn't see, the heart doesn't remember.

143. It's best just to forget it. Thee's nothing you can do about it.

144. Enjoy yourself now. Who cares about tomorrow?

145. Do your own thing.

146. If you're too happy, something bad is bound to happen.

147. Fate is against me.

148. It is the nail that stands out that gets hammered the hardest.

149. To succeed is to die.

Emotional

150. I feel confused and disoriented.

151. I feel overwhelmed.

152. I try not to let anything affect me.

153. I avoid feeling too sad about this.

154. I feel detached and separate from others.

155. I feel dissatisfied with everything.

156. I feel bored with life.

157. I refuse to wallow in self-pity.

158. People irritate me easily.

159. I get angry at myself.

160. I feel frustrated.

161. I'm fed up with spending so much time on this.

162. If I let myself, I get so unhappy I can't stand it.

163. I deserve to be punished for what I contributed to this loss.

164. I get upset with myself for the way I have behaved.

165. I'm ashamed of the way I've behaved.

166. I am revolted by the way people have responded.

167. It disgusts me to think of how it happened.

Physical

168. I don't want to be touched.

169. I get hurt more.

170. I'm more clumsy and accident prone.

171. I am sick a lot.

172. I have felt sick to my stomach.

173. There is a bitter taste in my mouth.

174. I exercise less.

175. I sleep more.

176. I don't watch what I eat.

Spiritual

177. I wish I could be saved from having to deal with this experience.

178. I doubt that anything or anyone can give my life meaning again.

179. I wonder what point there is in going on.

180. I can't imagine anyone ever being as important to me.

181. No one could ever pay enough for causing this loss to happen.

182. I've given up believing that my life has any particular significance.

183. My life doesn't seem to have a purpose.

184. It's hard for me to trust anybody.

185. Nobody cares how I am doing.

186. Nothing has really made any difference, so why do I bother?

187. There's no sense thinking or worrying about what happened.

188. I've realized that nothing could have prevented it.

189. I've lost respect for myself.

190. I wonder if I'm really a disgusting, worthless person.

191. If people important to me knew my contribution to this loss, they would be shocked.

192. I don't remember any dreams.

193. I've had fantasies of being dead.

194. I dream that I destroyed what/who I lost.

195. It wasn't my fault this happened.

196. No one can blame me for the way it turned out.

197. I can't be expected to be responsible at times like this.

198. I deserve to be taken care of after what's happened.

AWARENESS

Behavioral

199. It's been hard to concentrate.

200. I am scattered and ineffective.

201. I get so preoccupied that I forget where I am going.

202. I forget to do routine, everyday tasks.

203. It's hard for me to make decisions.

204. I never seem to know what to do with myself.

205. I am less confident.

206. I have very little to say.

207. I talk about how it's been for me since the time of this loss.

208. I do less of the things I enjoyed before.

209. I avoid being in new situations.

210. I've not been interested in meeting anyone new.

211. I avoid getting close to others.

212. I lack love, affection and companionship.

213. My friends have been avoiding me.

214. I've lost friends.

215. My friends avoid talking about my loss.

Cognitive

216. My thinking has been slower than usual.

217. I lose track of what's going on.

218. I am unable to find anything to look forward to.

219. I can't imagine how things will get better.

220. I forget how it used to be before this happened.

221. I'm struck by how trivial everyday life seems.

222. I'm struck by how other people seem to go on with their lives while I cannot.

223. I am overwhelmed at how real and inescapable this loss seems.

224. I know I cannot bring it back.

225. It seems hopeless to try to understand what really happened.

226. There's no way I can fully understand why it happened.

227. I think about how my life has been changed.

228. I am aware of what is no longer a part of my life.

229. I'm reminded how little I really control.

230. I think about what's missing in my life.

231. I think about the dreams that will never come true.

Emotional

232. The tears are hard to stop.

233. My feelings just come.

234. I long for what (whom) I've lost.

235. I really miss it/him/her.

236. It's hard to express what I feel in words.

237. I miss expressing my love.

238. I miss feeling happy.

239. Joy is missing in my life.

240. I feel a great deal of hurt or emotional pain.

241. I feel sad.

242. I feel helpless.

243. I feel empty, like a shell, like I am just existing.

244. I feel lonely and alone.

245. Music can stir up my feelings.

246. Being in certain places stirs up feelings unexpectedly.

247. Looking at old photos arouses painful feelings.

248. Certain odors (e.g. perfumes, old houses) can trigger feelings.

Physical

249. I feel restless.

250. I feel tense.

251. I use up much more energy than I did before.

252. My body feels heavy.

253. I am exhausted by any effort.

254. I've had no energy to do anything.

255. I feel pangs.

256. I feel numb.

257. I cry.

258. I sigh.

259. I sob.

260. I wake up feeling stiff and achy, as if I'd been tense all night.

261. I have difficulty getting to sleep.

262. I wake up during the night.

263. I am more tired than usual.

264. My dreams remind me of my loss.

265. I have trouble getting up in the morning.

266. I lack a sex life.

267. I lack touching, holding and hugging.

268. When someone touches me, my feelings come to the surface.

269. It's like I've been hit in the stomach.

270. I feel sick.

271. I feel tight in my throat, like there is a lump in it.

272. My stomach really churns.

273. I hurt all over.

274. I have aches and pains which remind me of my loss.

275. I don't know if I can stand the physical pain for one more day.

Spiritual

276. I would rather die than go on experiencing this.

277. I am at the lowest point I have ever been.

278. No amount of money could ever replace it.

279. Everything else seems trivial and meaningless.

280. The future seems empty.

281. There is nothing positive or redeeming about this loss.

282. What I value most in life has been destroyed.

283. My beliefs don't give me the comfort they use to give me.

284. I question the existence of the God I used to believe in.

285. My faith has been shaken.

286. I cannot continue life the same way as before.

287. I don't have the kind of love I had.

288. My life will never be totally free from pain and suffering.

289. Life is fragile.

290. I will lose things and people important to me.

291. I've lost my sense of innocence.

292. Parts of me are missing.

293. My belief in myself as a good and honest human being has been shaken.

294. I am not the loving, caring, trusting person I was.

295. There is a great emptiness in my life.

296. When I'm convinced things can't get any worse, they do.

297. It is easier to realize that someday I will die.

298. I have lost my desire to live.

299. I've lost my fear of dying.

PERSPECTIVE

Behavioral

300. Hearing about other's experiences with similar losses helps.

301. I like to be with friends who know what I've been through.

302. There is at least one person I can count on for support.

303. It helps to be with a friend who accepts me as I am.

304. Being by myself has been healing.

305. It helps when I don't have anything to do.

306. I take long walks and just daydream.

307. There is a special place which is healing for me.

308. Activities like getting a massage, painting or music are soothing.

309. I've found ways to enjoy myself.

310. Talking or writing about it gives me relief and release.

311. I can take what comes.

312. I can let things turn out the way they will.

Cognitive

313. I can think about other things than this loss now.

314. I realize that I've lost a lot, but I haven't lost everything.

315. What I have left in my life is enough to keep me going.

316. I think about how I have changed, what is different.

317. There are some things I will never understand about this.

318. I'm not as responsible as I thought I was for what happened.

319. I wasn't the only one who contributed to this loss.

Emotional

320. I have already passed the lowest point.

321. It's easier to let myself just experience this loss.

322. My fears about dying are less.

323. My feelings make sense when I think about them.

324. I am able to express my feelings about the loss.

325. I don't need to struggle to accept what has happened.

326. My feelings still catch me by surprise, but they don't last as long.

327. I still hurt, but the pain has lessened.

328. My guilt has lessened.

329. My shame has lessened.

330. I'm not so sad.

331. My feelings of anger are not as strong anymore.

332. My disgust over what happened has lessened.

333. My feelings can be ones of "sweet sadness."

334. I realize that sadness and peacefulness can coexist.

335. It feels good to be able to laugh again.

336. I can enjoy simple pleasures of life again.

Physical

337. My body is healing from the stresses of this experience.

338. The aches and pains I used to have with this loss have lessened.

339. I'm able to relax.

340. I enjoy being touched and held once again.

341. My energy level has improved since the time of the loss.

342. It takes less energy to do things than it used to.

343. I am more aware of myself physically than I was before the loss.

344. I notice how things smell and taste again.

Spiritual

345. My imagination has returned.

346. I have learned to accept that losses and changes are a part of life.

347. There are limits on what I lost.

348. My life will continue.

349. I've decided to go on living.

350. My dreams seem to help me understand and accept what happened.

351. Someone or something powerful and loving has helped me make it.

352. My faith or spiritual understanding helped me with this experience.

353. Something good could come out of this.

354. My life does seem to have meaning.

355. No one is totally to blame for what happened.

356. Whatever I contributed to this loss, I did not want it to happen.

357. I believe there is some good in every person.

358. Life seems more fragile and precious.

359. There are quiet places in my life now.

360. My past will always be a part of me.

361. A part of me will always be connected to what/who I lost.

362. The fond memories are there along with the painful ones.

363. What I've lost will always have a place in my life.

INTEGRATION

Behavioral

364. I've found ways to get back my integrity.

365. I've changed.

366. I don't depend as much on others.

367. I don't need to be so much in control of things.

368. I've remembered what I really want to remember about it.

369. I've done everything I can do right now about this loss.

370. I've finished things related to my loss as completely as I can.

371. At least one person knows that I've forgiven myself.

372. I've taken steps to forgive those involved.

373. I've restored relationships that were disrupted by it.

374. I am making restitution for my contributions to this loss.

375. I've completed my good-by to this loss.

376. I like being with people again.

Cognitive

377. There are ways that I have both gained and lost.

378. Putting my thoughts into words has helped me recover.

379. I realize how important it is to say good-by to what/who is gone.

380. It's important to have times of celebration and remembrance before it's too late.

381. I have as good an understanding as I can right now.

382. My life has more to it.

Emotional

383. I've had many feelings.

384. I've felt all I can feel about this loss.

385. I've experienced the loss as fully as I can.

386. I've found effective ways to express my feelings.

387. I've learned a lot from my feelings about this loss.

388. I've experienced this loss in ways that were healing.

389. I no longer feel shame.

390. I've let go of the guilt.

391. I've let go of my sadness.

392. I've let go of the anger.

393. I no longer feel disgust.

Physical

394. I can make sense out of the messages from my body.

395. I don't neglect my body.

396. I don't push my body beyond limits.

397. I have the energy I need.

398. I relax.

399. I feel better.

400. I sleep well.

401. I exercise.

402. I eat sensibly.

403. I take care of the way I look.

404. I can be sexually or romantically interested.

405. Passion is a part of my life.

Spiritual

406. I know my life is important.

407. This experience has meaning for me.

408. My dreams are restful, playful and helpful.

409. Some of my dreams of the future have survived this loss.

410. I've restored or regained part of what I had lost.

411. I am finding ways to fit this experience into the rest of my life.

412. I feel the presence of what/who I lost.

413. This loss has opened me to love and friendship.

414. I have forgiven myself for what happened.

415. I have been forgiven for what I contributed to this loss.

416. I have forgiven others for what happened.

417. I've made peace with those involved in this loss.

418. I would not want my loss reversed if it meant giving up all my growth from it.

419. Life is worth living again.

420. I feel confident enough in myself to move on to other things.

421. It's time for me to get on with life.

REFORMULATION

Behavioral

422. It takes less effort and thought to do what I need to do.

423. I do things on the spur of the moment.

424. I enjoy being alone.

425. I spend time by myself.

426. I'm nicer to myself.

427. I can laugh at myself.

428. I'm not as serious a person.

429. I'm more assertive.

430. I'm able to take risks again.

431. I like being challenged.

432. I'm more self-disciplined.

433. I discovered what I want in life.

434. I don't place limits in front of myself as readily as I did before this loss.

435. I've started new relationships.

436. I am more able to give to others.

437. I can care for me and for others.

438. I have time for my family and friends and time for me.

439. I listen to, play music, or sing.

440. I can express myself in many ways.

Cognitive

441. I am efficient and creative at doing things.

442. I can appreciate the paradoxes and seeming contradictions in my life.

443. I'm more open to possibilities.

444. I feel more confident.

445. I'm more patient.

446. I've grown.

447. I've changed in ways that would not have happened otherwise.

448. I see the past as just as important as what is happening now.

449. I don't spend as much time thinking about the loss.

450. Past, present and future are equally important.

451. I'm more creative in my approach to life.

452. I feel challenged to keep on going.

453. I enjoy having dreams as much as I do reaching for them.

454. I trust my ways of thinking.

455. I know what I need to do to move my life forward.

Emotional

456. I don't avoid my feelings.

457. I believe my feelings are valid.

458. I've found new ways to express my feelings.

459. I am at peace.

460. I feel loving and affectionate.

461. I can feel both joyful and sad.

462. Sadness reminds me how important this loss was to me.

463. I can get angry.

464. I am curious about many things.

465. It's hard to be bored.

Physical

466. I listen to what my body tells me.

467. I take my time.

468. I enjoy making love.

469. I enjoy touching and being touched.

470. I feel strong.

471. The messages from my body can make sense.

472. I am active in caring for myself physically.

473. I get the exercise I need.

474. What I eat is healthy.

475. I make sure I have time to relax.

476. I feel warm all over.

Spiritual

477. I'm no longer searching for answers to everything.

478. I have what is meaningful within me.

479. I act on what I believe and understand.

480. I've learned to respect myself.

481. I am not as hard on myself when I make mistakes.

482. I feel like a whole person.

483. I like the way I am.

484. I've discovered that there is more to me than meets the eye.

485. I feel a part of something much bigger than me.

486. My dreams make sense.

487. I trust my intuition to let me know what I need to know.

488. I live as fully as I can.

489. I am more consistently aware of what's important.

490. What is important to me has changed.

491. I can love and be devoted to another without losing myself.

492. I have fewer conditions on my love.

493. Death is only one of many transitions I'll make in life.

494. I realize I can do destructive things.

495. I have some degree of control over how and when I die.

496. I feel lovable.

497. Some kind of inner wisdom has been guiding me.

TRANSFORMING LOSS

498. I've challenged and altered some of my most cherished and long-standing assumptions and beliefs.

499. I've found a balance between my personal growth and my relationships.

500. I want other people in my life.

501. I have something to share with others.

502. I want to share with others who have these life experiences.

503. I've discovered that the most important parts of my loss remain alive inside of me.

504. What I own isn't as important.

505. I can get along with less than I have needed in the past.

506. The cycles of life have times of birth and death.

507. I feel a deep connection to people who are no longer alive.

508. I am sometimes surprised by what I know and say.

509. There is someone or something more powerful, loving, lasting and wise than any single human being.

510. I feel connected to the world and to nature.

511. I don't have to have all the answers for why I am alive.

512. Things in my life can change and life can still be meaningful.

513. I am curious about my death.

514. I am curious about what will happen after I die.

515. This is the right place for me right now.

516. I can't live without loving myself.

517. I feel connected to what I've lost in ways I never expected.

518. I discovered some essential parts of me.

519. I have peaceful moments.

520. My life has times of joy.

Appendix III
INTEGRA:
The Association for Integrative and Transformative Grief

Mission:

The purpose of INTEGRA is to develop and maintain resources for supporting educational, research and human service approaches to increase an understanding of the grieving process.

The development of INTEGRA builds on the following assumptions:

- Grieving involves mind, body and spirit.

- Growth from grief is possible and needs to be better understood.

- The nature of loss affects the grieving process.

- Validation of grief can come from education, creative expression, support groups, identification of resources and counseling.

- People help others with their grief by their willingness to explore their own grief and through training.
- Research into the grieving process promotes better understanding and more effective training of helping professionals.

Goals:

1. Create opportunities to bring together resources from around the world in order to establish working relationships and provide support and inspiration for those working with grief as a transformative process.

2. Develop potential research instruments to study the grieving process.

3. Provide comprehensive teaching, consultation and training programs in loss, grief, life cycle development for groups, families and individuals.

4. Identify grief-related human service resources for community, state and nation.

For further information, contact:

Susan Zimmerman
INTEGRA
PO Box 6013
East Lansing, MI 48826

Index